The Coronation and the Constitution in the British Tradition

Noel Cox

The Coronation and the Constitution in the British Tradition

The Political, Legal and Theological Function of the Ceremony

palgrave
macmillan

Noel Cox
Auckland, New Zealand

ISBN 978-3-031-88959-2 ISBN 978-3-031-88960-8 (eBook)
https://doi.org/10.1007/978-3-031-88960-8

This Palgrave Macmillan imprint is published by the registered company Springer Nature Switzerland AG
The registered company address is: Gewerbestrasse 11, 6330 Cham, Switzerland

I respectfully dedicate this work jointly to His Grace Edward Fitzalan-Howard, GCVO DL, 18th Duke of Norfolk, Earl Marshal and Hereditary Marshal of England, the Great Officer of State who has for long centuries had the principal responsibility and privilege of organising the solemnity of the coronation of a new King or Queen Regnant in Westminster Abbey, and to the Very Reverend Dr. David Hoyle, KCVO MBE, Dean of His Majesty's Collegiate Church of Saint Peter, Westminster, who ancient duty it is to instruct the Sovereign on all matters connected with the service and assists the Archbishop of Canterbury.

In nomine Patris et Filii et Spiritus Sancti.

Acknowledgements

I wish to express gratitude to all those who have assisted in the creation of this book. I thank all those who took the time to discuss various questions and themes related to the book's content, including those who did so anonymously. I want to make it clear that all who have helped, whether named or not, are equally appreciated and valued.

Additionally, I acknowledge the support of my wife, Katy, who played an important role in the writing process and provided unwavering support throughout. I recognise that without Katy's support, completing the book would have been much more challenging. I also express my thanks to my son, Christopher, who proved a valuable distraction during the latter stages of completing the work.

Finally, I pay tribute to my late twin brother John, who was a valuable source of inspiration and discussion on many of the topics covered in the book. I acknowledge the importance of John's contributions and the impact they had on shaping the work.

The Coronation and the Constitution, by The Revd Dr Noel Cox, A Foreword by Archbishop Sir David Moxon

One of the most poignant, paradoxically private yet globally public moments in the coronation of King Charles III, was the anointing of the King with holy oil. The new king was stripped of most of his robes, and his heart as it were was consecrated. Millions around the world watched on television. There was a fascination with the choreography, the symbols, the ancient words and the people involved. It was as if many groups and cultures were sensing something seminal, something crucial to one tap root of the human story was being displayed. It was re-presenting ancient and modern terms of service, duty, the common good, and an intuitive focus for unity in a vastly increasing social diversity.

In this fascinating and unique book, Noel Cox argues in a meticulous and widely researched approach, that monarchy as a constitutional reality still has a vital role. Crucially, this role is described as primarily spiritual: involving and symbolizing spiritual values, embodying the sacred against private gain, and acting as a focal point in a centrifugal society around which many may gather.

In 'The Coronation and the Constitution', Archbishop Rowan Wiliams is quoted as saying "It is there so that we can gather around something other than our preferences and anxieties and prejudices; around a gift of "kinship" in which we can stand together before God." The word King partly derives from the word for 'kin'. In this way, Noel argues, a society is held together by its internal agreement about the sacredness of certain fundamental moral standards. Even if these standards are deeply located or un-noticed at times within the ancient humus around the tap roots of our heritage and many storied history, they provide a moral nutrient that can be life giving. This has to include the legitimacy of government, through the secular and religious aspects of recognition or acclamation, coronation oath, anointing, investiture with regalia, crowning, enthroning, and homage.

A coronation and constitution tradition is described as a possible avenue of communication with the realm of the sacred values. "Within its society, popular constitutional monarchy can enjoy almost universal recognition in this capacity". This tradition is therefore enabled to heighten the moral and civic sensibility of the society and to infuse society with role models of self-giving and reaching out, in the name of our democratic citizenship and mutuality in a constitutional monarchy. Interestingly the sacred heart of this experience, contrasts strongly with the imposition of empire and colonisation.

Even though they are intermittent, this timely book reminds us that the coronation rituals of the original Anglo Celtic tradition, as they have morphed and evolved over time, can still move and inspire society and many communities of interest. This book describes a heritage offers a once and future vision of what upholds the common good and our highest responsibilities within hearth and home, parliament and state. Some prefer a republic in this day and age, but this book outlines the seminal and unique role that a coronation can still play, potentially, as a great act of national communion for many across the board.

Contents

CHAPTER 1

Introduction

Introduction

The death of Her late Majesty Queen Elizabeth II in 2022, the first demise of the Crown in more than 70 years, was a watershed moment in modern British constitutional history. The term demise was originally a law French term used for the transfer of real property, whether by lease or sale. Blackstone notes that this term for the transfer of property then became used on the death of the monarch to mean the kingdom is transferred or demised to his successor. Demise in this sense is not referring to the monarch's death, but to the automatic transfer of the monarchy to the heir, by operation of law.[1] This understanding is constitutionally significant.

In 1952, when Her Majesty succeeded her late father, King George VI, on the throne of the United Kingdom, the nascent Commonwealth

[1] For the definition of "demise" see Blackstone, Sir William, *Commentaries on the Laws of England* (1st ed., 1979), Book the First, p. 181.

N. Cox, *The Political, Legal, and Theological Functions of the Ceremony in the British Tradition*,
https://doi.org/10.1007/978-3-031-88960-8_1

of Nations was then but three years old[2]; even the United Nations organisation was then only four years older,[3] though both were revived and restructured versions of earlier institutions.[4] Other associated political and constitutional institutions and their accompanying rituals were far from new. The monarchy itself, and the coronation, were two such things, the one arguably dating back as far as the governance of Britain can be traced, and the other at least 1500 years old, and more ancient still in its origins, inspiration, functions, and rituals.

In 2022 the world was a very different place to what it had been in 1952. The Commonwealth was now well established, and had even grown to encompass some countries which had never, historically, been in the British empire or even within its broader sphere of geo-political influence.[5] The majority of member states of the Commonwealth were now republics or national monarchies,[6] though 14 (in addition to the United Kingdom) still recognised the Sovereign as their head of state—twice as many as had done so back in 1952.[7]

The United Kingdom, and of course the monarchy, had changed markedly in the intervening seventy years. The monarchy had adapted to new circumstances and conditions, as it had always done. In turn it

[2] The Commonwealth of Nations, "the Commonwealth" for short, was established by the London Declaration 28th April 1949, although it can be traced to the Balfour Declaration of 19th November 1926, as the British Commonwealth of Nations; Wheare, K. C., *The Constitutional Structure of the Commonwealth* (1960).

[3] The United Nations was created by the UN Charter 26 June 1945. The United Nations can be seen as the successor to the League of Nations (1920–1946).

[4] The Commonwealth was successor to the third British Empire, which existed during the nineteenth and twentieth centuries (and based in large part on India, and also Africa), and the second British Empire, which dates from the eighteenth and nineteenth centuries (predominantly Oceania), which in its turn evolved from the first, which dated from the seventeenth and eighteenth centuries (particularly North America); See Keith, A. B., *Constitutional History of the First British Empire* (1930); Halstead, J. P., *The Second British Empire* (1983).

[5] These currently include Mozambique (1995), Rwanda (2009), Gabon (2022), and Togo (2022).

[6] National monarchies in 2023 included Brunei Darussalam, Lesotho, Malaysia, Swaziland, and Tonga.

[7] The dominions in 1952 were Australia, Canada, Ceylon, New Zealand, Pakistan, and South Africa. In 2022 they were Antigua and Barbuda, Australia, the Bahamas, Belize, Canada, Grenada, Jamaica, New Zealand, Papua New Guinea, Saint Kitts and Nevis, Saint Vincent and the Grenadines, Solomon Islands, and Tuvalu.

might be anticipated that the coronation (the "Solemnity of Our Royal Coronation at Westminster", as it was described in the 2022 proclamation making the weekday following the coronation of King Charles III in 2023 a public holiday[8]) too would change and adapt. Coronations had inevitably always changed, albeit within strictly confined limits and bounds imposed by tradition, the dictates of constitutional probity, and liturgical custom and practice, to suit the contemporary circumstances.[9] Just as the state of society and politics in 1952 influenced some aspects of the coronation the following year (such as the role assigned to the High Commissioners of the dominions), so too it might be expected that any subsequent coronation would reflect the changes in society, in addition to the vital continuity of the solemnity of the coronation. Thus, the devolution of varying but extensive power to Edinburgh, Cardiff and Belfast,[10] in the last years of the twentieth century, and the early years of the twenty-first century, would inevitably lead to greater emphasis on the constituent parts of the United Kingdom, in what was, historically and practically, essentially the English coronation writ large. The coronation is thus not an empty ritual, but is rather a constitutional solemnity reflecting the state of the realm, and the relationship between King and peoples.

A coronation may be defined as a political, ceremonial and often, though not invariably, religious ceremony at which a new monarch is formally installed, celebrated and otherwise publicly welcomed to their new position.[11] It differs from the inauguration of a president of a republic (whether executive or primarily ceremonial), in that the latter

[8] "By The King a Proclamation appointing Monday 8th May 2023 a Bank Holiday in England, Wales and Northern Ireland Charles R.", 11th November 2022. For the first time in many years there was no proclamation of the coronation itself, and the announcement was made by a Buckingham Palace press release 11th October 2022; Torrance, David, "The Coronation: history and ceremonial" (House of Commons Library Research Briefing, number CBP9412, 6 December 2022), p. 20; HC Deb 17 November 2022 vol 722 c 820 (coronation of King Charles III).

[9] Bradshaw, Paul, "On Revising the Coronation Service" (1993) 96(770) Theology 130–137.

[10] By the Government of Wales Acts 1998 and 2006, and the Scotland Act 1998 and Northern Ireland Act 1998.

[11] The Coronation of King Charles III, although held on a Saturday, was marked by a public holiday, on the following Monday; "By The King a Proclamation appointing Monday 8th May 2023 a Bank Holiday in England, Wales and Northern Ireland Charles R", 9th November 2022. This was a statutory rather than prerogative proclamation, under s 1(3) of the Banking and Financial Dealings Act 1971.

ritual usually does not include religious aspects, and is generally devoid of any elements evoking any sense of fealty, homage or allegiance. It would not, for instance, include the anointing of the ruler with holy oil.

This book is an exploration of the conceptual functions of a coronation in the British context. It is not a history of the English coronation (although perforce much of its contents savours of this), but rather an analysis of its role, in a wider western and international historical context. It proceeds with the proposition that a coronation is still a vital legal, political and theological requirement for every new Sovereign of the United Kingdom. Whilst the strict legal need for a coronation was considered (perhaps obliquely)—and ultimately dismissed—by a court of law several centuries ago, the political and theological necessity for a coronation is, it will be argued, more nuanced than that comparatively simple answer might suggest. In part this is because of the political, constitutional, and theological role and status of the Sovereign, and their relationship with the broader body politic, as well as the organic nature of the constitution. Likewise, the legal necessity for a coronation deserves to be re-assessed in light of a fuller (and more holistic) understanding of its function, and of its relationship to the constitution, as well as the nature of the constitution itself, and the relationship of the coronation to law, politics, and theology.

The coronation is a core constitutional rite of passage, for both monarch and people, and its importance increases, rather than decreases, when there are national (or even personal) challenges, political, constitutional, or financial. The constitutional function of the coronation is to confirm, affirm and set aside the Sovereign, for their subsequent constitutional role. The constitutional status of the coronation is, of course, set in the context of an unwritten constitution, one whose essential features are continuity and flexibility.

The complexity of the function, and arguable necessity for a coronation, partly stems from the manner in which the position of Sovereign has evolved through the centuries, and can be traced to the earliest times in the British Isles—predating by some centuries the Norman Conquest and arguably even the post-Roman Saxon invasions and settlement of Britain. The existence of a king (the expression king is hereafter in this book to be taken as including queen regnant, where appropriate, and vice versa, and likewise for the pronouns he and her) has also influenced the development of the concept of the state in the English tradition of government, as the evolution of the common law, and of the constitution, has altered both the nature of kingship and its function. The role of the Sovereign is therefore inextricably linked with that of the political entity to which he or she belongs. Within that state, as we may now loosely call it, the king was first seen as the sacred head of the state, though his function included, from the earliest times, acting as a law-giver, as well as the leader of its army. The kingship was so intricately entwined in the apparatus of government, and so central to the polity, that its key rituals, and especially the coronation, augmented and reflected national identity, and were not merely ornamentation; they served, and continue to serve, deep constitutional and sociological purposes.

Likewise, the advent of feudalism in the early mediæval period meant everywhere in Europe an increased emphasis upon the coronation as a sacring and dedication of the new king and the formation of formal feudal bonds of fealty. In addition, feudal kingship, in England at least, reflected a centralised concept of governance. But, at the same time, it encouraged a pluralist view of government, one which was to lead in time to the evolution of Parliament and then finally to politically accountable and responsible Parliaments. The subsequent development and extension of democracy as a legitimating force in the constitution (though certainly not the only one) does not, however, inherently displace the central role of the Sovereign, nor the vital importance of the coronation. Conversely, the latter may serve to emphasise the importance of the sacred in government, and the position of the Sovereign as the embodiment of the political and social entity we understand today as the sovereign state.

Even the question of the strict legal necessity for a coronation is more complex than the (*obiter dicta*) judicial answer given by the courts in *Calvin's Case* (also known as the *Case of the Postnati*),[12] in the early seventeenth century, a case already alluded to. This answer was that the automatic succession to the throne of the heir apparent, upon the death of the last king, renders a coronation strictly unnecessary because the royal title is complete upon the legal demise of the Crown. This judicial conclusion is partly justified because the coronation itself never created a man a king, but rather exalted him as such. It is also true that the concept of the automatic succession to the Crown is one which only dates from the late mediæval period. But that concept also ignores, or obscures, much of the constitutional significance of the coronation.

[12] (1608) 7 Co Rep 1a; 77 ER 377.

In a specifically Christian context, the church had an additional role in anointing and crowning the new Sovereign, whatever the precise nature of the relationship between church and state might have been or indeed is today. The recent evolution of the United Kingdom into what has many of the attributes of a facto federal state, with Scotland, Wales, and Northern Ireland having varying degrees of self-government,[13] has done nothing, it is suggested, to diminish the role of the Crown, and conversely has enhanced the importance of the Sovereign as a unifying element in the realm and therefore the coronation as a uniting social, political and even religious ritual, in a pluralist nation (or nations).

Through constitutional changes throughout the centuries, the coronation continued both as a religious service and a political inauguration and spectacle—a solemnity—one which at once emphasised and proclaimed the unity of the kingdom and the authority of the king, within this evolving but organic and complex constitution. Although at times relatively neglected, in that aesthetics and decorum, or even competent liturgics, were sometimes absent or neglected, nevertheless the necessity for a coronation as a crucial, if not wholly indispensable, solemnity of the realm, was very largely unquestioned, at least before the nineteenth century.

In a constitutional context where the king (or, more rarely, queen regnant) is the linchpin of the constitutional order—and even where this is not de facto or even de jure the case—the choice, accession and proclamation of the Sovereign is of paramount importance to political stability. In England the method of selection of the Sovereign has been settled for many centuries—almost a thousand years—though not without the occasional upheaval (most recently in 1936). But the present primarily statutory basis for succession did not originally exist—perforce since, in the earliest years a Parliament, even loosely defined, did not itself yet exist. As a general rule, the early kings, in the sub-Roman[14] and Saxon

[13] The United Kingdom arguably cannot, since the passage of the Government of Wales Acts 1998 and 2006, and the Scotland Act 1998 and Northern Ireland Act 1998, be considered a truly unitary state, though the Crown and the prerogative is unitary. Even the Union with Scotland Act 1707 (6 Anne c. 11) created a state which was only partially unitary.

[14] The term sub-Roman is here preferred to Dark Ages, which suggests a period of unremitting chaos, barbarism and paganism between the end of the western Roman empire and the rise of neo-Roman imperial authority in the west; Lot, Ferdinand, *The End of the Ancient World and the Beginnings of the Middle Ages* (1931).

eras, were chosen from amongst the members of the royal family, and a form of quasi-elective kingship, within the royal house, was customary (though there was some experience of the descent of the Crown by Will, in the later Saxon period—and an anachronistic attempted revival of it in the sixteenth century, by Edward VI). Ultimately, the strictly hereditary title prevailed, as a more formalised and institutionalised monarchy, and later state, evolved. Parliament's right to confirm—and later to alter—the succession, was asserted from time to time, once that body became a permanent constitutional feature. Even today the law and practice of the accession and coronation both reflect the dichotomy between hereditary title, and parliamentary title. The coronation served a vital role in establishing the authority of the king, and was not solely or even primarily a public (or private) spectacle or arcane religious ritual.

In this broad constitutional context, the coronation involves the setting aside and consecrating of a new Sovereign, their presentation and proclamation to "the great and good" (however that might be understood in the time), and a grand public spectacle—as well as being a constitutional event of great antiquity and significance. This work will argue that this remains true today, although the respective weight of the legal, political and theological aspects of the coronation has changed over time, just as the role of the monarchy itself has changed through the centuries.

This work is not the first foray into the field of the coronation. There have been many works on English and later British coronations—in recent times usually written in time for one—most significantly varying from the early twentieth century researches of the father and son team of John and Leopold Wickham Legg, and the comprehensive 1937 history by the German scholar Percy Schramm, to numerous shorter and more popular (and unfortunately often hasty and derivative) works. The later lesser works have, however, included short books by Randolph Churchill (son of Sir Winston Churchill),[15] Brian Barker (a civil servant),[16] and others who were personally involved in a coronation, albeit often in a relatively junior capacity; Barker, who was Chief Information Officer of the Ministry of Works, was a Gold Staff Commander, whilst Churchill was a Gold Staff

[15] Churchill, Randolph, *The Story of the Coronation* (1953).

[16] Barker, Brian, *When the Queen was crowned* (1976).

Officer, for the coronation.[17] Each of these works has contributed something to a rich tapestry of our knowledge of past coronations, so that our understanding of what happened at coronations, at least over recent centuries, is comprehensive. Less has been said on their nature, or of their constitutional significance.

There had not, until recently, been a major work which brings up to date the scholarship of the past century or so. This is particularly unfortunate in light of the great amount of scholarship now extant in the fields of liturgical and ritual studies, and of monarchy and courts more generally. In the first years of the twenty-first century Sir Roy Strong, former director of the Victoria and Albert Museum, and of the National Portrait Gallery in London, and one of the foremost British arts critics, writers and broadcasters, helped to fill this gap. He brought us what can, with some justification, be called the definitive history of the coronation to date,[18] though the book was, to some extent, idiosyncratic.

Strong took us through the history of the coronation (the subject of his work was the coronation in Westminster Abbey, technically His Majesty's Collegiate Church of Saint Peter, Westminster, so Scottish coronations received comparably slight and peripheral attention).[19] His coverage was always with an eye to the contemporary context, but at the same time emphasised continuity. Indeed, as Strong rightly observed, the English coronation service showed remarkable resilience, with the form of the coronation of King Edgar in 973 (the earliest for which comprehensive details are available, and which was also politically one of the most

[17] Gold Staff Officers were ushers at the coronation, used since 1761. In 1953 there were 400, appointed by the Earl Marshal. The Gold Staff Commanders were team leaders of the ushers.

[18] Strong, Sir Roy, *Coronation* (2005).

[19] Pope John XVII granted the kings of Scots the right to be crowned and anointed in 1329, although their practice was considerably older—being a fusion of the ceremonies of the kings of Dál Riata (or Dalriada), based on the inauguration of Aidan in 574, and that of the Picts, from whom the Stone of Destiny allegedly came; Thomas, Andrea, "Coronation Ritual and Regalia", in Julian Goodare and Alasdair A. MacDonald (eds.), *Sixteenth Century Scotland* (2008), pp. 43–68, 46–47. See Shaw, Dougal, "Scotland's Place in Britain's Coronation Tradition" (2004) 9(1) The Court Historian 41–60

important, at the apogee of Old English kingship)[20] being clearly recognisable as the prototype, template and forerunner of King Charles III's coronation in 2023.

That is not to say, however, that the symbolism, and the purpose (let alone content and structure), of the coronation has not changed substantially over time. In the early mediæval period the coronation, in England as elsewhere, owed much to the blending of pagan tribal kingship (and even early Roman republicanism)—with its acclamation, and formal bestowal of a helmet and other regalia[21]—into a Christian tradition, with eclectic borrowings from, inter alia, Israel, Francia, the Holy Roman Empire, and the eastern Roman empire. The European coronation of the early middle ages was primarily a religious ceremony (perhaps unsurprisingly in an era dominated by the church, east and west), with the heir becoming fully king through their anointing and crowning by the agency of a prelate of the church. Not every European country included anointing in the coronation (which generally required the papal *imprimatur*), but crowning was early to be ubiquitous; girding with a sword, or crowning with a circlet was the norm in the duchy of Normandy, for instance.[22] But however much the details differed, each borrowed very largely from each other in a sort of constitutional and ceremonial "arms race", the prize being unquestioned legitimacy and what we later termed sovereignty, but which was often referred to as *imperium*, after the old Roman concept.[23] For instance, if one kingdom obtained papal authorisation for anointing, others might wish to obtain that also, so that they might not be thought inferior in any way.

Although the right to rule was not dependent upon being crowned and anointed—many early kings were to have a coronation comparatively late in their reign—the coronation served to significantly consolidate their

[20] Jones, Adrienne, "The Significance of the Regal Consecration of Edgar in 973" (1982) 33(3) The journal of ecclesiastical history 375–390.

[21] Regalia refers to the physical insignia of sovereignty, derived from *jura regalia*; Blackstone, Sir William, *Commentaries on the Laws of England* (1st ed., 1979), Book the First, p. 234.

[22] Cannon, John and Ralph Griffiths, *The Oxford Illustrated History of the British Monarchy* (1988), p. 116.

[23] Richardson, John, "The Meaning of *imperium* in the Last Century BC and the First AD", in Benedict Kingsbury, and Benjamin Straumann (eds.), *The Roman Foundations of the Law of Nations* (2010).

status, as well as conferring the *imprimatur* or authority of the church.[24] King Edgar's coronation in 973 may perhaps be seen more as a culmination and pinnacle of his reign, almost a triumphal procession in the Roman sense,[25] than as the endorsement of his right to rule. It may indeed not have been his first coronation—multiple coronations were not uncommon in mediæval times. A contrast may be made with ancient Egyptian coronations, which emphasised the assumption of authority of the new pharaoh (the term by which we usually know the ancient Egyptian kings, as distinct from the later khedives and sultans, styled king after 1922[26]), in a series of political and religious ceremonies which reminded the people at once of the role of the king as preserver of continuity, and also as the sacred embodiment of the state. A second coronation, from this perspective, would be unthinkable.

As with much of the constitutional law, the origins of the coronation lie in the laws of England, adopted and translated into the broader United Kingdom context. In this understanding, this book focusses on the coronation ceremony held in Westminster Abbey since 1066 (and earlier still at other locations), rather than the coronation of the King of Scots,[27] or indeed the investiture of the Prince of Wales (which savours more of the investiture of peers than the coronation of a Sovereign). The most recent investiture of a Prince of Wales was in 1969 and there appear, as of 2023, to be no plans for a future investiture. The modern practice, in any event, only dates from 1911, and that of 1969 was only the second modern investiture.[28] The Scottish coronation is very much older but has not been held since 1651.

[24] Edgar reigned 959–975, and was only crowned in 973; Williams, Ann, "Edgar (called Edgar Pacificus) (943/4–975)", in *Oxford Dictionary of National Biography* (2004); Huscroft, Richard, *The Norman Conquest* (2013), p. 21.

[25] The *triumphus* was a civil ceremony and religious rite of ancient Rome, held to publicly celebrate and sanctify the success of a military commander who had led Roman forces to victory; Beard, Mary, *The Roman Triumph* (2007).

[26] Hassan, H., *In the House of Muhammad Ali* (2000).

[27] The last of which was in 1651; Gross, George William Cullen, "1651: The Last Coronation in Scotland — An Anomaly?" (2021) 26(3) The Court Historian 229–245.

[28] Ellis, John Stephen, *Investiture* (2008). The investiture of peers was abolished in 1621, being replaced by the introduction; Wagner, Sir Anthony and J. C. Sainty, *The Origin of the Introduction of Peers in the House of Lords* (1967), pp. 132–134.

Methodology and Structure

Coronations as understood in the traditional western European sense, are, in those countries which remain monarchies, increasingly rarely found, though they are far from extinct. They indeed may be seen as an exceptional survival of a vanishing era, an age dominated by kingship and Christianity—although some non-Christian kingdoms retain, have adopted, or once had, comparable inaugurations. But the coronation, as the term is generally understood in the context of the United Kingdom, is a unique hybrid of election, tribal inauguration, political acknowledgment and sacred setting apart, which make its legal, political and theological roles highly significant.

The fact that the United Kingdom is one of the few monarchies which retain (or ever had) coronations, does not diminish the importance of the coronation—indeed, rather the opposite. The country is also the last of the great monarchies of Europe, excepting Spain (which never had a coronation), so it would perhaps be surprising if it did not retain such an ancient ritual and solemnity. It is in the context of its historical setting its theological and political underpinnings and rationale, and indeed a more modern sociological understanding of the role of ritual, that the importance of the coronation as a constitutional ritual of the highest importance is to be understood, and therefore its necessity may be considered.

This book takes the form of a discursive interpretive study. It seeks to evaluate the thesis, which it advances, that the coronation remains, in the United Kingdom, an essential public ritual for legal, political and theological reasons, and is not merely an historical antiquarian relic, or preserved for the benefit of the tourism sector (however valuable each may otherwise be). The respective weight to be ascribed to each of these three key elements has, as was suggested above, changed through the centuries. Perhaps today, when the Christian religion arguably plays a lesser role socially, legally, economically, ethically, morally and politically in Europe than it has for centuries, the theological aspect of the coronation is lessened (though this is by no means inherently so).

Conversely, with the growth in the importance of state ceremonial as an assertion of political legitimacy, it might be argued that the political aspect of the coronation today predominates. Yet, it will be suggested, such an interpretation is insufficiently nuanced, failing to consider the ways in which the various aspects of the coronation are interwoven into the fabric of society, church and state, over a timeframe of more than a thousand years. Each element therefore augments the others, and none can be dismissed as irrelevant or of no contemporary importance in light of the conditions of the country today.

It is a strange dichotomy, but perhaps a false one, to suggest that the constitutional or legal, political or realpolitik, and theological or ecclesiological aspects of the coronation, are in opposition to one another, though there may at times be tension between the legal, political and theological arguments for and against the strict necessity for a coronation, or for the inclusion or exclusion of particular elements and details—or individuals. The coronation is as much a political and legal occasion as it is a religious one, though it has always contained elements of each. It has evolved to the extent that it carries its own constitutional status and importance, justifying its own continued existence through its unquestioned (or almost unquestioned) pedigree and self-fulfilling purpose of king-enhancing and national (or perhaps kingdom-wide) and indeed transnational and international—and previously imperial—image building.

Because the coronation is a political, legal and religious event, it is necessary to consider its role from these three perspectives. Each will be examined in turn. But we will commence with a review of the broader history of coronations, their nature and something of their structure, from the wider perspective of their origins in the near east and Mediterranean basin. This is necessary to help understand the origins and function of the coronation, and the role which it played across the wide sweep of Mediterranean, Near Eastern and European civilisation, all of which exhibited common elements grounded in the common purpose of a coronation as a constitutional ritual, a rite of passage, and guarantor (or so it was hoped) of a successful political succession from one ruler to the next.

Chapter 2, coronations in context, canvasses the development of the coronation, as a sacred state rite, from its earliest appearance in the ancient near east, through the Roman Empire, east and west, the Germanic kingdoms and the early mediæval European monarchies, and its appearance and early evolution in Britain. The emphasis is upon continuity and commonality of themes and elements, and in particular the conscious and unconscious cross-fertilisation and borrowings across countries and civilisations and through the centuries. The evolution of coronations, and their very deliberate borrowing from traditions around the Mediterranean basin and Europe, was to reflect the conscious and subconscious desire to establish and maintain authority and legitimacy. The strongest claims later came to be the twin pillars of descent from imperial Rome, and the support of the hierarchy of the Christian church, exemplified by the crowning of the eastern emperors by the Œcumenical Patriarch in Constantinople, and of the Holy Roman Emperors by the Patriarch of the West in Rome.[29] Any European ruler who aspired to recognition of equality to the Holy Roman emperor or the eastern emperors needed to both mimic the state rituals of the imperial courts,[30] and to invoke equivalent ecclesiastical approbation.

In chapter 3, the background to the legal function of the English and later British coronation is examined, in particular its constitutive function. This chapter considers in detail the law and practice in respect to the succession. Although the evolution of the law of succession to the Crown was to ultimately favour a strictly hereditary title, augmented by statutory limitations, nevertheless the coronation served a vital purpose in establishing, proclaiming and endorsing the choice of king.

Chapter 4 draws together the constitutional steps which occur between the demise of the Crown and the coronation. The coronation is the fulfilment of a series of events which occur upon the demise of the Crown, to pass sovereignty from one person to the next. Most importantly, not only was authority conveyed, but it was conveyed to the true and rightful heir, as determined by a pre-existing criteria or process.

In chapter 5 the political function of the coronation is explored, particularly in relation to the unity of the state and the symbolic and practical role of the monarch. In particular, it is concerned with the establishment and preservation of legitimacy. This is a Weberian historical legitimacy,[31] based in continuity and conformity, rather than the legitimacy of the ballot box, or the force of arms or mere might. This political function has been particularly significant as a response to constitutional changes,

[29] In 2024, Pope Francis reinstated the title, reversing Pope Benedict XVI's 2006 renunciation of it; Wooden, Cindy, "'Patriarch of the West' reappears as papal title in Vatican yearbook". *National Catholic Reporter*, 11 April 2024.

[30] Even to the extent of adopting a so-called imperial crown—one with arches—which mimicked that of the Holy Roman Empire; Twining, Edward Lord, *A History of the Crown Jewels of Europe* (1960).

[31] Collins, Randall, *Weberian Sociological Theory* (1986); Weiler, Björn, "Describing Rituals of Succession and the Legitimation of Kingship in the West, ca. 1000–ca. 1150", in Alexander Beihammer, Stavroula Constantinou, and Maria G. Parani (eds.), *Court Ceremonies and Rituals of Power in Byzantium and the Mediæval Mediterranean* (2013), pp. 113–140.

not least the establishment of the United Kingdom in 1801,[32] and the ongoing development of a de facto if not de jure federal state since the late twentieth century.[33] The unifying function of the monarchy, and of the coronation, has increased significance, as other institutions, hitherto fulfilling a unifying function, may be unable to do so any longer.

In chapter 6 the theological character of the coronation is examined. In this chapter the connection between church and state is discussed, as well as the spiritual character of the person of the monarch. This aspect is both the most ancient—anointing was used in both Egyptian and Israeli coronations—and perhaps the most likely to be questioned in a pluralistic, increasingly secular society. Yet the continuity of the sacring, largely unchanged despite the Reformation, served and continues to serve a key role in establishing and declaring the role of the Sovereign as the divinely sanctioned servant of God and the country. Even—and arguably especially—in a pluralist society the role of the church as a source of spiritual, religious and moral authority remains of great importance. And who can forget the words of William Shakespeare?

> Not all the water in the rough rude sea / Can wash the balm off from an anointed king; The breath of worldly men cannot depose / The deputy elected by the Lord.[34]

The Conclusion addresses the combined effect and consequences of the various legal, political and theological functions of the coronation, and ends the work with a review of the primary thesis—that the strength and importance of the coronation lies, not in any single political, legal, constitutional or theological function, but rather in the combination of all of these factors. Ultimately, in the British tradition, the coronation is a constitutional ritual *par excellence*, exhibiting features from a multitude of sources, cobbled together over more than a thousand years, adapting to changing expectations, priorities and needs, and serving to unite the kingdoms, even if only for a day, in a solemnity of national rejoicing and commitment.

[32] Union with Scotland Act 1707 (6 Anne c. 11); Union with Ireland Act 1800 (39 & 40 Geo III c 67).

[33] Government of Wales Acts 1998 and 2006, the Scotland Act 1998 and Northern Ireland Act 1998.

[34] *Richard II*, Act III, Scene 3.

CHAPTER 2

Coronations in Context

Introduction

Once widespread amongst the sovereign states of Europe and copied—and with independently evolved analogous examples elsewhere in the world—today there remains but one example of what might loosely be described as the classic European coronation, that of the Sovereign of the United Kingdom. The latter is, in large part, the ancient English coronation adapted for a wider purpose. This study is largely confined to that specific example—the British coronation—for the political, constitutional and religious contexts of other states and civilisations are often markedly dissimilar, and any comparisons fraught with conceptual and practical difficulties. Specifically, any comparison with other contemporary examples of coronations, or historical comparisons with other analogous traditions, beyond exploring their formative influences on the British coronation (where this occurred), ought generally to be avoided.

The British coronation comes from a long Christian tradition, which largely shapes it in principle and in practice. But not all coronations share this tradition. In non-Christian states, coronation rites evolved from a variety of sources, and under many influences, often related to the religious beliefs and cultural and historical traditions of that particular nation. Buddhism, for instance, influenced the coronation rituals

N. Cox, *The Political, Legal, and Theological Functions of the Ceremony in the British Tradition*,
https://doi.org/10.1007/978-3-031-88960-8_2

of the Kingdom of Thailand,[1] although a Hindu influence is also apparent. A Buddhist tradition also predominated in the Kingdom of Cambodia,[2] and in the Kingdom of Bhutan,[3] while Hindu rituals played a significant role in the now abandoned Nepalese coronation rites.[4]

Shinto rites influenced the Japanese coronation ceremony,[5] which is of particularly ancient origins—although, as with all coronations and inaugurations, also now contains more modern (and indeed in some cases alien) accretions, which are however broadly in harmony with the overall structure, form and nature of the indigenous ceremony. The Emperor of Japan, or Tennō ("heavenly sovereign"), was formerly regarded as a living ***arahitogami*** or ***kami***, or deity, in the state religion, Shinto.[6] Even though his divinity was officially denied at the conclusion of the Second World War—although the precise meaning of the statement supposedly having this effect is controversial—the coronation of the Japanese emperor remains steeped in traditional custom and beliefs, and its structure, rationale and content remains of a traditional nature, with no obvious intention of

[1] In Thailand the most recent coronation was held on 4 May 2019 for King Vajiralongkorn; "Coronation of HM King Maha Vajiralongkorn to be held May 4–6: palace". The Nation. January 2019.

[2] Cambodian King Norodom Sihamoni's coronation was 29th October 2004, and compared to Thai coronations—or earlier Cambodian one's—was comparatively simple; "Cambodia's muted coronation", BBC News, 29 October 2004.

[3] The coronation of the *Druk Gyalpo* ("Dragon King") of the Kingdom of Bhutan, Jigme Khesar Namgyel Wangchuck, was held 6th November 2008; "Lavish coronation for Bhutan king", BBC, 6 November 2008; "Bhutan to crown its fifth king in November", 23 July 2008, In.reuters.com.

[4] The last Nepalese coronation was held on 4th June 2001 for King Gyanendra; "The once and future king", 15 June 2001–21 June 2001, *Nepali Times*.

[5] The enthronement (*Sokui no rei*) of the Japanese Emperor dates from enthronement of Emperor Kanmu in 781 (traditionally the 50th emperor, in a line dating back to 660 BC, though more historically certain to the 3rd to 6th centuries); Holtom, D. C., *Japanese Enthronement Ceremonies* (1972).

[6] This was purportedly renounced in 1946 in The Humanity Declaration (*Ningensengen*), also known as the *Imperial Rescript on the Construction of a New Japan* (*Shin Nippon Kensetsu ni Kan suru Shōsho*), *Imperial Rescript on National Revitalization* (*Nentō, Kokuun Shinkō no Shōsho*), and *Imperial Rescript Denying His Divinity*. The correctness of this understanding has, however, been challenged; Dower, John, *Embracing Defeat* (1999), pp. 314–317.

departing from the legitimacy of time-honoured ritual.[7] This concept of the legitimacy and tenacity of ritual is one which repeats itself in most, if not all, traditions, and is a principle feature of coronations world-wide.

The ceremonies used in the modern countries of Malaysia and Brunei, were shaped by strong Islamic influences, but also incorporated local cultural and political traditions, as well as exhibiting some—generally more recently added—western influences. Tonga's modern coronation ritual combines some ancient Polynesian influences (such as *kava* drinking and the presentation of feast animals) with more overtly western and Christian elements, such as crowning and anointing.[8] This reflects the fact that the monarchy, though of ancient Pacific Islands origin, only assumed its present form in the nineteenth century, under European (and predominantly British) influence.

The coronations in (modern) Egypt,[9] and Iran,[10] were, like those in Malaysia and Brunei, strongly Islamic in nature, whilst also incorporating significant native traditions. In contrast, the Ethiopian coronation ceremony was exclusively Christian—although the Ethiopian empire contained within its borders a considerable Muslim population—and uniquely included seven anointings, with seven different oils.[11] Like the coronations in every other state which has them, it also exhibited particular local features, and it was also notable for the antiquity of some of these, unsurprising for a monarchy with legendary origins in the persons

[7] Emperor Naruhito's enthronement took place 22nd October 2019; Katsuhisa, Saitō, "Pomp and Pageantry: Emperor Naruhito's Enthronement Ceremony", 21 October 2019, nippon.com.

[8] King Tupou VI of Tonga was crowned 4th July 2015, almost three years after his accession. The King was anointed with holy oil, adorned with a ring, and presented with a sceptre. The crown was then placed on his head by the Reverend D'Arcy Wood, a retired Uniting Church in Australia minister; Fox, Liam, "Tonga crowns King Tupou VI in lavish public coronation, parties", 4 July 2015, Nuku'alofa, ABC News.

[9] The last coronation in Egypt was that of 20th July 1937 for the 16-year old King Farouk I; Stadiem, William, *Too Rich* (1991), pp, 155–156.

[10] In Iran, the coronation, on 26th October 1967, occurred 26 years after the accession of Shāhanshāh Mohammad Reza Pahlavi; Steele, R., "Crowning the 'Sun of the Aryans': Mohammad Reza Shah's Coronation and Monarchical Spectacle in Pahlavi Iran" (2021) 53(2) International Journal of Middle East Studies 175–193.

[11] Timothy, I., *The Coronation of H.I.M. Emperor Haile Selassie I* (1983).

of the Queen of Sheba and King Solomon.[12] Whatever the traditional basis of each monarchy's coronation, most coronations, past and present, have some common elements, derived from their function, as well as borrowing from the traditions of other states, especially those within the cultural, political or religious orbit of the country.

Indigenous sub-national monarchies also preserve, or preserved until comparatively recently, various forms of coronation or inauguration, often drawing on traditional cultural and religious practises and beliefs, occasionally with additional elements derived from Christian, Muslim, Buddhist, or other imports. Religious influences were often of paramount importance, and in many cases still remain so, in determining the structure, content and purpose of the coronation.

At its heart a western coronation may be seen as a melding of national (or sub-national) political and cultural beliefs within the context of an overarching religious belief system. A coronation may be further distinguished from a mere inauguration of a king or queen in that the latter ceremony, by whatever term it may be described, omits the central element, the formal placing of the crown (or equivalent headdress) upon the head of the newly installed Sovereign, and their anointing with holy oil (though the latter was never ubiquitous). The crown—the physical crown rather than a heraldic representation[13]—was latterly present at the inauguration of the King of Sweden, for instance, but was not placed upon his head, nor worn, as it had been at the former Swedish coronations.

Coronations, however defined, and in their various forms, have existed since earliest antiquity in the Near East; equivalent rituals are to be found in other parts of the world, but as the focus of this study is English (and later British) coronations, the emphasis will be on the historical and conceptual lineage to which that belongs. Coronations, as understood in the above terms, evolved from origins in the ancient near east—primarily Egypt and Israel—through the practice of the Roman empire (east and

[12] Kaplan, Stephen, "Solomonic dynasty", in Bausi, Alessandro, Appleyard, David L., Uhlig, Siegbert, Kaplan, Steven, & Hahn, Wolfgang (eds.), *Ethiopia* (2017), pp. 111–112.

[13] In heraldry a crown or coronet, denoting rank, need not necessarily reflect the actual appearance of any particular crown; Cox, Noel, "The Coronets of Members of the Royal Family and of the Peerage" (2000) 22 The Double Tressure, the Journal of The Heraldry Society of Scotland 8–13.

west, though principally the former), and then through early post-Roman western Europe.

From the fourth century onwards, Christian elements began to appear in coronations, until they became pre-dominant in the late mediæval period. Concurrently, tribal customs, especially Germanic, and national and regional cultural traditions, added to the varied mixture, at least in some countries. The complexion of coronations in Europe varied considerably, depending to a greater or a lesser extent on local influences, but common elements remained clearly discernible. Today, the British coronation may be described as a rich and complex blend of ancient Israeli, early mediæval Eastern Roman (Byzantine), Frankish, late mediæval western European, and uniquely English elements. Later Scottish, and more recently still Commonwealth elements were included, whilst the ritual as a whole remained faithful to the earliest models, content and purpose. The core remains the structure used at the coronation of King Edgar in 973, and which probably had significantly earlier origins.

Coronations serve multiple purposes in each civilisation, state or other political entity in which they appear. However, elements exist which are largely common to all. In each, historical continuity is generally highly regarded, as a necessary legitimising aspect of the ritual—the new Sovereign's authority depends not on their individual might or merit but on their stepping into the shoes—or perhaps rather assuming the crown—of their predecessors. The approbation of the religious establishment, and of the political and social elite (whatever form that may take) is also fundamentally important. The rituals themselves vary considerably, but as we shall see, enjoy a considerable degree of cross-fertilisation, embedded in the historical, religious, political and cultural traditions of each state, but also influenced by the coronation rituals of neighbouring states, friend or rival alike.

A look at the evolution of coronations from their early origins in the near east helps us to understand both the evolution of the ritual and its conceptual elements. These origins illustrate both the historical precedents and the lingering quest for legitimacy and public and private authority. We shall now briefly canvass the development of the coronation as a ritual, from its origins in the ancient near east.

Ancient Near Eastern Coronations

Kingship in the ancient near east varied according to the religious, political and social conditions, and the various kingdoms were far from identical; the Canaanite and Egyptian monarchies were quite dissimilar from one another. However, there were common elements that can be identified, although much more is known of some monarchies than others. The view was generally or at least widely held that there was a direct relationship between the king and the deity (or deities). This might take the form of the king being divine, or the son or descendant of a god, or it might be that the king, though not himself divine, was the god's representative on earth, or the god's (or gods') chosen servant. The implications of this were profound and far reaching and have significantly affected the common modern perception that near eastern monarchy was autocratic—a view, indeed, which was to have a major effect on imperial Roman attitudes to the east.

The king, as the deity's elect, or a son of a god, was not an autocrat per se. His power over his subjects was not arbitrary—nor derived from mere force nor threat of force—but based on the principle of his authority being the embodiment of a god's will for humanity, and specifically for that state. It was thus a delegated authority, which might, in certain circumstances, be revoked by the god, if the king angered or dissatisfied them and was subsequently unable or indeed unwilling to assuage the latter's righteous anger.

Supplication and appeasement of the gods was often a daily part of the role of a king, and the neglect of such services could and generally did have dire consequences, not simply for the king, but for his kingdom as well. The Old Testament recounts the histories of numerous Israelite kings who allowed the proper worship of God to lapse or be neglected, and therefore inhibited or impeded the fullness of the kingdom and the peoples' relationship with God. All such kings paid the price for so doing, though sometimes belatedly. Gaining—and subsequently retaining—the favour of the deity was central to obtaining and preserving political power. The relationship between king and god was crucial, and if the king himself was descended from the god or gods, or otherwise divine, so much the better; the higher their personal status the greater their bargaining power in their role as intermediary between god(s) and humanity. A comparison may be made with Japan, whose emperor, as has been noted, was formerly, if not today, regarded as a deity.[14]

Not all kings in the near east were of course regarded as personally of a divine status. Sumerian kings were not generally regarded as themselves being divine, but kingship itself was nevertheless introduced from heaven, rather than being an earthly or merely human creation; an analogy may be seen with later Saxon kingship, where kingship was generally traced from a pagan god. This gave Sumerian kingship an institutional legitimacy which extended well beyond the status of the individual king, however great his individual merit and profound his political, military, architectural, and other earthly achievements might have been.[15] The office, rather than the individual, was the focus, and this meant that there was an emphasis upon institutional continuity. Rituals, particularly those of regnal inaugurations, or of the seasonal appeasement (especially of capricious gods), were essential.[16]

Based on the limited archaeological evidence available, it is possible to believe that the coronation of a new Canaanite king may have involved some kind of ritual procession or ceremony in which the new ruler was presented to the people and blessed by the priests or other religious figures. The king may also have been anointed with oil or other sacred substances to symbolise his status as the chosen representative of the gods.[17]

Egypt

In contrast to Sumerian kingship, in the Egyptian theo-political model, kingship itself was divine, not simply because like Sumerian kingship it was introduced from heaven, but because, in addition, it was a vital part

[14] See the Humanity Declaration (*Ningen-sengen*), *Imperial Rescript on the Construction of a New Japan* (*Shin Nippon Kensetsu ni Kan suru Shōsho*), *Imperial Rescript on National Revitalization* (*Nentō, Kokuun Shinkō no Shōsho*), and *Imperial Rescript Denying His Divinity*; Dower, John, *Embracing Defeat* (1999), pp. 314–317.

[15] Crawford, Hariet, *The Sumerian World* (2013).

[16] Erickson, Kyle, "The early Seleucids, their gods and their coins" (2010) University of Exeter PhD thesis.

[17] Day, John, "The Canaanite inheritance of the Israeli monarchy", in John Day (ed.), *King and Messiah in Israel and the Ancient Near East* (2013), pp. 72–90.

of the order of creation. The king was not merely a representative of the gods, but had divine powers and authority—and responsibility—whilst here on earth. Again, as in Sumeria, failure to perform the proper rites might have dire consequences for king and kingdom alike. But, unlike in Sumerian kingship, it was not so much to appease the gods, but rather to maintain the cosmic balance and harmony; something only a king who was himself divine could achieve. It is quite likely that this conception was influenced by the development of Egyptian kingship in the context of a hydraulic civilisation,[18] one based, like those of Mesopotamia and the Indus Valley, on the use and control of water. The balance of humanity and nature, human and divine, was essential to life, and the order brought from heaven was mediated through the kings. They were truly *in loco deos*. The divide between human and divine was bridged by and in the kingship of the pharaohs. Though their power, secular and spiritual (if such a division were possible to conceive in such a system) was great, so too were their responsibilities.

These divine, or divinely inspired, powers and responsibilities were reflected in the iconography and ceremonial of the Egyptian kingship. A number of images of Egyptian coronations, including those of the Pharaohs Rameses II and Seti I in the thirteenth century BC, have survived to the present time,[19] though written texts are rarer.[20] Set within the context of a divine, and divinely descended, monarchy, these served at once a political and a religious function—an aspect which remained common in the much later European coronation theory and practice. Indeed, there was rarely a strict separation between political power and status and religious authority and legitimacy, and this conceptual unity was to survive, to a greater or lesser extent, in the development of coronations in both the near east and in Europe. The Egyptian kings were often crowned with the joint crowns of Upper and Lower Egypt, symbolising in their person and in their attire the unity of the kingdom. The embodiment in one person of the unity of the state has long been a central aspect of the coronation. The sacred nature of the kingship was reflected in the ritual

[18] See Cox, Noel, *Constitutional paradigms and the stability of states* (2012).

[19] See "The Coronation of Ramses II in the presence of his father Seti and the Theban Triad. Qurnah Temple of Seti I", in Keith C. Seele, *The Coregency of Ramses II with Seti I and the date of the great hypostyle hall at Karnack* (1940), p. 28.

[20] Gardiner, Sir Alan, "The Coronation of King Ḥaremḥab" (1953) 39(1) The Journal of Egyptian Archaeology 13–31.

of the coronation, both in the participation of priests and in the nature of the ritual itself. The notion of the separation of church and state, so beloved of many modern theorists, was quite alien to the Egyptian mind, as indeed it was in many civilisations throughout the long centuries for which we have recorded histories.[21]

Because the Egyptian king—or pharaoh—had both religious and political functions, and was a pivotal part of the created order, the ritual surrounding the succession to the throne was of fundamental political and religious significance. Immediately upon the death of the reigning pharaoh, his successor was named (assuming that all was well in the state, and the succession was both prompt and unchallenged), so that the kingdom's cosmic protection would continue unbroken. While the new monarch ascended the throne the very next day, the coronation ceremony did not take place until the first day of a new season. This was probably both for practical reasons—so that arrangements for a suitably splendid ceremonial might be made, and the necessary political and religious elite could be present—as well as for symbolic reasons (the beginning of a new season was appropriate for the commencement of a new regime).

In later centuries the ceremony was usually carried out at Memphis by the high priest of Ptah, who invested the new king with the necessary powers to continue his predecessors' work of mediation between gods and humanity. The *imprimatur* of the priests was vital to the legitimacy of a claim to divine status. Ptah was an Egyptian creator god who conceived the world and brought it into being through the creative power of speech.[22]

The central role of the priests of Ptah was to be preserved even under the reign of the Hellenistic Ptolemies, until the end of the ancient Egyptian monarchy in 30 BC, when the kingdom became a province of the Roman Empire. The retention of the pivotal role of Ptah in the Egyptian coronation under the Ptolemies was one of many examples where the legitimacy of a regime, which might otherwise be questioned—the Ptolemies were not native Egyptians, but descended from one of Alexander the Great's generals, and were of Macedonian ancestry—was

[21] See, for example, Cox, Noel, *Church and State in the Post-Colonial Era* (2008).

[22] Allen, James P., *Genesis in Egypt: The Philosophy of Ancient Egyptian Creation Accounts* (1988), pp. 38–41.

reinforced and bolstered symbolically and practically by careful adherence to both the form and substance of the constitutional practices of the *ancien regime*. Royal ritual and ceremonial were called upon to fulfil a political purpose, specifically, to reinforce legitimacy and reflect continuity and conformity with tradition. No pharaoh, or his advisers, dared ignore the important role of the religious establishment of the high priests of the senior gods, or the need to conform with previous practice—the fate of Pharaoh Akhenaton[23] would have been shared by many more rulers had others too presumed to depart from tradition in a similarly revolutionary manner. Radically altering, or attempting to alter, the structures, concepts and traditions which underpin any ruler's own authority threatens, inevitably, their own legitimacy and claim to authority.

Egyptian coronation rituals established, in their political and religious aspects, many of the themes later echoed in European coronations (though often for very different reasons, and of course in wholly different political, theological and cultural contexts). Although the most significant record of Egyptian coronations is contained in the Palermo stone, chronicling the succession of pharaohs from the first to the fifth dynasties of the Old Kingdom,[24] nevertheless we can obtain a relatively clear picture of at least some of the rituals involved throughout the age of the pharaohs. What might be called the coronation proper formed but a small part of the whole ritual. Essentially this latter took place over the course of a year—the coronation year. The year of the coronation marked the beginning of the new regnal era. Rites were celebrated to emphasise equally the political power of the pharaoh, his divine attributes, and his popular rule. In a British—or any later European—coronation, these ancient rites might be said to be reflected respectively in the crowning and investing, anointing, and acclamation and homage, packaging, as it were, the ceremonials which in Egypt covered a whole year, into a series of rites which occupied a few short hours.

The king's divine attributes were celebrated in the emblematic rite of the suckling of the young king (by the goddess Isis), as if he—the king—were the successor in spirit of the child god Horus. He would be purified

[23] Dodson, Aidan, *Amarna Sunrise: Egypt from the Golden Age to Age of Heresy* (2014); O'Connor, David B. and Eric H. Cline (eds.), *Amenhotep III* (1998).

[24] The stone is one of seven surviving fragments of a stele known as the Royal Annals of the Old Kingdom of Ancient Egypt; Wilkinson, Toby, *Royal Annals of Ancient Egypt* (2000).

with water and anointed with oil. This emphasised not merely the sacred origins of kingship but also the individual pharaoh's ongoing relationship with the divine. This made him, if not a god, a foster child of the gods, able to mediate on familiar terms with the gods—or as familiar as mere mortals can achieve. The transformation of the new pharaoh from a royal son into the divine king was both immediate upon his succession and gradual, in that he assumed the attributes of his divinity in a series of public (and some private) rituals. Like later conceptions of European kingship, a sacred status was not acquired solely by the mere act of accession, or indeed at the coronation, but through a more fluid process. It can perhaps best be thought of as a journey, a transformation.[25] Once complete, the king could assure the preservation of the cosmic balance, provided the proper rites were performed.

The very existence of Egypt as a state and as a civilisation depended upon the preservation of this balance, and the king alone could ensure this—if anyone could—by their necessary intercession and mediation with the gods. It required a divine king to intercede with sufficient authority with the gods; a lesser mortal would have inadequate standing to mediate successfully, and might indeed incur the wrath of the gods upon such an upstart—and therefore upon the kingdom of Egypt itself.

The rites of the coronation included elements which reflected the status of the king, Each Egyptian crown, alone or in combination, represented either a territory, or an attribute, and sometimes both. Thus, the *Deshret* (red crown), containing the *uraeus* (a rearing cobra), represented the pharaohs of Lower Egypt and the desert Red Land, and the deities Horus, Wadjet and Neith. Likewise, the *Atef*, the crown of Osiris, was a combination of Upper Egypt's white crown, the *hedjet*, and ostrich feathers on either side. It also often had a golden disc at its tip. The ostrich feathers, similar to those representing *ma'at*, symbolised truth, justice, morality, and balance. They also represented the cultic centre of Osiris, which was in Busiris, in Lower Egypt.[26] The *atef* was typically worn atop a pair of ram or bull horns as a circlet. The *uraeus* was a symbol for the goddess Wadjet,[27] who was the patroness of the Nile Delta and the

[25] Hunt, Alice, "British Coronation: A History", Gresham College, 2 May 2023.

[26] Located at the present-day Abu Sir Bana; Gomaà, Farouk, "Busiris (Abu Sir Bana)," in *Encyclopedia of the Archaeology of Ancient Egypt* (1999), p. 207.

[27] Herodotus, *The Histories*. translated by Mensch, Pamela, with notes by James Romm (2014), B:152; 155; 156.

protector of all of Lower Egypt.[28] The pharaohs wore the uraeus as a head ornament, to indicate *Wadjet*'s protection and reinforced the pharaoh's claim over the land.

The combination of crowns represented both the inherent syncretism of Egyptian theology and politics, and the symbolic unity of the state under the rule of the pharaoh. It can also be seen as a precursor of the occasional later European practice of incorporating elements from various constituent states into the crown or other insignia of a Sovereign. One very recent example is the 1821 sword of offering, in which the stones are arranged to form roses, thistles, shamrocks, oak leaves and acorns, to represent the constituent parts of the United Kingdom.[29]

Israel

Although the Egyptian kingship was for long centuries the pre-eminent example of monarchy in the near east, it was most certainly not alone. Nor was it the only example of a tradition which included coronations as a central royal practice. Almost 300 years after the Pharaohs Rameses II and Seti I reigned, according to the Hebrew *Bible*, kings David and Solomon and their successors were crowned and anointed, mostly by a high priest, sometimes by a prophet, and occasionally by both. The Jewish tradition of kingship was distinct from that of Egypt, as was its ritual of inauguration; similarities however existed, due to the inherent requirements of a public political and religious ritual, and to some degree of mutual influence. Both Egyptian pharaohs and Jewish kings were anointed, for example.

The earliest Jewish kings were inaugurated in a manner which reflected at once their sacred kingship and their close association with the high priests, though, as Ishide argues, Israeli kingship was dynastic from the start, in imitation of other near eastern monarchies.[30] The anthem "Zadok the Priest," recalling the anointing of King Solomon, has for centuries been sung at British coronations during the anointing. It had however been in use from long before the supremely glorious setting by Handel was composed (for the 1727 coronation of King George II). The

[28] Dunand, Françoise, and Christiane Zivie-Coche, *Cosmonogies, Creation, and Time: Order and Disorder in Creation* (2004), p. 347.

[29] Keay, Anna, *The Crown Jewels* (2011).

[30] Ishide, Tomoo, *The Royal Dynasties of Ancient Israel* (1977).

text of "Zadok the Priest," a loose translation of the antiphon "*Unxerunt Salomonem*",[31] had been used since the coronation of King Edgar at Bath in 973,[32] an event which is often described as the most significant early English coronation, if not the first, and the prototype for all subsequent British coronations to this day. The biblical precedent was consciously followed, in the use of 1 King's 1:45:

> And Zadok the priest and Nathan the prophet have anointed him king in Gihon: and they are come up from thence rejoicing, so that the city rang again. This is the noise that ye have heard.

Zadok was High Priest of Israel during the reigns of David and Solomon.[33] The Biblical tradition of kings being anointed—and sometimes, though not invariably, also crowned—was clear. It was also, like much of the Israeli kingship, derived from a Canaanite model.[34] The use of the passage was a reminder of the scriptural origins, not simply of the coronation, but of kingship itself. Old Testament Scripture also tells of the anointing of Jehu as king of Israel.[35] Saul and David were both anointed and both were immediately inspired by the spirit of God (1 Samuel 9:1, 1 Samuel 16:13), having assumed the status of rulers chosen by God. In later centuries, as in England, so to in France Zadok was commemorated at coronations in a similar manner.[36]

The relationship of the religious and political aspects of kingship are significant in Jewish tradition, just as it was in Egypt, and are reflected in the nature of the inauguration of the kings. Although at times kingship was seen as controversial, in that it was questioned whether the people

[31] Hughes, Andrew, "Antiphons and Acclamations: The Politics of Music in the Coronation Service of Edward II, 1308" (Spring 1988) 6(2) The Journal of Musicology 150–168. Antiphons are short chants, sung as a refrain, usually for the introit, offertory or communion.

[32] Range, Matthew, *Music and Ceremonial at British Coronation* (2012), p.10; "Guide to the Coronation Service", Westminster Abbey. <https://www.westminster-abbey.org/about-the-abbey/history/royalty/coronations>.

[33] 2 Samuel 8:16–19.

[34] "The Canaanite inheritance of the Israeli monarchy", in John Day (ed.), *King and Messiah in Israel and the Ancient Near East* (2013), pp. 72–90.

[35] 2 Kings 9:1–6.

[36] Jackson, Richard A., *Ordines Coronationis Franciae* (1995–2000).

could have a king and still remain different from all the nations, nevertheless the king was generally seen as divinely ordained (a *mitzveh*).[37] The Hebrew Testament largely ignores kingship, with some notable exceptions, as in the Book of Deuteronomy (17:14–20, the laws of the kings, and 28:36, where the king goes into exile with the people), perhaps reflecting an ambivalent attitude to the office. The tension between the direct relationship between a tribal people and God, ruled by priests and prophets, and the near eastern tradition, well known to the Jews, of kings as the god's or gods' representative, was to influence the development of Jewish kingship. Attempts by Gideon and his son Abimelech to establish a hereditary kingship ran contrary to a long Jewish tradition of generally living without an intermediary between God and humanity, except for the priests and prophets (Judges 8:22–23, 1 Samuel 8:7). But the traditions of Solomon and David had a long-lasting influence, both in Israel and later abroad.

Scripture is explicit with respect to the specific detail of Jewish coronations. Aside from the high priest Zadok and the prophet Nathan anointing King Solomon (1 Kings 1:33–48), we are told that the prophet Samuel anointed Saul to be Israel's first king,[38] though here as elsewhere there is no record of his being crowned then or subsequently. However, Saul later followed the ancient near eastern tradition, already strong elsewhere even in those early times, of wearing a crown or diadem upon his head, as a sign of his authority. On Saul's death in turn, a crown that had been on his head was presented to David.[39] The symbolic and spiritual descent of authority from one king to another could not be clearer.

Further detailed accounts of coronations in ancient Judah are found in Scripture, for example that in which the then seven-year-old King Jehoash (Joash) is crowned in an attempt to unseat the usurper Athaliah.[40] The ceremony took place in the doorway of the Temple in Jerusalem, at the king's pillar. Jehoash was crowned, and the "testimony" —*edut* (2 Kings 11:12) —given to him. The latter was the covenant, law, and statutes

[37] Polish, David, "Rabbinic views on kingship—a study in Jewish sovereignty" (Spring 1991) 3(1/2) Jewish Political Studies Review 67–90.

[38] In 1 Samuel 10:1.

[39] 2 Samuel 1:10.

[40] 2 Kings 11:10–20 and 2 Chronicles 23:11.

(Exodus 31:18, 2 Kings 17:15, Psalms 19:8, 132:12), though its exact form is now unknown. He was then anointed by the high priest and his sons. The acclamation "God save the King" was shouted by the assembled throng, as trumpeters proclaimed the king's coronation. Professional singers sang hymns of praise, whilst music played.[41] There are grounds for believing that psalms 20, 101 and 110 were originally hymns sung at coronations,[42] so these may well have been sung for the young king Jehoash.

It is likely that each of these elements represented, to a greater or lesser extent, what was then customary practice, as such would be vital to establishing the legitimacy of Jehoash's reign. Legitimacy was, after all, the one strength that an aspiring genuine claimant to a throne had over any usurper. The hereditary principle prevailed over other models.[43] It is of particular note that the use of a crown is recorded.

The anointing of the king with oil by a priest in the temple (as Jehoashaz, 2 Kings 23:30), the king seating himself on a throne in the royal palace, and the presentation of regal insignia, were all common near eastern practices. In this instance, the insignia included a crown (2 Samuel 1:10, Psalms 89:20, 132:18), and the *edut*. Each of the above features, the acclamation, the singing, trumpets, crowning, anointing, and even the presentation of a sacred text, were later to be found in many European coronations. All Christian coronation rites continued to borrow from these liturgical and ceremonial elements of ancient Israel, usually through intermediary usage elsewhere, particularly in west Francia.

The Israelite kingship and its associated coronation rituals hold substantial influence on the understanding of British coronations, as both systems reflect the intertwining of religious and political authority. As O'Donovan argues, there is no necessary distinction between secular and sacred, politics and religion.[44] In Israel, the kingship was not merely a political office but also a divinely sanctioned role, with the king often considered a mediator between God and the people. The coronation rituals symbolised divine approval, as the king was anointed with

[41] 2 Kings 11:4, 2 Chronicles 23:3, 2 Kings 11:12, and 2 Chronicles 23:11.

[42] Gerstenberger, Erhard S., *Psalms* (2001).

[43] Ishide, Tomoo, *The Royal Dynasties of Ancient Israel* (1977).

[44] O'Donovan, Oliver, *The Desire of the Nations* (1996).

sacred oil, signifying his consecration to God. These rites were rich with theological significance, linking the ruler's authority directly to divine will.

This theological underpinning profoundly shaped British coronation ceremonies, as it did western understanding of kingship generally. In Britain, the monarchy was also seen as having divine endorsement, especially during coronations, where the monarch is similarly anointed with holy oil. This ritual, derived from ancient biblical practices, underscores the monarch's role as both a political and religious figure. The British coronation mirrors many elements of Israelite ceremonies, such as the invocation of divine blessing, prayers for wisdom, and the use of symbols like the crown, sceptre, and orb, which signify the monarch's responsibility to rule justly under God's guidance. Thus, the legacy of Israelite kingship is central to understanding the sacred dimension of British coronations, where the monarch's authority is portrayed as coming from both the people and God.

Coronations in the ancient near east were not confined to Israel and Egypt; Scripture relates the crowning of Esther as consort of Ahasuerus, king of Persia.[45] Although (as in Israel) the anointing rather than the crowning appears to have been central to the Persian ritual, the latter was perhaps growing in significance as a reminder of the political power of the king, as distinct from his religious status and role.

In Plutarch's *Life of King Artaxerxes II*, we learn that the king was required to go to the ancient Persian capital of Pasargadae for his coronation ceremony. There he entered a temple dedicated "to a warlike goddess, whom one might liken to Artemis", and there divested himself of his own robe, substituting the ancient one worn by Cyrus I at his crowning (c. 600 BC, some 700 years before Plutarch was writing, and 200 years before Artaxerxes II was himself king of Persia).[46] The assumption of the robes of a prior ruler, particularly a famed one, was a common feature of later coronations in a number of countries. In England, for example, for centuries kings assumed St Edward's robe,[47] one of the supposed survivals of the original coronation attire of St Edward the Confessor, at their coronation.[48] The rituals of the Persian coronation

[45] Esther 2:17.

[46] Section 3.1.

[47] Hunt, Alice, Drama of *Coronation* (2008).

[48] Keay, Anna, *The Crown Jewels* (2011).

as a whole, as in Egypt and Israel, at once emphasised continuity and the link between the king and the divine, and between the king and his royal predecessors.

The imagery found in coronations also found its way into a wider arena. One of these was on coinage, where the depiction of a crowned or otherwise similarly adorned prince was widespread from the fourth century BC. At first, these depict mainly deities and not kings, for example, the Mother of Gods wearing the turreted crown (Rhea-Kybele is often depicted wearing the "turret crown",[49] and is also given the title of *Mater turrita* by Ovid),[50] However, just as the use of crowns in coronations became more common, so too did they begin to appear more frequently on coins, worn by rulers rather than gods or goddesses. From the early third century the heads of the kings of the Hellenistic empire begin to appear on their coins, which were based on Athenian originals via the coinage of Alexander the Great. They typically are shown wearing a headband or diadem.[51] The imagery of the king became more elaborate as their political roles became more dominant and central to the governance of their states.

In all of these—and other—near eastern coronations, the use of anointing and a crown dominated (though neither were ubiquitous). Legitimacy, and divine approbation, were essential to the success of the accession, and both were aided through a properly conducted coronation. Continuity, and linking the new king with the preceding constitutional heritage, was fundamental to the inauguration of a new king. This theme became dominant elsewhere, and proved a common element in later European coronations.

Roman Coronations

Somewhat later, and further to the west, parallel developments were underway to those which had occurred in the near east, though they were by no means identical. In the long history of the Roman Republic, and for

[49] Lucretius, *On the Nature of Things Cybele*; Bonnie A. Catto, "Venus and Natura in Lucretius: "De Rerum Natura" 1.1–23 and 2.167–74" (1988) 84(2) The Classical Journal 97–104.

[50] Ovid, *Metamorphoses.* translated by A. D. Melville, Introduction and notes by Edward John Kenney (2008), p. 686.

[51] Ogden, Daniel, *The Legend of Seleucus* (2017).

some time under the early empire, there were no equivalent ritual inauguration practices to that of the ancient kings of Israel, nor indeed to that of Egypt. This is for sensible and wholly explicable socio-political and religious reasons, not least of which was the succession method, particularly under the empire. As the Roman *principate* constituted a deliberate rejection of kingly office—though the illusion became increasingly meaningless over time—this omission was scarcely surprising. Even as the republican veneer of the empire was gradually to wither, this appearance was to change but slowly. In part this may be explained by the Roman fondness for honouring the traditions of their ancestors. Most of all, however, it is likely a reflection of the nature of the imperial office.

In contrast to then well-established near eastern practice, the early emperors were habitually acclaimed by the Senate or by a legion speaking for the armies as a whole (or for themselves) and were subsequently confirmed without any special ritual. In theory this was because they were not monarchs in the near eastern—or even ancient Roman—sense, but rather chief magistrates, chosen by the senate and people of Rome. The process of selecting the emperor was for long arguably both the greatest strength and the greatest weakness of the empire.[52] It was a strength because it allowed for and even encouraged the rise to the *imperium* of the strongest soldier or most astute politician of the generation. Conversely, it was a weakness precisely because of the uncertainty this engendered; some emperors, such as Otho, briefly and futilely literally bought the *imperium* through bribes to the Praetorian Guard (in existence 27 BC-312 AD),[53] the imperial bodyguard, which many times, like the later Janissaries of the Ottoman empire, 1363–1826,[54] itself decided the fate of the empire.[55] In such a situation, rituals of accession were often of the most prosaic nature.

However, political reality under the principate was such that the Roman empire was soon a de facto monarchy, even if the outward form of republican government was long preserved. The empire rapidly became the property of dynasties of rulers, but that did not inherently mean it was

[52] Heather, Peter, *The Fall of the Roman Empire* (2005).

[53] Greenhalgh, P. A. L., *The Year of the Four Emperors* (1975).

[54] Nicolle, David, *The Janissaries* (1995).

[55] De la Bédoyère, Guy, *Praetorian* (2017).

a monarchy.[56] To some extent that was the result of a loose association of the imperial rule with a family, initially the Julio-Claudian dynasty, 27 BC to 68 AD.[57] Although certain families dominated, for a time, they never acquired a perpetual claim to hereditary rule, and the approval of senate and army remained vital. The emperor of the Roman Empire, like that of the later Holy Roman Empire, was never strictly hereditary in nature; the longest surviving Roman dynasty was ironically to be the very last, the House of Palaiologos, which reigned for 194 years (1259–1453)[58]; in the west no one dynasty reached even 100 years. Like the Roman dynasties, those of the Holy Roman Empire were short-lived, mostly around 100 years; the last, the Hapsburgs, lasted from 1440 to 1806, an impressive 366 years.

The imperial title was also not simply an individual office, but an accumulation of several key positions, including the chief priest or *Pontifex Maximus*.[59] It is worth noting that the *rex sacrorum* ("king of the sacred"), the senior Roman priest, outranked even the *Pontifex Maximus*, and fulfilled at least some of the sacral duties of kingship. In the Roman government there was a division of responsibilities, with the consuls assuming political power and military command, as well as some sacral functions.[60] This was not a true separation of powers,[61] and the notion of combining in the one office the responsibilities of government, civil and military, was well developed during the early Roman empire, even if individual dynasties did not last long. In contrast, the lineage of the Hapsburg emperors of the (notionally elective) Holy Roman empire can be traced to the tenth century, and the held the imperial throne from 1440 to the dissolution of the empire in 1806.[62]

[56] Compare the crowned republic of the Dutch; Van der Burg, M., "Transforming the Dutch Republic into the Kingdom of Holland" (2010) 17(2) European Review of History 151–170.

[57] Matyszak, Philip, *The Sons of Caesar* (2006).

[58] Nicol, Donald M., *The Last Centuries of Byzantium, 1261–1453* (2nd ed., 1993).

[59] Nicholson, Oliver and David Gwynn, "Pontifex Maximus", in Oliver Nicholson (ed.), *The Oxford Dictionary of Late Antiquity* (2018).

[60] Beard, Mary, J. A. North and S. R. F. Price, *Religions of Rome* (1998).

[61] Montesquieu, Charles Louis de Secondat Baron de, "The Spirit of the Laws", in Arend Lijphart (ed.), *Parliamentary versus Presidential Government* (1992), pp. 48–51.

[62] Wandruszka, Adam, *The House of Habsburg* (1964).

Partly under the increasing influence of the eastern part of the empire, and partly, perhaps, because of the growing acceptance that the imperial office was properly that of a monarch (as the ancient Roman hostility to monarchy declined), eastern royal traditions gradually made significant inroads in Rome. This had symbolic and ceremonial implications, both at the beginning of a reign, and during its course. The emperor Diocletian (reigned 285–305) greatly developed the ceremony surrounding the Roman emperor. He was said to have worn a gold crown and jewels (as a sign of his authority and not simply for decoration). In addition, he forbade the use of purple cloth to all but the emperors[63]; an early, but by no means the first, example of a sumptuary law, regulating the use of particular colours and fabrics, as a means of distinguishing and preserving distinctions between social classes.[64] The eastern diadem, which had been worn by the Achaemenid rulers of Persia, was introduced to Rome by Aurelian (ruled 270–275).[65] It did not truly become part of the emperor's regalia until the reign of Constantine I (emperor 306–337),[66] who wore it habitually throughout his reign,[67] and was thereafter worn by all subsequent rulers of the later Roman Empire. This reflected a gradual eastward shift in the geopolitical priorities of Rome, as much as an evolving acceptance of eastern political imagery, and the reality of the changing nature of the Roman state.

In addition to the eastern crown, derived from that of the Persian empire, there was an additional crown, worn by later Roman emperors. This was particularly as part of the cult of *Sol Invictus*, part of the imperial cult as it developed during the third century. This *corona radiata*, the "radiant crown" is probably known best today from the Statue of Liberty

[63] Corcoran, Simon, "Before Constantine", in Noel Lenski, *The Cambridge Companion to the Age of Constantine* (2006), pp. 35–58, 43. Potter, David S., *The Roman Empire at Bay, AD 180–395* (2004), p. 290.

[64] Cox, Noel, "Tudor sumptuary laws and academical dress: An Act against wearing of Costly Apparel 1509 and An Act for Reformation of Excess in Apparel 1533" (2006) 6 Transactions of the Burgon Society 15–43.

[65] "Ch. 1: "The Empire From Constantine to Justinian the Great", subsection "Reforms of Diocletian and Constantine", *A History of the Byzantine Empire*. Ellopos.net. Retrieved 26 September 2008.

[66] Thurston, Herbert, "Coronation", in Charles Herbermann (ed.), *Catholic Encyclopedia* (1913).

[67] "*Caput exornans perpetuo diademate*"; Aurelius Victor, Ep. lx, Dufraigne, P., *Aurelius Victor* (1975).

in New York. It was perhaps worn by the Helios that was the Colossus of Rhodes, and was of religious rather than political origins, marking the sacred nature of kingship, perhaps expressing the concept that either the king is himself divine, or is ruling by divine right.[68] Its use by the Roman emperors, who were monarchs in all but name, but not kings, is an example of the sort of syncretism which was a characteristic both of the ancient Egyptian monarchy and of later Roman civilisation.

Despite the gradual introduction of imperial insignia, no specific Roman coronation ceremony was observed at first, with emperors assuming power through a rather more informal (indeed often chaotic and occasionally bloody) process. They might, however, be ceremonially inducted into certain offices, such as that of *Pontifex Maximus*,[69] or of consul.[70] However, a form of coronation gradually evolved over the course of the fifth century, as the monarchical nature of the imperial office was finally officially acknowledged.

The unique nature of the office of emperor, meaning that it depended upon the support of Senate, army and people, was acknowledged; divine approbation was but one element, though an important one, and heredity also played a part. The emperor Julian was hoisted upon a shield upon his proclamation, reflecting at once the choice and support of the military, and his future role as war leader. He was crowned with a gold necklace provided by one of his standard-bearers[71]; a symbol, perhaps, of senatorial or popular endorsement. He later wore a jewel-studded diadem, more redolent of eastern monarchy. This example was followed by subsequent emperors, who were crowned and acclaimed in a similar manner, in a coronation ritual presided over by the Patriarch of Constantinople (who

[68] Bardill, Jonathan, *Constantine, Divine Emperor of the Christian Golden Age* (2012), p. 114; Stewart, Andrew, *Faces of Power* (1993), p. 246; Sebesta, Judith Lynn and Larissa Bonfante (eds), *The World of Roman Costume* (2001), p. 82.

[69] Nicholson, Oliver and David Gwynn, "Pontifex Maximus", in Oliver Nicholson (ed.), *The Oxford Dictionary of Late Antiquity* (2018).

[70] Beck, Hans, Antonio Duplá, Martin Jehne et al. (eds.), *Consuls and Res Publica* (2011).

[71] Thurston, Herbert, "Coronation", in Charles Herbermann (ed.), *Catholic Encyclopedia* (1913).

himself was officially later styled the Archbishop of Constantinople, the New Rome, and Œcumenical Patriarch).[72]

By the reign of Leo II, who as a child of six was crowned emperor by the Patriarch Acacius in the Hippodrome of Constantinople (Ἱππόδρομος τῆς Κωνσταντινουπόλεως) in 473,[73] the decision was taken to permit the Patriarch of Constantinople to physically place the crown on the emperor's head (rather than the emperor himself assuming the crown),[74] as a sign at once of the Church's approval of the choice of emperor, and of the divine status of the Sovereign. The new emperor's tender years may also have played a part in this decision. In later centuries, after receiving their crown from the Patriarch of Constantinople, Eastern Roman emperors placed it upon their own head, symbolizing that their dominion came directly from God,[75] and minimising the hierarchical authority of the church.

The ritual included recitation of prayers by the Patriarch over the crown, a further—and important—development in the liturgy of the coronation. The endorsement of the church, symbolising the divine choice and the emperor's religious status, had become pre-eminent in the rite of the coronation. The Eastern Roman coronation ritual, from at least 795 onwards, also incorporated the vesting of the new emperor in various items of explicitly imperial dress prior to his entrance to the cathedral. Following his entrance into the Hagia Sophia,[76] he received the prostrations of the Senators and other patricians (a survival of ancient Roman senatorial acclamation). The church then assumed responsibility from the state, with the Patriarch commencing to read a set of lengthy

[72] Charanis, Peter, "Coronation and its constitutional significance in the later Roman empire" (1940) 15 Byzantion 49–66.

[73] Dagron, Gilbert, *Emperor and Priest* (2003), p. 69.

[74] Croke, Brian, *Roman Emperors in Context* (2021), ch 5, "The imperial reigns of Leo II", pp. 153–159.

[75] Wister, Robert J., "The Legitimation of Authority Divine and Human", (4 December 2002). Retrieved 26 September 2008; See also Owen, Matthew and Ingo Gildenhard, *Tacitus, Annals, 15.20–23, 33–45* (2013), vol. XV, p. 29.

[76] Ἁγία Σοφία (Holy Wisdom), was built 532–537 by Emperor Justinian I, as a state church, to replace the second church on the site, destroyed during the Nika riots of 532. The first church was built c.346–360. The building was a mosque 1453–1931, a museum 1935–2020, and controversially a mosque once again from 2020; Mainstone, Rowland J., *Hagia Sophia* (reprint ed., 1997); "Turkey turns iconic Istanbul museum into mosque", BBC News, 10 July 2020.

prayers. While he was doing this, the emperor was invested first with the *chlamys* (χηλαμψσ) and then with the crown. The *chlamys* was a cloak doubled or pinned over the shoulder. It consisted of a woollen cloth oval three times the length of the wearer, worn halved along its length and draped in complicated folds.[77] It was the *paludamentum* of the general in the field. Following the crowning, the emperor himself received Holy Communion, followed by formal acts of homage.[78] From the moment of his coronation, the Byzantine—or rather Roman—emperor was regarded as holy; as a symbol of this, while the Patriarch was holding the crown over the emperor's head, the attending people repeatedly cried: "Holy!".[79]

Despite its ancient origins, in Egypt and Israel, anointing was only added to the Eastern Roman coronation ritual comparatively late.[80] It first appeared after the eleventh century, later than in the west, with the new emperor receiving the Sign of the Cross on their forehead from the Patriarch.[81]

The purple *chlamys* disappeared from the coronation rite during this time period, being replaced with the *mandyas* (μανδψασ), or cope.[82] The early history of the cope can be traced variously to the *lacerna*, the *byrrus*, and the *pluvial*, parents of the *cappa nigra*. The *cappa nigra* was (and still is) worn as an outdoor garment by the clergy and was originally without liturgical significance. By the eighth century the cope began to travel along the same path of development as other vestments; better quality materials, including silks, were used, and colours were gradually introduced, often contrary to sumptuary laws. Over the next two centuries the cope evolved in style similar to the vestment that is now so readily

[77] Cox, Noel, "The Coronation Robes of the Sovereign" (1999) 5(1) Arma 271–280.

[78] Thurston, Herbert, "Coronation", in Charles Herbermann (ed.), *Catholic Encyclopedia* (1913); Constantine VII Porphyrogenitus, de Cerimoniis Aulae Byzantinae, I, 38 (ed. Johann Jakob Reiske, 1751, vol I, pp. 191–196; ed. Albert Vogt, 1935, vol II, pp. 1–5, cc. 47–8.

[79] Sedlar, Jean W., *East Central Europe in the Middle Ages, 1000–1500* (1994).

[80] Nicol, Donald M., "Kaisersalbung. The unction of emperors in late Byzantine coronation ritual" (1976) 2 Byzantine and Modern Greek Studies 37–52.

[81] Macrides, Ruth, J. A. Munitiz and Dimiter Angelov, *Pseudo-Kodinos and the Constantinopolitan Court* (2013), pp. 120–123.

[82] Thurston, Herbert, "Coronation", in Charles Herbermann (ed.), *Catholic Encyclopedia* (1913).

recognised. Its use by the emperors, especially in place of the *chlamys*, may be seen as another example of the increasing emphasis on the sacred nature of the imperial office.

The imperial innovations, particularly those which contained ritual affirmations of church, popular, military or senatorial approval, were to prove to have a lasting influence on the developments of coronations in western Europe in the course of the late dark ages and early middle ages, and survive today in the British coronation, most notably in the robes worn by the king or queen regnant. It is also instructive to reflect on the preservation, in eastern Roman coronations, of vestiges of approval by senate and people, with that of the army being perhaps replaced with the approval of the church. Thus it may be said that the coronation reflected an imperial authority and legitimacy derived at once from several discrete sources.

Later Byzantine, Frankish and Germanic Developments

The Eastern Roman empire, predominantly though not exclusively centred on Constantinople, survived the fall of Rome by almost a thousand years, depending upon which date is chosen for the fall of the west. The final fall of the eastern empire, by contrast, may be precisely dated to the capture of Constantinople (the surviving rump of the empire) by the invading Ottoman Turks, on 29th May 1453; the years 476 to 1453 is a convenient, if perhaps largely symbolic, year range. Over that time the power, prestige and longevity of the eastern Roman empire exerted an influence well beyond its ever-changing borders. This was partly because of its association with the glories of ancient Rome, and partly because of its own merits as the new, in later years largely Hellenised, and Christian, Roman Empire—the term Byzantine empire was not in contemporary use and is of comparatively modern origin. It was, according to Anthony Kaldellis, first used by an Athenian, Laonikos Chalkokondyles, in the mid fifteenth century,[83] but was only in general use in the western world from the mid-nineteenth century.[84] The residents of Constantinople would not

[83] Kaldellis, Anthony, "From 'Empire of the Greeks' to 'Byzantium'", in Jake Ransohoff and Nathanael Aschenbrenner (eds.), *The Invention of Byzantium in Early Modern Europe* (2022), pp. 349–367.

[84] Rosser, John H., "Introduction", *Historical Dictionary of Byzantium* (2011).

have called themselves anything other than Romans—and in such matters, symbolism carries great weight.

The influence of the Roman Empire, east and west, formed the basis for the imperial and royal ambitions of rulers from Britain to Russia, and many places in between. This widespread influence applied in many aspects of governance, but was especially notable in respect of the imperial office. The legacy of Rome survives today in many guises, from the Romance languages (Spanish, Portuguese, French, Italian, and Romanian, as well as regional languages such as Catalan, Occitan and Sardinian)[85] to the civil law system.[86] It also survives in some aspects of the British coronation, and especially in the crowning and in the style of robes worn by the sovereign.

The Eastern Roman coronation ceremony began to influence what had been Barbarian kingdoms in the West, in keeping with their acceptance of Christianity, and their common—though not ubiquitous—seeking after the trappings of Roman or sub-Roman authority. The so-called Iron Crown of Lombardy—which studies show contains no iron—is traced in legend to Constantine himself (but more likely dates to the much later though still comparatively ancient eighth or ninth centuries).[87] It was used for the coronations of the Kings of the Lombards, the Kings of Italy, and the Holy Roman Emperors (as Kings of Italy and later as Kings of Lombardy and Venetia), from at least as early as the fourteenth century, and probably the eleventh, to 1838.[88] The use of the emblems of Roman royalty by Barbarian, and sub-Barbarian, kings reflects the desire to assume or to be associated with, not merely the trappings, but also the substance, legitimacy and authority of imperial Rome.

In the areas that are now known as the Iberian peninsula and south east France, the Visigothic king Sisenand was crowned in 631 in succession to King Suintila (ruled 621–631), as the king of Hispania, Septimania and Galicia, in accordance with a Byzantine-influenced coronation

[85] Alkire, Ti and Carol Rosen, *Romance Languages* (2010).

[86] Glenn, H. Patrick, *Legal Traditions of the World* (2014).

[87] Twining, Edward Lord, *A History of the Crown Jewels of Europe* (1960); Buccellatin, Graziella and Holly Snapp (eds.), *The Iron Crown and Imperial Europe* (1995).

[88] Twining, Edward Lord, *A History of the Crown Jewels of Europe* (1960).

ceremony.[89] As a usurper—he was a leading nobleman, who spearheaded a rebellion against Suintila—he may have felt the need for additional legitimacy, although his rule was later to be legitimised by the Fourth Council of Toledo (633), when Suintila himself was accused of various iniquities, forced to renounce his power, excommunicated, stripped of his possessions, and exiled along with his family.[90] In 672, Wamba, king of the Visigoths, was the first occidental king to be anointed as well as crowned (by the archbishop of Toledo[91]), well before anointing had become standard practice in Constantinople itself.

West Francia, the western part of the Frankish empire established by Charlemagne, was divided under the Treaty of Verdun in 843, following the death of Charlemagne's son, Louis the Pious. It eventually evolved into the nascent Kingdom of France, and lasted from about 840 until 987, from Charles the Bald (843–877) to Louis V of France (986–987).[92] Like the eastern and western parts of the Roman empire, and the later Holy Roman empire, in the West Frankish polity kingship was nominally elective. The kings were elected by the secular and ecclesiastical magnates. As with the other empires, dynastic influence tended to prevail, so that, for the half-century between 888 and 936, candidates from the Carolingian and Robertian houses were alternately chosen as monarchs. The Robertians, after becoming counts of Paris and dukes of France, eventually became kings themselves and established the Capetian dynasty after 987, later providing all of the kings of France until the final collapse of the kingdom in 1848. As with other rulers of this era and later, they sought to augment their legitimacy by associating with long-standing imperial practices, as well as newer religious rites.

In May 849 Charles the Bald, the first West Francian king, was crowned "King of the Franks and Aquitainians" in Orléans. Archbishop Wenilo of Sens officiated at the coronation, which included the first instance of anointing with royal unction in the territory that had become West Francia. The idea of anointing Charles may

[89] Crouch, Jace T., "Isidore of Seville and the Evolution of Kingship in Visigothic Spain" (1994) 4 Mediterranean Studies 9–26.

[90] Barbero, A. and M. I. Loring, "The Catholic Visigothic Kingdom", in Paul Fouracre (ed.), *The New Cambridge Mediæval History I* (2005), p. 353.

[91] Collins, Roger, *Early Mediæval Spain* (1995).

[92] Nelson, Janet L., "Kingship, Law and Liturgy in the Political Thought of Hincmar of Rheims" 92 English Historical Review 241–279.

be traced to Archbishop Hincmar of Reims, who composed at least four *ordines*, describing appropriate liturgies for a royal consecration, suggesting that coronations were well entrenched in the socio-theological and political landscape by then, from the time of the Carolingian empire (800–888), if not earlier.[93] Anointing carried political as well as religious significance, in England as in West Francia.

It was only under the Carolingian dynasty in what was now to become France that crowning and anointing became standard practice, and also began to exhibit Christological attributes.[94] To help to legitimise his deposition of the last of the Merovingian kings, Pepin the Short, King of the Franks 751–768 was twice crowned and anointed, at the beginning of his reign in 752, and for the first time by a pope in 754 by Pope Stephen II, in the Abbey of Saint-Denis.[95] The anointing was perhaps inspired by Virgil of Salzburg, an Irish monk who was an adviser to Pepin, on the basis of the *Collectio canonum Hibernensis*,[96] a systematic Latin collection of Continental canon law, scriptural and patristic excerpts, and Irish synodal and penitential decrees.[97]

As is often the case when one's political legitimacy might be questioned, it was prudent to bolster the claim to the throne by whatever means available; and coronations, and especially the anointing, provided an extra level of authority and therefore protection. It was also something that a de facto ruler might undertake, provided the needed prelates were willing, at comparatively little cost (financial and political) —compared, for example, to raising an army, or quelling an insurrection. It was also harder for a challenger to unseat an anointed king.

The anointing was to assume primary significance, where used. A modern authority even suggests that a British monarch cannot be

[93] Ibid, reprinted in *Politics and Ritual in Early Mediæval Europe* (1986), pp. 133–172, 137–138.

[94] Alaichamy, Martin, "An Incarnational Christology of Kingship: The Theological Meaning of Carolingian Royal Unction (751–877)" (2022) Trinity International University PhD dissertation.; Jacobson, Paul A., "Sicut Samuhel unxit David: Early Carolingian Royal Anointings Reconsidered", in Larson-Miller, Lizette (ed.), *Medieval Liturgy* (Routledge, Abingdon, 2019), pp. 267–303

[95] Waitz, Georg (ed.) "De unctione Pippini regis nota monachi sancti Dionysii" (1887) 15(1) Monumenta Germaniae Historica, Scriptores 1.

[96] Enright, M. J., *Iona, Tara, and Soissons* (1985), pp. ix, 198.

[97] Flechner, Roy, *The Hibernensis: Volume 2* (2019).

crowned nor receive the regalia without being anointed first.[98] This would appear a logical consequence of the crown jewels—those elements of the regalia reserved for use in the coronation—along with the rest of the regalia, being heirlooms of the Crown,[99] and inalienable,[100] and therefore only available for use by an anointed king.

Occasionally, as in ancient Rome, authority might be shared or an heir prepared for succession by anointing them—or even crowning them—during the lifetimes of their fathers. The young sons of Pepin the Short, Charles—later Charlemagne—and Carloman, were anointed alongside their father in 754.[101] The one known English example was Henry the young king (1155–1183), who was crowned at Westminster Abbey titular King of England, Duke of Normandy, Count of Anjou and Maine 14th June 1170, and again in Winchester Cathedral (alongside his new wife, Margaret of France) 27th August 1172 by Rotrou, Archbishop of Rouen, during the lifetime of his father, King Henry II.[102] King Stephen had earlier still (1143) attempted to have his son Eustace IV, Count of Boulogne, crowned, but failed to obtain papal support for this.[103] Papal authorisation was deemed essential for what was widely seen as a sacrament.

Constantine VI, emperor 780–797, was the final ruler to be generally recognised as Roman emperor, being recognised as such by both the Empire which he ruled in the east, the papacy and the western European powers over which the pope held suzerainty. After Constantine VI's blinding and deposition by his mother Irene (born Irene Sarantapechos (Εἰρήνη Σαρανταπήχαινα)), she subsequently controversially assumed the

[98] Legg, L. G. W., *English Coronation Records* (1901), p. xxxiv.

[99] "the ancient jewels of the crown are heirloomes and shall descend to the next successor and are not devisable by testament"; Sir Edward Coke, cited by Nash, Michael L., "The Jewels of the Kingdom", in *Royal Wills in Britain from 1509 to 2008* (2017), pp. 61–86.

[100] Their inalienability is a consequence of their status as *jura majora*; Bogdanor, Sir Vernon, *The Monarchy and the Constitution* (1995), p. 190.

[101] Waitz, Georg (ed.) "De unctione Pippini regis nota monachi sancti Dionysii" (1887) 15(1) Monumenta Germaniae Historica, Scriptores 1.

[102] Heslin, Anne, "The coronation of the Young King in 1170" (1965) 2 Studies in Church History 165–178; Warren, W. L., *He7nry II* (1973), p. 111.

[103] Strickland, Matthew, *Henry the Young King* (2016), pp. 89–90.

status of empress regnant 797–802.[104] Due to the irregular situation, and the inability of the eastern empire to protect the papacy in the wake of the advance of the Muslim Arabs, the Patriarch of the West sought protection from the Franks, and in Old St Peter's Basilica in Rome on Christmas Day 800,[105] Pope Leo III proclaimed and crowned Pepin the Short's son Charlemagne emperor of what he perceived, or could legitimately argue, was the vacant throne of an undivided Roman empire.[106]

Thereafter it was generally accepted that a papal coronation was required to acquire the imperial title (possibly to mirror the practice of coronations of the eastern Emperors by the Patriarch of Constantinople). This remained so until 1508, when Maximilian I was unable to make the journey to Rome, as his route was blocked by the Venetians. As a result, he was instead proclaimed emperor-elect by Pope Julius II at Trent,[107] thus recognising the right of Germanic monarchs elected by the prince-electors to use the imperial title, without papal coronation being a prerequisite; concurrently, imperial coronations as King of the Germans were moved from Aachen to Frankfurt Cathedral from the 1562 coronation of Emperor Maximilian II (1562–76).[108] By this time the pretence of the Holy Roman Empire to be the successor of Rome was much weakened by the decline of the authority of the emperors, the growth of the independence of the constituent states of the empire, and its confinement largely to German lands. The conceptual death knell of the empire was arguably at the Peace of Westphalia in 1648, where the sovereignty of immediate tenants of the emperor was acknowledged.[109] The *coup de grâce* was later delivered by Napoleon.[110]

[104] Garland, Lynda, *Byzantine Empresses* (1999).

[105] Mayr-Harting, Henry, "Charlemagne, the Saxons, and the Imperial Coronation of 800" (1996) 111 (444) The English Historical Review 1113–1133; Romano, John F., "The Coronation of Charlemagne as a Liturgical Event" (2020) 82 Mediaeval Studies 149–181.

[106] Collins, Roger, *Charlemagne* (1998).

[107] Stollberg-Rilinger, Barbara, *The Emperor's Old Clothes* (2020), p. 13.

[108] Conley, Thomas, "The Speech of Ibrahim at the Coronation of Maximilian II" (2002) 20(3) Rhetorica 263–273.

[109] Osiander, Andreas, "Sovereignty, International Relations, and the Westphalian Myth" (2011) 55(2) International Organization 251–287.

[110] Wilson, Peter H., "Bolstering the Prestige of the Habsburgs: The End of the Holy Roman Empire in 1806" (2006) 28(4) The International History Review 709–736.

Increasingly, in direct or indirect competition with one another, kings were inspired or compelled to introduce or emulate the latest innovation from other kingdoms—especially those which suggested or implied a sacred connection or divine approbation. Just as with the Carolingian dynasty in France, the tradition of crowning and anointing a ruler acquired a constitutive function, not simply reflecting already acquired authority, but amounting to the inauguration and making of the Sovereign.

Coronations in mediæval Christian Europe were influenced by the practice of the Roman Emperors, as it had developed from late antiquity. This was as true of the kings of England as it was of the Holy Roman Emperors; for this purpose at least one might charitably acknowledge the claim of the Holy Roman emperors to be successors to the western emperors. The exact term Holy Roman Empire was not used until the thirteenth century,[111] but the emperor's legitimacy always rested on the concept of *translatio imperii*, that he held supreme power inherited from the ancient emperors of Rome.[112] Voltaire's quip that "This body which was called and which still calls itself the Holy Roman Empire was in no way holy, nor Roman, nor an empire" was only partly true even when he was writing (1773).[113]

Later Developments

The later European coronation ceremonies descended from rites initially created in Byzantium, Visigothic Spain, Carolingian France, and the Holy Roman Empire, and rose to their liturgical and political apogee during the early mediæval era. Thus, they contained elements intended to affirm divine approbation of the new sovereign—such as the anointing, and the central role of prelates—and also the approval and support of the key men of the realm. The public nature of the occasion was also important even if few men or women, other than the political and religious elite,

[111] Garipzanov, Ildar H., *The Symbolic Language of Authority in the Carolingian World (c.751–877)* (2008).

[112] Whaley, Joachim, *Germany and the Holy Roman Empire* (2012), vol. I, pp. 17–21; Kantorowicz, Ernst, *The King's Two Bodies* (1957); Huizinga, Johan, *Autumntide of the Middle Ages* (2020); Cantor, Norman F., *The Civilization of the Middle Ages* (1993).

[113] Voltaire, "Chapitre LXX", *Essais sur les mœurs et l'ésprit des nations* (in French). Vol. 3 (nouvelle ed., Neuchâtel, 1756), p. 338

were close enough to see or hear well, or were even present at all. The details of coronations varied greatly however, depending upon a number of religious, political, cultural and historical factors. Central to all was the legitimacy conferred by a coronation. The source of this legitimacy might have varied, but always included an element of divine approval, popular acknowledgement, and political acceptance, as well as a sacring or setting aside of the king in some manner.

In some European countries of Celtic or Germanic origin, prior to the adoption of Christianity, upon his election the new king was raised on a shield and, while standing upon it, was borne on the shoulders of several chief men of the nation (or tribe) in a procession around his assembled subjects. This was said to traditionally be performed three times.[114] Following this, the new king was given a spear, and a diadem made of silk or linen (not to be confused with a crown) was bound around his forehead as a token of his regal authority.[115] Though possibly of north European tribal origin, it also resembled the Roman practice of army or senatorial approval of a new ruler. The passing of royal insignia normally followed the acclamation, thus confirming that the new Sovereign was invested with authority through the will of their subjects and the approval of heaven, as well as through any claim by strict heredity or by family compact, or indeed election from amongst the eligible members of the extended royal family. The resemblance to more modern, Christianised—or Christian-framed—coronations in Europe is clear.

The European coronation ceremonies of the Middle Ages were essentially a combination of the Judeo-Christian rite of anointing with additional, often regional, elements. These ceremonies in mediæval Christendom, both eastern and western, were also deeply embedded in the Christian world. They were directly or indirectly influenced by Biblical accounts of kings being crowned and anointed.[116] Following Europe's conversion to Christianity, crowning ceremonies became more

[114] Teitler, Hans, "Raising on a shield: Origin and afterlife of a coronation ceremony" (2002) 8 International Journal of the Classical Tradition 501–521.

[115] Maine, Sir Henry Sumner, *Early Law and Custom* (1890).

[116] Giesey, Ralph E., "Inaugural Aspects of French Royal Ceremonials", in János M. Bak (ed.), *Coronations* (1990).

and more ornate, depending on the country in question, and their Christian elements—especially anointing—became the paramount component.[117] In part this may have been because of the central role assumed by prelates in planning, organising and conducting coronations (as well as recording them), but it also reflects the dominance of religious feelings and concerns in early mediæval European political thought.[118]

Crowns and sceptres, used in coronations since ancient times, took on an explicitly Christian significance, together with the orb (particularly in its *globus cruciger* form, with a cross above the orb), as symbols of the purportedly divine order of things, with the monarch as the divinely ordained overlord and protector of his dominions.[119] Although the *globus cruciger* was used as early as Constantine I, and there are images on coins and seals of kings from Edward the Confessor onwards bearing orbs,[120] English kings only undoubtedly used them at their coronation from the time of Henry VIII in 1509.[121] Each element of the regalia had a specific symbolic justification in the coronation. During the Middle Ages, this rite was considered so vital in some European kingdoms that it was sometimes referred to (and especially the anointing) as an eighth sacrament.[122] The origin of the early mediæval understanding of Coronation rituals being sacraments in their own right is that the blessing, by unction, of the candidate, enacts the outpouring of the Spirit, which confirms God's action and authoritative gift, in the rite.

The newly anointed ruler was thereafter viewed as a *persona mixta*, part priest and part layman, but never afterwards wholly either.[123] This

[117] Thurston, Herbert, "Coronation", in Charles Herbermann (ed.), *Catholic Encyclopedia* (1913).

[118] Morris, Colin, *The papal monarchy* (1989).

[119] Carile, Maria Cristina, "Globus cruciger", in Dale C. Allison, Jr, Christine Helmer, Volker Leppin, Choon-Leong Seow, Hermann Spieckermann, Barry Dov Walfish, and Eric J. Ziolkowski, (eds.), *Encyclopedia of the Bible and Its Reception*, Vol. 10, Genocide—Hakkoz (2015).

[120] Keay, Anna, *The Crown Jewels* (2011), p. 32, Davenport, Cyril, *The English Regalia* (1897), pp. viii, 17–18.

[121] Rose, Tessa, *The Coronation Ceremony and the Crown Jewels* (1992), p. 45.

[122] Coulombe, Charles A. "Coronations in Catholic theology". Charles. A Coulombe (9 May 2005).

[123] Hunt, Alice, "The Bright Star of the North: James I and his English Coronation", in M. Twycross, P. King, S. Carpenter, and G. Walker (eds.), *Mediæval English Theatre: 38 The Best Pairt of our Play. Essays presented to John J. McGavin* (2017), Part II, pp. 22–37.

notion persisted into the twentieth century in Imperial Russia, where the Tsar was considered to be wedded to his subjects through the Russian Orthodox coronation service.[124] Even today this notion is not extinct; in an interview with the BBC, the Archbishop of Canterbury, Justin Welby, speaking on the Platinum Jubilee of Queen Elizabeth II, was quoted as follows:

> The archbishop likened her role as monarch to a lifelong religious vocation and the coronation to the vows for religious ministry.
>
> > "The coronation service is a form of ordination, in a liturgical sense, and she lives that out without a grumble."
> > "It is priestly—the language, the structure, it's very similar to an ordination of a priest or a bishop," he said.[125]

The priestly aspects of rulers in this conception should not be exaggerated, but equally it is not absent, and should be duly considered. A number of aspects of coronations past and present serve to illustrate this. Crowning ceremonies arose or at least were later influenced by a worldview in which monarchs were seen as ordained by God,[126] to serve not merely as political or military leaders, nor as figureheads, but rather to occupy a vital spiritual place in their dominions as well.[127] Although dissimilar in many ways, this echoes the role of the Egyptian kings and their own divinely ordained place in the created universe.

The attitude to the sacred nature of the coronation varied across Europe, despite the common legacy of a Frankish origin and Eastern Roman augmentation and ornamentation.[128] But there was, at least in the pre-modern era, a widespread if not ubiquitous understanding of the sacred nature of kingship, and this was everywhere reflected in the coronation ritual, to a greater or a lesser extent.

[124] Oldenburg, Sergei S., *Last Tsar* (1975), pp. 59–60.

[125] Sean Coughlan and Nicholas Witchell, "Justin Welby: Queen set example at Philip's funeral", BBC News, 5 February 2022, <https://www.bbc.com/news/uk-60231239>.

[126] Christian references include 1 Peter 2:13,17 and Romans 13:1–7. For an Islamic perspective, see Ghazali, Ghazālī, *Book of Counsel for Kings* ("Nas'īat al-mulūk") transl. by F. R. C. Bagley (1964).

[127] Coulombe, Charles A. "Coronations in Catholic theology". Charles A. Coulombe (9 May 2005).

[128] Hunt, Alice, *Drama of Coronation* (2008), Chap 1, pp. 12–38.

Coronations in the British Isles

Little is known of pre-Saxon coronations, or inaugurations, or indeed those of Britons prior to or under Roman rule (if indeed such occurred), or even of sub-Roman kingship, though some hints of the latter survived amongst the early Welsh princes. It is likely that the inauguration of pre-Roman and Roman era princes resembled tribal inaugurations of Celtic and Germanic peoples elsewhere rather more than they did later coronations. The period after 410 cannot with any fairness still be termed the Dark Ages, but it is certainly the case that records are more fragmentary and political, social and economic circumstances were more disordered than at any time since Claudius's invasion 400 years earlier. It is also likely that social, economic and political circumstances would have precluded elaborate ceremonials such as were later to become standard.

After c.500 politics in Britain were dominated by kings with territorial kingdoms,[129] whose boundaries were constantly changing due to the upheavals of the age, especially the invasions and settlements of the Anglo-Saxons and the westward movement of the remaining British—or Celtic—states. But in both the Saxon territories and those of the Britons, the legitimacy of the kingship, and of the king, was of paramount importance to the stability or even the survival of the polity.[130] The legitimate attainment of power had to be by dynastic inheritance or military proficiency (the latter ideally backed by some dynastic connection to the previous king)[131]; mere murder and usurpation, for instance, would have been an unsatisfactory means of acquiring the throne, even for a member of the royal family. The dynastic element remained central, and this led to some important and interesting contrasts between the Saxon and the post-Roman British kingship. The British ruling classes in what was later to become Wales continued to emphasise Roman ancestors (and not simply earlier native rulers) within their pedigrees as a way to link their rule with the old imperial Roman order, suggesting stability and continuity derived from association with that old order.[132] In contrast the Anglo-Saxon royal

[129] Davies, Wendy, *Patterns of Power in Early Wales* (1989), p. 32.

[130] Davies, Wendy, *Wales in the Early Middle Ages* (1982), p. 122.

[131] Ibid, pp. 121–125; Davies, Wendy, *Patterns of Power in Early Wales* (1989), p. 38.

[132] Davies, John, *A History of Wales* (1993); Ward-Perkins, Bryan, "Why Did the Anglo-Saxons Not Become More British" (2000) 115 English Historical Review 513–533.

pedigrees generally traced their descent from Wōden (Odin).[133] Both were tracing descent from a worthy ancestor, one imbued with authority, sacred or secular, who might be looked upon to confer status upon their descendants, and impart upon them some of their legitimacy.

While political theory was therefore far from absent, at this time coronations, in the later eastern Roman (or west European) tradition, remained rudimentary in the British Isles; an imperial coronation had gradually evolved over the course of the fifth century, too late to directly influence developments in what we now call Wales, or indeed elsewhere in Britain. The inauguration of rulers therefore looked to native tribal and kingly tradition, influenced by recollection of Roman rituals, rather than the (new) Roman imperial practice. However, this was to slowly change, partly through the influence of the church, whose Europe-wide networks allowed and indeed encouraged the diffusion of knowledge, including of liturgy and ritual, and of the scriptural basis of coronations. Coronations, along with earlier forms of inaugurations, were never empty rituals, but always served a political and religious purpose.

It was not long after the withdrawal of the legions and the collapse of central authority in the British provinces of the Roman empire, that the first evidence appears of a coronation rite, inspired by the church's accounts of ancient Hebrew kingly inaugurations. According to Adomnán of Iona (who died 704), the king of Dál Riata (a political entity covering the west coast of Scotland and north-east Ireland), Áedán mac Gabráin, came to the monastery at Iona in 574—or possibly the hill of Dunadd—to be crowned by St Columba. This is the earliest recorded coronation in Britain and Ireland,[134] but it is likely not the first, even allowin for doubts of the historisity of the anointing.[135] Even though Adomnán was writing over one hundred years after the event, the abbot's knowledge may well have been based on contemporary records in the abbey, as Adomnán was abbot of Iona. In any event, it suggests an appreciation, by the late

[133] Sisam, Kenneth, "Anglo-Saxon Royal Genealogies" (1953) 39 Proceedings of the British Academy 287–348.

[134] Adomnan of Iona, *The life of St Columba* ed. Richard Sharpe (trans.) (1995), vol 3, 5 and translator's note 358; Broun, Dauvit, "Aedán mac Gabráin", in Michael Lynch (ed.), *The Oxford Companion to Scottish History* (2001), p. 5; Byrne, Francis John, *Irish Kings and High-Kings* (1973), p. 159; Yorke, Barbara, *The Conversion of Britain* (2006), p. 241.

[135] Enright, M.J., *Iona, Tara, and Soissons Ritual* (1985).

seventh century, if not the sixth century, of the significance of coronations, and especially of their Christian aspect, though it remains uncertain of what, exactly, the rite comprised.

It was no longer sufficient to rely solely on any traditional tribal inauguration; after the conversion to Christianity a scripturally-based ritual, presided over by a prelate, was almost mandatory. Ironically, at this time, in Constantinople, coronations, as later understood, were still only in their comparative infancy.

In what later became England there was also, with the Christianisation of the kingdoms of the Anglo-Saxons, the gradual development of interest in assuming what were seen as the general if not universal attributes of kingship, including crowns and coronations. It was some time before coronations became a standard ritual in the British Isles, and then possibly because of external influences. The first known English coronation (the kingdom of Dál Riata not being in what we now term England) was in 787, for Ecgfrith, son of King Offa of Mercia (who himself ruled 757–796). Ecgfrith himself was to rule for only 141 days, after his father's death in 796.[136] As the heir to the throne, it was probably in imitation of the consecration of Charlemagne's sons by the pope in 781[137]; it could also have been an attempt to associate Ecgfrith in the government, just as Roman emperors had done. Additionally, although there is no record of Offa himself having been crowned and/or anointed, at this time or earlier, it is likely that this had occurred. Ecgfrith himself may not have been anointed or crowned after his own accession.

In 796, more than 200 years after Áedán mac Gabráin was crowned—or at least consecrated—as king of Dál Riata by St Columba, the Anglo-Saxon king Eardwulf of Northumbria was consecrated and enthroned.[138] It is probably too much of a logical jump to assume any certain pre-Saxon connection between the Saxon kingdom of Northumbria and sub-Roman political entities, but it is worth noting that the kingdom of Northumbria (established 654) comprised two core areas, the kingdoms of Bernicia

[136] Swanton, Michael, *The Anglo-Saxon Chronicle* (1996), p. 50. Reigning from 29th May that would put his death on or around 17th December.

[137] Williams, Ann, "Ecgfrith king of Mercia", in Ann Williams, Alfred P. Smyth and D. P. Kirby (eds.), *A Biographical Dictionary of Dark Age Britain* (1991).

[138] The Anglo-Saxon Chronicle records that he was consecrated by Eanbald I, Archbishop of York, and Bishops Æthelberht, Beadwulf and Hygebald, at York Minster on 26th May 796; Swanton, Michael, *The Anglo-Saxon Chronicle* (1996), Ms. D, s.a. 796.

(existing before c.547 to 654) and Deira (existing c.450–654),[139] which may have originally been sub-Roman Celtic British entities occupied by later Anglo-Saxons, rather than merely the creation of newly arrived Germanic settlers.[140] Nonetheless, contact with, and fertilisation from Europe, were leading the development of coronations, just as they were wider social, political and religious changes, though it may be supposed that the first generation of pagan Saxon kings were not crowned as that concept is now understood, but rather inaugurated in tribal ceremony.

This was to soon change. The first English *ordo* (religious order of service) is found in the Leofric Missal. Janet Nelson has shown that this service represents an English, or perhaps a Wessex, version of the early ninth century Carolingian anointing ritual.[141] She concludes that it was probably written in England before the mid ninth century, but that it was later transmitted back to the Continent when it was used by Hincmar of Reims. This was when Hincmar composed an *ordo* for the coronation of Judith, the daughter of Charles the Bald, who married King Æthelwulf in 856. Nelson argues that evidence of its antiquity includes the use of a helmet (*galea*) to crown the king, rather than a crown, as well as the role played by the magnates (*principes*) in the ceremony. The helmet may be exemplified by the superb Sutton Hoo helmet, discovered in 1939 and dating from the early seventh century, possibly the property of Rædwald, King of East Anglia.[142] This form of the coronation service passed out of use after the first half of the ninth century, when it was replaced by the Second English *ordo*. This latter is largely but not entirely comprised of materials drawn from the *ordines* used in western Francia in the late ninth century.[143] The native—to the Saxons—traditions gave

[139] Rollason, David W., *Northumbria, 500–1100* (2003).

[140] Fleming, Robin, *Britain after Rome* (2010).

[141] Nelson, Janet L., "Carolingian Coronation Rituals: A Model for Europe?" (2004) 9(1) The Court Historian 1–13.

[142] Bruce-Mitford, Rupert, *The Sutton Hoo Ship-Burial, Volume 2* (1978).

[143] Nelson, Janet L., "The Earliest Surviving Royal Ordo: Some Liturgical and Historical Aspects", in B. Tierney and P. Linehan (eds.), *Authority and Power* (1980), pp. 29–48; reprinted in Janet L. Nelson, *Politics and Ritual in Early Mediæval Europe* (1986), pp. 341–360; Nelson, Janet, "The First Use of the Second Anglo-Saxon *Ordo*", in Julia Barrow and Andrew Wareham (eds.), *Myth, Rulership, Church and Charters* (2008), pp. 117–126, 125–126.

way before a broader evolving European form of coronation. This second *ordo* provides the form and template for all subsequent ones.[144]

Over one hundred years after Eardwulf of Northumbria was consecrated and enthroned, Æthelstan (styled King of the Anglo-Saxons 924–927 and then King of the English 927–939) was crowned and anointed 4th September 925.[145] Æthelstan was crowned at Kingston-upon-Thames, perhaps due to its symbolic location on the border between Wessex and Mercia, by Athelm (or Æthelhelm), Archbishop of Canterbury, who himself probably designed or organised a new *ordo* in which the king wore a crown for the first time instead of a helmet. The new *ordo*—commonly referred to as the Second *Ordo*—was in turn to become one of the sources for the mediæval French *ordo*.[146]

Æthelstan's position must be seen in the context of wider political developments. As the first King of the English, or King of England (the styles were interchangeable for several centuries more), he also overtly claimed some form of suzerainty over the whole of the island of Britain. On his coins and charters he is described variously as *Rex totius Britanniae*, or "King of the whole of Britain", or *Bretwalda*, perhaps a conscious attempt to link himself with Roman or sub-Roman political institutions and traditions. He also used the style "*basileus et curagulus*" (king and custodian), *basileus* being jealously guarded until this time by the eastern Roman Empire and reserved for their own emperors. In charters from 931 Æthelstan is called.

> king of the English, elevated by the right hand of the almighty to the throne of the whole kingdom of Britain.[147]

[144] Pratt, David, "The making of the Second English Coronation Ordo" (2017) 46 Anglo-Saxon England 147–258.

[145] Foot, Sarah, *Æthelstan* (2011), pp. 73–74.

[146] Nelson, Janet, "The First Use of the Second Anglo-Saxon *Ordo*", in Julia Barrow and Andrew Wareham (eds.), *Myth, Rulership, Church and Charters* (2008), pp. 117–126, 125–126. For a fuller account of the various recensions see Pratt, David, *English Coronation Ordines in the Ninth and Early Tenth Centuries* (2023).

[147] Foot, Sarah, *Æthelstan* (2011), pp. 212–213; Ortenberg, Veronica, "The King from Overseas: Why did Æthelstan Matter in Tenth-Century Continental Affairs?", in David Rollason, Conrad Leyser and Hannah Williams (eds.), *England and the Continent in the Tenth Century* (2010), pp. 211–236, 215.

It is likely his coronation was part of his attempts to consolidate his claimed authority. This was to influence later kings; Edgar's coronation in 973 consolidated the role of the ritual of coronation in England. The coronation was not simply a ceremony or rite, it served a vital political and religious function. The constitutive function was early seen in England, particularly in late Saxon times, with both kings Harold Godwinson (Harold II, crowned 6th January 1066) and William the Conqueror crowned in Westminster Abbey on 25th December 1066, to complete their acquisition of the crown, albeit acquired in different circumstances. Harold was the first English king known to likely have been crowned in Westminster Abbey (rather than in Westminster Old Palace[148]); William was the first Norman king so crowned.[149] Both were incorporating indigenous elements with what were seen, however erroneously, as ubiquitous components of a classic European coronation, and thus bringing the ruler the status of equality with other sovereigns. Cultural, political, and religious differences existed, but were largely subsumed into the greater format of the coronation ceremony.

The secular aspects of the coronation in the middle ages, especially the political, were perhaps relatively less significant than the religious (though important nonetheless, especially the acclamation and the homage). Since only a relatively few people could actually be present at a coronation, only the political and religious elite, and those with particular roles which required their presence, could witness it first-hand. The homage, in particular, was crucial in a feudal era. The legal significance of the coronation, especially after the acceptance of the concept, in 1399, that "the king never dies", and thus there is automatic accession to the throne, was less than its political significance. Again, however, whilst feudalism prevailed, the homage created, or at least cemented, ties of fealty and obedience between king and subject. The coronation oath, of especial importance in England from pre-Norman times, also held particular relevance, echoing perhaps the *edut* (the covenant, law, and statutes) of the kings of Israel.

[148] The building was consecrated on 28 December 1065, making the argument that he was crowned in the Palace rather than the new Abbey plausable but unlikely, since the Abbey was complete by 1060; Page, William, "Benedictine monks: St Peter's abbey, Westminster", in *A History of the County of London* (1909), vol. 1, "London Within the Bars, Westminster and Southwark", pp. 433–457; Carr, Wesley, *Westminster Abbey* (1999); Cannadine, Sir David (ed.), *Westminster Abbey* (2019).

[149] Huscroft, Richard, *The Norman Conquest* (2009), pp. 131–133.

No king's title was seen as complete without a coronation, however perfunctory, and the greater the power of the new sovereign—or their ambitions—the greater the spectacle of the coronation was likely to be.

But whether it was legally, politically or theologically mandatory for a new Sovereign to undergo a coronation, there were a number of what were seen as essential elements in a mediæval coronation, as there are still today. In this there are parallels with classical practice, the coronation of the Eastern Roman emperors cemented their hold on the throne, however questionable their title might originally have been. These elements may be seen to form the seven key components of an English coronation. These are the recognition or acclamation, the oath, the anointing, the investiture with regalia, the crowning, the enthroning, and the homage, commonly, but not inevitably, in that sequence. It was also generally (if not invariably) set within the context of a mass or eucharist. Indeed, the centrality of the eucharist to the coronation rite has been emphasised by a recent dean of Westminster Abbey.[150] On only two occasions was it arguably not eucharistic, the coronation of King John 27th May 1199 (as the king left the abbey before taking communion),[151] and that of King James II 23rd April 1685 (as a Roman Catholic, he was unable to take communion from the Anglican Archbishop of Canterbury, so Archbishop Sancroft omitted the eucharist).[152]

By 1200 coronations in England were essentially a rite of passage for the new king, from *Dominus Anglorum* to *Rex Anglorum* (from mere de facto ruler, to de jure King); similarly, the Holy Roman Emperor was only King of the Romans prior to his coronation by the pope, only assuming the style of emperor upon his coronation; they were previously crowned and anointed as King of the Romans.[153] The Archbishop of Canterbury bestowed unction—using holy oil or chrism[154]—transforming a candidate from merely *Dominus* (ruler) to being *Rex Dei Gratias* (King by the

[150] Carr, Wesley, "This Intimate Ritual: The Coronation Service" (2002) 4(1) Political Theology 11–24, 22.

[151] "John", Westminster Abbey, <https://www.westminster-abbey.org/abbey-commemorations/royals/john>.

[152] Harris, Tim, *Revolution* (2006), p. 45.

[153] Watanabe-O'Kelly, Helen, "The Last Habsburg Coronation and What it Means to be Anointed", in Klaas Van Gelder (ed.), *More than Mere Spectacle* (2021), pp. 303–312.

[154] The anointing for most Monarchs was done with the oil of catechumens; but by Papal permission, those of France, England, Scotland, Sicily, and Jerusalem were done with chrism; Coulombe, Charles, "An Eighth Sacrament?", <https://onepeterfive.com/eighth-sacrament/?fbclid=IwAR3d-UhwahXmtHlZ6I-nuE6-nMA086GcIayqtDKHtVIVi4UIFIPBea0Ie2g>.

grace of God). This practice echoed the early use of oil in baptism and confirmation, with the Church using oil for anointing Christian kings, but also reflecting and acknowledging the scriptural origins of anointing kings in ancient Israel. Anointing, though today even rarer than crowning, was long thought of pivotal significance in establishing Christian monarchy, and significant efforts were made to ensure that the proper oil was used, and correctly administered, even at the cost of inventing origin myths of increasing improbability, such as that in mediæval France, a myth which met its match in a similar legend concocted for English King Henry IV in 1399.[155] Henry's coronation was, of course, a example of royal ritual used for political purposes.[156]

There were also components which occurred outside Westminster Abbey, such as the procession into London, and the coronation banquet,[157] which were essentially ceremonial and social rather than of religious or directly political significance (although being seen by the people on such an occasion, and in such a setting, often enhanced an otherwise shaky relationship with the citizens of London, in particular). The coronation was not subject to some form of *rigor mortis*, unchanging from generation to generation, but exhibited, for clear reasons, a remarkable degree of continuity in form and content. Like the coronations of early mediæval Europe, of Israel, and of Egypt, central to the coronation was the establishment of legitimacy.

Over time the importance of each of the key components of an English coronation changed, to reflect differing expectations and requirements, but the seven key components enumerated above remained. The main role of the coronation became rather more secular than sacred, but both

155 Oppenheimer, Sir Francis, *The Legend of the Ste. Ampoule* (1953); Cartwright, Mark, "The Coronation Ceremony of the British Monarchy", *World History Encyclopedia*. https://www.worldhistory.org/article/1533/the-coronation-ceremony of the british-monarchy/.

156 Favorito, Rebecca, "Constructing Legitimacy: Patrimony, Patronage, and Political Communication in the Coronation of Henry IV" (2016) The Ohio State University PhD thesis.

157 The coronation banquet in Westminster Hall—the only significant surviving part of the ancient Palace of Westminster, built 1097—were held from 1194 to 1821, but the celebratory coronation banquets have been held in Buckingham Palace since the nineteenth century; in 1953 these were held on the 3rd and 4th June, in the Ballroom, for 400 guests each; Strong, Sir Roy, *Coronation* (2005), p. 62.

aspects were always present and could not be readily separated; the Reformation did not materially change that (it would be an over-simplification, an error which some authors have fallen into, to categorise the liturgy of a coronation as Anglican, although changes made in 2023 perhaps increased the validity of such a charge[158]). As the Crown lost much of its spiritual status and political power in the course of the eighteenth century, so it increasingly sought to gain psychological and sociological authority—which also required the occasional "manifestation of magnificence", if not the invention of tradition.[159] By the early twentieth century, when the invention or reinterpretation of tradition assumed new heights, there was plentiful material in the order of a coronation to render any innovation almost superfluous.

The Coronation Ordo

For the coronation service proper—that occurring in Westminster Abbey—the liturgies for each was recorded in a series of manuals, the best known of which is the *Liber Regalis*, used in 1382 for the coronation of Anne of Bohemia (and possibly in 1308 for the coronation of Edward II). This shows a considerable degree of commonality of broad structure between the coronation of Edgar in 973, and that of Charles III in 2023. The First Recension of the pre-Conquest *ordines* (coronation order or service) may never have been used in England. This was the *Pontificale Egberti*, supposedly written by Ecgbert, Archbishop of York 732–766. It was the Second Recension which was used for the coronation of Edgar by St Dunstan in 973. This was subsequently used by later Anglo-Saxon and early Norman kings; William the Conqueror was determined to emphasise the continuity of his reign with that of his Saxon predecessors, from whom he claimed title.[160] No contemporary English account corroborates the Norman justification for the Conquest, so the degree to which

[158] *The Authorised Liturgy for the Coronation Rite of His Majesty King Charles III For use on Saturday 6th May 2023, 11:00am at Westminster Abbey* (2023).

[159] Hobsbawn, Eric and Terence Ranger, *The Invention of Tradition* (1983).

[160] Garnett, George, "Coronation and propaganda: some implications of the Norman claim to the throne of England in 1066" (1986) 36 Transactions of the Royal Historical Society 91–116.

William's claim was accepted by English contemporaries remains uncertain.[161] It was unquestionably politically expedient for him to be crowned according to English custom—although in the event the coronation of William I in the new abbey church very nearly prematurely ended his reign, due to the disorder which ensued. The rite was also presided over by Ealdred, archbishop of York, because Stigand, archbishop of Canterbury, had been excommunicated for pluralism,[162] and because of doubts over the validity of his appointment.[163]

The Third Recension of the coronation service was probably compiled during the reign of Henry I and was first used for the coronation of Stephen in 1135. Whilst maintaining considerable continuity with earlier services, this recension also borrowed heavily from the coronation ritual of the Holy Roman Emperors, the *Pontificale Romano-Germanicum*, a liturgical text compiled in Mainz in 961. The tradition or custom of deliberate borrowing from imperial practice, first from Constantinople, and then from Germany,[164] echoed the custom of the Saxon kings adopting imperial styles; Edgar styled himself *Albionis Imperator Augustus*,[165] and Æthelstan variously used the styles *basileus* and *imperator*, as well as *rex*.[166] These apparently alien importations were not surprising given the European-wide political environment in which England was embroiled at this time; Stephen's rival, Maude (or Matilda), was the widow of Henry V, Holy Roman Emperor 1111–1125. It was also consistent with a tradition already at least several hundred years old, and possibly still more

[161] Garnett, George, "William's coronation", in *The Norman Conquest* (2009), pp. 19–39.

[162] Rex, Peter, *1066* (2011), pp. 94–95.

[163] Huscroft, Richard, *Ruling England 1042–1217* (2005), p. 48; Chibnall, Marjorie, *Anglo-Norman England 1066–1166* (1986), p. 39; Walker, Ian, *Harold the Last Anglo-Saxon King* (2000), pp. 136–138; Blumenthal, Uta-Renate, *The Investiture Controversy* (1988), pp. 148–149.

[164] Whereas a coronation may occur anywhere, English coronations have been held in London since 1066—indeed in the same venue, Westminster Abbey. Likewise, Eastern emperors were generally crowned in Constantinople.

[165] Cannon, John and Ralph Griffiths, *The Oxford Illustrated History of the British Monarchy* (1988), pp. 14–16.

[166] Foot, Sarah, *Æthelstan* (2011), pp. 212–213; Ortenberg, Veronica, "The King from Overseas: Why did Æthelstan Matter in Tenth-Century Continental Affairs?" in David Rollason, Conrad Leyser and Hannah Williams (eds.), *England and the Continent in the Tenth Century* (2010), pp. 211–236, 215.

ancient, of kings symbolically attempting to associate their legitimacy with the corporate status and glory of imperial Rome, and particularly the *translatio imperii*, the supreme power purportedly inherited by the Holy Roman Emperors from the ancient emperors of Rome.[167]

The Fourth Recension of the coronation order (contained in the *Westminster Missal* and the *Liber Regalis*) was the basis of all modern coronations, and was first used for the coronation of Edward II in 1308, after several decades of development. The *Liber Regalis* was probably prepared for the Coronation of Anne of Bohemia, the wife of Richard II, in 1382. In its essence the service conveyed the message that only when he was enthroned aloft on a raised stage, kissed by the officiating clergy, and had received fealty from the supporting magnates, could a would-be king be seen as having authority over both Church (as far as that was ever acknowledged) and people.[168] It was influenced by contemporary French practice, but also emphasised the balance between king and nobles, and the coronation oath, both of which were distinctly English aspects of the coronation. The enthroning, where the Sovereign, who previously sat in King Edward's chair, is today symbolically lifted up into the throne by the archbishops, bishops and peers, reminds as how the early kings were raised on a stone.[169]

The acclamation—when the assembled congregation expressed their collective acceptance of the king-elect—grew in importance when the title of the king was slightly suspect, or downright dubious (as for example, and much later, with King William III and Queen Mary II).[170] In the

[167] Whaley, Joachim, *Germany and the Holy Roman Empire, Volume I* (2012), vol. I, pp. 17–21.

[168] Each of these elements were enacted in 2023, albeit in simpler form than hitherto. King Charles III was enthroned aloft on a raised stage (the coronation chair was placed on the Cosmati Pavement, but the throne chair of the king was raised up one step), kissed by the officiating clergy (the Archbishop of Canterbury knelt and swore fealty to the king), and had received fealty from the supporting magnates (the Prince of Wales knelt, swore homage, and kissed the king on the cheek, followed by a taking of the oath of allegiance by those present—and elsewhere in the world—who chose to do so); *The Authorised Liturgy for the Coronation Rite of His Majesty King Charles III For use on Saturday 6th May 2023, 11:00am at Westminster Abbey* (2023).

[169] See *Supplement to the London Gazette*, 20 November 1953, p. 6250.

[170] Modern practice is for the presentation of the monarch to the people by the Archbishop of Canterbury accompanied by the Lord High Chancellor, the Lord Great Chamberlain, the Lord High Constable and the Earl Marshal, with Garter Principal King of Arms preceding them, and the recognition of the monarch by the people.

case of William the Conqueror, it is well known that the acclamation almost caused a disaster, as the enthusiasm of those in the Abbey was misunderstood by the Norman soldiers on guard duty outside. A king who wished to emphasise his divine right to the Crown might subtly downplay the importance of this part of the ceremony. This could be done without deleting it, which itself would cause offence and risk alienating key supporters. In a similar way, and somewhat earlier, sixth century Eastern Roman theorists focused not on the coronation of the Roman emperor itself, but on the "election" and the consent as crucial elements in the imperial inauguration. This was the divine choice through officials, senators and people, the fundamental basis of imperial authority from the Roman principate onwards.

The *Liber Regalis* was translated into English for the first time for the coronation of James I in 1601, partly as a result of the Reformation in England enjoining if not requiring religious services to be understandable by the people,[171] but also in an attempt by contemporary antiquarians to recover, as they perceived it, a lost English identity from before the Norman Conquest.[172] They sought, and found, elements of the coronation dating from the time of King Edgar in 973—and, as we now know, arguably considerably earlier than that. King James I's coronation was an exemplar of continuity and legitimacy, despite the use of English rather than Latin, to bolster the standing of a Scots king whose title to the crown was not as strong as he might have wished,[173] even though his title was largely unquestioned. A century later the Latin text was resurrected anew for the 1714 coronation of the German-speaking King George I, since it was the only language common to both the king and the clergy involved in the ceremonial. Most of the service perforce had to be conducted in Latin,[174] not for any theological or political reason, but out of shear necessity.

[171] Gosling, Lucinda, *Royal Coronations* (2013), p. 10.

[172] Strong, Sir Roy, *Coronation* (2005), p. 244.

[173] Hunt, Alice, "The Bright Star of the North: James I and his English Coronation", in M. Twycross, P. King, S. Carpenter, and G. Walker (eds.), *Mediæval English Theatre* (2017), Part II, pp. 22–37.

[174] *The London Gazette*, issue 5270, 19 October 1714.

Coronation Oath

One element which has long remained especially important (and particularly English) is the coronation oath. The coronation as a whole incorporated and perpetuated features which put limits and conditions on the king's reign. The coronation oath emphasised the idea that the king was a servant of God (and therefore of the Church) and had assumed important Christian duties. It also stressed loyalty to the king's person and to the office which he held, as a consequence of the assumption of those duties. The claimant had been put in possession of the Crown, throne, and kingdom as securely and as publicly "as the wit of man could devise". His power had been legitimised; *Potestas* was converted into *auctoritas*. He had also been given a new character, and was now different from other men; women in the rare case of a queen regnant. He was required to swear that he would ensure that the Church of God and the whole Christian people within his dominions would be kept in true peace. Further, he swore that he would forbid impure and wrongful acts to "men of every degree", and that he would order that justice and mercy should be observed in all legal judgements.

The exact wording of the earlier oaths is generally lost, but there is no doubt of the contemporary importance with which they were treated. In the late eleventh century kings swore a triple oath—to protect the Church and people, to offer justice to all, and to act with mercy.[175] To this day the coronation oath is a formal legal requirement under both the Act of Settlement 1700,[176] and the Coronation Oath Act 1688.[177] The effect, however, of these latter provisions is to change the emphasis of the coronation oath; prior to the addition of an explanatory introduction in 2023, the preservation of the independence of the church predominated.

The different kings had varied interest in and attachment to discrete parts of the ritual of the coronation. King James I and Charles I both regarded the coronation oath, for instance, as not being strictly binding upon them, since their title to the Crown was, in their eyes at least, by divine right.[178]

[175] Cannon, John and Ralph Griffiths, *The Oxford Illustrated History of the British Monarchy* (1988), p. 117.

[176] 12 & 13 Will III c 2.

[177] 1 Will. III & Mary c. 6.

[178] Legg, L. G. W., *English Coronation Records* (1901), pp. xxix.

But despite this attitude, in general kings were always expected to honour their coronation oath, and not a few reissued their oaths later in their reigns; to some extent the history of Magna Carta is the history of the coronation oath, and the consequences for a king who neglected to keep his oath.[179] Oaths in a feudal society were inviolable, even if there was no direct sanction—only an indirect divine one—on a royal oath-breaker, still they were in some manner bound. Equally, the magnates and prelates bound themselves to the new king in the homage service. This form of allegiance survived the decline and death of feudalism, as it has origins predating that economic, political and social system.

With the accession of William and Mary the Crown was in a quite different situation to what it was, for instance, under Charles I. There was a renewed (though perhaps temporary) emphasis upon the elective nature of kingship, the coronation oath, and the public acclamation and political and ecclesiastical homage and fealty. However, as Brightman lamented, perhaps unfairly, the efforts of Henry Compton, Bishop of London, to revise the rite meant that "nothing of the ancient order remained in its place without change; and very little of it was left at all."[180] However, even in an age of parliamentary sovereignty, the coronation oath plays an important legitimising role, as can be seen in the discussion in chapter 4.

Coronation Spectacle

Whilst the oath was of importance to the magnates, the politicians and the senior clerics, for most people it was largely irrelevant. For them the coronation meant a grand public spectacle. In Tudor times at least.[181] Queen Elizabeth I took care to meet the people's expectations in this respect with her pre-coronation procession.[182] Just as the acclamation

[179] Richardson, H.G., "The English Coronation Oath" (1941) 23 Transactions of the Royal Historical Society 129–158; Watt, G., "The Coronation Oath" (2017) 19(3) Ecclesiastical Law Journal 325–341.

[180] Brightman, F.E., *Chronicle* JTS iv (1902–3) p. 152 quoted in Peter Hinchliff, "Frederick Temple, Randall Davidson and the Coronation of Edward VII" (1997) 48(1) Journal of Ecclesiastical History 71–99, 76.

[181] Loach, Jennifer, "The Function of Ceremonial in the Reign of Henry VIII" (1994) 142 Past & Present 43–68.

[182] Haugaard, William P., "The Coronation of Elizabeth I" (1968) 19(2) The Journal of Ecclesiastical History 161–170; Stróbl, Erzsébet, "The City as Stage: The Coronation Entry of Elizabeth I in 1559" (2021) Art in Urban Space 191

within the Abbey was part of the king-making process, so too was the procession, though in a different manner. By 1603, perhaps under the influence of Calvinism, as Strong believed, the coronation as a whole was seen as a royal ornament, a solemnisation of the royal title. Symbolism remained important, but it was the symbolism of the court, not of the Church or the people.

Kings James I and Charles I both neglected the procession into London—the latter to the extent of cancelling it altogether. He thereby incurred the resentment of City burghers, who lost the traditional opportunity to express their loyalty to him (and also profit from increased trade), and arguably remembered this to his disadvantage a decade later. The danger of changing elements of the coronation—even external ones like the procession—without a clear appreciation of the function and purpose for which they existed, is all too apparent. It was perhaps not too much of an exaggeration to say that changing the focus of the coronation from an outward, public, spectacle, to an inward focussed court ritual, weakened the legitimacy of both kings.

An Arminian clique of higher clergy under King Charles I, led by William Laud,[183] were interested in developing a distinct Anglican ecclesiology—not a doctrine distinct from the Universal Church, but one which marked the English church as both catholic and reformed. The coronation could have given them an opportunity to apply their views in practice, but King Charles I was crowned in 1626 by George Abbot, Archbishop of Canterbury, a Calvinist, and only appointed William Laud to the position of Archbishop of Canterbury in 1633. The King was not able, so soon after his succession, to avoid this scenario, as the ordinary minister of the coronation is the Archbishop of Canterbury, unless prevented by imprisonment, incapacity or vacancy.

The Caroline divines differed from the Puritans in devotional rather than doctrinal approach.[184] Laud did not concentrate upon doctrine because it was not of central interest to him—he was not primarily a theologian and regarded these questions as settled. He was.

> devoted to the Church of England, that is to a church of apostolic antiquity, that part of the universal Catholic Church which had preserved the

[183] Chadwick, Owen, *The Reformation* (1972), p. 225.

[184] Ibid, p. 226.

> purity of the primitive church by casting off the corruptions and accretions of Roman superstition".[185] In the one work of theology which he published, Laud declared a faith in Christ "as it was professed in the ancient Primitive Church and as it is professed in the present Church of England.[186]

Had Charles I been able to successfully promote his liturgical vision it is possible that the coronation of his successors might have emphasised a more outward facing spectacle, and one more aligned with pre-Reformation liturgy; equally, however, contemporary secular fashion encouraged a focus on the court.

However inspired, changes have always occurred, sometime to keep up with fashion, occasionally on principle, or on a royal whim—and periodically, due to necessity. The investiture with items of regalia, and the crowning, underwent detailed changes over time, but its function remained largely unchanged. Even the destruction of almost all the regalia by the Parliamentary forces in 1649—only the anointing spoon, and the three swords of spiritual justice, temporal justice, and mercy survived[187]—did not cause significant changes to be instigated at the next coronation. Indeed in 1661 a new spirit of antiquarian inquiry ensured that the best efforts of the time were made to recreate the regalia in as authentic a manner as was then possible.[188] There was no taste for reckless innovation. Reinforcing the authority of the restored kingship necessitated an emphasis upon ancient, unquestioned, royal ritual. Indeed, an emphasis upon history, legitimacy, and continuity, were and remain near universal aspects of coronations. Coronations do not occur for the personal amusement of the primary royal personage present (although we may, perhaps unfairly, accuse George IV of having exhibited that apparent intention[189]), but for the establishment of their full title to reign.

Likewise, the coronation of 1689 did much to legitimise the new order, with King William and Queen Mary crowned in the traditional manner, but jointly as king and queen regnant (rather than as king and

[185] Sharpe, Kevin, "Archbishop Laud" (August 1983) History Today 26–30, 27.

[186] *Conference with Fisher the Jesuit*, cited in Sharpe, Kevin, "Archbishop Laud" (August 1983) History Today 26–30, 27–28.

[187] Blair, Claude (ed.), *The Crown Jewels* (1998), vol 1.

[188] Rose, Tessa, *The Coronation Ceremony and the Crown Jewels* (1992).

[189] Gosling, Lucinda, *Royal Coronations* (2013).

queen consort). The oath enjoyed particular importance, due to the so-called "Glorious Revolution" that had immediately preceded it, and the new parliamentary supremacy which that brought about. We start to see the coronation serving a different function to the king-making it had occasionally exhibited in past centuries.

After 1685 the constitutional and social significance of the coronation went into general decline. The hallowing by the Church remained important for both religious reasons, but there were increasingly large numbers of spectators in Westminster Abbey,[190] whose interest perhaps lay more in the show of the investiture with the regalia and the later coronation banquet in Westminster Hall, than in the principles underpinning the anointing, oath-taking, or homage. Nevertheless, although it spoke to the masses in very different ways to how it had spoken to the social and political elite in the Abbey, yet it still spoke to them, helping to bind Sovereign and people in a—hopefully—unbreakable bond.

The downward trend continued and the coronation ceremonial was treated, as Strong argued, in a rather cavalier fashion in the 1700s and early 1800s. King George I succeeded not by divine right or even popular choice but by the will of Parliament. A more prosaic, less principled attitude prevailed, much less one of religious piety; it is not a coincidence that the Church of England was also in the doldrums at this time. Hanoverian coronations lacked the attention to detail that characterised many of those of earlier periods, though they did bring us some of Handel's incomparable music, most notably the anthem, "Zadok the Priest".

The coronation of King William IV was perceived publicly as a mean affair (to his ultimate disadvantage); even that of Queen Victoria was only marginally better. Both paled into insignificance in contrast to the magnificence of King George IV's coronation, with its Georgian antiquarian extravagance,[191] but arguable relative absence of a spiritual core. Thankfully for the Exchequer the cost was met to a large degree by the French war indemnity of one hundred million French francs,[192] although that money might have been spent more wisely, or at least less ostentatiously. By the time of Queen Victoria's coronation, however, there were

[190] The number of attendees has of course varied over time. In 1953 it was 8,261, and in 1902 it was 5,873; Strong, Sir Roy, *Coronation* (2005).

[191] Huish, Robert, *An Authentic History of the Coronation of George IV* (1821).

[192] Strong, Sir Roy, *Coronation* (2005), pp. 372–374.

signs of a desire for the revival of a ceremony of some genuine splendour, to emphasise the setting aside by anointing of the Sovereign with holy oil, as popular embodiment of both Crown and nation. The ancient role of the coronation was being rediscovered, in place of the court ritual or profane public entertainment that had hitherto dominated for a century or more.

The pre-coronation procession into London was discarded after 1661, but was replaced in effect by the (military) parade to the Abbey. The coronation parades of the twentieth century (even that of 1953) far exceeded the earlier efforts for size. For splendour the twentieth century parades may have been at something of a disadvantage compared with their mediæval and later counterparts, but now they were aimed at showing the nature of a popular monarchy, dependent not on the choice of God hallowed by Holy Church, or even the choice of Parliament, but on the approbation of the people. They also, at the height of imperial growth (particularly in 1902, 1911 and 1937) reflected an emphasis upon national and international power and majesty. Even in 1953 there were 29,000 service personnel in the procession, including numerous Admirals of the Fleet, Field Marshals, and Marshals of the Royal Air Force[193]—mostly in carriages—and another 15,800 personnel lined the route,[194] including contingents from the dominions and colonies. This was the last occasion upon which the British Empire, gradually transforming into the Commonwealth, was able to embody imperial might and authority. Subsequent parades would have to be limited, perforce, to represent a post-imperial reality—and a much smaller military. In 2023 there were 4000 personnel in the Coronation procession, including 20 bands, and 400 personnel from 45 Commonwealth countries, including 21 from

[193] In 1953 there were 6 Admirals of the Fleet, 6 Field Marshals, and 8 Marshals of the Royal Air Force involved in the coronation, all but one taking part in the coronation parade, a total of 20 individuals. In 2023 there were only six in total—1 Admiral of the Fleet (Sir Benjamin Bathurst); 3 Field Marshals (Lord Walker of Aldringham, Lord Guthrie of Craigiebank, and the Duke of Kent); 2 Marshal of the Royal Air Force (Lord Craig of Radley, and Lord Stirrup), three of whom were in their late 80s or 90s.

[194] See *Supplement to the London Gazette*, 17th November 1953 (HMSO, London, 1953), pp. 6223–6270 "Ceremonial of the Coronation of Her Majesty Queen Elizabeth II". At that time there were 868,000 regular military, air and naval personnel in the British armed forces; https://www.statista.com/statistics/579773/number-of-personnel-in-uk-armed-forces/.

New Zealand,[195] 40 from Australia,[196] and 50 from Canada.[197] As a proportion of the size of the military, it was comparable to 1953.

Coronation Attire

In the course of the twentieth century the form of service was improved to recover from the "slash and burn" treatment under King James II and William and Mary, and much attention was given to reviving ancient, hallowed, aspects—not simply for show, or for the amusement of a rarefied elite group of scholars, but from an appreciation of the substance. As an example, scholarly attempts were made to better understand the detail of the coronation, in both ritual and dress.[198]

The latter is particularly interesting. The oldest extant coronation order with a definite English connection, dating from the ninth century, makes no mention of the royal coronation robes.[199] The second oldest extant coronation order, of the eleventh century, which may have been that used by both Harold II and William the Conqueror, is equally silent on the question of dress. The Bayeux Tapestry however shows Harold wearing a yellow tunic, a green dalmatic and a purple mantle.[200] Whilst this source should be treated with caution, nevertheless the artists' rendering may reflect the expected attire, even if not that actually used. It is only in the twelfth century that a surviving order specifically mentions the coronation vestments. This refers to the *armillae* or bracelets, and pallium or

[195] Press Release, "Armed Forces personnel to feature in Coronation", Ministry of Defence, 16th April 2023; Baker Wilson, Kim, "NZ Defence Force contingent heading to London for King's coronation", *1 News*, 23 April 2023.

[196] Press Release, Australian Defence Force, "Defence set to honour Coronation of the King and Queen Consort", 23 April 2023. The personnel would be from Australia's Federation Guard.

[197] Ferreira, Jennifer, "Here's how Canada plans to celebrate King Charles III's coronation", 24 April 2023. www.ctv.ca. Bell Media.

[198] For one example of many, see Schramm, Percy, *A History of the English Coronation*, trans. Leopold G. Wickham Legg (1937).

[199] This is in the Leofric A manuscript; "The Earliest Surviving Royal Ordo: Some Liturgical and Historical Aspects", in B. Tierney and P. Linehan (eds.), *Authority and Power* (1980), pp. 29–48.

[200] Hicks, Carola, *The Bayeux Tapestry* (2006).

mantle.[201] The Armills are understood to bind the Sovereign to his or her people, but Woolley suggests they are a later Western version of the Eastern Roman priestly stole.[202]

Richard III's *Little device*, his coronation order which was later copied for Henry VII and Henry VIII, specified that a king would be arrayed in two shirts, "of lawn, and of crimson tartaryn."[203] He was also to wear breeches, hosen, coat or cassock of crimson satin,[204] a surcoat of crimson with a hood, a mantle of crimson, and a cap of estate.[205] For the anointing, he was divested of the outer robes as far as the crimson cassock, then invested with linen[206] gloves, "tabard of white tartaryn shaped in the manner of a dalmatick" (the *colobium sindonis,* Latin for "shroud tunic), linen coif (an ancient form of headdress),[207] long coat wrought with "great images of gold" (similar to the tunicle or dalmatic), hose and sandals, armils, and pall royal (*pallium regale*). The *colobium sindonis*, for centuries, was that worn by Edward the Confessor at his coronation in 1043, until it was destroyed during the Civil War.[208]

The royal attire was eventually settled as comprising a coif, buskins and sandals (as for a bishop), the *colobium sindonis* (comparable to the alb), tunic and dalmatic (as for a bishop), belt or girdle (comparable to the bishop's girdle), cope or mantle called *pallium regale*, and a stole (as worn

[201] See Wilson, H. A., "The English Coronation Orders" (July 1901) The Journal of Theological Studies 481–504, 490–491.

[202] Woolley, Reginald Maxwell, *Coronation Rites* (1915).

[203] *The Rutland Papers* (Camden Society, London 1842) vol 21 (Henry VII); Legg, L. G. W., *English Coronation Records* (1901), pp. 219–239. Lawn is usually more closely woven and stiffer than cambric; Beck, William, *The Draper's Dictionary* (1886).

[204] Satin, with a glossy surface and dull back, is a closely-woven silk fabric showing much of the warp. Satinette, or satinet, is of a cotton warp, and woollen weft.

[205] The cap of estate is thought to have been first worn by Edward III (1327–77), in place of his crown. It was, like the Cap of Maintenance, a badge of rank. It was placed under the crown by Henry VII, no doubt for reasons of comfort. Subsequently, all crowns and coronets have invariably been set on such a cap; Cox, Noel, "The Coronation Robes of the Sovereign" (1999) 5(1) Arma 271–280.

[206] A fabric woven from the fibres of flax. Cotton, or a cotton mix is now more usual.

[207] Compared to the amice of a bishop, the distinctive cap of the now obsolete grade of serjeants at law from whom the common law judges were recruited. Although this was a common enough item of dress in the thirteenth century, the coif came to be symbolic of membership of the Order of the Coif.

[208] Gosling, Lucinda, *Royal Coronations* (2013), pp. 42–43.

by a priest or bishop, in later days). These were accompanied by a ring (as for a bishop), sceptre (equivalent to the crozier), rod, and of course the crown—itself said to be comparable to the mitre of a bishop, although its origins and evolution were very different. The attire was particularly significant in its form. According to William Wyndewode,[209] the king was a clerk (or cleric). The common law under Edward III held that an anointed king had spiritual jurisdiction[210] (reiterated, of course, in the reign of King Henry VIII, in rather different circumstances[211]). Influenced also by practice in Constantinople, it was little wonder that the king came to be attired in a manner reminiscent of a cleric.[212]

At the end of the service, the king was disrobed, leaving only coat and shirt, then arrayed with hose, sandals, the other robes of estate similar to those in which he walked to church, but of purple and of finer material. He also wore the crown over his cap of estate, and carried a sceptre, which is of Saxon origin. This manifested the change in status from de facto and putatively de jure king to anointed and undoubtedly de jure king.

According to an inventory of regalia by Sporley, a monk at Westminster Abbey in the mid-fifteenth century, there were then preserved in the abbey, from the time of the sainted King Edward, a tunic, supertunic, armil, girdle,[213] embroidered mantle (*paleum brudatum*), a pair of buskins or boots (*par caligarum*), and a pair of gloves (*par cerotecaman*).[214] These were early examples of coronation attire, which later was to evolve along antiquarian lines, rather than in accordance with contemporary fashion.

Any surviving coronation dress was lost during the Civil War, and had to be replaced after the restoration of the monarchy in 1660. The seventeenth century was perhaps not a favourable time from an aesthetic perspective, and the wardrobe furnished the new king with even less taste and knowledge than did the goldsmiths. However, the succeeding period,

[209] *Provinciale* (1433) lib. iii. Ut clericalis, etc (1505).

[210] Legg, J. Wickham, *The Coronation of the Queen* (1898), p. 6.

[211] See, for example, the Ecclesiastical Appeals Act 1532 (24 Hen VIII c 12), the Submission of the Clergy Act 1533 (25 Hen VIII c 19).

[212] Hope, W. H. St John, "The King's Coronation Ornaments" (April 1901) 1 Ancestor 127–159.

[213] Styled *zona* in the Latin of the period.

[214] Legg, L. G. W., *English Coronation Records* (1901), p. 191.

prior to the twentieth century, was one of gradual degradation, so that each coronation produced something a little worse, until a nadir was arguably reached with the coronation of Queen Victoria in 1838.[215] The twentieth century at least saw a more serious scholarly approach generally being taken to the planning of the coronation—contemporaneous with the growth of the modern approach to the revival and use of ceremonial.[216] This strong emphasis upon institutional memory and precedent was not, however new; it was perhaps just that the role of the antiquarian and liturgist prevailed, in tune with a more formalised, sympathetic and scholarly approach to ceremonial.

George III's coronation robes, now in the Royal Ceremonial Dress Collection, Kensington Palace, are the oldest now surviving. The robe, surcoat and tipit required 36 yards of crimson velvet,[217] and 36 yards of purple velvet. In addition, 63 yards of open chain lace were used. For the two robes, two surcoats, and two tippets 116 yards of broad gold lace trimming were used. The two tippets, or stoles were both laced down before and round the bottom with two rows of the same gold lace and the same gold chain between the two rows. George III's coronation also required a purple and a crimson silk sheet, each fringed all round with a rich gold fringe. A purple and a crimson velvet bag, each laced with broad gold lace, gold tassels and cords, were also used.[218]

Over the crimson and scarlet surcoats of a king (or coronation dress for a queen regnant) the order of wear is firstly the *colobium sindonis*, then the *supertunica*, the royal stole, and then the *pallium regale*, or imperial mantle. The purple robe of estate is donned last, replacing the scarlet robe of state worn upon arrival in the Abbey.[219] Each element of

[215] Hope, W. H. St John, "The King's Coronation Ornaments" (Jul 1902) 2 Ancestor 63–81.

[216] Hobsbawn, Eric and Terence Ranger, *The Invention of Tradition* (1983).

[217] Velvet, the most elaborate of the plain weaves traditionally made from silk, has a short plush pile surface, and is used for the gowns of some office-holders, and for the hats of some doctors. Velveteen is a cotton or mixed cotton and silk imitation.

[218] Legg, L. G. W., *English Coronation Records* (1901).

[219] In 2023 King Charles wore the scarlet robe of state made for King George VI in 1937, and then donned the purple robe of estate made for King George VI in 1937. Queen Camilla wore the scarlet robe of state made for Queen Elizabeth II in 1953, and a new robe of estate made by Ede and Ravenscroft and embroidered by the Royal School of Needlework; Press Release, "A first glimpse at Their Majesties' Coronation robes", The Royal Family, 29 April 2023.

dress, as every piece of regalia, contributed some symbolic or representational aspect to the coronation, however poorly understood or badly rendered. Cost-cutting (or the occasional extravagance, as under George IV); fashion, and ill-judged antiquarian enthusiasm, also contributed to the mix.

The English coronation, both in its seven key elements or stages, and in the vestments and insignia, reflected a combination of elements from Anglo-Saxon England, Byzantium, continental Europe, and ancient Israel. Its function and details changed over time, in response to political and religious requirements. However, as a fundamental assertion of legitimacy and continuity, and the union of king and people with the blessing of heaven, no sovereign could afford to dispense with it or even make radical changes, for fear of undermining their legitimacy.

Further, the nature of the coronation is a remarkably eclectic combination of Christian and tribal, secular and religious, political and legal ritual, which always served, and continues to serve, multiple purposes. To the people, it was a spectacle, a chance to celebrate; to the political elite an opportunity to highlight their allegiance to the new sovereign, perhaps in hope of reward. The church enjoyed the centrality of their role in endorsing the new rule, and displaying at the same time the ultimate subservience of all, even kings, to God. They also obtained renewed assurances of protection. The kings themselves, perhaps personally awed by the ritual,[220] were reminded, especially in the acclamation and in the oath, but also in the anointing, that they held a sacred trust.

Conclusion

The earliest coronations as we understand them today can be traced to the ancient near east. Kings were inaugurated in accordance with indigenous rituals, but there was a degree of cross-fertilisation amongst the kingdoms across the region. The Egyptian and Israeli kingdoms were to prove most influential in the later development of coronations in Europe. Later still, the eastern Roman empire developed a theologically and ecclesiologically rich tradition of coronations, and this proved influential in Francia and Britain. Mediæval European practice, according to a significant religious tradition, was also to be strongly influenced by Israeli tradition.

[220] Butcher, Catherine and Mark Greene, *The Servant Queen and the King she serves* (2016).

Over time, regional and national accretions, borrowings from other traditions, and the exigencies of public life, coupled with the regular revision of coronation orders of service, led to the general form that European and especially English coronations had assumed by the late middle ages.

For coronations everywhere continuity has always been an important element, for various (often overlapping) political and religious reasons. Whether in ancient Israel or Egypt, mediæval France or the modern United Kingdom, coronations were never regarded as an occasion for mere spectacle—though George IV's 1821 coronation tended towards being seen as that, despite the ostensible goal of being a unifying national ritual after the devastation of the French revolutionary and Napoleonic wars[221]—nor merely an antiquarian extravaganza. They were not even primarily an exercise in political propaganda—though that too was almost invariably an important element, especially in the parades (as in the twentieth century, where the parades' emphasis was undoubtedly on expressing imperial power—national and certainly not personal to the particular king). The Roman *triumphus* served a not dissimilar (though more limited) purpose many centuries earlier.[222] Even Napoleon's coronation, with its rich Roman imagery, was a conscious attempt to legitimise a *parvenu* regime by linking it to a ubiquitous imperial past.[223]

By the modern age western coronations remained primarily religious occasions at which the Sovereign was anointed and hallowed for their role—though now to a rather different role than to that in the middle ages, let alone in the time of Edgar or earlier kings, or earlier still, the Egyptian pharaohs and Jewish kings. In some countries—though not all—the coronation became associated with autocracy, though not in England, at least in large part due to the significant limiting elements in the coronation, most conspicuously the coronation oath, but also the acclamation and arguably other elements too, such as the homage, and even the crowning itself, at which the peers of the realm donned their coronets at the same time as their king was crowned. The latter element, unfortunately, was rendered problematic by the evisceration of the House of

221 Huish, Robert, *An Authentic History of the Coronation of George IV* (1821).

222 The *triumphus* was a civil ceremony and religious rite of ancient Rome, held to publicly celebrate and sanctify the success of a military commander who had led Roman forces to victory; Beard, Mary, *The Roman Triumph* (2007).

223 Dwyer, Philip, "'Citizen Emperor': Political Ritual, Popular Sovereignty and the Coronation of Napoleon I" (2015) 100(339) History 40–57.

Lords by the House of Lords Act 1999. For the 2023 coronation of Charles III those few peers present wore parliamentary robes, or coronation robes without coronets[224] (the wearing of the latter was a practice unique to England), whilst other participants wore uniform, morning dress, or dark lounge suits—or their national or feminine equivalents.

By the twentieth century—and indeed probably much earlier—the British coronation had become a national and indeed international act of commitment. The coronation was retained despite, if not because of, the changing role of the Sovereign. In the face of growing twenty-first century iconoclasm and scepticism, it might be anticipated that it would come under attack. But it would be expected that King Charles III, having succeeded Queen Elizabeth II, would have a coronation essentially unchanged from that of his royal mother. This indeed proved to be largely the case. In this age of the advancing destruction of much of our ancient heritage in the name of modernisation—or simply of destruction for its own sake—arguably it is even more important to recognise that coronations are not merely desirable, but indispensable, and that significant changes are made to them only with due, if not indeed extreme, caution.

This is true despite (or perhaps because of) the fact that the British coronation remains the last great coronation; many countries never had coronations, or dispensed with them for various reasons. For example, Denmark in 1849, Norway in 1908, Sweden in 1907 and the Holy See in 1978 all abandoned coronations, though each in turn for very different reasons.[225] In the case of Sweden and the Holy See there was no formal abolition of the rite, which could theoretically be revived by a future Sovereign or Pope. Such a revival is, however, equally unlikely in each case, due respectively to a modern social democratic tradition which

[224] Initially only parliamentary robes, or business suits, were to be worn; Ward, Victoria, "Peers to wear coronation robes in last minute Palace U-turn", The Telegraph, 3 May 2023.

[225] The last coronations were, Denmark 1840, Norway 1906, Sweden 1873, Holy See 1963, respectively; Hoffman, Erich, "Coronation and Coronation Ordines in Mediæval Scandinavia", in János M. Bak (ed.), *Coronations* (1990), pp. 125–143. Other examples of states which utilised coronations as understood in a European sense are Brazil (1 December 1822 Dom Pedro I, Rio de Janeiro, 18 July 1841 Dom Pedro II, Rio de Janeiro, using a crown of 1822, which is still in Brazil); France 1825; Hungary 1916; Iran 1967, Portugal 1640, and Poland 1795. The last coronation in Bohemia was that of Emperor Ferdinand I in 1836, and the last in Yugoslavia, that of 1904.

grudgingly relegates the king to figurehead status, at most, and an exaggerated, and seemingly inexorable tendency to emphasise the humility of the popes, after long centuries of embracing and expounding an imperial papacy rivalling if not exceeding the Roman imperial court for splendour, regal magnificence, and the overt manifestation of *imperium*.[226]

Some more recently constituted European countries (such as the Netherlands and Belgium[227]), and miscellaneous sovereign states which were not kingdoms (such as Andorra, Liechtenstein, and Luxembourg[228]) never had coronations at all, and only the ancient great kingdoms, especially France, England, and also the Holy Roman Empire (and the Eastern Empire), had full scale coronations, including anointing, although the precise details differed.

Prior to the modern age, and particularly to the decline both of monarchy as a conceptual and operational form of government, rather than the modern form of so-called constitutional monarchy (which have often been characterised as crowned republics), and of organised mainstream religion, the coronation fulfilled a clear political and religious function, if not a social role, in European states. It enjoyed a lineage longer than any single European state had been in existence—though in some cases (as in England) it was a close leader—and was regarded as

[226] Pennington, Kenneth, *Pope and Bishops* (1984); Morris, Colin, *The papal monarchy* (1989).

[227] The Netherlands was long notionally a republic from 1581 (though, like the Holy Roman empire, dominated by one dynasty), and a kingdom from 1806, and Belgium was only constituted in 1830, having hitherto been part of the Netherlands; Kossmann, E. H., *The Low Countries, 1780–1940* (1988).

[228] Created by Charlemagne, Andorra was constituted an independent principality in 1278, though ruled jointly by the count of Urgell (then the Bishop of Urgell from 988), and French princes from 1095; Vila, Linda Armengol, *Approach to the History of Andorra* (1989). The claim of the President of France to be co-prince, though incorporated in the 1993 Constitution, might be questioned.

Liechtenstein was a fief of the Holy Roman empire from around 1000, with the southern part (Vaduz) gaining imperial immediacy in 1396 (having previously been enfeoffed to the Counts of Hohenems), and raised to the status of principality in 1719, after the Princes of Liechtenstein also acquired the Lordship of Schellenberg (1699) and the County of Vaduz (1712), and thus finally obtained immediacy for themselves; Raton, Pierre, *Liechtenstein* (1970).

Luxembourg, acquired by the Luxembourg dynasty in 1059, was a county from 1214, and a duchy 1353–1797 (as a fief of the Holy Roman empire), and was briefly part of France, and then an independent grand duchy from 1815, though in a personal union with the Netherlands 1839–1890; Arblaster, Paul, *A History of the Low Countries* (2005).

an indispensable rite of passage for a ruler. It comprised elements drawn from a long tradition of royal and imperial authority, in the context and subject to the profound influence of Christian notions of kingship, as well as even more ancient traditions of the sacred and political office of ruler. Continuity, and congruity with a wider European tradition, offered an invaluable boost to legitimacy—conversely, where a departure from heritage is sought, for whatever reason, the coronation is an obvious target for abolition.

Specifically in the British context, it will be argued that the coronation, in all its glory and ancient complexity, is essential, not because of its formal legal necessity to establish kingly title (for that is automatic), but for broader, and far more ancient reasons, legal, political and theological. These reasons start with the relationship between the law and the coronation; what may be seen as the legal rationale for a coronation. The solemnity of the coronation is primarily a constitutional procedure and ritual of the first importance.

Having briefly considered the historical evolution of the coronation in its English and wider European, Mediterranean and near eastern origins, we will now turn our attention specifically to the English and later British coronation, looking firstly at its legal function, and in particular its role in proclaiming and establishing a new king in possession of his throne and kingdom.

CHAPTER 3

The Right to the Throne

Introduction

The coronation, being influenced by multiple factors over the course of the centuries, despite the inherently conservative form and nature of the ritual, has served many different functions. In some instances—as for the coronation of George IV—it served a broad social and political purpose, in that case emphasising tradition and continuity after decades of the French and American revolutions and the Napoleonic wars.[1] Sometimes, as with the coronation of Henry VII, the coronation served a more overtly constitutive function, reinforcing if not creating a sounder legal basis for the de facto and de jure authority of the new monarch.[2] As Brightman stated

> A coronation rite is ideally the process of the creation of the monarch, even though in course of time, through a change in the theory of succession, it may come to be rather the ratification of an accomplished fact than the means of its accomplishment.[3]

[1] Gosling, Lucinda, *Royal Coronations* (2013).

[2] Penn, Thomas, *Winter King* (2012).

[3] Brightman, F. E., "Byzantine Imperial Coronations" (1901) II(7)(Old Series) Journal of Theological Studies 359–392, 359.

N. Cox, *The Political, Legal, and Theological Functions of the Ceremony in the British Tradition*,
https://doi.org/10.1007/978-3-031-88960-8_3

The legal function of the coronation must be seen through the holistic lens of its nature as an ancient ritual, in which a new king—or more rarely, queen regnant—is acknowledged, invested, anointed, crowned and receives the homage of the lords temporal and the fealty of the lords spiritual. The legal function of a coronation can only be evaluated through a careful assessment of the different aspects of the constitutional role which a coronation fulfils. This includes consideration of the coronation as the endorsement of the elect of God, the chosen candidate of the *Witan* (the Saxon assembly approximating to a form of proto-parliament) and later assemblies, or people, or the heir of the late Sovereign, depending upon which perspective is taken, the customs of the times and the exigencies of the circumstances.

In strict law, since the fourteenth century acceptance of the doctrine that the king never dies, and that a lineal descendant (or other heir at law) of the late Sovereign become king—or queen—automatically upon the death of the late Sovereign—the coronation would not appear to be a legal necessity to formally make a new Sovereign. Case law—admittedly a single judgement (*Calvin's Case*[4]), if we discount the very exceptional and specific judgement concerning George IV's consort, Queen Caroline—also supports this contention that the coronation does not make the heir apparent or presumptive (or anyone else for that matter) the Sovereign. This seems a reasonable conclusion, although for a thousand years every Sovereign has had a coronation—except Edward V (and Lady Jane Grey), due to the shortness and uncertainty of their reigns, and Edward VIII, who abdicated before he could be crowned. Contrary to what Brightman suggests, the coronation, in the late Dark Ages to the early middle ages—such as, for example, that of King Edgar in 973—was rarely, if ever, deemed to constitute a man the king, though it might enhance his status, and endorse his rule, even if, as in the case of Edgar, he had already ruled for many years. It was, however, rarely, if ever, questioned whether a coronation was necessary.

There have also been occasions when the coronation was deemed expedient to establish beyond reasonable challenge a claim to the Crown which might be impugned by another claimant, or for other technical reasons. For instance, Richard II (1377), who succeeded at the age of 10 years, was crowned early for the very specific purpose of avoiding a

[4] (1608) 7 Co Rep 1a; 77 ER 377.

royal minority, a protectorate led by the king's uncles being avoided, in favour of the more informal mechanism of a series of continual councils,[5] which ruled in his name. So it was with Henry VI (1422), whose regency (under Humphrey, Duke of Gloucester), which started when Henry inherited the crown aged nine months, had formally ended with his coronation at the still tender age of seven years.[6] The implication was that although a coronation did not automatically give the king greater independent authority—Henry VI remained unable to govern independently until he came of age at 16 in 1437—it at least suggested that possibility. The constitutional theory, of course, was that the king was never in law, a minor,[7] even prior to his coronation, whatever his temporal age might be. In practice, for a young king, provision had to be made for the conduct of government until he became old enough to exercise discretion himself; likewise, for an aged or infirm king provision had also sometimes to be made for augmented assistance in government.[8]

Half a century later, at the accession at the age of 12 years of Edward V (1483), elder of the unfortunate Princes of the Tower, the Council felt that a speedy coronation was desirable, thus obviating the need for a protectorate. Edward IV's Will had nominated his brother, Richard, Duke of Gloucester (later King Richard III) as the protector of his son

[5] Pollard, A. J., *Richard III and the Princes in the Tower* (1991).

[6] Allmand, Christopher T., "The Coronations of Henry VI" (30 April 1982) 32(5) History Today 28–33.

[7] Holdsworth, Sir William S., *A History of English Law* (3rd ed., 1923), vol 3, p. 464; Blackstone, Sir William, *Commentaries on the Laws of England* ed. E. Christian (1978), part IV.D.

[8] Pre-1840 regencies were generally governed by ad hoc arrangements, although for much of the early eighteen century Lords Justices were required from time to time due to the Sovereign's absence in Hanover. Since 1937 the absence, illness or incapacity of the Sovereign has been dealt with in the United Kingdom by the Regency Acts 1937 (1 Edw VIII & 1 Geo VI c 16), 1943 (6 & 7 Geo VI c 42), and 1953 (2 & 3 Eliz 2 c. 1), and the Counsellors of State Act 2022. Earlier legislation included section XI of the Treason Act 1554 (1 & 2 Ph & M c 10) made King Philip, the husband and co-ruler of Queen Mary I, regent if Mary died and her heir was male and under 18 or an unmarried female under 15; Regency Act 1705 (4 Ann. c 8); Succession to the Crown Act 1707 (6 Ann c 41); Regency During the King's Absence Act 1728 (2 Geo. II c. 27); Minority of Successor to Crown Act 1751 (24 Geo. II c. 24); Minority of Heir to the Crown Act 1765 (5 Geo. III c. 27); Care of King During his Illness, etc. Act 1811 (51 Geo. III c. 1); Regency Act 1830 (1 Will. IV c. 2); Lords Justices Act 1837 (7 Will. IV & 1 Vict. c. 72); Regency Act 1840 (3 & 4 Vict. c. 52); and the Regency Act 1910 (10 Edw. VIII & 1 Geo. V c. 26).

during his minority. Richard, however, successfully managed to delay the coronation of his nephew,[9] against the wishes of the Council—and the ultimate interests of Edward V and his younger brother Richard. The rest, as they say, is history, though whether Edward V and his brother fell victim to their uncle Richard, or to another actor (Henry Tudor, later King Henry VII, has been suggested as a possible regicide, for instance), we will probably never be sure.[10] One might speculate, however, about the course of history had Edward V been crowned early, as the Council, in its wisdom, had wished. Such an academic exercise, however, is ultimately futile.

As with almost anything concerning an institution or ritual as venerable as the coronation, predating as it does even the English state, the position is more complicated than the question of whether the coronation is a legal necessity to create a king. A coronation does not make a man a king, or a woman a queen, but it can be argued that without one their status is different; the fullness of sovereignty requires a coronation. There are some early instances of coronations being delayed for some years, but also of them being repeated[11]; and we have just discussed examples of coronations being held early to end a regency or protectorate during a royal minority. The election and homage elements of coronations were particularly important in this respect; a king whose title was uncertain or challenged might (re-)assert his status by being crowned with all the solemnity that was possible—the combined forces of church and state proclaimed his kingship.

The legal function of a coronation is thus to be seen as part of a process of acquiring, asserting and establishing authority and legitimacy. It was never a question of brute force, although during the Anarchy (1138–1153), the Wars of the Roses (1455–1487), and most recently, after the so-called Glorious Revolution (1688–1689), the process by which the Crown was acquired might have been less than smooth or regular. The underlying principle is that a Sovereign owes their title to a set of laws,

[9] McKisack, May, The *Fourteenth Century* (1959), pp. 399–400; Tuck, Anthony, "Richard II (1367–1400)", *Oxford Dictionary of National Biography* (2004).

[10] Pollard, A. J., *Richard III and the Princes in the Tower* (1991).

[11] Henry III in 1216 (in Gloucester, as London was controlled by rebels) and 1220, Henry VI in 1429 and separately as King of France in 1431, and Charles I in 1625 and again as King of Scots 1633; Ridgeway, H. W., "Henry III (1207–1272)" *Oxford Dictionary of National Biography* (2004).

known as the law of succession. Today this includes elements derived from the royal prerogative, the common law, and statute law, and is truly *sui generis*. Once a Sovereign succeeds to the Crown, on the demise of the Crown, their title is legally complete. But there remain a number of practical and legal steps which are required, in a process collectively known as the accession. Some of these, such as the coronation oath, overlap with the coronation itself.

In order to consider the legal function of a coronation, it is first necessary to review the law of succession, that set of principles, common law and statute law, which establish who is the next Sovereign after the death (or much more rarely, legal demise by other means, such as abdication) of the king or queen regnant. It is this legal title which the coronation affirms and endorses. The development of the law of succession influences and has been influenced by the coronation; both are integral parts of the constitution. The occasional uncertainty in the law of succession, or departure from it, raised the importance of the coronation as a vital constitutional and legal instrument; conversely, if the succession is wholly unexceptional, the legal and constitutional role of the coronation is less constitutive and more emblematic.

Becoming the King—The Law of Succession

The individual who is invested with the insignia of royalty at a coronation, is anointed and enthroned, and who is proclaimed and receives the homage and fealty of the Lords Temporal and Spiritual, is the person whom the law of succession identifies as the heir to the throne of the late deceased monarch.[12] It is commonly said that the title to the Crown was governed at common law,[13] by the feudal rules of hereditary descent

[12] The crowning of the Queen Consort is not to be so interpreted, though it too sets them apart for their sacred role in support of the King.

[13] *Halsbury's Laws of England* (4th ed, 1974), vol 8 para 845.

formerly applicable to land.[14] They were however subject to the distinctions that the ancient doctrines relating to the exclusion of the half-blood from the inheritance to land had no application to the Crown, and that, in the case of females, the title to the Crown devolved upon the eldest daughter alone and her issue, according to the doctrine which excluded the land law principle of coparcenary.[15]

Unlike the emperor of the Roman Empire (or even the Holy Roman Empire), which were nominally not hereditary, the descent of the English and later British kingship was consistent with the great majority of states and relied upon hereditary descent confined to a royal house. Like the kingdom of France, whose kings were descendants of Hugh Capet (987), so too in England the royal descent was confined to those with an hereditary claim, although aberrations did occur. The descent of King Charles III may be traced to the House of Wessex (established in the early sixth century)—a span of some 1,500 years—although several times the male line has died out, and irregular succession has occurred more than once.[16] Although there is a general division into the Houses of Wessex (also Denmark, and Godwin), Norman, Blois, Plantagenet (Angevin, Lancaster, and York), Tudor, Stuart (also Orange), Hanoverian, Windsor (Saxe-Coburg-Gotha, and Schleswig–Holstein-Sonderburg-Glücksburg), the royal descent has been confined to one dynasty, with brief interludes of Danish rule, Harold II and the Interregnum 1649–1660. Like the

[14] This is the substance of the rule as deduced by Sir William Blackstone (see *Commentaries on the Laws of England* ed. E. Christian (1978), pp. 192, 193). The principal authority for the existence of the rule is to be found in the course of descent in the past, and in the fact that where the rule has been broken, or where any doubt as to the validity of the title has existed, it has usually been found necessary to fortify the title by statute. See 7 Hen IV c 2 (Succession to the Crown) (1405-6); 1 Mar sess 2 c 1 (Legitimacy of the Queen) (1553); 1 Eliz I c 3 (Recognition of the Queen's Title to the Crown) (1558-9); 1 Jac I c 1 (Recognition of the King's Title to the Crown) (1603-4) (all repealed); and the Succession to the Crown Act 1707 (6 Ann c 41).

[15] Unlike real property inheritance, for example, it is generally accepted that in the case of female heiresses, the title devolved upon the elder daughter of the king alone, and her issue, and was not subject to coparcenary. This is stated by Blackstone to be of necessity (he gave no other authority). In the case of land, the title devolved upon all the daughters equally as coparceners (Coke, Sir Edward, *Coke upon Littleton* ("*First Institutes*") (1979) 135a; Blackstone, Sir William, *Commentaries on the Laws of England* ed. E. Christian (1978), p. 194. See Farran, C. d'Olivier, "The Law of the Accession" (1953) 16 Modern Law Review 140–147. Queen Elizabeth II succeeded in accordance with Blackstone's rule.

[16] Weir, Alison, *Britain's royal families* (2008).

Japanese monarchy, and unlike that, for instance, of Thailand (which dates from a usurpation by a general in 1782, who admittedly also reunified the divided kingdom),[17] the royal house can be traced back to a legendary and mythical time, rather than to a usurpation.

The late Saxons and early Normans

In the 1050s and early 1060s, Duke William of Normandy became a contender for the throne of England then held by his near kinsman, Edward the Confessor. According to the *Vita Ædwardi Regis*, Edward had commended his widow and the kingdom to Harold's "protection" on his deathbed in January 1066.[18] Subsequently the Witenagemot chose Harold, in preference to Edward's great-nephew, Edgar the Ætheling, who was still a minor,[19] even though Harold appears to not himself have been an ætheling; ætheling, or aetheling, atheling or etheling, was an Old English word (æþeling) used in Anglo-Saxon England to designate princes of the royal dynasty who were eligible for the kingship.[20] As Edward the Confessor had no male heir apart from Edgar the Ætheling, whose interest he appears to have failed to have taken steps to uphold, claimants had readied themselves for his death. William II of Normandy, Sweyn II of Denmark and Harald III of Norway were all candidates for the Crown of England, and Edgar the Ætheling, as a boy with no powerful adult to support his cause, was rejected by the Witenagemot in favour of the mature and experienced—though still young—Harold. The Witenagemot was accustomed to choosing the new king from amongst the æthelings, so this was a revolutionary choice, given that Harold Godwinson was not a member of the House of Wessex. It was nonetheless not entirely an unsurprising decision, as he was probably the only man capable of resisting the various foreign claimants, and his election was likely thus seen as a necessary expedient to preserve the kingdom from continued (or revived) alien domination, such as from

[17] Wyatt, David K., "The Bangkok monarchy and Thai history" (9185) 2(2) Crossroads: An Interdisciplinary Journal of Southeast Asian Studies 131–139.

[18] Barlow, Frank, *Edward the Confessor* (1970).

[19] Barlow, Frank, *The Godwins* (2013).

[20] Originally referring to anyone who could prove royal descent, after King Ælfred it was limited to the King's sons and brothers—Edgar was exceptional due to an absence of closer relatives in the male line; Abels, Richard, "Royal Succession and the Growth of Political Stability in Ninth-Century Wessex" (2002) 12 The Haskins Society Journal: Studies in Mediæval History 83–97.

the Danes. Upon his selection by the Witenagemot Harold was immediately crowned, most likely in Westminster Abbey, which would make him the first king to be crowned in the church newly built by Edward the Confessor.[21]

William's claim to the English throne was based on his assertion that, in 1051, Edward the Confessor had promised him the throne (ignoring the question of illegitimacy—which was not then quite the bar to inheritance it was later to become[22]—he was a first cousin once removed to the childless Edward the Confessor[23]). Harold II—having allegedly sworn in 1064 to uphold William's right to succeed to the throne—was therefore himself a usurper and an oath breaker. Though the legally stronger claim to the throne may have been conquest (which was recognised as a legitimate basis for a claim to sovereign authority),[24] this emphasis upon legal right was nonetheless important historically and practically.

William's victory at Hastings confirmed, in the eyes of many, that God had endorsed his claim to the throne. Edgar the Ætheling, perhaps unsurprisingly, acquiesced in the situation, even if he might at times have perhaps entertained thoughts of how events might have unfolded otherwise. Already bypassed by the Witenagemot in favour of Harold Godwinson, William I's decisive victory at Hastings probably ensured that Edgar the Ætheling himself never dared challenge the new order—in a manner analogous to the Chinese concept of the Mandate of Heaven,[25] the Norman rule was settled, established and practically unassailable.

[21] Between 1042 and 1052, King Edward the Confessor began rebuilding St Peter's Abbey to provide himself with a royal burial church. The building was consecrated on 28 December 1065; Page, William, "Benedictine monks: St Peter's abbey, Westminster", in *A History of the County of London* (1909), vol. 1, "London Within the Bars, Westminster and Southwark", pp. 433–457; Cannadine, Sir David (ed.), *Westminster Abbey* (2019).

[22] McDougall, Sara, "Illegitimacy and the Making of Mediæval Dynasties *c.*900–*c.*1050", in *Royal Bastards* (2016), pp. 94–115.

[23] Emma of Normandy (Ælfgifu), daughter of the Norman ruler Richard the Fearless (ruled 942–996), was Queen of the English during her marriage to King Æthelred from 1002 to 1016. Edward the Confessor was her son, as were Ælfred Aetheling and Hardicanute (King of England 1040–1042), the later with her second husband, Cnut the Great; Campbell, Alistair and Simon Keynes, *Encomium Emmae Reginae* (1998); O'Brien, Harriet, *Queen Emma and the Vikings* (2006).

[24] Brookfield, F. M., "Some aspects of the Necessity Principle in Constitutional Law" (1972) University of Oxford DPhil thesis.

[25] Jiang, Yonglin, *The Mandate of Heaven and The Great Ming Code* (2011).

Despite the invasion, and the subsequent wholesale redistribution of land, and the depredations of the Normans, particularly in Northumberland and elsewhere in the north, the Norman claim to legal continuity from the Saxon kingdom was to have lasting implications. Though an invader, William's claim to the throne was dressed in legal form, and his adoption of the customs of the realm—or some of them—and especially his coronation, were pivotal in the process of consolidating his hold on power.

The Plantagenets and later mediæval dynastic developments.

The principal authority for the existence of the rules as to the succession to the Crown is to be found in the course of descent in the past. It is also seen in the fact that where the rules have been broken, or where any doubt as to the validity of the title has existed, it has usually been found necessary to fortify the title by statute, augmented by the coronation. Once crowned, a king was far more settled in his title than he had been previously. To use another land law analogy, the heir was possessed at all times of a right to an estate even before succession, but once seisin was obtained over that land, legal ownership was complete.[26] The coronation constituted the completion of the title to the Crown, just as seisin did for land.[27]

At the 1199 coronation of King John, Hubert Walter, the Archbishop of Canterbury, supposedly made a speech that offered, for the last time, the theory of a king's election by the people (or rather the magnates).[28] Whilst it is likely the address or sermon was designed to bolster the new king's somewhat shaky legal title to the Crown ahead of his nephew, nonetheless that such a sermon could be given at all suggests both that the Archbishop or his advisors had some knowledge of the law of succession, and that the multifaceted nature of the succession had not yet been wholly forgotten.

By the time of the accession of Richard II (1377), influenced by the arguably misleading (but increasingly influential) analogy of land law, the then developed rule of representative primogeniture was applied fully to

[26] Nenner, Howard, *The Right to be King* (1995), p. 32; Bracton, Henry de, *De legibus et consuetudinibus Angliæ* (1968–77), fo. 39b, 40, 44, 44b.

[27] Nenner, Howard, *The Right to be King* (1995), p. 32.

[28] Petit-Dutaillis, Charles, *The Feudal Monarchy in France and England*. transl E. D. Hunt (1964), pp. 117–118.

the Crown.[29] But the true political nature of the Crown, and the continuing right of the magnates to regulate the succession to it, was re-asserted, not twenty years later, by the deposition of the king. The reality, which the constitution never forgot nor the coronation ignored, was that the title to the Crown was never solely a manner of formal and unadulterated hereditary inheritance, as if the realm were merely real property, and the king a landowner.

In the absence of statutory limitations, therefore, the Crown would descend lineally to the issue of the reigning Sovereign, males being preferred to females, and subject to the right of primogeniture amongst both males and females of equal degree, whilst children would represent their ancestors *per stirpes in infinitum*.[30] Upon the failure of lineal descendants, the Crown would pass under this rule to the nearest collateral relation descended from the blood royal.[31]

The first formulation of the doctrine of the demise of the Crown can be dated with some particularity to a date between 25 and 29th September 1399. This doctrine was held to invalidate the parliamentary writs that had been issued by the authority of the former king. The last Parliament of Richard II had become the first of Henry IV, and a new Parliament was afterwards called on the demise of the Crown without the issue of writs until 1867.[32] After 1399 there was to be no interregnum on the death of a king, and the succession of the next. One might infer that a coronation was not, therefore, legally necessary thereafter, as title to the Crown was already established on the death of the previous king. But this was incorrect both then and now, as the coronation itself had never created a man king, but was rather his formal hallowing; the fact that so many early kings were crowned some years after their accession, or were crowned more than once, supports this hypothesis. Had anyone suggested that Henry V (1413), the first king to succeed after 1399, did not need to be crowned, their contention would likely have been met with a mixture

[29] Taswell-Langmead, Thomas, *English Constitutional History* (9th ed., 1929), p. 169.

[30] Blackstone, Sir William, *Commentaries on the Laws of England* ed. E. Christian (1978), p. 194.

[31] Ibid, p. 202; *Willion v Berkeley* (1561) 1 Plowd 223, 245; 75 ER 339); Coke, Sir Edward, *Coke upon Littleton* ("First Institutes") (1979), at 15b).

[32] Lapsley, Gaillard, "The Parliamentary Title of Henry IV", in Geoffrey Barraclough and Helen Cam (eds.) *Crown Community and Parliament in the Later Middle Ages* (1951), pp. 273–336, 336.

of disbelief, offence, ridicule and incredulity. Such a principle was also found elsewhere; in Hungary no ruler was regarded as being truly legitimate until he was physically crowned with St Stephen's Crown (the Holy Crown, or *Szent Korona*) by the archbishop of Esztergom in Székesfehérvár Cathedral.[33] Between 1000 and 1527 37 kings and 39 queens were crowned there.[34]

Once accession was deemed to occur upon the death of the king, succession was now direct and automatic. It followed that there ought also to be no need for parliamentary intervention, to designate or inaugurate the new king—or to reinforce their title to the Crown, for the accession to be proclaimed, or indeed for a coronation. But the common law right of inheritance was always liable to be defeated by parliamentary grant, or—in earlier centuries—by the election of the *Witan* or *Commune Concilium*.[35] Thus parliamentary intervention normally took place when the king's ability to rule (or in some cases his right to rule) was challenged. This was not specific to the Crown, as Parliament from the earliest times exercised the role of correcting errors or addressing gaps in the existing law, and providing clarification as required, as for example, in the Treason Act 1351.[36] It could in principle, therefore, change any law, and deprive anyone of property or title. The coronation could not make a Sovereign unless the law—including Parliament—had already played its part, even if that part were restricted or latent in nature. The Crown now descends according to the statutory limitations, but retains its hereditary and descendible qualities as at common law, subject to these statutory provisions.[37]

Title by descent, and title by choice of Parliament expressed two different views of kingship, but not two views which are necessarily in

[33] Yonge, Charlotte, "The Crown of St. Stephen", in *A Book of Golden Deeds Of all Times and all Lands* (1867), pp. 290–304; Woolley, Reginald Maxwell, *Coronation Rites* (1915).

[34] Zupka, Dušan, "Power of rituals and rituals of power: Religious and secular rituals in the political culture of mediæval Kingdom of Hungary", in *Historiography in Motion* (2010), pp. 29–42.

[35] *Halsbury's Laws of England* (4th ed, 1974), vol. 8, para 846.

[36] 25 Edw 3 St 5 c 2.

[37] These are contained in the Act of Settlement 1700 (12 & 13 Will III c 2), and His Majesty's Declaration of Abdication Act 1936 (1 Edw VIII & 1 Geo VI c 3. The Legitimacy Act 1959 (7 & 8 Eliz II c 73) does not affect the succession to the Throne (s 6(4)).

conflict. But the potential for conflict came to the fore particularly and most dramatically under James II, and the solution settled the supremacy of the statutory title over any other. The question as to whether the king could vacate the throne by his misconduct, as James was held to have done, is not one which can be examined here. Suffice to say, the king was no longer in situ. So far as the succession was concerned the immediate solution was a return to the ancient device of election by the magnates, or as it now was, by Parliament, *ex post facto.* Although to some extent revolutionary, it was not unprecedented or unique. In such a situation, as even Wentworth and Fitzwilliam acknowledged, a coronation would be more than a formal nicety, and would be a constitutional necessity due to the exceptional circumstances.[38]

From 1399 we have two competing but complementary views of the title to the Crown: by inheritance, and by grant of Parliament. A king relying in fact on one would invoke the other to reinforce or augment his title. For several centuries more there remained conflict between title by parliamentary choice, and title by inheritance. The old form of election gave way to parliamentary title, but several kings claimed hereditary title despite statutory bars, apparent or real, procedural or substantive, James I among them.[39] The accession, once accepted—and validated and given the stamp of approval at a coronation—was however, largely unquestioned.

Dunham and Wood have argued that two centuries of depositions led to the formulation of a new theory of parliamentary monarchy, based on the principle that any aberrant settlement of the succession had to be justified by the consent of the estates of the realm. They concluded that by 1485 it had

> established and then reiterated principles that were, in the end, to form a constitutional doctrine legitimating a right to depose and a right to rule.[40]

[38] Wentworth, Peter, *A Pithie Exhortation to Her Majestie for Establishing Her Successor to the Crowne* (1598), p. 54; Hunt, Alice, *Drama of Coronation* (2008), chap 1, pp. 12–38.

[39] Indeed, the succession of James in such circumstances appeared to suggest that hereditary right was indeed indefeasible. He was also an alien, and thereby debarred by common law from possessing land in the kingdom; Nenner, Howard, *The Right to be King* (1995), p. 3.

[40] Dunham, W. H. and T. Wood, "Right to Rule in England: Deposition and the Kingdom's Authority, 1327–1485" (1976) 81 American Historical Review 738–761.

But the Crown was not yet at the disposal solely of Parliament, and nor was the coronation constitutionally unimportant; indeed, in this scenario the latter was arguably more important than ever before.

The Tudors

At the conclusion of the bloody and complex series of conflicts known as the Wars of the Roses, the newly victorious dynasty benefitted from the competing conceptions of the authority to rule. The Tudor dynasty could appeal neither to the theory of hereditary right which had been the basis of the Yorkist claim, nor the statute law on which a Lancastrian claim might have been maintained. It was not clear by what right Henry VII was king, but there could be no denying that he was king. Heredity, election, nomination, conquest and prescription could each have been pleaded, but reliance on too many grounds showed the weakness of the title. But Henry VII was at least de facto king.[41] De facto authority can give rise to de jure authority, as was well understood in both civil and canon law.[42] There is no assertion of hereditary right in the Act for the Recognition of the title of Henry VII 1485,[43] but nor is it denied. It merely recognises a fact; it does not elect or create the king.[44] That the Parliament which passed the statute was summoned by a usurper—even if one with a weak claim—did not necessarily matter since he was at least de facto king. Henry relied on possession, though he was not without a claim which might be otherwise justified, of victory in battle against his rival. Such a title (like that of William the Conqueror four centuries before) might be less than an undisputed hereditary title, but it was better than none at all. Henry VII also acted astutely to reinforce his title in any way available, including in his coronation. In some respects, this stratagem

[41] Under an Act to regulate the Succession 1405-6 (7 Hen IV c 2), Henry VII's line were legitimate, but excluded from the succession. Henry VII did not claim the Throne by inheritance, neither did Elizabeth (though hers was a legitimate birth subsequently invalidated).

[42] Brookfield, F. M., "Some aspects of the Necessity Principle in Constitutional Law" (1972) University of Oxford DPhil thesis.

[43] Act for the Recognition of the title of Henry VII 1485 (1 Hen VII c 1), printed at the beginning of the Statutes of Henry VII in *Statutes of the Realm* (1816), vol II, p. 499.

[44] Keir, Sir David Lindsay, *The Constitutional History of Modern Britain since 1485* (8th ed, 1966), p. 8.

echoed Roman practice, but its true origins lay in Saxon and early English constitutional history.

Henry VII's coronation, as attested to by the *Little Device*,[45] was in no particular manner markedly different from that of Richard III. Indeed, as Legg observes, the *Little Device*, a guide to the service including details of purchases of materials required, was a copy of that used for the former king. It was so poorly edited that the text, which is corrupted, includes the name of King Richard, and details of a coronation for the Queen, although the new king had not yet married.[46] When a title might be weak or suspect, or where there might be a challenge, it was especially important to ensure that the coronation ritual was complete, faithful to tradition, and consistent with the previous practice. Likewise, William I had chosen to be crowned in the new Saxon coronation church, in accordance with native custom, to confer an element of legitimacy upon himself. Such a deliberate appropriation has often been used, as, for instance, by Napoleon, Emperor of the French (1804),[47] and Bokassa I, Emperor of Central Africa (1977),[48] both of whom elevated themselves to an imperial throne of their own invention.

Matters were easier for the next generation after Henry VII. As the son of Elizabeth of York (one of the last survivors of the losing dynasty in the Wars of the Roses), Henry VIII arguably had the best hereditary claim of anyone then alive. Largely because of apprehension about the succession to the Crown of the newly established Tudor dynasty—and doubtless unspoken fears of a revived Wars of the Roses—Parliament was quite willing to accede to the king's proposals for securing the succession. The new king obtained from Parliament a power to dispose of the Crown by will, and devised it, failing issue of his son Edward (VI), or daughters Mary or Elizabeth, to the grandchildren of his younger sister. The reigns of Henry's three children all relied on statutory right. This was necessarily the case, since the statute of 1536,[49] making Mary and Elizabeth

[45] Legg, L. G. W., *English Coronation Records* (1901), pp. 219–239; British Museum Add. 18,669.

[46] Ibid.

[47] Dwyer, Philip, "'Citizen Emperor': Political Ritual, Popular Sovereignty and the Coronation of Napoleon I" (2015) 100(339) History 40–57.

[48] Titley, Brian, *Dark Age* (2002), pp. 82–98.

[49] 28 Hen VIII c 7.

illegitimate, was not repealed.[50] The first Act of Succession of Henry VIII in 1534,[51] declared the king's marriage to Katherine of Spain void and annulled, and affirmed that to Anne Boleyn.[52]

Each time the king made a change to the succession through Parliament he arguably weakened hereditary claims to the Crown, and strengthened the role of Parliament. However, even in this context, the role of the king was still preserved, and still remained crucial. Indeed, in one special case it was markedly increased. An Act fixing the succession 1544 refers to the statute of 1536, and makes Jane's heirs the king's heirs, and enacted:

> that the King should and might give, will, limit, assign, appoint or dispose the said imperial Crown and the other premises ... by letters patent or last will in writing.[53]

The king bequeathed the Throne to the Suffolk line, descendants of his younger sister Mary, by Will in 1546. Not since early Plantagenet times had the king's presumed to bequeath the kingdom to his heir (admittedly here with parliamentary sanction), though it had in the Saxon era been more usual.

The succession of Mary was unprecedented, apart from the brief reign, if it can be so called, of Lady Jane Grey. Jane was not crowned, her possession of the Crown being too short and uncertain. The disastrous reign of Matilda, the only earlier instance of a female Sovereign in England, tended to reinforce the idea that while a man could inherit the throne through a woman, a woman was not fit to herself reign.[54] Queen Mary's coronation helped seal her claim to the Crown. Mary's coronation did not

[50] Mary was legitimated by statute (1 Mar St 2 c 1), and also relied on a statute to confirm her title to the Throne (1 Mar St 3 c 1). Elizabeth remained illegitimate in canon law, and therefore in the eyes of her Roman Catholic subjects, as well as under 28 Hen VIII c 7 (although her title to the Throne was also confirmed, by 1 Eliz c 3).

[51] 25 Hen VIII c 22.

[52] The First Act of Succession of Henry VIII 1534 (25 Hen VIII c 22).

[53] 35 Hen VIII c 1 (Succession to the Crown Act 1543-4).

[54] According to John Knox, because of Eve's perfidy in seducing Adam with the forbidden fruit, women were forever to be subject to the dominion of men; Knox, John, *First Blast of the Trumpet*, in David Laing (ed.), *The Works of John Knox* (1846–1864), vol. IV, pp. 377–378.

constitute a return to pre-Reformation practice[55]; it was based on that of Edward VI (despite the latter's substantially revised form[56]). There was even a suggestion, not acted upon, that the coronation be deferred until after Parliament had met and declared her Queen.[57] Such a move would have been unprecedented, not in relying upon parliamentary title, but in putting this ahead of the sacred rite of coronation. The new Queen's title by common law succession, as the eldest surviving child of the king, was deemed sufficient, and the coronation a certain means of making assurance doubly sure. Like other Tudor coronations, continuity and conformity outweighed short-term religious reforms and controversies.[58]

However, even holding the coronation was not at all simple. The new queen was crowned and anointed by Stephen Gardiner, Bishop of Winchester (who was also Lord Chancellor), as Thomas Cranmer, the Archbishop of Canterbury, was then a prisoner in the Tower of London. A new supply of holy oil was provided by the Roman Catholic Bishop of Arras, and the pope provided a new coronation chair (unfortunately now lost), on the grounds that the old oil and coronation chair had been polluted and corrupted by use in the coronation of the Protestant Edward VI. Other aspects of the 1547 liturgy were amended as the queen thought they were offensive. For example, she did not carry the orb except in the outgoing procession, and she likewise did not wear St Edward's robe,[59] one of the supposed survivals of the original coronation attire of St Edward the Confessor, and therefore sacred secondary relics of the saintly king.[60]

In her turn, Elizabeth I claimed the Crown under the third Act of succession of Henry VIII.[61] Elizabeth I's coronation, described by

[55] Page, Daniel Bennett, "Anointing Judith: Liturgy, Music, and the Coronation of Mary I", in Valerie Schutte and Jessica S. Hower (eds.), *Mid-Tudor Queenship and Memory* (2023), pp. 69–96.

[56] Hunt, Alice, *Drama of Coronation* (2008), chap 3, pp. 77–110.

[57] Ibid, chap 4, pp. 111–145; Hunt, Alice, "The monarchical republic of Mary I". (2009) 52(3) The Historical Journal 557–572.

[58] Hoak, Dale, "The Coronations of Edward VI, Mary I, and Elizabeth I, and the Transformation of the Tudor Monarchy", in C. S. Knighton and Richard Mortimer (eds.), *Westminster Abbey Reformed 1540–1640* (2003), pp. 115–151.

[59] Hunt, Alice, *Drama of Coronation* (2008).

[60] Keay, Anna, *The Crown Jewels* (2011).

[61] Succession to the Crown Act 1543-4 (35 Hen VIII c 1).

Dillon as "primal scene of monarchical self-representation", was largely unchanged from her immediate predecessors.[62] Her succession was comparatively smooth, and her coronation, by the relatively junior Owen Oglethorpe, Bishop of Carlisle (most episcopal sees being vacant or occupied by Roman Catholic appointees of Queen Mary), was likewise unremarkable. It is noteworthy, however, that there was a comparatively short space of time between her accession (17th November 1668) and coronation (15th January 1559). This was due, in part, to the need to counter the First Succession Act of 1533,[63] and the Second Succession Act of 1536,[64] which had declared both Mary and Elizabeth to be bastards and excluded them from the line of succession. As noted above, although the Third Succession Act of 1544–45,[65] had restored their place in the succession, it had not restored their legitimacy. Sir Nicholas Bacon, the Lord Keeper of the Great Seal, advised that following her coronation, Elizabeth's right to rule would be beyond question since.

> the English laws have long since pronounced, That the Crowne once worn quite taketh away all Defects whatsoever.[66]

Whether Bacon was quite correct in his advice, the principle he enunciated appears consistent with that expressed on other occasions, before and since. It is primarily an assertion that although the coronation does not make someone king, it is essential as an endorsement and proclamation of their new status. It also imparts to them an indelible character, something to be considered further in chapter 6.

[62] Dillon, Janette, "The Monarch as Represented in the Ceremony of Coronation", in *Representations of Elizabeth I in Early Modern Culture* (2011), pp. 125–139.

[63] Succession to the Crown Act 1533 (2 Hen VIII c 22), repealed by the Succession to the Crown: Marriage Act 1536 (28 Hen VIII c 7) s 1 and the Legitimacy of the Queen Act 1553 (1 Mar sess 2 c 1) s 2 [repealed by Statute Law Reform Act 1948].

[64] 28 Hen VIII c 7.

[65] 35 Hen VIII c 1.

[66] Duncan, Sarah and Valerie Schutte (eds.), *The Birth of a Queen* (2016), p. 80.

The Stuarts

Although James I was not seriously opposed as the successor to Elizabeth I,[67] it was necessary to reinforce his title by statute, since it contravened an earlier Act.[68] The Act of Recognition of the King's title 1603–1604[69] was an attempt to explain the contravention of the Succession to the Crown Act 1543–1544,[70] an assertion that the hereditary title was stronger than the statutory one.[71] This was probably correct, at that time. Later years were to show, however, that once Parliament was used as a means of reinforcing a claim to the throne, it might also be used in depriving someone of the throne, or at least to bar their hereditary right to it. James' coronation, although in English for the first time, was otherwise a model of antiquarian legitimacy and continuity.[72] His motive was clearly to emphasise that he was, by birth right, king of England as he had been king of Scots; hereditary title trumped any statutory title. Parliament, whether in Edinburgh or London, had a constitutional role to play, but it was plainly subordinate to that of the king himself, and his hereditary title.

Both Charles I and Charles II were to have a similar approach to that of James I to their coronations, though neither were faced with any doubts as to the legitimacy of their respective titles. Though King Charles II succeeded his martyred royal parent in 1649, he was not to be crowned in England until 23rd April 1661, after the 1660 Restoration of the monarchy; he had however previously been crowned King of Scots 1st January 1651 at a solemn Presbyterian service in Scone.[73]

[67] James was proclaimed king "by law, lineal succession, and undoubted right"; Larkin, James and Paul Hughes (eds.), *Stuart Royal Proclamations* (1973), vol. I, pp. iv, 2–3.

[68] A point not lost on his contemporaries; Harbin, George, *Hereditary Right to the Crown of England Asserted* (1713), pp. 208–209.

[69] Act of Recognition of the King's title 1603-4 (1 Jac I c 1).

[70] 35 Hen VIII c 1.

[71] Sir Thomas Craig, a Scots legal scholar, exhaustively laid the ground for James's hereditary claim in *The Right of Succession to the Kingdom of England* (1703). James was, in any case, practically the only reasonable choice.

[72] Hunt, Alice, "The Bright Star of the North: James I and his English Coronation", in M. Twycross, P. King, S. Carpenter, and G. Walker (eds.), *Mediæval English Theatre* (2017), Part II, pp. 22–37.

[73] Gross, George William Cullen, "1651: The Last Coronation in Scotland — An Anomaly?" (2021) 26(3) The Court Historian 229–245.

The London coronation was delayed for a year because of the necessary preparations, which included providing a new set of regalia. The coronation itself, as might be expected after two decades of civil wars and strife, and an ill-fated republic which soon descended into military dictatorship, was to follow the time-honoured format, and was intended as a strong affirmation of a return to legitimate government according to the ancient constitution.[74] The rule of the major-generals, 1655–1657, was a particularly unpleasant recollection for most people,[75] and a reminder of a past golden age was widely welcomed.

Charles II was the last sovereign to make the traditional procession from the Tower of London to Westminster Abbey the day before the coronation. His younger brother, James II, abandoned the tradition of the pageant and progress from the Tower to the Abbey[76]—started by Richard II in 1377, as a means of inspiring loyalty among the burghers—according to Strong, to pay for jewels for his queen at his coronation in 1685.[77] Equally plausibly, it was likely also because between 1666 and 1676 the innermost ward of the Tower of London was transformed and the surviving but much neglected palace buildings were removed,[78] thus depriving the new king of any suitable starting point in the Tower, and offering a practical reason for dispensing with this part of the ceremony. From the coronation of William IV onwards there has been a replacement procession from St James's Palace, later Buckingham Palace, to the Abbey.[79]

Although Charles II's title to the Crown was unassailable, that of his brother was less clear. Although undoubtedly the next in line to succeed Charles II, who had no legitimate children of his own,[80] James Duke

[74] Hunt, Alice, "All Forms Accustomed': Ritual, precedent and the past at the coronation of Charles II", in *Remembering the English Civil Wars* (2021), pp. 101–121.

[75] Barnard, T. C., *The English Republic 1649–1660* (2014).

[76] Edie, Carolyn A., "The Public Face of Royal Ritual: Sermons, Medals, and Civic Ceremony in Later Stuart Coronations" (1990) The Huntington Library Quarterly 311–336.

[77] Strong, Sir Roy, *Coronation* (2005), pp. 133–135.

[78] Parnell, Geoffrey, *The Tower of London* (1993), p. 65.

[79] Strong, Sir Roy, *Coronation* (2005), p. 401.

[80] He had at least 20 illegitimate children, of which he acknowledged 14; The most well known was James Scott, Duke of Monmouth; Powell, Roger and Peter Beauclerk, *Royal Bastards* (2008).

of York presented a problem for the political elite as he was a Roman Catholic. Parliamentary attempts were made to exclude the Duke of York and "all other popish successors", and it was proposed "that no King shall marry a popish Queen".[81] This Exclusion Crisis lasted from November 1679 till March 1682.[82] Ironically, a doctrine condemned as papist in the sixteenth century was now adopted by protestants. It was supposed that a Roman Catholic monarch would not respect the law, and so could not be effectively bound to preserve the Protestant Church of England.

In two of the three Parliaments from 1679 to 1681 bills intended to exclude the Duke of York from the succession were introduced and debated in the House of Commons.[83] The bill of May 1679 was worded so as to include Scotland and Ireland, in case their respective Parliaments neglected to enact similar measures. In 1680 a similar measure was introduced, and received three readings in the Commons, but was defeated in the House of Lords.[84] Had it been passed, and received the royal assent (itself an unlikely occurrence), the subsequent constitutional development of Britain might have taken a very different path.

Anti-Exclusionists argued indeed for a heritable Crown, but saw in it features of a life tenancy that made it impossible for the king to affect the disposition of the estate after his death; Edward VI's failure in this regard was doubtless still in mind. The Exclusionists argued that there was no law of succession (or at best there was a hereditary expectation to succeed), and that the king and Parliament were empowered to make one (or that the hereditary expectation to succeed was rebuttable by Parliament for cause). While denying that there was a fundamental law of succession, they maintained that there was a fundamental right of self-defence against a king who was opposed to the liberty of the Protestant Church.[85] They

[81] Cobbett, William (ed.), *The parliamentary History of England* (1806–1820), vol. IV, pp. 1132, 1196, 1250, 1332.

[82] Locke himself was involved, see Ashcraft, Richard, "The Two Treatises and the Exclusion Crisis", in J. G. A. Pocock and R. Ashcraft (eds.), *John Locke* (1980), pp. 25–114.

[83] Nenner, Howard, *The Right to be King* (1995), p. 10.

[84] Cannon, John and Ralph Griffiths, *The Oxford Illustrated History of the British Monarchy* (1988), p. 414.

[85] W. G., *Case of Succession to the Crown of England Stated* (1679), p. 14. Sovereignty became an issue because in countering the assertions of a fundamental law of succession the Exclusionists were pressed to contend for the even more basic right of self-protection.

would have acknowledged their debt to Hobbes but that he stood for secular absolutism. An elective monarchy could have led to an arbitrary and uncertain succession.[86]

The Jesuit Robert Parsons had stated in 1594 that:

> no man is King or Prince by instrument of nature, but every King and kings sonne hath his dignity and preheminence above other men, by authority only of the common wealth.[87]

In the 1590s Peter Wentworth proposed that Parliament, as the High Court of Parliament, be charged to sort through the potential complex of hereditary claims, to choose whoever had the best right, though not itself to elect the heir.[88] The opportunity to formulate a rule for future successions was, however, lost, with the relatively seamless succession of James I upon the death of Elizabeth I. What was a heresy in late Tudor times came to be orthodoxy in the next century. Sir Algernon Sidney was less concerned in who should succeed as who should decide the question.[89]

On the flight of James II in 1688, all those who had served as members of the Parliaments of Charles II, together with the Court of Aldermen and members of the Common Council of the City of London assembled on 26th December 1688, at the desire of the Prince of Orange. They requested the said Prince to take over the civil and military administration and the disposal of the public revenue, and likewise to summon a Convention Parliament.

A Convention Parliament was accordingly summoned by the Prince of Orange by letters directed to the Lords Spiritual and Temporal (being Protestants), and to the coroners, clerks of the peace, and others. This Convention Parliament met on 22nd January 1688 (old style). On 28th January the Commons so convened recorded that:

[86] Comber, Thomas, *Religion and Loyalty Supporting each other* (1681), pp. 11, 34.

[87] Specifically, he argued that the presumption of the hereditary right of the next in blood could be rebutted in some circumstances; Doleman, R., *Conference About the Next Succession* (1594), pp. 142, 198–199.

[88] Wentworth, Peter, *A Pithie Exhortation to Her Majestie for Establishing Her Successor to the Crowne* (1598), pp. 5, 48, 51.

[89] Scott, Jonathon, *Algernon Sidney and the Restoration Crisis, 1677–1683* (1991), p. 53. Sidney argued that unless the succession could be grounded in the consent of Parliament, there was no hope of political stability; *Discourses concerning Government* ed. Thomas West (1990), chap 2 sect 11 pp. 136–137.

> King James II having endeavoured to subvert the constitution of the kingdom by breaking the original contract between the King and people and by the advice of Jesuits and other wicked persons having violated the fundamental laws; and having withdrawn himself out of this kingdom; has abdicated the government; and that the Throne is thereby vacant.[90]

This declaration is of particular significance because it asserts that the throne might be vacated by misconduct—a view doubtless shared by the Regicides of Charles I, a very different body of men, though scarcely 40 years earlier—and because it appeared to reject, or ignore, the well-established principle that the throne is never vacant.

On 12th February a declaration was drawn up and agreed by the Lords and Commons affirming the rights and liberties of the people, and settling the Crown and regal government of England, France and Ireland upon William and Mary of Orange, during their joint lives and the life of the survivor. The further limitations were: (first) to the heirs of the body of Mary; (second) to the Princess Anne of Denmark and the heirs of her body; and (third) to the heirs of the body of William, Prince of Orange.

This declaration was offered on the following day to William and Mary, who accepted its terms, and the declaration was then published to the nation in the form of a proclamation.[91] The declaration was subsequently enacted with certain additions in the form of the Bill of Rights 1689,[92] and the Acts of the Convention Parliament were also subsequently ratified and confirmed by the Crown and Parliament Recognition Act 1689,[93] which also acknowledged the new king and queen.

Since William and Mary were monarchs de facto at the time Parliament was summoned, it was validly summoned (whereas the Convention Parliament was not), and the confirmatory Act was legally effective to do what it purported to do, namely to validate the royal title and the Acts of the Convention Parliament.[94] The Bill of Rights, being thus confirmed by

[90] Commons Journals dated 28 January 1688.

[91] Commons Journals dated 12 February 1688 and 13 February 1688.

[92] 1 Will III & Mary sess 2 c 2.

[93] 2 Will & Mary c 1.

[94] So far as the royal title was concerned, the Act merely "recognised and acknowledged" title, whereas enacting rather than declaratory language was used in confirming the Acts of the Convention Parliament. See Brookfield, F. M., "Some aspects of the Necessity Principle in Constitutional Law" (1972) University of Oxford DPhil thesis, Parliaments

a Parliament summoned in the constitutional manner, acquired the force of a legal statute, and appears upon the statute books as such. It may also be argued that the Lords temporal and spiritual, forming part of the Convention Parliament, had constituted a *magnum concilium*—more on that later—which inherited the *Witan*'s elective role, and which therefore had the power to elect a new Sovereign from amongst the eligible heirs.

Once proclaimed, and their title confirmed, the new king and queen were crowned. Unsurprisingly, the coronation of William and Mary contained a number of unusual aspects, partly on account of it being a joint coronation of King and Queen regnant, but also because of the difficult times in which it occurred—in the recognition, the words "rightful, by the laws of God and man", were omitted.[95] The *Bible* was presented for the first time, and the coronation was once again incorporated within the structure of the communion service, for the first time since the first recension. This latter change was particularly significant as showing a careful consideration of the structure and nature of the coronation. The choral presentation of "*Firmetur manus tua*" ("let your hand be firm"), used from the second recension onwards, was abandoned.[96] Prayers consecrating the king before the anointing, except for "*Deus qui populis*", at the end of the litany, were omitted. Other prayers were rewritten.[97] Crucially, the oath was rewritten. The queen was crowned and invested with insignia at the same time as the king, being a queen regnant rather than queen consort. A queen consort is usually crowned and anointed

of the de facto king, 278. They could have claimed the Crown by conquest, but William and Mary disavowed any intention to do so.

[95] Legg, L. G. W., *English Coronation Records* (1901), p. 317.

[96] Ibid, p. xvii; Hughes, Andrew, "Antiphons and Acclamations: The Politics of Music in the Coronation Service of Edward II, 1308" (Spring 1988) 6(2) The Journal of Musicology 150–168.

[97] Legg, L. G. W., *English Coronation Records* (1901), p. 317.

after the king,[98] as is proper given her secondary and derivative position. Queens were consecrated from the mid-eighth century.[99]

Despite the events of 1688–1689, the right of Parliament to vary and limit the descent of the Crown, in cases of misgovernment amounting to a breach of the original contract between the Crown and the people, cannot be said to be admitted as a definite constitutional principle. But due weight must be attributed to the fact that the tenure of the Crown since 1688 has depended upon the action taken by the Lords and Commons convened at that time in an irregular manner.[100]

The Glorious Revolution settlement

The present succession is still affected largely by the Revolutionary Settlement.[101] As from the dates of the Unions of England with Scotland and Ireland, the succession of the imperial Crown of the United Kingdom of Great Britain, and of Great Britain and Northern Ireland respectively, was to be as it then stood limited and settled under the Act

[98] The earliest known coronation of a Queen was that of Judith, wife of Æthelwulf, King of Wessex, in 856; Wilson, H. A., "The English Coronation Orders" (July 1901) The Journal of Theological Studies 481–504, 482. Judith, daughter of Charles II, King of West Francia (and later Emperor of the Romans) ("Charles the Bald"), was the first to be styled Queen, and was crowned and anointed by Hincmar, Archbishop of Rheims, as part of the wedding, at Verberie-sur-Oise, on 1st October 856; Nelson, Janet L., *The Annals of St-Bertin* (1991).

[99] Smith, Julie Ann, "The Earliest Queen-Making Rites" (1997) 66(1) Church history 18–35.

[100] Maitland, Frederic, *The Constitutional History of England—a course of lectures* (1931), pp. 283–285.

[101] *Halsbury's Laws of England* (4th ed., 1974), vol 19, at para 847.

of Settlement.[102] Thus succession is vested in the heirs of the body of the Princess Sophia,[103] who are Protestants.[104]

The settling of the succession on the heirs of the Electress Sophia was an extension of this broadly elective approach, but the succession thereafter proceeded by inheritance. The Succession to the Crown Act 1707[105] itself expressly affirmed the power of Crown and Parliament to limit and bind the succession—though not necessarily to determine the individual claim of a specific heir.

After the triumph of hereditary title over election in the early middle ages, the possibility of intervention by the successors of the *Witan* remained. It was asserted in the sixteenth, seventeenth and early eighteenth centuries. The modern position is that the statutory provisions settle the Crown in the present line of succession, and provides certain statutory conditions on the acquisition of tenure.[106]

The descent of the Crown in the present Protestant line is secured by the Act which regulates the succession, the Act of Settlement 1700.[107] William Henry Duke of Gloucester, son of Anne, died in 1700 at the age of eleven, raising the prospect once again of a foreign-born Sovereign.

[102] Union with Scotland Act 1706 (6 Anne c 11), art II; Union with Ireland Act 1800 (39 & 40 Geo III c 67) art 2; Ireland Act 1949 (12 & 13 Geo VI c 41) s 1 (1). In Scotland a convention offered the Throne jointly to William and Mary, though conditional upon the abolition of episcopacy and the institution of a Presbyterian church order.

[103] The Princess Sophia having predeceased Anne, the Crown descended, under this provision, to George I, son of Sophia. It then descended lineally to George IV, from George IV to his brother William IV, from whom it descended to Queen Victoria, niece of William IV, then lineally to Edward VIII, who on 10th December 1936, executed an Instrument of Abdication, and, on 11th December 1936, gave his assent to His Majesty's Declaration of Abdication Act 1936 (1 Edw VIII & 1 Geo VI c 3). Thereupon His Majesty ceased to be king, and the Crown passed to George VI (s 1 (1)).

[104] As to the effect of the Act of Settlement 1700 (12 & 13 Will III c 2) and the subsequent statute, 4 Anne c 4 (Princess Sophia, naturalisation) (1705) (otherwise 4 & 5 Anne c 16) (repealed) on the lineal descendants of Princess Sophia, see *Attorney-General v Prince Ernest Augustus of Hanover* [1957] AC 436, [1957] 1 All ER 49, HL (lineal descendants are British subjects). Indeed, Blackstone maintained that this Act actually reasserted the rule of hereditary succession; Blackstone, Sir William, *Commentaries on the Laws of England* ed. E. Christian (1978).

[105] 6 Ann c 41.

[106] *Halsbury's Laws of England* (4th ed., 1974), vol. 19, at para 850.

[107] Act of Settlement 1700 (12 & 13 Will III c 2) s 1.

The Act of Settlement[108] was introduced to respond to this situation, although other restrictions were also added. Consent would be required for the king to engage in war or to leave the country. Privy counsellors were to sign any advice which they gave (the origin both of ministerial countersignatures and ministerial responsibility, although the latter was already discernible during the reign of Charles II). No foreigners were to be allowed to hold office under the Crown, or occupy a seat in Parliament.[109] No person holding an office of profit or a pension from the Crown were to be a Member of Parliament. To limit the Crown's hitherto unfettered freedom to appoint ministers of their choice no pardons were to be available on impeachment by Parliament.[110]

Anyone who adhered to the Roman Catholic Church, or who married such a person, could not inherit the Crown, nor could they remain Sovereign if they were disqualified after succeeding to the Crown. In such a case the people were absolved of their allegiance, and the Crown was to descend to such person or persons, being Protestants, as would have inherited it in case the person so reconciled were dead.[111] This statutory provision allowing for the future demise of the Crown was the first time this had ever been done. As a consequence of the wording used in the Act of Settlement 1700,[112] there was no requirement that someone whose spouse joined the Roman Catholic Church after marriage lost their right to the Crown.[113] However it would appear that the operation of the

[108] 12 & 13 Will III c 2.

[109] This prohibition is the subject of some consideration in the Report of the Justice and Law Reform Committee on the Imperial Laws Application Bill (1988) Explanatory Material pp. 57–60, 58; Section 3 would appear to prevent New Zealanders (and others of Her Majesty overseas subjects) from being appointed members of the Privy Council.

[110] Cannon, John and Ralph Griffiths, *The Oxford Illustrated History of the British Monarchy* (1988), p. 440.

[111] This is the joint effect of the Act of Settlement 1700 (12 & 13 Will III c 2) s 2, as amended by the Accession Declaration Act 1910 (10 Edw VII & 1 Geo V c 29), and the Bill of Rights 1689 (1 Will III & Mary sess 2 c 2) s 1, as amended by the Juries Act 1825 (6 Geo IV c 50) s 62.

[112] 12 & 13 Will III c 2.

[113] Thus, Prince Edward Duke of Kent retained his position in the line of succession despite his wife Katharine having been received into the Roman Catholic Church on 11th January 1994. However, their son George Earl of St Andrews lost his right to the Throne when he married the Roman Catholic Sylvana Palma Tomaselli 9th January 1988.

Act was irreversible, although to be effective the marriage must be a legal one.[114]

The law of succession, whether perceived as primarily or solely statutory in nature, or as a mixture of ancient elective, constitutive, or hereditary title, presents a problem for any suggestion that the coronation serves no legal purpose. Even Earl Fitzwilliam, in his assessment in 1838 that the coronation served no purpose, limited his conclusion to those circumstances where the Crown was not in contest.[115] Since title to the Crown depends on more than simply hereditary title, or parliamentary grant, the coronation, where the various sources of legitimacy are highlighted, combined and celebrated, still serves a vital confirmatory if not constitutive function. This is especially so in the acclamation and homage, where the magnates, lords spiritual and temporal, acknowledge and accept their new king.

Today, although not necessarily popularly well known, the law of succession is well understood by scholars, and is settled—even if some conceptual uncertainty remains. As we have seen, the law has not always been clear, nor invariably followed even when clear. The greater the uncertainty of the claim to the throne, the greater the role for the coronation. Although the coronation does not make a Sovereign, as such, nonetheless their status is enhanced or augmented by a coronation. Omitting a coronation was previously unthinkable, and nor were any significant changes considered appropriate, although over time the coronation has evolved markedly, even if its basic structure remains intact after a thousand years. It remains a central constitutional ritual, a rite of passage, and a personal and national dedication, the "solemnity of our royal coronation". It was and remains an assertion of authority based on constitutional history and practice, and not primarily a thing of personal or public fashion. This is an important safeguard of legitimacy, which is especially important at any time of change or uncertainty.

Similarly, Prince Michael of Kent lost his own right to the Throne when he married Baroness Marie-Christine von Reibnitz in 1978.

[114] Thus, the marriage of George Prince of Wales to Mrs Maria Fitzherbert, a devout Roman Catholic and twice a widow, did not disqualify him from succeeding as king in 1820, as the marriage was contrary to the Royal Marriages Act 1772 (12 Geo III c 11), and therefore legally null and void; Farran, C. d'Olivier, "The Law of the Accession" (1953) 16 Modern Law Review 140–147.

[115] Hunt, Alice, *Drama of Coronation* (2008), chap 1, pp. 12–38.

Even settled succession law can be subject to change, change which has the potential to once again raise at times difficult questions, including of certainty. Provisions designed to achieve a single simple alteration to the law may have the potential to create altogether different issues. In the more than 300 years since the passage of the Act of Settlement there have been but two statutory alterations of the succession law. The demise of the Crown in 1936 was a case of succession upon an abdication, although the new King, George VI, was the heir apparent of Edward VIII.[116] His Majesty's Declaration of Abdication Act 1936[117] was passed in accordance with the procedures of the Statute of Westminster 1931.[118] This had the effect of ending the reign of King Edward VIII in the United Kingdom and the dominions, without Edward VIII ever having been crowned; the planned date of his coronation became that of the new king George VI. The second change to the law of succession, albeit of greater long-term consequence, was much less dramatic in immediate effect. It too was superficially unrelated to the question of the coronation.

Changes to the Succession Law

On 28th October 2011, proposed reforms to the succession to the throne were announced during the Commonwealth Heads of Government Meeting in Perth, Australia. The heads of government of the then 16 Commonwealth realms[119] agreed to change the rules of succession to the Crown by replacing male preference primogeniture with absolute primogeniture, in which the first-born child of a monarch would be heir apparent regardless of gender.[120] Similar changes occurred in a

[116] There was however some consideration given to the Duke of Kent succeeding, as he had a son and heir. See also the Accession Proclamation of His Majesty King George VI 12 December 1936.

[117] 1 Edw VIII & 1 Geo VI c 3.

[118] 22 & 23 Geo V c 4.

[119] Barbados subsequently became a republic on 30 November 2021, though without the benefit of a referendum on the question; Constitution (Amendment) (No 2) Act, 2021.

[120] Ironically, given greatly lengthened life expectancy, and the increased probability that an heir will be of comparatively advanced age upon succeeding to the throne, a case could be made for the adoption of a system of ultimogeniture (also known as postremogeniture or junior right) rather than succession of the first-born, as an alternative to primogeniture. Such a system sees the youngest child—usually son—succeeding. Known

number of western and northern European monarchies at around the same time, although for different, indigenous reasons. These included the kingdoms of the Netherlands (1983),[121] Belgium (1991),[122] and Denmark (2009),[123] and the grand duchy of Luxembourg (2011).[124] It was introduced in Norway in 1990,[125] replacing male-preference cognatic primogeniture, which was the rule between 1971 and 1990, and agnatic primogeniture, which had been the principle prior to 1971.

Only the small principalities of Andorra, Liechtenstein, and Monaco, and (most crucially) the kingdom of Spain, have not yet altered their laws of succession in response to modern concepts of gender equality; in Andorra's case neither co-prince is in any event today hereditary. Spain has used male-preference cognatic primogeniture from the eleventh century—in the successor states to the Visigothic kingdoms—until 1700 and since 1830. It is this system which hitherto prevailed in England, and Scotland, and later the United Kingdom. Monaco, like Spain, uses male preference primogeniture (since 1454).[126] Succession in Liechtenstein alone remains according to male primogeniture.[127]

The proposed change to the British order of succession and that of all the realms of Queen Elizabeth II would only apply for persons born after October 2011. It was also proposed to end both the prohibition on marriage to Roman Catholics and the requirement for those in line

as Borough English, it was abolished by the Administration of Estates Act 1925 (15 & 16 Geo V c.23); Blackstone, Sir William, *Commentaries on the Laws of England* ed. E. Christian (1978), section III, p. 73.

[121] Constitution for the Kingdom of the Netherlands, Article 25.

[122] Daalder, Hans, "The monarchy in a parliamentary system" (1991) 1 Res Publica, TijdschriftvoorPolitologie, Revue de Science Politique, Belgian Journal of Political Science 70–81. According to Article 91 of the Belgian constitution, the heir accedes to the throne only upon taking a constitutional oath before a joint session of the two Houses of Parliament.

[123] Act of Succession 1953, amended 2009.

[124] BY Grand Ducal Decree; Décret grand-ducal du 16 septembre 2010 introduisant l'égalité entre hommes et femmes en matière de succession au trône, Memorial Journal Officiel du Grand-Duché de Luxembourg/Memorial Amtsblatt des Großherzogtums Luxemburg B—N° 55, 719, 23 June 2011.

[125] Article 6, The Constitution of the Kingdom of Norway 1814.

[126] Princely Law 1.249 of 2 April 2002.

[127] Constitution of the Princely House of Liechtenstein of 26 October 1993.

to the throne to gain the permission of the Sovereign to marry.[128] However, the requirement for the Sovereign to be in communion with the Church of England was proposed to remain, as well as the specific ban on Roman Catholics sitting on the throne. These two provisions were deemed central to the maintenance of the monarchy as a non-Roman Catholic, and overtly Anglican—at least in England—institution, linked to the continuing establishment of the church in England (and a parallel, though distinct, arrangement in Scotland, with respect to the established Church of Scotland).

New Zealand chaired a working group to determine the process for reform. Depending on individual constitutional arrangements, the proposed reforms needed to be approved by the parliaments of most of the realms. However, in some realms such as Papua New Guinea and Tuvalu, the reforms did not require direct legislation and would become automatic if and when the changes were implemented in the United Kingdom.[129]

In December 2012, it was announced by the Deputy Prime Minister of the United Kingdom that all the realms had agreed to implement the proposals that had been outlined, and that the new legislation would also end the prohibition on anyone in the line of succession marrying a Roman Catholic. The United Kingdom's proposed legislation was published on 13th December 2012, and the Bill was passed early in 2013.[130]

Outside the United Kingdom, the local news media tended to regard this as a matter for the British authorities, or as one which could somehow be resolved by non-legal means. But, whilst this discussion was often misguided and incorrect, it was also a debate which raised important constitutional issues for all the realms, though it did not constitute a significant political or legal discourse in very many.

At a meeting of the Council of Australian Governments (COAG) in mid-December 2012, Prime Minister Julia Gillard and the premiers of five states agreed that each state legislature would be asked to pass a law permitting the federal parliament to alter the law of succession for the Commonwealth and all the states. However, Queensland Premier

[128] Under the Royal Marriages Act 1772 (12 Geo III c 11).

[129] This was because their constitutions specified that the Sovereign was that of the United Kingdom.

[130] Succession to the Crown Act 2013.

Campbell Newman disagreed, citing Sect. 7 of the Australia Act 1986 (UK) and concluding from it that each state is sovereign and each should therefore pass its own legislation affecting the succession laws in its jurisdiction. Accordingly, the Queensland state government introduced its own Succession to the Crown Bill in the Queensland Legislative Assembly on 13th February 2013. The federal government stated that if Queensland were to proceed with the Bill, it would override the state's legislation in favour of national legislation. Following an agreement at a COAG meeting in April 2013, Queensland on 2nd May 2013 amended its Bill to add permission for the Commonwealth to act on behalf of the state, and the federal Bill was accordingly passed the same day. The other state legislatures passed similar enabling legislation.

In Canada, the Canadian federal government's Succession to the Throne Act, 2013, was tabled in the Canadian House of Commons as Bill C-53 on 31st January 2013 and passed by that body on 4th February. It was then approved by the Senate on 26th March 2013 and received Royal Assent on the following day. It would then come into force on a date that would be fixed by order of the Governor General-in-Council, in a similar manner to the United Kingdom legislation; 26th March 2015 was chosen.

The position taken by the federal Cabinet was that Canada's monarch is automatically whoever is monarch of the United Kingdom and the Canadian Parliament need only assent to the changes made to the laws of succession in the United Kingdom by that realm's Parliament, which can be achieved by ordinary legislation, without the approval of the provinces. The Canadian Act gives assent to a bill that had been laid before the United Kingdom Parliament and which, as later amended, was given Royal Assent there on 25th April 2013, as the Succession to the Crown Act 2013.

However, in Canada as in Australia, there was disagreement over this process, mainly on whether the rules of succession involve the office of the Queen thus requiring a constitutional amendment under Sect. 41(a) of the Constitution Act, 1982. The question was firstly, whether, by the principle of received law, by statute law, or both, the Bill of Rights 1689,[131] the Act of Settlement 1700,[132] and the Royal Marriages Act

[131] 1 Will III & Mary sess 2 c 2.

[132] 12 & 13 Will III c 2.

1772,[133] were a part of the Canadian constitution. Secondly, it was asked whether Canada had or could assent to the Succession to the Crown Bill 2012 as had been presented to the United Kingdom Parliament or the Bill as amended by that body and subsequently passed into law as the Succession to the Crown Act 2013. In practice the Federal Government and Parliament proceeded with a Bill. The Canadian law was challenged, unsuccessfully, in the Quebec Superior Court, over its alleged failure to follow the amending procedure set out in Sect. 41 of the Constitution Act, 1982.[134]

Elsewhere among the realms the process was generally easier. According to Lord Wallace of Tankerness, who sponsored the British government's Succession to the Crown Bill in the House of Lords, the governments of Jamaica and Belize had outlined that neither country required domestic legislation to give effect to changes to the lines of succession to their thrones, as those lines were left by Belize's and Jamaica's constitutions to the law of the United Kingdom. Lord Wallace of Tankerness expressed the view on 13th March 2013 that the British government expected that the parliaments of Jamaica and Belize would not be consulted further by their governments.[135]

In addition, of Antigua and Barbuda, Barbados, the Bahamas, Grenada, Saint Lucia, Saint Vincent and the Grenadines, and Saint Kitts and Nevis, it was also said by Lord Wallace of Tankerness, that

> We believe that it would be open to the other Caribbean realms to take a similar view [as Jamaica and Belize], but it is, of course, for them to decide how best to give the changes effect.[136]

All of these realms ultimately implemented the changes, by whatever means they chose.

The whole process of change in 2011–2015 was predicated on the belief that the succession to the throne was the responsibility of the United Kingdom Parliament, or the parliaments of the realms. As we

[133] 12 Geo III c 11.

[134] Rhèal Sèguin, "Changes to royal succession face legal fight in Quebec". *The Globe and Mail* (7 June 2013).

[135] Lord Wallace of Tankerness. Parliamentary Debates (Hansard) (United Kingdom: House of Lords). col. 310. 13 March 2013.

[136] Ibid.

have seen, this is not wholly correct. There was little discussion of the niceties of the law of succession, beyond the obvious questions, such as disqualifications, gender, and the mechanisms required for implementing any changes in each realm and in the United Kingdom itself. Nor was there evidence of in-depth thought of the role of the monarch, or of the nature of the relationship between the realms, or between the realms and the United Kingdom. Internal questions in Canada and Australia tended to dominate such discourse as occurred, largely inspired by pre-existing domestic political agendas.

Likewise, there was no apparent consideration given to the wider constitutional implications of the proposed changes, including those affecting the establishment of the churches in England and Scotland. The Church of England, and other churches, kept a relatively low-key approach to the question of the reform of the law of succession, despite the significant religious element present.

Today, descent is by primogeniture, the heir succeeding immediately upon the demise of the Crown.[137] The principle of primogeniture has now been abolished with respect to real property,[138] and remains only in respect of the Crown (subject to the recent change in favour of treating males and females as equal) and dignities such as peerages and baronetcies.[139]

Conclusion

A coronation is a legal necessity, not because it makes a Sovereign, for even in the earliest times it did not do so, but because it proclaims the legal reality. It is thus a ritual which contains within its core a profoundly significant constitutional function.

[137] As is reflected in the wording of the Accession Council, that lineal descendant of the Anglo-Saxon *Witan* (see the Appendix, Accession Proclamation 1952).

[138] Administration of Estates Act 1925 (15 & 16 Geo V c 25) (UK); cf. Administration Amendment Act 1944 (NZ).

[139] *Nevil's Case* (1604) 7 Co Rep 33a; 77 ER 460; *R v Purbeck (Viscount)* (1678) Show Parl Cas 1, 5; 1 ER 1; *Norfolk Earldom Case* [1907] AC 10; *Rhondda's (Viscountess) Claim* [1922] 2 AC 339. A peerage is descendible as an estate in fee tail; *Ferrers' (Earl) Case* (1760) 2 Eden 373; 28 ER 942.

The case which has been hitherto regarded as good authority for the principle that the coronation is not a legal necessity, *Calvin's Case*,[140] did appear to suggest that a coronation, as a consequence of hereditary succession, was not a legal necessity (as there was by then automatic and immediate succession). However, it is to be doubted whether a Sovereign would be fully accepted without a coronation, as may be seen with the still-current common attitude towards King Edward VIII ("the uncrowned king"); the succession remains a combination of hereditary title, parliamentary grant, and consent—as we were forcibly reminded in 1688–1689, and indeed again in 1936. Even the 2013 changes, which involved the participation of all the realms to a greater or lesser extent, illustrates that the completeness of title depends upon a bringing together of various elements, and it is at a coronation that this occurs in its fullness. Prior to the acceptance of the maxim, "the King is dead, long live the King!", the coronation signified the ending of the interregnum or uncertainty following the death of the previous Sovereign.[141] Thereafter it still had a symbolic function in proclaiming the new reign.

It is overly simplistic to conclude that because succession is hereditary and the heir apparent becomes the Sovereign automatically upon the death of their predecessor, that there is no need for a coronation. As an example, Queen Elizabeth II succeeded in accordance with Blackstone's rule on coparcenary heiresses. Henry VIII provided for the succession of his daughters by statute, but it was therein said that the Crown should pass to females "according to their ages, as the Crown of England has been accustomed, and ought to go in cases where there be heirs female to the same".[142] But this—the succession of Elizabeth II—was the only time a woman had succeeded, a younger sister being still alive, apart from the case of Mary—which itself was not without doubts, bloodshed and

[140] (1608) 7 Co Rep 1a; 77 ER 377.

[141] In France (which also followed automatic succession), by tradition the new king ascended the throne when the coffin of the previous monarch descended into the vault at Saint Denis Basilica, and the Duke of Uzès proclaimed *"Le Roi est mort, vive le Roi!"* ("The King is dead, long live the King!"); Giesey, Ralph E., "Inaugural Aspects of French Royal Ceremonials", in János M. Bak (ed.), *Coronations* (1990). The Duke of Uzès were Seigneur d'Uzès from the twelfth century, Vicomte d'Uzès from 1318, and Duc d'Uzès from 1565. They became a peerage of France in 1572 (the vast majority of nobles were not peers), and were the premier peerage, ranking after the Princes of the Blood.

[142] 25 Hen VIII c 22.

insurrection. The coronation helped put to rest any uncertainty, if indeed any existed in 1952.

Earlier still, Richard II and Henry VI were crowned in an attempt to end their formal dependence on protectors (or at least strengthen their claim to the throne), and this was also considered for Edward V. The coronation is an essential element in the succession to the Crown, since the title to the Crown passes in accordance with a mixture of principles, being primarily political in nature rather than simply the descent of property, personal or real.

The title to the Crown may be characterised as being determined by common law principles as modified by Act of Parliament from time to time, but it is probably more correct to say that it is *sui generis*. Whatever basis the title may have derived from, it culminated in the ceremony of the coronation. Aspects of election, heredity and parliamentary mandated succession combine—and this unique amalgamation is reflected in the coronation, with its seven key elements of the recognition or acclamation (election), the oath (today the parliamentary title particularly), the anointing, the investiture with regalia, the crowning, the enthroning, and the homage. The oath, as a specific aspect of the coronation, highlights, as does the homage, and indeed the acclamation, the reciprocal nature of kingship. The changed nature of the oath was reflected in 2023, with a reworded and expanded introduction; in place of "Madam, is Your Majesty willing to take the oath?" the Archbishop of Canterbury asked

> Your Majesty, the Church established by law, whose settlement you will swear to maintain, is committed to the true profession of the Gospel, and, in so doing, will seek to foster an environment in which people of all faiths and beliefs may live freely. The Coronation Oath has stood for centuries and is enshrined in law. Are you willing to take the Oath?[143]

The new words would seem calculated to explain that the Coronation Oath need not compromise the King's commitment to a multifaith society, as well as explaining why the King was still required to take the oath—because it was a legal requirement. Indeed, it (the oath) was now couched in terms of the role of the church promoting a multifaith society, very much a modern understanding of its function.

[143] *The Authorised Liturgy for the Coronation Rite of His Majesty King Charles III For use on Saturday 6th May 2023, 11:00am at Westminster Abbey* (2023).

The first promise was slightly changed, to reflect constitutional changes, but its substance remained unaltered

> Will you solemnly promise and swear to govern the Peoples of the United Kingdom of Great Britain and Northern Ireland, your other Realms and the Territories to any of them belonging or pertaining, according to their respective laws and customs?[144]

This alteration was doubtless to accommodate the changing names of realms.

The legal function of the coronation is in the inauguration of the new Sovereign, complete with the constitutionally significant acclamation, oath, anointing, investiture, crowning, and homage. Each element has a legal significance, from the acclamation or recognition of the duly succeeded Sovereign (whose title is derived from statutory provisions and common law hereditary principles), and the oath forming part of a social compact between king and people. The anointing, as a setting aside of the king in a sacred dedication to service confers upon the Sovereign a *sui generis* legal status, while the symbolic conferment of insignia of regal power, including the crown, emphasise the political and religious authority of the Sovereign (and ultimately, of his government). The homage, like the acclamation, represent and enact the bond between king and people (in the persons of the magnates, as the Lords spiritual and temporal). All of these steps, ancient as they are, are particularly important when there has been a departure from the normal succession, or where the new Sovereign might face opposition. It not merely celebrates the advent of a new Sovereign, but it also emphasises the orderly transition from the previous king or queen. Continuity and legitimacy are central to the ritual of the coronation, and as such it has both a constitutive function and a distinct role to play in implementing and inaugurating a new regime.

This continuity, especially important after any change to the law of succession, is also reflected in the steps which occur immediately upon the demise of the Crown, and which continue for some time up to and including the coronation itself. Like the Egyptian coronation year, the

144 Ibid.

period between the accession and the coronation collectively marks the beginning of the new regnal era.[145]

The right to the throne being once determined by the law of succession—including all the elements which that entails—there are certain steps which follow which also contribute to establishing the new Sovereign on the throne. These steps at once emphasise the legal and constitutional continuity of the system, and also the relationship between the Sovereign and the law, the church, and the people. These also reflect the vital constitutional role which the ceremonies surrounding the death, accession and coronation of the Sovereign exhibit.

[145] Until 1963 statutes in the United Kingdom were dated in accordance with the regnal year; Acts of Parliament Numbering and Citation Act 1962 (10 & 11 Eliz. 2. c. 34). This is still the practice in Canada; Bishop, Olga B., *Canadian Official Publications* (2016), p. 117.

CHAPTER 4

From the Demise of the Crown to the Coronation

Introduction

The law of succession, based on hereditary descent, limited by parliamentary provisions, and subject to *sui generis* rules, identifies the individual who is king—or queen regnant—upon the demise of the Crown. Succession is automatic and immediate—there is no interregnum or delay whilst an election takes place from amongst the eligible heirs, as is retained in some (non-European) monarchies. However, there remain a number of practical and legal steps which are required upon the demise of the Crown, in a process collectively known as the accession. Some of these, such as the coronation oath, overlap with the coronation itself. The latter is of such ancient origin that a series of legal provisions also applied to the arrangements for a coronation, including the Court of Claims, convened specifically to determine disputes as to customary service at a coronation. Like the ancient Egyptian year of the coronation, the Sovereign acquires their status on the death of their predecessor, but their title had to be confirmed, validated and endorsed by a series of rituals and ceremonies. The key ceremony, in English (and later British) kingship, is the coronation, but this is but one step.

These steps are a combination of the practical and the legal—the latter both statutory and customary—and have changed somewhat over time. Today they include the accession proclamation, the Sovereign's accession

N. Cox, *The Political, Legal, and Theological Functions of the Ceremony in the British Tradition*,
https://doi.org/10.1007/978-3-031-88960-8_4

declaration, and the two statutory oaths under the Act of Union 1706,[1] and the Accession Declaration Act 1910.[2] The coronation itself follows most of these steps, nowadays after a suitable interval allowing for a period of state and private mourning for the late Sovereign, and sufficient time to plan and implement arrangements for a suitably grand coronation. These plans include not only the ceremonial and liturgical, but also such key questions as who should be invited to attend the coronation—and formerly the coronation banquet. This is not simply a matter of who had sufficient public eminence to merit an invitation, but rather a question of who, for constitutional and public reasons, ought to be included, and how interest groups, such as civic and religious representatives, should be chosen. Such a decision-making process, we shall see, is also applied to the membership of and invitation to the Accession Council.

In 2022, for the first time, the preliminary, pre-coronation, steps were all conducted in public, broadcast to the world, as part of a concerted effort to bring the process into the context in which it is placed; a public proclamation of a change of regime. The accession proclamation, the Sovereign's declaration, and the two statutory oaths, were brought to a much larger and more diverse audience than was possible even 10 years earlier, let alone 70 years before, when Queen Elizabeth II ascended the throne. They were public, as their purpose was a very public one, namely to proclaim the new Sovereign, and establish the parameters under which they would reign. This is unquestionably a constitutional procedure of great significance, rooted in the law and practice of the realm, and leading up to the coronation as the culmination and climax. The period between the demise of the Crown and the coronation is a time of public and private preparation, reflecting in its several stages, the transition from one Sovereign to another. It is both the proclamation and acknowledgement of the new reign and an opportunity for the restatement of some core constitutional principles.

[1] Union with Scotland Act 1706 (6 Ann c. 11), art. xxv.

[2] Accession Declaration Act 1910 (10 Edw VII & 1 Geo V c 29).

Steps Undertaken on the Accession

Today there are four key constitutional steps or procedures which are undertaken upon the demise of the Crown, before the celebration of the coronation itself. The procedures which are involved in each, and their legal effect, vary considerably. These steps are the accession proclamation, the Sovereign's declaration, and the two statutory oaths respectively under the Act of Union 1706,[3] and the Accession Declaration Act 1910.[4] The final oath, the coronation oath, is made at the coronation itself, as may indeed be the Accession Declaration Oath, as it was in 2023.

The Sovereign is nowadays proclaimed as soon as possible after the demise of the Crown, although it would appear that the now ubiquitous practice of proclaiming a Sovereign prior to the coronation only arose on the accession of King Edward VI in 1547,[5] and their proclamation by a council of the great and good without the king's presence only dates from the time of King James I. The decision to proclaim Edward VI's accession was perhaps reflecting the diminished importance Thomas Cranmer, Archbishop of Canterbury, wished to ascribe to the first post-Reformation coronation.

The accession of James I was different from the usual for other reasons—most significantly his absence from London (he was in distant Scotland), and the union of the English and Scottish Crowns which his accession inaugurated. With Queen Elizabeth I clearly dying, in March 1603 Sir Robert Cecil, Secretary of State, sent James a draft proclamation of his accession to the English throne. Elizabeth died in the early hours of 24th March, and James was proclaimed king in London later the same day.[6] Thus, although proclaimed in his absence, the new king had approved the form of his proclamation in advance, as later became customary. He did not rush to travel south, and took his time to undertake something of a triumphal march to London.[7]

The proclamation of a Sovereign is, at least theoretically, no more than a statement of established fact, that the late Sovereign has deceased, and

[3] Union with Scotland Act 1706 (6 Ann c. 11), art. xxv.

[4] Accession Declaration Act 1910 (10 Edw VII & 1 Geo V c 29).

[5] Hunt, Alice, *Drama of Coronation* (2008), Chap 3, pp. 77–110.

[6] Croft, Pauline, *King James* (2003), p. 49; Willson, David Harris, *King James VI & I* (1963), p. 158.

[7] Courtney, Alexander, *James VI* (2024), p. 239.

the new one ascended the throne. That can of course be, as in the case of James I, an important intimation of an uncertainty resolved, and civil war or rival claims averted. Today the prospect of a disputed or uncertain succession is remote—though any changes to the law of succession, as in 1936 or 2013, potentially raise that theoretical possibility, however unlikely it may be. Such pretender movements have existed elsewhere in comparatively recent times.[8]

The first public intimation of the death of the Sovereign is nowadays greatly aided by electronic media; whilst the death of the monarch has come, in the course of the twentieth century, to be announced in a formal printed and framed notice placed on the railings of Buckingham Palace, in 2022 the death of Queen Elizabeth II was first announced on Twitter and on newswires (at 1830 hours 8th September),[9] and then by the customary black edged notices—which were also placed on the railings of the Palace of Holyroodhouse, in Edinburgh. The death was announced one minute after the Twitter and newswire statements, by Huw Edwards, senior news presenter, simultaneously on the BBC News channel and BBC 1 television. It repeated three minutes later on all BBC TV channels, which had suspended their regular separate scheduled programming.[10] BBC Radio 4 and BBC Radio 5 Live made announcements at 1832.[11] The death

[8] Such as, for instance, Carlism in Spain. They take their name from Carlos V, son of Ferdinand VII, who was a pretender to the throne of Spain with his declaration to be rightful heir on 1st October 1833. Traditionally, all but one of the Spanish kingdoms allowed the succession of daughters in the absence of sons and of sisters in the absence of brothers. The one exception, Aragon, tended to favour semi-Salicism; Holt, Edgar, *The Carlist Wars in Spain* (1967).

[9] https://twitter.com/RoyalFamily/status/1567928275913121792.

[10] Torrance, David, "The Accession of King Charles III" (House of Commons Library Research Briefing, number CBP9621, 29 September 2022).

[11] Buckingham Palace had announced concern for the Queen's health at 1230, and BBC One ran continuous coverage from 1240, clearly anticipating the eventual outcome; "Queen under medical supervision at Balmoral". BBC News. 8 September 2022. All times are BST. Although the public announcement was made at 1830, Her Majesty had died at 1510, and Elizabeth Truss, the newly appointed Prime Minister of the United Kingdom, was notified at 1630.

In the realms, a similar story unfolded. The announcement of HM's passing was first carried at 0535 on AM Early TV on Three, and on the TVNZ 1 ticker at 0540, and then a bulletin one minute later, just a few minutes after the United Kingdom. The Prime Minister of New Zealand was notified, by message from the Cabinet Secretary at approximately 0450, about an hour after Ms Truss was informed.

of Elizabeth II was the first death of a Sovereign in Scotland since King James V in 1542, and in certain respects the steps which followed were affected and influence by the enhanced Scottish aspect which this created. It was al the first which was primarily covered by social media.[12]

When the new Sovereign's accession is followed in rapid succession by a coronation, there is perhaps little need to announce the accession; and even in much earlier times, when the coronation was not necessarily immediate, or in the era when coronations were often left until later in a reign, the fact of the accession of a new king would soon be known through his public appearances and law-making, and even through his coinage.[13]

The King's Address

In an age of almost instantaneous communications, in 2022 the new Sovereign was able, twenty-four hours after the death of his predecessor, and (significantly) prior to the gathering of the Accession Council, which was called to proclaim the new Sovereign, to give an Address, broadcast in both Chambers of Parliament, and televised, as well as broadcast on the Internet. In the King's Address, King Charles III stated (in a speech which doubtless had passed through numerous iterations in draft form over recent years) that.

> I speak to you today with feelings of profound sorrow. Throughout her life, Her Majesty The Queen – my beloved Mother – was an inspiration and example to me and to all my family, and we owe her the most heartfelt debt any family can owe to their mother; for her love, affection, guidance, understanding and example.
>
> Queen Elizabeth was a life well lived; a promise with destiny kept and she is mourned most deeply in her passing. That promise of lifelong service I renew to you all today.
>
> Alongside the personal grief that all my family are feeling, we also share with so many of you in the United Kingdom, in all the countries where The

[12] Darwish, Ibrahim M., Abdulaziz A. Alzoubi, and Noora Q. Abu Ain, "The Death of Monarchs: Front-Page Reporting of Queen Elizabeth II's Death" (2024) 14(7) Theory and Practice in Language Studies 2046–2052.

[13] Coins have often borne the image of the ruler who had them minted since at least Phoenician times, since the time of Alexander the Great usually on the obverse; Sear, David, *Greek Imperial Coins and Their Values* (1982).

> Queen was Head of State, in the Commonwealth and across the world, a deep sense of gratitude for the more than 70 years in which my Mother, as Queen, served the people of so many nations [...] In her life of service we saw that abiding love of tradition, together with that fearless embrace of progress, which make us great as Nations. ...
> As The Queen herself did with such unswerving devotion, I too now solemnly pledge myself, throughout the remaining time God grants me, to uphold the Constitutional principles at the heart of our nation.
> And wherever you may live in the United Kingdom, or in the Realms and territories across the world, and whatever may be your background or beliefs, I shall endeavour to serve you with loyalty, respect and love, as I have throughout my life [...]
> On behalf of all my family, I can only offer the most sincere and heartfelt thanks for your condolences and support. They mean more to me than I can ever possibly express.
> And to my darling Mama, as you begin your last great journey to join my dear late Papa, I want simply to say this: thank you. Thank you for your love and devotion to our family and to the family of nations you have served so diligently all these years. May 'flights of Angels sing thee to thy rest'.[14]

From a constitutional perspective, the key points which may be gleaned from the address are they the new king is emphasising continuity, a commitment to uphold the "constitutional principles at the heart of our nation", and a model of Christian servant kingship (to "serve you with loyalty, respect and love").

The Accession Council

The King's Address, which was significant but had no legal effect—another innovation in an age of near instant and ubiquitous news and social media—was followed by the meeting of the first part of the Accession Council. This is formed of certain Privy Counsellors, Great Officers

[14] Royal Family website, "His Majesty The King's address to the Nation and the Commonwealth". <https://www.royal.uk/news-and-activity/2022-09-09/the-kings-address-to-the-nation-and-the-commonwealth>. The quote, "may flights of Angels sing thee to thy rest" is from Hamlet, Act 5 Scene 2, the final scene of the Shakespeare play. It is spoken by Horatio, who is paying tribute to his dying friend, Hamlet, Prince of Denmark. The full quote reads: "Now cracks a noble heart. Good night, sweet prince, and flights of angels sing thee to thy rest."

of State,[15] the Lord Mayor and High Sheriffs of the City of London, realm High Commissioners, some senior civil servants and certain others invited to attend, and is held (without the presence of the Sovereign) to formally announce the death of the Monarch and proclaim the succession of the new Sovereign and to make certain consequential Orders of Council, mainly relating to the Proclamation.[16] Orders of Council can be made by Privy Counsellors acting alone, as a corporate body; Orders in Council require the approval of the monarch "in Council". Whereas the regnal name of a Sovereign is normally revealed at the Accession Council, in 2022 this occurred, whether by design or otherwise, at the public statement by the newly appointed Prime Minister, Elizabeth (Liz) Truss, on the death of the Queen.[17]

The Accession Council is not a legal necessity, in that it is not required by statute.[18] The proclamation of the new Sovereign is an old tradition,

[15] For England and the United Kingdom these are the Lord High Steward (since 1421 appointed only for a coronation—in 2023 General Sir Gordon Messenger, Royal Marines—and for the trial of peers, a procedure abolished in 1948), the Lord High Chancellor (now concurrently the Secretary of State for Justice), the Lord High Treasurer (vacant since 1714), the Lord President of the Council (currently the Leader of the House of Commons), the Lord Keeper of the Privy Seal (currently the Leader of the House of Lords), the Lord Great Chamberlain (hereditary in gross, for the duration of a reign, currently Rupert Carington, 7th Lord Carrington, for the reign of King Charles III), the Lord High Constable (since 1512 appointed only for a coronation, in 2023 Admiral Sir Tony Radakin), the Earl Marshal (hereditary in gross, currently Edward Fitzalan-Howard, 18th Duke of Norfolk), the Lord High Admiral (mostly in commission since 1709, excepting for the Duke of Clarence 1827-28, and the Duke of Edinburgh 2011-2021, and held by the Sovereign 1964-2011 and [apparently] since 2021).

There are separate Great Officers of State, and Officers of the Crown, in Scotland, the former including the Lord Clerk Register (since 2007 Lord Mackay of Clashfern) and the latter including that of Lord High Constable, held since the thirteenth century by the Hay family, and currently by Merlin Hay, 24th Earl of Erroll.

[16] Privy Council Office, "The Accession Council". <https://privycouncil.independent.gov.uk/privy-council/the-accession-council/>.

[17] 10 Downing Street website, Prime Minister's statement on the death of Her Majesty Queen Elizabeth II, 8 September 2022.

[18] The proclamations of George I in 1714 and Victoria in 1837, were, however, statutory; Succession to the Crown Act 1707 (6 Anne c. 41), s. 10 and Regency Act 1831 (1 Will IV, c. 2), s. 2 respectively. The former was because of the need for provision for a smooth succession in troubled political times. The Act required privy counsellors and other officers, in the event of Anne's death, to proclaim as her successor the next Protestant in the line of succession to the throne, and made it high treason for any of them to fail to do so. The later was because of the possibility, anticipated in 1831, of the heiress

but the idea that an Accession Council makes it dates only to the accession of James I in 1603, when the fact that James I was in Scotland required immediate action in London, without waiting for the new king's specific consent or involvement—although as noted above—his prior consent had been obtained while the late Queen was still alive. Before 1603 the accession proclamations were made by the Sovereign himself.

The Accession Council called to proclaim the new Sovereign comprised, at its core, members of the Privy Council, but is not limited to that august body. It may also be recalled that the Accession Council, as principally composed of members of the Privy Council, descends from the ancient Council, and earlier still, the *Witan*, whose role it was, inter alia, to elect a new king from amongst the eligible members of the Royal Family, the ætheling. The Accession Proclamation, as a statement from the Accession Council, a body which—excepting its core, the Privy Council[19]—which has no explicit legal existence, has no constitutive legal role, and is a public statement of fact and law; with the death of one Sovereign, another has ascended the throne, and is now in their turn owed loyalty, fealty and homage. There is no reliance on any specific statutory or other law—the inference is that succession is by hereditary right (as modified or limited by statute)—and there is most definitely no suggestion that any legal steps are required to constitute the new Sovereign.

In 2022, as is customary, the Lord President of the Council presided over the Accession Council. Due to a recent change of Prime Minister—the appointment of Elizabeth Truss two days before the Queen's death

presumptive, Princess Alexandrina Victoria (now Queen Victoria), being supplanted by a posthumous heir or heiress born to Queen Adelaide, widow of William IV.

[19] In 1952 the members were advised on 6th February thus—

> Let the messenger acquaint the lords and others of Her Majesty's Most Honourable Privy Council, that the Accession Council is appointed to meet at the Court at St James's Palace (entrance Ambassadors Court) on Wednesday, the 6th day of this instant February at 5 p.m. of the clock.

On the 7th February 1952 members were advised that—

> The Accession Council (second part) will be held at St James's Palace on Friday 8th instant at 10 a.m. Entrance in Ambassadors Court. Ordinary Clothes. Visiting card should be handed to messenger on entering. F. J. Fernau, Clerk of the Council

was the last constitutional function she exercised—Penelope (Penny) Mordaunt had been appointed Lord President but not yet "declared" during a meeting of the "King in Council" (the Privy Council); the new ministry was in the course of being appointed. However, an Acting Lord President need only be a Privy Counsellor, which Ms Mordaunt was, although the actual Lord President that Mordaunt was apparently acting for, Mark Spencer, was also present at the Accession Council.[20] He was in the process of being replaced, a situation which doubtless must have added to the stress and complexity of preparing the business of the Accession Council.

The Accession Council for King Charles III met in London 10 am Saturday 10th September 2022, the previous Sovereign, Elizabeth II, having died at 3.10 p.m. in the afternoon of Thursday 8th September.[21] Over time various technological changes have aided in efficiently and speedily summoning members of the Accession Council. In 1936 privy counsellors were summoned via a radio broadcast, in 2022 the Privy Council Office website simply asked them to monitor their email inboxes. As with all Privy Council meetings since the time of Queen Victoria, proceedings were conducted with all in attendance standing.

The first part of the Accession Council meeting lasted for merely nine minutes, and in that time concluded business including the approval of eight Orders of Council. Attendance included selected privy counsellors, the Lord Mayor and Aldermen of the City of London,[22] and Commonwealth realm High Commissioners, a total of some 200 in all. In a break with tradition, not all Privy Counsellors (more than 700) were invited to Parts I and II. Instead, 177 were summonsed to attend either ex-officio or through having won a place in a ballot.[23] The meeting was held in the Picture Gallery of St James's Palace.

[20] Torrance, David, "The Accession of King Charles III" (House of Commons Library Research Briefing, number CBP9621, 29 September 2022).

[21] The *London Gazette Extraordinary*, 9 September 2022, no 63808 (announcement of death).

[22] According to the official list of attendees, three aldermen were present (of the 25 members of the Court of Aldermen, one of whom was the incumbent Lord Mayor, and another his successor. The third alderman present was the second Sheriff, thus both Sheriffs were in attendance; "Attendees at the Accession Council", 10th September 2022.

[23] Torrance, David, "The Accession of King Charles III" (House of Commons Library Research Briefing, number CBP9621, 29 September 2022).

The second part of the Accession Council, the holding by the Sovereign of his or her first Council, is attended by Privy Counsellors only. The Council met, as has become customary, in the Throne Room of St James's Palace. The formal business of the first meeting of the Privy Council of King Charles III included approving twelve prerogative Orders in Council[24] (additional to the eight Orders of Council made at the first part of the Accession Council). Additionally, several statutory Orders in Council were approved. The King's first Statutory Order in Council provided that the Sovereign Grant provisions would expire six months after the end of the present reign,[25] as certain provisions of the Sovereign Grant Act 2011 cease to have effect six months after the death of a monarch unless alternative provision is made by an Order in Council within six months of the new reign. This new statutory framework was the likely reason, it can be surmised, that the Sovereign Grant was referred to by the new King in his Declaration, the first time that royal finances had formed part of the business of a modern Accession Council. In 2022 the whole meeting of the second part of the Accession Council took only 16 minutes. The proceedings of both parts were televised for the first time (including being streamed on the Internet), in a sign of the significantly changed expectations—and technology—from 1952.

The Accession Proclamation

Although the various Orders in both the first and second parts of the Accession Council were legally, constitutionally or practically significant and necessary, the most important role constitutionally for the Accession Council—and one which occurs in the absence of the Sovereign—is the

[24] These authorised publication of the King's personal Declaration; the "transmission" of the two signed copies of the Scottish Oath to the Court of Session in Edinburgh and the Privy Council Office in London; the form of Proclamation for proclaiming King Charles III in the British Overseas Territories; and authorising the Lord Chancellor, Lord Privy Seal, Principal Secretaries of State, the Chancellor of the Exchequer, the Chancellor of the Duchy of Lancaster, the Secretary of State for Northern Ireland, the First Ministers of Scotland and Wales to make use of their respective Seals until replacements were prepared and authorised by The King; Torrance, David, "The Accession of King Charles III" (House of Commons Library Research Briefing, number CBP9621, 29 September 2022).

[25] The Sovereign Grant Act 2011 (Duration of Sovereign Grant Provisions) Order 2022.

proclamation of the new King. Yet the accession proclamation is, legally, no more than a public statement of what has occurred, not the cause of that change. It is, as it were, a press release or special news bulletin. This is shown by the words used in the accession proclamation. For example, the proclamation of Queen Elizabeth II in 1952 stated.

> Whereas it hath pleased Almighty God to call to His Mercy our late Sovereign Lord King George the Sixth of Blessed and Glorious Memory by whose Decease the Crown is solely and rightfully come to the High and Mighty Princess Elizabeth Alexandra Mary: We, therefore, the Lords Spiritual and Temporal of this Realm, being here assisted with these of His late Majesty's Privy Council, with representatives of other members of the Commonwealth, with other Principal Gentlemen of Quality, with the Lord Mayor, Alderman and Citizens of London, do now hereby with one voice and Consent of Tongue and Heart publish and proclaim that the High and Mighty Princess Elizabeth Alexandra Mary is now, by the Death of our late Sovereign of Happy Memory, become Queen Elizabeth the Second, by the Grace of God Queen of this Realm and of all Her other Realms and Territories, Head of the Commonwealth, Defender of the Faith, to whom Her lieges do acknowledge all Faith and constant Obedience, with hearty and humble Affection; beseeching God, by whom Kings and Queens do reign, to bless the Royal Princess Elizabeth the Second with long and happy Years to reign over us.
>
> Given at St. James's Palace this Sixth Day of February in the year of our Lord one thousand nine hundred and fifty-two.
>
> Simonds C. W. S. Morrison. Harry Crookshank. Norfolk, E.M.
> Winston S. Churchill. C. R. Attlee. Leathers. Ogmore.
>
> David Maxwell Fyfe. Waverley. Selbourne. James Griffiths.
> Woolton. Samuel. Davidson. Arthur G. Bottomley.[26]

The key words are that the Crown is "solely and rightfully come" to the new Queen, that the Accession Council "publish and proclaim" that

[26] The *London Gazette*, 8 February 1952, no 39462, p. 787. The signatories numbered 191 in total, led by the signed by the Lord Chancellor first, followed by the half dozen or so most senior Cabinet ministers and in no particular order thereafter by the remainder of the nearly 200 people attending the Accession Council; Morris, R. M., *Inaugurating a New Reign* (2018), p. 8.

the Crown "is now, by the Death of our late Sovereign", "become Queen Elizabeth the Second, by the Grace of God Queen of this Realm and of all Her other Realms and Territories, Head of the Commonwealth, Defender of the Faith", and that "Her lieges do acknowledge all Faith and constant Obedience". The Crown was no longer described as "imperial", as it had been in every accession proclamation since at least the time of Edward VI, an omission doubtless inspired by the independence of the Indian subcontinent, and the approaching dissolution of the remaining parts of the British Empire, a process which was largely complete within ten years. It may be observed, of course, that the word "imperial" is not, historically, to be taken to refer to the British Empire, as it predates that, and instead refers to the imperial status of the Kings of England; a distinction unlikely to have been well understood publicly or possibly even officially. Its removal in 1952 is thus not surprising, though it may be regrettable.

The proclamation of 1952 varied noticeably from the previous usual wording, partly due to constitutional and political changes in the years since 1936 (primarily the end of the British Empire). The style now included "Head of the Commonwealth", and the list of members of the Accession Council now included "representatives of the members of the Commonwealth". The expression "we do acknowledge" became "her lieges acknowledge"; and "become our only lawful and rightful Liege Lord/Lady" was now "become Queen". The Crown which came to the princess is unspecified. Most strikingly, the style under which she is proclaimed, "Queen of this Realm and of all Her other Realms and Territories [...]" was not the correct royal style (which was the same as that used for her father's accession, with "Emperor of India" omitted). This is probably due to the fact that the status of "Ireland" was politically sensitive since the proclamation of the Republic in 1949, but the style had not yet been officially altered (it would only be in May 1953, more than a year after the accession, that this was regularised). It must be noted, however, that in Canada Elizabeth II was proclaimed "our only lawful and rightful Liege Lady Elizabeth the Second by the Grace of God, of Great Britain, Ireland and the British Dominions beyond the Seas QUEEN, Defender of the Faith, Supreme Liege Lady in and over Canada"; she was also proclaimed queen of Ireland in South Africa.[27]

[27] See May, Henry, *The South African Constitution* (3rd ed., 1955), p. 164.

Unsurprisingly, the accession proclamation of King George VI was unique, given that his accession was not due to the death of his predecessor, but to his abdication—and that effected by Act of Parliament.[28] The wording was thus.

> Whereas by an Instrument of Abdication dated the Tenth day of December instant His former Majesty King Edward the Eighth did declare His irrevocable Determination to renounce the Throne for Himself and His Descendants, and the said Instrument of Abdication has now taken effect, whereby the Imperial Crown of Great Britain, Ireland, and all other His former Majesty's dominions is now solely and rightfully come to the High and Mighty Albert Frederick Arthur George : We, therefore, the Lords Spiritual and Temporal of this Realm, being here assisted with these of His former Majesty's Privy Council, with numbers of other Principal Gentlemen of Quality, with the Lord-Mayor, Aldermen, and citizens of London, do now hereby, with one Voice and Consent of Tongue and Heart, publish and proclaim, That the High and Mighty Prince Albert Frederick Arthur George, is now become our only lawful and rightful Liege Lord George the Sixth by the Grace of God, of Great Britain, Ireland, and the British Dominions beyond the Seas King, Defender of the Faith, Emperor of India: To whom we do acknowledge all Faith and constant Obedience, with all hearty and humble Affection: beseeching God, by whom Kings and Queens do reign, to bless the Royal Prince George the Sixth, with long and happy years to reign over Us.
>
> Given at St. James's Palace, this Twelfth day of December in the year of our Lord One thousand nine hundred and thirty-six.[29]

The usual recitation of the demise of the Crown was inapplicable due to the Abdication, and the wording simply states that the "Instrument has now taken effect"—there is no statement as to precisely what legal mechanism was used to affect the demise, although the words can be read—incorrectly—as to suggest that the Instrument of Abdication itself affected the demise of the Crown. This might therefore seem an unusual omission, except that the Accession Council does not concern itself with the legal or practical niceties of how a Sovereign becomes king or queen, only the fact that they are now the Sovereign.

[28] HM Declaration of Abdication Act 1936 (10 Edw VIII & 1 Geo VI c 3).

[29] *London Gazette*, 14th December 1937.

The wording of the Proclamation for King Charles III was slightly simplified from that of 1952. It was.

> Whereas it has pleased almighty God to call to his mercy our late Sovereign lady Queen Elizabeth II of blessed and glorious memory, by whose decease the Crown of the United Kingdom of Great Britain and Northern Ireland is solely and rightfully come to the Prince Charles Philip Arthur George. We, therefore, the lords spiritual and temporal of this realm, and members of the House of Commons, together with other members of Her late Majesty's Privy Council, and representatives of the realms and territories, aldermen, and citizens of London and others, do now hereby, with one voice and consent of tongue and heart, publish and proclaim that the Prince Charles Philip Arthur George, is now, by the death of our late Sovereign of happy memory, become our only lawful and rightful liege lord, Charles III, by the grace of God, of the United Kingdom and Northern Ireland, and of his other realms and territories, King, head of the Commonwealth, defender of the faith, to whom we do acknowledge all faith and obedience with humble affection, beseeching God, by whom kings and queens do reign, to bless His Majesty with long and happy years to reign over us.[30]

The changes in 2022 were largely stylistic, slightly shortening the text, whilst retaining other changes made in turn in 1952. However, "Members of the House of Commons" was added after "Lords Spiritual and Temporal", and "representatives of the Realms and Territories" substituted for "representatives of other Members of the Commonwealth". The phrase "other Principal Gentlemen of Quality" was omitted, as was mention of the Lord Mayor of London. The phrase "High and Mighty", which once preceded the new monarch's name, was also absent.[31]

"Members of the House of Commons", after "Lords Spiritual and Temporal" was doubtless added to reflect the increased significance and indeed dominance of the House of Commons at the expense of the House of Lords, not just because of the Parliament Act 1911[32] and

[30] *London Gazette*, 12th September 2022, no 63812, p. 1; Supplement No. 1 to *The London Gazette* Extraordinary of Friday, 9 September, 2022.

[31] Torrance, David, "The Accession of King Charles III" (House of Commons Library Research Briefing, number CBP9621, 29 September 2022).

[32] 1 & 2 Geo. V. c. 13.

the Parliament Act 1949,[33] but also the House of Lords Act 1999. The expression "representatives of the Realms and Territories" reflected the modern nature and constitutional significance of the Commonwealth, limiting attendance in London to those states which had the Sovereign as their head of state; "representatives of other Members of the Commonwealth" (itself new in 1952) being inappropriate today as the Commonwealth as a whole includes a majority of republics or indigenous monarchies. The phrase "other Principal Gentlemen of Quality" was omitted possibly because of its gender limitation, as updating it to "other Principal Gentlemen and Ladies of Quality" could still be seen as antiquated if not problematic from a social perspective. The phrase "High and Mighty" was probably abandoned for a similar reason, whilst the mention of the Lord Mayor of London was likely abandoned to reflect the diminished status of the office after the creation of the new London mayoralty in 2000.[34] It is likely that the text, complete with its additions and subtractions, had evolved over a long period of time.

The timing of the Proclamation has varied considerably, though in modern times it always follows Part I of the Accession Council. In the case of King Charles III, the conclusion of Part II of the Accession Council was followed, at 11 am Saturday 10th September 2022, by the reading of the Proclamation from the balcony overlooking Friary Court at St James's Palace. The Proclamation was read by Garter Principal King of Arms (David White), accompanied by the Earl Marshal, other Officers of Arms and the Serjeants at Arms. There was later a second London proclamation at the Royal Exchange.[35] Prior to 2022 additional proclamations were also made at Temple Bar and the Charing Cross.[36] These were possibly

[33] 12, 13 & 14 Geo. VI c. 103.

[34] Greater London Authority Act 1999.

[35] Both London proclamations were required by Order of Council passed by the first part of the Accession Council; "It is this day ordered in Council that the Kings of Arms, Heralds and Pursuivants do attend at the Court at St. James's to proceed with the usual ceremonies to proclaim His Majesty King Charles the Third", 10th September 2022; "It is this day ordered in Council that the Lord Mayor of the City of London, the Court of Aldermen, and Commons of London do attend at the Royal Exchange in order to proclaim His Majesty King Charles the Third", 10th September 2022.

[36] No statement was made about this. It is possible this was purely an economy measure, or it may have been in reflection of the diminished role of the City of London. The custom had been to lay the proclamation before the Court of Aldermen and to read it, after a ceremony at Temple Bar, London, at the corner of Chancery Lane, in Fleet

dispensed with as an economy measure and as redundant, or to reflect the reduced status of the City of London; by far the greatest number of people hearing and seeing the proclamations would have done so via electronic media of one sort or another. Whilst the number of London proclamations were reduced, additional emphasis was placed upon the proclamations in the constituent nations of the United Kingdom.

Reflecting the status of Scotland, and Northern Ireland (the latter as the surviving remnant of the Kingdom of Ireland), separate proclamations were made in Edinburgh and Belfast.[37] The Cardiff proclamation for the first time reflected the enhanced status of Wales.[38] The Lord Lieutenant for South Glamorgan, Morfudd Meredith, and Wales Herald of Arms Extraordinary, Thomas Lloyd, made the "Proclamation for Wales" in Welsh and English at 1200 on 11th September 2022. They did so from a dais in the grounds of Cardiff Castle. The Welsh Proclamation was as follows:

> FFURF AR BROCLAMASIWN AR GYFER DATGAN Y SOFRAN NEWYDD YN Y DEYRNAS UNEDIG
>
> Gan ei bod wedi rhyngu bodd i Dduw Hollalluog i alw i'w Ofal ein diweddar Sofran, yr Arglwyddes Frenhines Elizabeth yr Ail, o Fendigaid a Gogoneddus Goffadwriaeth, y mae Coron Teyrnas Unedig Prydain Fawr a Gogledd Iwerddon, oblegid ei Hymadawiad, wedi dod yn gwbl ac yn gyfiawn i ran y Tywysog Charles Philip Arthur George: Yr ydym ninnau, felly, Arglwyddi Ysbrydol a Thymhorol y Deyrnas hon ac Aelodau o Dŷ'r Cyffredin, ynghyd ag aelodau eraill o Gyfrin Gyngor Ei diweddar Fawrhydi, cynrychiolwyr y Teyrnasoedd a'r Tiriogaethau, Henaduriaid a Dinasyddion Llundain, ac eraill, yn awr yn datgan ac yn cyhoeddi drwy hyn yn unllais ac o Galon a Thafod unfryd fod y Tywysog Charles Philip Arthur George, bellach, oblegid Marwolaeth ein diweddar Sofran o Serchus Goffadwriaeth, wedi dod inni yn unig gyfreithlon a chyfiawn Ddyledog Arglwydd Charles y Trydydd, drwy Ras Duw, ar Deyrnas Unedig Prydain Fawr a Gogledd Iwerddon a'i Deyrnasoedd eraill, yn Frenin, yn Ben ar y Gymanwlad, yn

Street, and at the Royal Exchange. However, in 1952 the proclamation was read by Garter Principal King of Arms, Sir George Bellew, first at 11 a.m. from the Friary Court balcony, then in Trafalgar Square, in Fleet Street, and at the Royal Exchange.

[37] See the Union with Scotland Act 1707 (6 Anne c. 11), the Scotland Act 1998 and Northern Ireland Act 1998.

[38] See the Government of Wales Acts 1998 and 2006.

Amddiffynnwr y Ffydd, i'r hwn yr ydym yn datgan, ag Anwylserch gostyngedig, ein holl Ffydd a'n Hufudd-dod; gan atolwg ar i Dduw, drwy'r hwn y mae Brenhinoedd a Breninesau yn teyrnasu, fendithio Ei Fawrhydi â hir Oes hapus i deyrnasu drosom.

Rhoddwyd ym Mhalas St. James y degfed dydd o fis Medi ym mlwyddyn Ein Harglwydd dwy fil a dwy ar hugain.

DUW A GADWO'R BRENIN[39]

The United Kingdom (London) standard proclamation was also read in the overseas territories. In the Isle of Man, however, the proclamation differed in that it included a local title for the first time, doubtless reflecting the enhanced constitutional status of the Crown dependency since 1952.[40] During a ceremony at Government House in Onchan, the Lieutenant-Governor, General Sir John Lorimer, proclaimed The King.

Charles III by the grace of God of the United Kingdom of Great Britain and Northern Ireland and of his other realms and territories King, Lord of Mann, head of the Commonwealth, Defender of the Faith, to whom we do acknowledge all faith and constant obedience [...] God save the King, Lord of Mann.[41]

From 1399 the Kings and (from 1504) Lords of Mann were vassals of the kings of England. For several centuries the position was held by the Stanleys, Earls of Derby. In 1765 the title was revested in the Crown, after the last lord proprietor, the Duchess of Atholl, sold the title, which was subsequently assumed by the Sovereign.[42] A second Proclamation

[39] Welsh Government, FFURF AR BROCLAMASIWN AR GYFER DATGAN Y SOFRAN NEWYDD YN Y DEYRNAS UNEDIG. <https://llyw.cymru/sites/default/files/publications/2022-09/broclamasiwn-sofran-deyrnas-unedig.pdf>.

[40] See the *Royal Commission on the Constitution 1969–1973*, Volume I, Report (Cmnd 5460) (Report). London, 1973.

[41] Proclamation of the Lord of Mann at St. John's, 16th September 2022; <https://www.tynwald.org.im/about/tynday/Documents/20220914-Proclamation-Print-Format.pdf>.

[42] The Isle of Mann Purchase Act 1765 (5 Geo. III c. 26). Under the Isle of Man Purchase Act, the Atholl's still retained their manorial rights, the patronage of the bishopric, and certain other perquisites, until these in turn were sold in 1828; Duke of Atholl's Rights, Isle of Man Act 1825 (6 Geo. IV c. 34).

took place on Tynwald Hill in St John's on 16th September, this time in English and in Manx Gaelic.[43]

Equivalent proclamations occurred in the realms. For example, in Canada, the text for the proclamation of King Charles III in 2022 was as follows.

> TO ALL TO WHOM these presents shall come or whom the same may in any way concern,
> GREETING:
> Whereas our late Sovereign, Queen Elizabeth the Second, passed away on September 8, 2022, by whose death the Crown of Canada vests in His Royal Highness Prince Charles Philip Arthur George;
> We, the Right Honourable Mary May Simon, Governor General of Canada, assisted by His Majesty's Privy Council for Canada, proclaim that His Royal Highness Prince Charles Philip Arthur George is now, by the death of our late Sovereign, Charles the Third, by the Grace of God of the United Kingdom, Canada and His other Realms and Territories King, Head of the Commonwealth, Defender of the Faith, to whom we acknowledge faith and allegiance.
> Given under my Hand and Seal of Office at Ottawa, this tenth day of September, two thousand and twenty-two.
> Long Live the King[44]

Likewise, separate, unique, proclamations were made in Australia and New Zealand. In the first case it was.

[43] <https://www.tynwald.org.im/about/tynday/Documents/20220914-Proclamation-Print-Format.pdf> and <https://www.itv.com/news/granada/2022-09-16/lieutenant-governor-praised-for-speaking-manx-during-proclamation>.

[44] "Proclamation Proclaiming that His Royal Highness Prince Charles Philip Arthur George Is Now, by the Death of Our Late Sovereign, King Charles the Third: SI/2022-42". *Canada Gazette*, Part II, Volume 156, Extra Number 4. 10 September 2022.

Whereas because of the death of our blessed and glorious Queen Elizabeth II, the Crown has solely and rightfully come to Prince Charles Philip Arthur George.
We, therefore, General the Honourable David Hurley AC DSC (Retd), Governor-General of the Commonwealth of Australia, and members of the Federal Executive Council, do now proclaim Prince Charles Philip Arthur George to be King Charles III, By Grace of God, King of Australia and his realms and territories, Head of the Commonwealth, and with hearty and humble affection, we promise him faith and obedience. May King Charles III have long and happy years to reign over us.
Given at Canberra, this 11th day of September, 2022, and in the first year of His Majesty's reign.
Signed by me, as Governor-General and counter-signed by my command, by the Honourable Anthony Albanese MP, Prime Minister of the Commonwealth of Australia.
God Save the King[45]

In New Zealand the text of the proclamation was

Whereas by the death of our late beloved Sovereign Queen Elizabeth II, the Crown is solely and rightfully come to His Royal Highness Prince Charles Philip Arthur George.

We, therefore, The Right Honourable Dame Cindy Kiro, Governor-General of New Zealand, The Right Honourable Jacinda Ardern, Prime Minister of New Zealand, and Members of the Executive Council, assisted by members of Parliament, Judges, Representatives of the Realm, and numerous other representative citizens here present, hereby proclaim that His Royal Highness Prince Charles Philip Arthur George is now King Charles III, By the Grace of God King of New Zealand and of His Other Realms and Territories, Head of the Commonwealth, Defender of the Faith, to whom His subjects swear their faith and true allegiance, with hearty affection; wishing His Majesty King Charles III a long and happy reign.

Given under the hand of Her Excellency the Governor-General, and issued under the Seal of New Zealand, this 11th day of September 2022.

[45] The Australia Proclamation 11th September 2022, was also replicated, in slight variations, in all the states.

Jacinda Ardern, Prime Minister

God Save the King.[46]

In both Canada and New Zealand (as in Wales, and the Isle of Mann) the reading of the proclamation was in two languages, English and French, and English and Māori, respectively. This reflected the fact that in both countries these are official languages. In New Zealand the proclamation was also simultaneously translated into New Zealand sign language, this being also an official language.[47]

The Sovereign's Declaration

Like the accession proclamation, the Sovereign's declaration to the Accession Council is non-statutory, and although often referred to as the Accession Declaration,[48] must be distinguished from the statutory Accession Declaration and the other statutory oath which must be taken. The declaration follows no set form but normally relates to the death of the previous Sovereign. The declaration by Elizabeth II was as follows.

> Your Royal Highnesses, My Lords, Ladies and Gentlemen: By the sudden death of my dear Father, I am called to assume the duties and responsibilities of the Sovereignty. At this time of deep sorrow, it is a profound consolation to me to be assured of the sympathy which you and all my Peoples feel towards me, to my Mother, and my Sister, and to the other members of my Family. My Father was our revered and beloved Head, as he was of the wider Family of his subjects: the grief that his loss brings is shared among us all. My heart is too full to say more to you today than that I shall always work, as my Father did throughout his Reign, to uphold constitutional government and to advance the happiness and prosperity of my Peoples, spread as they are all the world over. I know that in my resolve to follow his shining example of service and devotion, I shall be inspired by the loyalty and affection of those whose Queen I have been called to be, and by the counsel of their elected Parliaments. I pray that God will

[46] *New Zealand Gazette*, 11th September 2022, no 3873.

[47] New Zealand Sign Language Act 2006.

[48] Hazell, Robert and R. M. Morris, *Swearing in the New King* (2018).

help me discharge worthily this heavy task that has been laid upon me so early in my life.[49]

The personal declaration by King Charles III was similar, but with a slightly different emphasis—for example, "happiness and prosperity" becomes "peace, harmony and prosperity", and "my Peoples, spread as they are all the world over" becomes "the peoples of these Islands and of the Commonwealth Realms and Territories throughout the world":

My Lords, Ladies, and Gentlemen.
It is my most sorrowful duty to announce to you the death of my beloved Mother, The Queen.
I know how deeply you, the entire Nation – and I think I may say the whole world – sympathise with me in the irreparable loss we have all suffered. It is the greatest consolation to me to know of the sympathy expressed by so many to my Sister and Brothers and that such overwhelming affection and support should be extended to our whole family in our loss.
To all of us as a family, as to this kingdom and the wider family of nations of which it is a part, my Mother gave an example of lifelong love and of selfless service.
My Mother's reign was unequalled in its duration, its dedication and its devotion. Even as we grieve, we give thanks for this most faithful life.
I am deeply aware of this great inheritance and of the duties and heavy responsibilities of Sovereignty which have now passed to me.
In taking up these responsibilities, I shall strive to follow the inspiring example I have been set in upholding constitutional government and to seek the peace, harmony and prosperity of the peoples of these Islands and of the Commonwealth Realms and Territories throughout the world.
In this purpose, I know that I shall be upheld by the affection and loyalty of the peoples whose Sovereign I have been called upon to be, and that in the discharge of these duties I will be guided by the counsel of their elected parliaments. In all this, I am profoundly encouraged by the constant support of my beloved wife.
I take this opportunity to confirm my willingness and intention to continue the tradition of surrendering the hereditary revenues, including the Crown Estate, to My Government for the benefit of all, in return for the Sovereign Grant, which supports My official duties as Head of State and Head of Nation.

49 *London Gazette* 12 February 1952, Declaration made on 8th February.

> And in carrying out the heavy task that has been laid upon me, and to which I now dedicate what remains to me of my life, I pray for the guidance and help of Almighty God.[50]

The most significant feature is that there is a specific reference to the Sovereign Grant,[51] the latest form of the arrangement for financing the operation of the monarchy, in place from 1760 with the Civil List,[52] and indeed in an earlier form from 1688.[53] The other changes served perhaps to reduce any emphasis upon ties of loyalty and the Sovereign-subject relationship, in favour of a greater emphasis upon harmony and affection. It is also, perhaps curiously, couched in terms of the new King notifying the Accession Council of the death of the late Queen—curious in that it occurred immediately after the second part of the Accession Council concluded. This might perhaps have been more logically placed before the Accession Council commenced its business.

The Statutory Oaths and Declarations

The steps which occur on the accession serve to illustrate the fact that succession to the Crown is not solely dependent upon parliamentary authority or approval, though Parliament is not uninvolved. These oaths reflect the constitutional structure of the United Kingdom. Apart from the Accession Proclamation, upon succeeding to the throne the new Sovereign must take certain oaths, including two statutory oaths relating to the establishment of the churches in England and Scotland.

One of the first acts of the new Sovereign after making his or her Declaration is to take and subscribe to the Oath relating to the security of the Church of Scotland as required by the 25th Article of the Act

[50] "His Majesty's Declaration", 10th September 2022; *Supplement No. 1 to The London Gazette* Extraordinary of Friday, 9 September, 2022. 12 September 2022 number 63812.

[51] Sovereign Grant Act 2011.

[52] Civil List Act 1760 (1 Geo. 3 c. 1).

[53] Reitan, E. A., "The Civil List in Eighteenth-Century British Politics: Parliamentary Supremacy versus the Independence of the Crown" (1966) 9(3) The Historical Journal 318–337, 323.

of Union 1706.[54] This Oath has been taken by every Sovereign at their Accession since King George I in 1714.[55] The wording is as follows.

> I, [INSERT TITLE] by the Grace of God of the United Kingdom of Great Britain and Northern Ireland and of My other Realms and Territories King, Defender of the Faith, do faithfully promise and swear that I shall inviolably maintain and preserve the Settlement of the true Protestant Religion as established by the Laws made in Scotland in prosecution of the Claim of Right and particularly by an Act intituled "An Act for securing the Protestant Religion and Presbyterian Church Government" and by the Acts passed in the Parliament of both Kingdoms for Union of the two Kingdoms, together with the Government, Worship, Discipline, Rights and Privileges of the Church of Scotland. So help me God.[56]

Apart from the requirement to take the oaths, any person coming into possession of the Crown must join in communion with the Church of England.[57] In practice, the Sovereign has also been a member of the Church of Scotland, and worships in accordance with the rites of the Established Church in Scotland whilst resident within that kingdom. There is however no legal requirement that the Sovereign be a member of the Church of Scotland.[58] The Sovereign is not head of the established church in Scotland, unlike in England,[59] although since 1690 he does annually appoint the Lord High Commissioner to the General Assembly, who is the Sovereign's personal representative to the General Assembly of the Church of Scotland (the Kirk), reflecting the latter's role as the national church of Scotland, and the Sovereign's role as a member of that

[54] 6 Anne c.11.

[55] Privy Council Office, "The Accession Council" <https://privycouncil.independent.gov.uk/privy-council/the-accession-council/>.

[56] Ibid. This was taken and subscribed to by King Charles III at the Accession Council on 10th September 2022; Supplement No. 1 to *The London Gazette Extraordinary* of Friday, 9 September, 2022. 12 September 2022 number 63812.

[57] Act of Settlement 1700 (12 & 13 Will. III c. 2), s. 3.

[58] Nor, indeed, need they be a member of the Church of England, merely in communion with it. Kings George I and George II were German Lutherans. Members of the Sovereign's family need not be in communion with, or members of, the Church of England. The Duke of Edinburgh, before marrying The Queen, was received into the Church, being previously as a member of the Greek Orthodox Church.

[59] Richardson, John, "No king but Caesar? The Headship of the Church in Anglican Theology" (2002) 116(4) Churchman 305–325.

Church.[60] It is, however, provided as a fundamental term of the union of England with Scotland that every person who succeeds to the Crown must take and subscribe the oaths for the preservation of the Established Church in England and the Presbyterian Church in Scotland.[61] These are separate oaths to the coronation oath and accession declaration.

The Accession Declaration should be in the form specified by Sect. 4.1 of the Bill of Rights 1689.[62] This is to the effect that he or she is a faithful Protestant, and will, according to the true intent of the enactments which secure the Protestant succession to the throne, uphold and maintain those enactments to the best of his or her powers according to law.[63]

This current wording is relatively benign, but it was not always so, and indeed the wording has caused discomfort and embarrassment to several generations of Sovereigns. According to s 2 of the Act of Settlement 1700,[64] the new Sovereign had to read out a declaration at their coronation in which he asserted his own orthodoxy and condemned the doctrine of transubstantiation. They also proclaimed from the throne that.

[60] Mechie, Stewart, *The Office of the Lord High Commissioner* (1957).

[61] See the Union with Scotland Act 1706 (6 Ann c. 11), art. xxv, and ss. 2-5. The oath for the preservation of the Established Church of England is now administered as part of the coronation oath. The oath for the preservation of the Presbyterian Church in Scotland was taken by Queen Elizabeth II at a meeting of the Privy Council held immediately after her accession, the instrument being subscribed in duplicate, and one part sent to the Court of Session to be recorded in the Books of Sederunt, and afterwards to be lodged in the Public Register of Scotland, the other part remaining among the records of the Council to be entered in the Council Book: see the *London Gazette Extraordinary*, 8th February 1952, p. 861.

[62] 1 Will. III & Mary sess. 2 c. 2.

[63] Bill of Rights 1689 (1 Will. & Mary sess. 2 c. 2), s. 1; Act of Settlement 1700 (12 & 13 Will. III c. 2), s. 2; Accession Declaration Act 1910 (10 Edw. VII & 1 Geo. V c. 29). The declaration was made by King George V at the opening of Parliament, and therefore the necessity for making it at the coronation did not arise: 7 H.L. Official Reports (5th series), col. 4. The same was true in the case of Queen Elizabeth II. King George VI made the declaration during the coronation service: see *Supplement to the London Gazette*, 10th November 1937, p. 7054. For the purposes of any enactment requiring an oath or declaration to be taken, made or subscribed by the Sovereign on or after the accession, the date on which the Sovereign attains the age of eighteen years is deemed to be the date of the accession: Regency Act 1937 (1 Edw. VIII & 1 Geo. VI c. 16), s. 1(2).

[64] 12 & 13 Will III. c. 2.

> the Invocation or Adoration of the Virgin Mary or any other Saint, and the Sacrifice of the Mass, as they are now used in the Church of Rome, are superstitious and idolatrous.[65]

Such words, of great significance in the sixteenth century, and central to the constitutional polity even in the eighteenth century, had become, by the twentieth century, not merely anachronistic but also embarrassing. This was not merely because of nineteenth century Roman Catholic emancipation, or even because the age of violent religious polemic had passed, but because the ecclesiological and theological complexion of the Church of England had changed, and there was now a more nuanced understanding of doctrine and ecclesiology. The understanding of orthodoxy and the relationship between the Church of England and the church universal had changed.[66]

Although the doctrine of transubstantiation was condemned in the formularies, it was accepted by many high church and Anglo-Catholic sections of the church.[67] Likewise, "the Invocation or Adoration of the

[65] The full wording was—
I, A. B., by the grace of God King (or Queen) of England, Scotland and Ireland, Defender of the Faith, do solemnly and sincerely in the presence of God, profess, testify, and declare, that I do believe that in the Sacrament of the Lord's Supper there is not any Transubstantiation of the elements of bread and wine into the Body and Blood of Christ at or after the consecration thereof by any person whatsoever: and that the invocation or adoration of the Virgin Mary or any other Saint, and the Sacrifice of the Mass, as they are now used in the Church of Rome, are superstitious and idolatrous. And I do solemnly in the presence of God profess, testify, and declare that I do make this declaration, and every part thereof, in the plain and ordinary sense of the words read unto me, as they are commonly understood by English Protestants, without any such dispensation from any person or authority or person whatsoever, or without thinking that I am or can be acquitted before God or man, or absolved of this declaration or any part thereof, although the Pope, or any other person or persons, or power whatsoever, should dispense with or annul the same or declare that it was null and void from the beginning.

[66] Cox, Noel, *Priest of the Church or priest of a church* (2021), chapter 1, pp. 1–32.

[67] Article 28 of the *Thirty-Nine Articles of Religion* (1562, confirmed 1571 by the Subscription (Thirty-Nine Articles) Act 1571 (13 Eliz. I c. 12)). For attempts to reconcile the Article see Newman, John Henry, *Essays and Sketches* ed. Charles Frederick Harrold (1948), in particular, Tract 90.

Virgin Mary or any other Saint", had, thanks to the work of the Tractarians and the Oxford Movement, become commonplace in the Church of England in the course of the nineteenth and twentieth centuries.[68] In addition, "the Sacrifice of the Mass, as they are now used in the Church of Rome", was no longer regarded as wholly abhorrent, and some Roman Catholic liturgical texts were even adopted in some Anglican parishes.[69] Liturgical studies had also led to improved understanding of the development and nature of the eucharist.[70] These developments, with increasing œcumenism,[71] made the original wording of the oath under s 2 of the Act of Settlement 1700[72] wholly unacceptable to the new Sovereign. King Edward VII was said to be so offended by the required wording that he recited it almost inaudibly,[73] to avoid giving offense but simultaneously complying with the requirements of the statute law.

In 1910 a revised declaration, introduced by the Accession Declaration Act 1910,[74] allowed the new King George V to merely affirm that he was a faithful member of "the Protestant Reformed Church by law established in England".[75] There was opposition even to this modest declaration, and a final revision, enacted 3rd August 1910, simply said that "I declare that I am a faithful Protestant and will uphold the Protestant succession".[76] In 2023 King Charles III took this oath at his coronation, rather than at the opening of the first parliament of the new monarch's reign (as with Queen Elizabeth II, on 4th November 1952), with the words.

> Archbishop of Canterbury: Your Majesty, are you willing to make, subscribe and declare to the statutory Accession Declaration Oath?

68 Nockles, Peter, *The Oxford Movement in Context* (1997).

69 Holbrooke-Jones, Stanley, "The Triumph of Anglo-Catholicism Challenged" (2005) 119(2) Churchman 159–178.

70 Bradshaw, Paul, *The Search for the Origins of Christian Worship* (2nd ed., 2002).

71 Cox, Noel, *Priest of the Church or priest of a church* (2021), chapter 7, pp. 93–108.

72 12 & 13 Will III. c. 2.

73 Lee, Sir Sidney, *King Edward VII* (1925–27), v. 2.

74 10 Edw. VII & Geo. V c. 29.

75 I [N] de solemnly and sincerely in the presence of God profess, testify and declare that I am a faithful Protestant, and that I will, according to the true intent of the enactments which secure the Protestant succession to the Throne of my Realm, uphold and maintain the said enactments to the best of my powers according to law.

76 Nicolson, Sir Harold, *King George the Fifth His Life and Reign* (1952), pp. 162–163.

The King: I am willing.

The King: I Charles do solemnly and sincerely in the presence of God profess, testify, and declare that I am a faithful Protestant, and that I will, according to the true intent of the enactments which secure the Protestant succession to the Throne, uphold and maintain the said enactments to the best of my powers according to law.[77]

The meaning of this oath of course is that the Sovereign must not be a Roman Catholic. Perhaps in order to pre-emptively respond to any possible offence that this might still engender, despite its wording being mild compared to its original form, in 2023 there was an addition to the coronation service, after an anthem. This was the new King's Prayer. This was.

God of compassion and mercy whose Son was sent not to be served but to serve, give grace that I may find in thy service perfect freedom and in that freedom knowledge of thy truth. Grant that I may be a blessing to all thy children, of every faith and conviction, that together we may discover the ways of gentleness and be led into the paths of peace. through Jesus Christ our Lord. Amen.[78]

This is possibly the first time in British history that such a personal prayer has been voiced so publicly by the Sovereign. The King's Prayer is entirely an innovation in 2023 and represents a significant departure from previous practice, since it seems calculated to allow the King to express his personal spiritual convictions. Significantly, it also highlighted the servant kingship model, a point to be discussed further in Chapter 6. It also sets a broader context for the statutory oaths with respect to the two established churches.

[77] *The Authorised Liturgy for the Coronation Rite of His Majesty King Charles III For use on Saturday 6th May 2023, 11:00am at Westminster Abbey* (2023).

[78] Ibid.

The coronation oath is also to be taken in the form provided by statute,[79] though unlike the Accession Proclamation, the Sovereign's declaration, the oath according to the provisions of the Accession Declaration Act 1910,[80] and the oath in accordance with the Act of Union 1706,[81] it is now likely to occur some considerable time after the accession (and thus allowing time for a change if deemed appropriate). The requirement of s 2 of the Act of Settlement 1700,[82] that the Coronation Oath shall be in accordance with the Coronation Oath Act 1688[83] has not been followed, as the oath has been amended in practice without legislative sanction.[84] There is now a significant divergence between law and practice in this respect,[85] a problem with uncertain implications.[86] Although it would be desirable to regularise this, through an amending statute, but it is unlikely to have a high priority in any government's legislative schedule, and might also raise contentious questions with respect to the precise wording. Fortunately, of course, the title to the Crown is not dependent upon the taking of the coronation oath, in

[79] Act of Settlement 1700 (12 & 13 Will. III c 2), s. 2. In terms of this provision the form of the oath is provided by the Coronation Oath Act 1688 (1 Will. & Mary sess 4 c. 6), s. 3, and must be administered by the Archbishop of Canterbury or York, or any other bishop of the realm appointed by the Sovereign for that purpose, in the presence of all persons attending, assisting or otherwise present at the coronation: s. 4.

[80] 10 Edw. VII & Geo. V c. 29.

[81] Union with Scotland Act 1706 (6 Ann c. 11), art. xxv.

[82] 12 & 13 Will. III. c. 2.

[83] 1 Will. III & Mary c. 6.

[84] *Report of the Justice and Law Reform Committee on the Imperial Laws Application Bill* (1988) Explanatory Material pp. 57–60.

[85] The form of the oath as at present administered differs from that provided by the act owing to the dis-establishment of the Irish Church (by the Irish Church Act 1869 (32 & 33 Vict. c. 42)), and by the provisions of the Union with Scotland Act 1706 (6 Ann c. 11), art. xxv.

[86] Watt, G., "The Coronation Oath" (2017) 19(3) Ecclesiastical Law Journal 325–341.

any particular form.[87] But that does not mean that taking the oath has no constitutional significance or role, a point we shall return to shortly.

The accession proclamation is important, if not now indispensable, but it is the coronation which publicly and formally hallows the new Sovereign, and provides a very public arena for the declaration of the Sovereign's religious orthodoxy and constitutional propriety. The coronation follows seamlessly after the accession and the steps associated with it; as has been observed, the whole bears some resemblance to the ancient Egyptian year of the coronation. The Accession Council, the proclamation of accession, the declaration of religious orthodoxy, and the coronation oath, all form parts of a series of actions designed to establish the new regime in accordance with settled tradition. Compliance with them is important for constitutional reasons, not simply for the sake of tradition, aesthetics, or mere conservatism.

The steps being duly followed, excepting the coronation oath to be taken at the coronation, preparation is underway for that event. Because the coronation is a very public ceremony, there has often been controversy over the various persons to be present and to witness the taking of the coronation oath—the Court of Claims was early established to resolve such disputes peaceably and systematically, based on proven grant

[87] The latest form of the Coronation Oath may be seen in the Proceedings of the Coronation of Her Majesty The Queen, 2nd June 1953:

> Archbishop of Canterbury—"Madam, is your Majesty willing to take the oath?"
> The Queen—"I am willing"
> Archbishop of Canterbury—"Will you solemnly promise and swear to govern the people of this United Kingdom of Great Britain and Northern Ireland and the other realms and territories, according to the statutes in Parliament agreed on, and the respective laws and customs of the same?"
> The Queen—"I solemnly promise to do so"
> Archbishop of Canterbury—"Will you, to the utmost of your power, maintain the laws of God, the true profession of the Gospel, and the Protestant Reformed Religion established by law? And will you maintain and observe inviolably the settlement of the Church of England and the doctrine, worship, discipline and government thereas by law established in England? And will you preserve unto the bishops and clergy of England and to the churches there committed to their charge, all such rights and privileges as by law do or shall appertain to them or any of them?"
> The Queen—"I will".

or prescription.[88] However, this also raises the important question of who is entitled to attend the coronation, if indeed anyone other than the Sovereign themself has any entitlement with respect to attendance at the coronation.

The Right to Attend a Coronation

In the course of planning a coronation, one factor which must be considered is the question of who may be included or excluded from attendance at a coronation, given its key constitutive and symbolic functions. Perhaps unsurprisingly, this question is one that is fraught with difficulties. In modern times attendance at a coronation is dependent upon invitation by the Earl Marshal, who has executive authority for organising and directing a coronation.[89] But this is not an unfettered discretion. For every coronation for some 645 years a Court of Claims had been held to hear petitions relating to attendance and service at coronations.[90] However, in 2023 no Court of Claims was instituted.[91] Likewise, no coronation commission was established (as had been customary), and there was no royal proclamation of the coronation (only of the Bank Holiday).[92]

[88] The Bishop of Durham and the Bishop of Bath and Wells, as bishops assisting the Sovereign, have this right by prescription; *Coronation of Her Majesty Queen Elizabeth the Second* (1952). They, and similar services, exist "by ancient customs and usages of the realm, as also in regard of divers tenures of sundry manors, lands and other hereditaments", see the *London Gazette Extraordinary*, 6 June 1952, p. 3165.

[89] Squibb, G. D., *The High Court of Chivalry* (1959). The planning and organisation of a coronation was historically assigned to a Coronation Commission, which in 1953 was chaired by the Duke of Edinburgh; HL Deb 27 January 1953 vol 180 c 4 (coronation arrangements). There were also coronation joint committee—for Commonwealth countries—and a coronation executive committee, both chaired by the Duke of Norfolk; for the executive committee, see the Order in Council dated 16 June 1952: *London Gazette*, 20 June 1952. The Order in Council appointing a Coronation Committee for the coronation of Elizabeth II was promulgated on 6 June 1952: *London Gazette*, 10 June 1952.

[90] See, generally, Wollaston, Sir Gerald, *Coronation Claims* (1903).

[91] Torrance, David, "The Coronation: history and ceremonial" (House of Commons Library Research Briefing, number CBP9412, 6 December 2022), p. 20.

[92] In 2022 a coronation committee was appointed, but no commission was proclaimed, nor was the date of the coronation itself proclaimed; Torrance, David, "The Coronation: history and ceremonial" (House of Commons Library Research Briefing, number CBP9412, 6 December 2022), p. 20; HC Deb 17 November 2022 vol 722 c 820 (coronation of King Charles III). The bank holiday was however proclaimed, 9th November

The legal framework surrounding the coronation in 2023 was thus largely absent. For the specific purpose of deciding ex officio and hereditary claims to perform services at the coronation, a Coronation Claims Office was established,[93] staffed by members of the Cabinet Office and overseen by Oliver Dowden, the Chancellor of the Duchy of Lancaster.[94] It was assisted by Garter Principal King of Arms, David White, as a ceremonial expert, the Archbishop's Coronation Planning Director, Danny Johnson, as an ecclesiastical expert, and two barristers, Andrew O'Connor, KC, and Catherine Dobson.[95] In principle such an administrative process would be simpler than the cumbersome procedure of the Court of Claims, which, being a court, followed strict judicial procedures.

In addition to determining who should have a role at the coronation, the administration of a coronation involves a wide range of

2022, and the traditional words used: "Whereas, We have resolved by the Favour and Blessing of Almighty God to celebrate the Solemnity of Our Royal Coronation at Westminster upon Saturday the sixth day of May in the year 2023 … ", Privy Council meeting, 9 November 2022.

[93] "Coronation Claims Office to look at historic and ceremonial roles for King Charles III's Coronation", Press Release, 5 January 2023. Cabinet Office and The Rt Hon Oliver Dowden CBE MP (Chancellor of the Duchy of Lancaster).

When looking at claims, the Coronation Claims Office will consider matters including whether the role or service was performed in 1953 or not, what the basis is for it to be performed now and the claimant's connection to those who previously performed the role or service.

Officials from the Coronation Claims Office will consult with ecclesiastical experts from Lambeth Palace and ceremonial experts from the Royal Household when considering claims.

[94] The Roll of Claims and Proceedings at the Coronation of His Most Sacred Majesty Charles the Third by the Grace of God of the United Kingdom of Great Britain and Northern Ireland and of His other Realms and Territories, King, Head of the Commonwealth, Defender of the Faith, and of Her Majesty Queen Camilla, His Consort (2024); ("Coronation Roll, 2023").

[95] Mr White had been Garter Principal King of Arms since 2021, and an Officer of Arms since 1995. Mr Johnson was Archbishop's Coronation Planning Director November 2022-August 2023, and was the Archbishop of Canterbury and the Church of England's Operational Lead for Operation London Bridge March 2021-October 2022. He was previously Hospitality Operations Manager to the Archbishop of Canterbury January 2018-September 2022, and the Archbishop of Canterbury and the Church of England's Operational Lead for Operation Forth Bridge March 2021-May 2021. Mr O'Connor was noted for his expertise in public law, especially inquiries. Miss Dobson was junior counsel acting for the Shadow Attorney-General in *R (Miller) v The Prime Minister* [2019] UKSC 41 (in a challenge to the Prime Minister's advice to the Queen to prorogue Parliament) and a constitutional law specialist.

government bodies. In 2023, in evidence to the Commons Public Administration and Constitutional Affairs Committee, Oliver Dowden said the King, "through Buckingham Palace", was "responsible for the content of the coronation, the guest list"—which included, in addition to foreign and Commonwealth royalty, Prince Rahim Aga Khan, and the King of the Ashantis Otumfuo Osei Tutu II,[96] and "all the other things associated with the coronation". The role of the Government, he added, was twofold:

> Through DCMS, the Government support ceremonials, as they did with the platinum jubilee and various other moments of national celebration. Through the Cabinet Office, I chair a cross-Government co-ordination Committee to make sure that the whole of the Government works properly to support the coronation, whether that is in relation to policing, security, the footprint of the coronation in terms of the roads, the involvement of the military or all the other things that come together to make this a wonderful day in our nation's history.[97]

The administration and planning of the coronation were entrusted to a Coronation Organising Committee chaired by Sir Clive Alderton, Principal Private Secretary to Their Majesties. The Committee was assisted by Lieutenant-Colonel Michael Vernon, Comptroller of the Lord Chamberlain's Office and Alexander Scully, Deputy Comptroller, Lord Chamberlain's Office. The specific roles and responsibilities of the Government and the Church were clearly defined. The Prime Minister delegated the Government's overall responsibility for the coronation to the Chancellor of the Duchy of Lancaster. Responsibility for the delivery of the coronation arrangements was delegated to the Secretary of State for Digital, Culture, Media and Sport, Michelle Donelan, and then Lucy Frazer, supported by the Cabinet Office on constitutional and ceremonial arrangements.[98]

We might also distinguish between those present for diplomatic, political or social reasons, and those present for more specific (or even prosaic)

[96] *Coronation Roll, 2023.*

[97] Public Administration and Constitutional Affairs Committee, Oral evidence: The work of the Cabinet Office; <https://committees.parliament.uk/oralevidence/12604/html/>.

[98] *Coronation Roll, 2023,*

reasons. In the British practice, apart from the ministers of the coronation—the Archbishop, assisting bishops, Dean of Westminster, Earl Marshal, Lord Great Chamberlain, and lessor officers, such as precentor, ushers, and choristers—certain individuals long had right or expectation of attendance due to their constitutional function. Such officers included the Lord Mayor of London (although the coronation actually has occurred within the jurisdiction of another territorial local authority, the City of Westminster, rather than the ancient "square mile", since the creation of the City of Westminster in 1540, when the Abbey was—briefly—constituted the cathedral of a new diocese of Westminster[99]). The existing offices connected with the coronation which have been allowed by the Court of Claims as hereditary in gross are those of Lord Great Chamberlain, the right to carry the great spurs, and certain Scottish and Irish offices,[100] as well as some associated with the defunct coronation banquet.[101]

In many cases attendees are required at a coronation because of their function in the service, such as the Archbishop of Canterbury[102]; in some instances the incumbent Archbishop was unavailable and a lesser ranking prelate was invited—or prevailed upon—to officiate instead.[103]

In 2023, of the 429 claims submitted to the Coronation Claims Office,[104] applications simply to attend the ceremony or for other

[99] "December 1540; Grants, No. 30", *Letters and Papers, Foreign and Domestic, Henry VIII*, British History Online, Vol. 16: 1540–1541 (1898), pp. 174–175.

[100] *Halsbury's Laws of England* (4th ed., 1974), vol. 12(1) para. 26.

[101] For example, the Grand Carver of England, allegedly held by the Feildings, Earls of Denbigh and Desmond, as well as the King's Champion.

[102] There is a statutory requirement for their presence, or that of the Archbishop of York, or another bishop of the realm duly appointed, to administer the oath; Coronation Oath Act 1688 (1 Will. & Mary sess 4 c. 6), s 2.

[103] In 1559 Elizabeth I appointed Owen Oglethorpe, the (Roman Catholic) Bishop of Carlisle, to preside at the coronation, although he was shortly afterwards to be deprived of his see for not swearing the oath of supremacy, as required under the Act of Supremacy 1558 (1 Eliz. I c. 2); Norrie, Aidan, "The Bishop and the Queen; Or, Why Did the Bishop of Carlisle Crown Elizabeth I?" (2019) 56(1-2) Northern History 25–45.

[104] More than 200 by early 2023; HC Deb 2 February 2023 Vol 727 c449 [Topical Questions], The Rt Hon Oliver Dowden CBE MP (*Chancellor of the Duchy of Lancaster); The Roll of Claims and Proceedings at the Coronation of His Most Sacred Majesty Charles the Third by the Grace of God of the United Kingdom of Great Britain and Northern Ireland and of His other Realms and Territories, King, Head of the Commonwealth, Defender of the Faith, and of Her Majesty Queen Camilla, His Consort (2024)* (Coronation Roll, 2023).

elements of the events taking place on the weekend of the Coronation were considered out of scope; 32 claims were considered within scope and subject to further consideration, of which 14 were allowed (compared to 16 of 21 in 1953[105]).

Those accepted were the Earl of Erroll (to bear a silver baton or staff as Lord High Constable of Scotland), the Barons of the Cinque Ports (through Mr Ian Russell, Registrar and Seneschal of the Cinque Ports),[106] Clerk of the Crown in Chancery (and Permanent Secretary of the Ministry of Justice) (to record the proceedings[107]), the Lord Great Chamberlain (Lord Carrington, assigned a role in investing the King with the regalia), Lord Hastings and the Earl of Loudoun (each of whom was to carry one of the Golden Spurs, the Bishop of Durham and the Bishop of Bath and Wells (Bishops Assistant to the King), the Dean and Chapter of the Collegiate Church of St Peter (instructing the monarch in the forms, rites and ceremonies), the Lord Mayor of London, the Earl of Dundee (to carry the Quartering of the Standard (Scotland)), the Lord Lyon King of Arms and Heralds and Pursuivants of Scotland (part of the King's procession), and The Walker Trust (who nominated the Anglican Bishop of Edinburgh), who previously performed the role of Heritable Usher of the White Rod.[108] Others were later allowed, such as the Honourable the King's Champion.[109]

The vastly increased number of claimants in 2023 may be ascribed to the large number of hereditary peers who sought to attend, in light of the

[105] Steafel, Eleanor, "Does your family history mean you're entitled to a Coronation ticket?", The Telegraph, 24 January 2023, <https://www.telegraph.co.uk/royal-family/2023/01/24/king-charles-iii-coronation-could-family-get-ticket/>.

[106] For the significant political role played by the ports, see Murray, K. M. Elisabeth, *The Constitutional History of the Cinque Ports* (1935).

[107] *The Roll of Claims and Proceedings at the Coronation of His Most Sacred Majesty Charles the Third by the Grace of God of the United Kingdom of Great Britain and Northern Ireland and of His other Realms and Territories, King, Head of the Commonwealth, Defender of the Faith, and of Her Majesty Queen Camilla, His Consort* (2024) (the *Coronation Roll*, 2023).

[108] "People who will play historic roles at the heart of the Coronation Service announced", 9 April 2023 <https://www.gov.uk/government/news/people-who-will-play-historic-roles-at-the-heart-of-the-coronation-service-announced>.

[109] Press Release, "Roles to be performed at the Coronation Service at Westminster Abbey". The Royal Family. 27 April 2023.

exclusion of all but a handful,[110] and also doubtless the non-legal and less complex procedures adopted for making a claim. The claim of the Earl of Shrewsbury and Waterford, the Lord High Steward of Ireland, was allowed, but he did not attend as the role was not required.

In the twentieth century attempts were made to widen the range of attendees. A number of key roles, being non-hereditary, were assigned to leading military, naval and air officers, such as (in 1953), the Lord High Steward, Admiral of the Fleet Viscount Cunningham of Hyndhope, who carried St Edward's Crown into the Abbey, Field Marshal Viscount Alanbrooke, who was Lord High Constable and Field Marshal Commanding Coronation Troops, the bearer of the sceptre with the Cross, Marshal of the Royal Air Force Viscount Portal of Hungerford, and the bearer of the orb, Field Marshal Earl Alexander of Tunis.[111]

In a more diverse allocation of these roles, in 2023 these were respectively, the Lord High Steward, General Sir Gordon Messenger, Royal Marines (Constable of the Tower of London), who carried St Edward's Crown into the Abbey, Admiral Sir Tony Radakin (Chief of Defence Staff), who was Lord High Constable, the bearer of the sceptre with the Cross, the Duke of Buccleuch and Queensberry, and the bearer of the orb, Dame Elizabeth Anionwu. Other roles were assigned to General Sir Patrick Sanders, carrying the Queen Consort's Sceptre, Lord Chartres, carrying the Queen Consort's Ring, the Keeper of the Jewel House, Brigadier Andrew Jackson, carrying the Sovereign's Ring, Air Chief Marshal the Lord Peach, carrying the Sword of Mercy (the Curtana),[112] General the Lord Richards of Herstmonceux, carrying the Sword of Spiritual Justice, and General the Lord Houghton of Richmond, carrying the Sword of Temporal Justice.[113]

[110] Ward, Victoria, "Coronation officials forced to get tough after hundreds demand role in ceremony", The Telegraph, 2 February 2023, <https://www.telegraph.co.uk/royal-family/2023/02/02/king-charles-coronation-officials-forced-get-tough-hundreds/>.

[111] *Supplement to the London Gazette*, 17th November 1953 (HMSO, London, 1953), p. 6223–6270 "Ceremonial of the Coronation of Her Majesty Queen Elizabeth II".

[112] Ditmas, E. M. R., "The Curtana or Sword of Mercy" (1966) 29(1) Journal of the British Archaeological Association 122–133.

[113] Press Release, "Roles to be performed at the Coronation Service at Westminster Abbey". The Royal Family. 27 April 2023.

The selection in 2023 was more diverse than ever before, both racially and in the allocation of prominent roles to women. Dame Elizabeth Anionwu was a nurse, health care administrator, lecturer, and Emeritus Professor of Nursing at the University of West London, and of Irish and Nigerian ancestry. She was joined by Baroness Benjamin, a Trinidadian-British actress, singer, presenter, author, businesswoman, and politician, who carried the Sceptre with the Dove, Baroness Kennedy of The Shaws, who carried the Queen Consort's Rod, Baroness Manningham-Buller, who carried St Edward's Staff, Petty Officer Amy Taylor, who carried the Jewelled Sword of Offering, Penny Mordaunt (the Lord President of the Council), who carried the Sword of State, and Cadet Warrant Officer Elliott Tyson-Lee, who carried the flag of the United Kingdom.[114] The most significant were perhaps the choices of Petty Officer Taylor, and Cadet Warrant Officer Tyson-Lee, who were respectively an Aircraft Engineer from 845 Naval Air Squadron at RNAS Yeovilton where His Majesty originally trained and served as a pilot, and from the Royal Air Force Air Cadets. In 1953 the Flag of the United Kingdom was borne, not by an air cadet, but by Captain John Dymoke, Royal Lincolnshire Regiment, who was The Queen's Champion. The Jewelled Sword of Offering was borne on that occasion by Lord Hardinge of Penshurst, who had been the late King's Private Secretary 1936–43.

In 2023 it was explicitly stated that "those presenting [the regalia] have been chosen on the advice of Government". These included the Lord Carrington (Lord Great Chamberlain), presenting the Spurs, Lord Kamall, presenting the Armills, Baroness Merron, presenting the imperial mantle or Robe Royal, the Archbishop of Armagh, presenting the Sovereign's Orb, Lord Patel, presenting the Sovereign's Ring, Lord Singh of Wimbledon, presenting the Coronation Glove, the Bishop of Moray, Ross and Caithness and Episcopal Primus of Scotland, presenting the Sceptre with Cross, and the Archbishop of Wales, presenting the Sceptre with Dove.[115] Those presenting Regalia to Her Majesty were Rose Hudson-Wilkin (Bishop of Dover), presenting the Queen Consort's Rod, Lord Chartres (former Bishop of London), presenting the Queen Consort's Sceptre with Cross, and Brigadier Andrew Jackson (The Keeper of the Jewel House at HM Tower of London), presenting the Queen

[114] Ibid.

[115] Ibid.

Consort's Ring. The Archbishop of Canterbury performed the crowning with St Edward's Crown and Queen Mary's Crown for the King and Queen respectively.[116]

The inclusion of the Church in Wales, the Church of Ireland, and the Episcopal Church of Scotland, as well as female bishops (and one, Rose Hudson-Wilkin, also non-white), was a conscious effort at broadening episcopal participation beyond the traditional Church of England. Non-Christian faiths were also represented—Lord Kamall was a Muslim, Baroness Merron a Jew, and Lord Patel a Hindu and Lord Singh of Wimbledon a Sikh.

Some other choices suggested some personal preferences of the Sovereign; the standard-bearer of the England quartering of the Royal Arms was the 7th Duke of Westminster.[117] He was a close friend of William Prince of Wales and Prince Harry Duke of Sussex, a godparent of William's first son, Prince George, and himself a godson of King Charles III.[118] The influence of the Sovereign themselves on the planning and arrangement of the coronation probably depends as much on their personal interest in the ceremony as anything else. The Standard of the Ireland Quartering of the Royal Arms was borne by the Earl of Caledon, who had been Lord Lieutenant of Armagh since 1989. Still other selections of participants conferred upon members of the hereditary peerage the traditional role of attendance, which was otherwise denied almost all peers, hereditary and life alike. For instance, the Standard of the Principality of Wales was borne by the Marquess of Anglesey, the Duke of Buccleuch and Queensberry carried the Sceptre with Cross, and the Duke of Wellington bore Queen Mary's Crown.[119]

Including those with an official role to play, the total attendance has in the recent past been very great—in 1953, for instance, there were some 8,200 people in the Abbey,[120] greatly in excess of the usual capacity of the building, which is approximately 2200. The additional seating was made

[116] Ibid.

[117] Ibid.

[118] Rayner, Gordon, "Prince George christening: profiles of the godparents". *The Daily Telegraph*. 23 October 2013.

[119] Press Release, "Roles to be performed at the Coronation Service at Westminster Abbey". The Royal Family. 27 April 2023.

[120] Brooke-Little, John, *Royal Ceremonies of State* (1980), p. 55.

possible by installing temporary tiered seating in the nave, aisles, and transepts, within the Abbey, a process which necessitated the closure of the Abbey for six months; the construction of such tiers and galleries, and the central coronation platform, traditionally forms part of turning the church into a theatre of state.[121] This work usually included the construction of many temporary structures, inside and out, although the Abbey had been rebuilt in the mid-thirteenth century with its role as a coronation church expressly in mind. Much of the construction work was of a temporary nature, due to the needs of a ritual divided between Westminster Palace (procession, and court celebrations, until 1661), Westminster Hall (the coronation banquet, until the last in 1821), and Westminster Abbey (the coronation proper). In 2023, as an indication of the smaller scale of attendance, the Abbey church was closed for only a week.[122]

From the earliest times coronations everywhere had a wide range of attendees, including members of the Royal Family, prominent lay and religious leaders, and (at least in some traditions) distinguished foreign guests—the latter often for the diplomatic purpose of impressing them with the might and glory of the kingdom. Indeed, many of the nobles present also were there for political purposes, including to pre-empt any treasonous thoughts of over-mighty subjects, who might presume to compete with or even threaten the king's authority.

Ultimately, those invited to witness or participate in the coronation were included for a mixture of reasons, but these always included political expediency, as the primary purpose of the coronation was to uphold the status of the new king.

The Claims of the Peerage to Attendance

Peers of the realm have long been amongst the largest group present at a coronation. This was not as mere observers. Aside from the now largely removed membership (for hereditary peers) of the House of Lords, there were other miscellaneous—but sometimes still important—privileges attaching to the possession of a peerage. These include special

[121] Coldstream, Nicola, "The Abbey and Palace as Theatres for Coronation", in Warwick Rodwell, and Tim Tatton-Brown (eds.), *Westminster Part I* (2015).

[122] 28th April to 8th May inclusive. "Abbey to close in late April for Coronation preparations", <https://www.westminster-abbey.org/abbey-news/abbey-to-close-in-late-april-for-coronation-preparations>, 6th March 2023.

positions in the order of precedence,[123] the right to certain distinctions in their coats of arms, to wear coronation and parliamentary robes (the latter when members of the House of Lords), and of course to use the style and titles of peerage. They are not however legal privileges in the same sense as the exemption from appearing as a witness,[124] or of access to the Sovereign,[125] which relate to the constitutional functions of the peerage.[126] The former are ceremonial or honorific in nature, and do not in any way alter the peers' standing or status vis-à-vis commoners (which latter category includes members of the Royal Family who are not peers), peeresses in their own right, or the Sovereign.

There is, however, one exception to this principle that most peerage privileges are merely ceremonial or honorific in nature, where a "minor" privilege actually reflects the constitutional role of the peerage, and which may indeed be said to be an example of the right of peers to have access to the Sovereign. This is the right to attend a coronation. This remains a very great privilege, and one that, like the (albeit uncertain) privilege of being hereditary counsellors to the Sovereign, would appear to be distinct from the right of membership of the House of Lords—indeed it predates the House, andParliament itself, by many centuries. It is not, however, certain that such a right exists.

There would potentially be many peers who would petition the Court of Claims—if this were convened[127]—for an invitation to a coronation, and it is doubtful that the Court could rightly exclude them arbitrarily, although ultimately the Earl Marshal could simply decline to issue an invitation. This complication was neatly avoided in 2022 by omitting to convene a Court of Claims, despite it having been consistently convened for every coronation for at least 645 years. In the event the coronation claims office rejected all claims made by peers to merely attend a coronation. This was despite the fact that, aside from the Archbishops and Bishops, and members of the Royal Family, the peerage have been the

[123] Squibb, G. D., *Precedence in England and Wales* (1981).

[124] Parliamentary Privilege, First Report, 31 March 1999, para 330.

[125] Ibid.

[126] See also Cox, Noel, "The British Peerage: The Legal Standing of the Peerage and Baronetage in the Overseas Realms of the Crown with Particular Reference to New Zealand" (1997) 17(4) New Zealand Universities Law Review 379–401.

[127] Torrance, David, "The Coronation: history and ceremonial" (House of Commons Library Research Briefing, number CBP9412, 6 December 2022), p. 20.

most regular participants in the coronation service for a thousand years—and arguably not in their legislative capacity,[128] but rather their (now almost wholly obsolete) executive role as counsellors to the Sovereign.

The privilege of access is no longer exercised,[129] but it is possibly still retained by peers whether members of the House of Lords or not.[130] The original collective assembly of what we now know as the peerage, the *witan*, and later the *magnum concilium*, as distinct from the *commune concilium*, and which itself was to evolve into Parliament, was increasingly rarely called, and was last summoned in 1640, after Charles I's defeat in the Bishops' War.[131] However, the collective role of the hereditary peerage—or perhaps more correctly, the peerage whether hereditary or otherwise—was distinct from the later legislative function of membership of the House of Lords.

Although membership of Parliament has always been central to peerage, it is not the total extent of its nature. Indeed, there have always been members who were not peers, and peers who were not members. The nature of peerage relates more to its identity as a title or dignity created by the Crown[132]; the Sovereign cannot himself hold a dignity,[133] A peerage is also in the form of inalienable (or normally inalienable) property. English law—and the law in Scotland (and formerly also Ireland[134])

[128] See the *Coronation of Her Majesty Queen Elizabeth the Second* (1952). Office-holders were generally only excluded where their services were not needed, because of the abolition of the coronation banquet.

[129] *History of Parliament* (2007), Part 1: "The House of Lords and the Peerage".

[130] Cox, Noel, "The rights of peerage" (2007) 5 HPA Newsletter: Journal of the Hereditary Peerage Association 1–3.

[131] Maddicott, J. R., *The Origins of the English Parliament, 924–1327* (2010).

[132] The last time hereditary peerages were regularly conferred was 1965 (Baron Margadale). After a considerable hiatus, several new peerages were created in the early 1980s. Viscounts Whitelaw and Tonypandy were conferred in 1983—both to men without heirs—and the Earldom of Stockton in 1984. Royal peerages continue to be conferred: the Dukes of York (1986), Cambridge (2011) and Sussex (2018), and the Earldom of Wessex (1999). Cambridge was the first created since the House of Lords Act 1999—the Earldom of Wessex was created 19th June 1999, and the Act came into force 11th November 1999.

[133] *Buckhurst Peerage Case* (1876) 2 App. Cas. 1, per Lord Cairns LC; considered by *Rhondda's (Viscountess) Claim* [1922] 2 A.C. 339.

[134] The peerage actually comprises five distinct peerages, those of England (created prior to 1707), Great Britain (1707-1801), United Kingdom (since 1801), Scotland (prior to 1707) and Ireland (last created 1898).

in relation to peerages differs from that in England and Wales in some respects[135]—recognises a peerage as an incorporeal and impartible hereditament, inalienable and descendible according to the words of limitation in the grant, if any.[136]

The House of Lords Act 1999 excluded hereditary peers and peeresses per se from membership of the upper house, and the House of Lords (Hereditary Peers) Act 2024 completed the process, but neither statute deprived them of their status as peers, nor affected their other rights and privileges—including the official recognition of their titles. Membership of the House of Lords was a central function of the peerage for many centuries, but it was not its sole, or perhaps even principal, purpose.

The House of Lords Act 1999 implicitly preserves existing privileges of peerage. This is an interpretation supported by the Explanatory Note to the House of Lords Act 1999, para 9.

> The Act does not affect the rights of holders of a hereditary peerage excluded from the House of Lords to keep all the other titles, rights, offices, privileges and precedents attaching to the peerage which are unconnected with membership of the House of Lords.

The privilege of peerage is the body of privileges that belongs to peers, their wives and their widows who have not remarried. The privilege is distinct from parliamentary privilege, and applies to all peers, not just members of the House of Lords. It still exists, although "occasions of its exercise have now diminished into obscurity."[137] Parliamentary privilege is a distinct matter.

Members of the House of Lords enjoyed similar privileges and burdens to those of the House of Commons, subject only to differences inherent upon the permanent nature of membership of the upper house. Temporal and spiritual peers enjoyed their privileges for the same reasons as their more transitory colleagues in the Commons, to promote the work of the

[135] See Cox, Noel, "The British Peerage: The Legal Standing of the Peerage and Baronetage in the Overseas Realms of the Crown with Particular Reference to New Zealand" (1997) 17 (4) New Zealand Universities Law Review 379–401.

[136] *Nevil's Case* (1604) 7 Co Rep 33a; 77 E.R. 460; *R* v. *Purbeck (Viscount)* (1678) Show Parl Cas 1, 5; 1 E.R. 1; *Norfolk Earldom Case* [1907] A.C. 10; *Rhondda's (Viscountess) Claim* [1922] 2 A.C. 339.

[137] *Companion to the standing orders and guide to the proceedings of the House of Lords* (2007), p. 202–203.

House. But because of the differences between an elected "knight of the shire", and a hereditary peer, peers enjoyed certain additional privileges, not necessarily related to membership of Parliament.

The Privilege of Peerage extends to all temporal peers and peeresses regardless of their position in relation to the House of Lords; Scottish and Irish peers, therefore, had, and retain, the Privilege of Peerage. Lords Spiritual do not have the Privilege of Peerage, as they are Lords of Parliament, and not peers. This was not always so. In 1621, to clarify their status, the House of Lords adopted a standing order that, in its present form, reads "Bishops to whom a writ of summons has been issued are not Peers but are Lords of Parliament".[138]

As stated in the First Report on Parliamentary Privileges, "The extent of the privilege [of peerage, rather than parliamentary privilege] has long been obscure and ill-defined, and for that reason alone the present situation is unsatisfactory".[139] Three of its features survived into the twentieth century. The first was the right of trial by peers, which was abolished by the Criminal Justice Act 1948,[140] and will not be considered further here. The second privilege is the right of access to the Sovereign at any time. The third is freedom from arrest in civil causes (which was both a parliamentary privilege and also a privilege of peerage). The Committee recommended that privilege of peerage should be abolished, without however having considered the nature of the second privilege, that of access to the Sovereign.[141] It might also be said that they did not draw a clear distinction between parliamentary privilege, and the privilege of peerage, as the latter was outside their remit. There are other, minor privileges.

In many respects the most important privilege of peerage remaining—if not, in fact, the only one (we of course exclude here the parliamentary privileges)—is perhaps also the least well understood. It was generally accepted that peers, being the hereditary counsellors of the Sovereign,[142]

[138] Standing Orders of the House of Lords (27 March 1628), "Lords and the manner of their introduction", 6.

[139] "First Report on Parliamentary Privilege" 30th March 1999, para 329.

[140] 11 & 12 Geo. VI. c. 58.

[141] Ibid.

[142] See, generally, Pike, Luke, *Pike's Constitutional History of the House of Lords* (1894), pp. 251–254.

have freedom of access to the Sovereign in relation to public affairs.[143] Pike believed that the claim that peers were individually hereditary counsellors to the Sovereign only dated from relatively late times, being based upon the original role of the *curia regis*. However, the idea led to King Charles I summoning the peers to York in 1640 for advice, and to the meeting of the peers in 1688 when King James II had fled. The peers' right of access is said to be based upon the articles in the accusations against Hugh le Despenser the elder and younger, in the reign of Edward II, and is of doubtful authority. However, whatever its origins, its existence was rarely doubted.

Members of the House of Commons enjoy this right of access collectively, but only those individual members of the Commons who are Privy Counsellors or members of the Royal Household enjoy it individually. These latter include the Government whips in the House of Commons, including the Treasurer, Comptroller, and Vice-Chamberlain of the Household. This privilege is not, for peers, a parliamentary privilege, but a privilege of peerage. It is also unaffected by the House of Lords Act 1999, and arguably would survive the final expulsion of the remaining hereditary peers (or even life peers) from the House, since it is unrelated to membership of the House of Lords.

Peers formed the *magnum concilium*, or Great Council, which was one of the four councils belonging to the Sovereign. The most famous of the King's councils is the Privy Council (traditionally dated to King Ælfred in 895). Another council is Parliament, which was the *commune concilium*, or Common Council. Finally, judges are considered counsellors of the Sovereign on legal matters.

A council composed only of peers was often summoned by some early English Kings. Such a council, having been in disuse for centuries, was revived in 1640, when, as noted above, King Charles I summoned all of the Peers of the Realm using writs issued under the Great Seal of the Realm. Though such a council has not been summoned since then, each peer remains a counsellor of the Sovereign, and, according to Sir William Blackstone, has the right "to demand an audience of the King, and to lay before him, with decency and respect, such matters as he shall judge of

143 Anson, Sir William, *The Law and Custom of the Constitution* (1886), vol. 1, p. 227; Stubbs, William, *The Constitutional History of England in its origin and development* (4th ed., 1906), vol. 2, p. 515; *Report as to the Dignity of a Peer of the Realm* (1829), vol. I, p. 14.

importance to the public weal".[144] This privilege would appear to have been very rarely exercised in modern times, if at all.

Whether hereditary peers are still counsellors of the Sovereign, even though they are not *ipso facto* members of Parliament, is admittedly uncertain. The nature of the peerage was intimately linked with their political role. It was for this reason that it might be said that "the whole kingdom has an interest in a peerage".[145] The same may be said of Scottish peers.[146] This role included both legislative and executive aspects. Membership of the House of Lords represented one; the right to be hereditary counsellors to the Sovereign is another. It is the latter, rather than the former, which was the basis for the attendance of peers at a coronation. It must also be recalled that it was once the magnates who acclaimed and rendered homage to a new King, after having chosen him or confirmed his title to the Crown.

It is probably difficult to be sure what the precise scope of the privilege of access to the Sovereign is, but it would appear to allow individual peers the right of access to the Sovereign. Eldon thought that peers could only tender advice, not, as of right, carry an address or petition to the Sovereign.[147] In practice, an audience must be sought through an officer of the Royal Household, but there would appear to be a strong argument that such a request should not be declined without good cause to do so. The question whether the role of peers as counsellors to the Sovereign alone justifies a claim to a right to attend a coronation is an interesting one, and one which reflects the constitutional role of the peerage, collectively and individually.

No one has an absolutely certain right to attend a coronation—except the King or Queen Regnant[148]; any claim accepted by the Court of

[144] Blackstone, Sir William, *Commentaries on the Laws of England* (reprint 1978 of 1783 edn), Bk. 1 pt. 2, pp. 228–229.

[145] *Calvin's Case* (1607) 7 Co Rep 156 16a; 77 E.R. 377, 396. Also considered in *Earldom of Norfolk Case* [1907] A.C. 10 (H.L.) and the later cases such as *Rhondda's (Viscountess) Claim* [1922] 2 A.C. 339.

[146] Nicholas, Sir Harris, *History of the Earldoms of Strathearn, Monteith and Airth* (1842), pp. 100–108.

[147] Colchester, Charles Lord (ed.), *The Diary and Correspondence of Charles Abbot Lord Colchester* (1861), vol. III, p. 606 (12 March 1829).

[148] King Edward VIII was not of course crowned, owing to his abdication a few months before his planned coronation, nor was King Edward V (one of the Princes in the Tower), and both were still unquestionably kings.

Claims might still be rejected by the Sovereign or his or her responsible minister, the Earl Marshal. In 1953, for the first time, only a representative group of peers were invited to attend the coronation, on the advice (probably sound) that the peerage as a whole had no absolute right to attend.[149] The large size of the peerage precluded the inclusion of all peers; from 1902, aside from the royal dukes, only the senior peer of each degree—duke, marquess, earl, viscount, and baron had rendered homage personally to the new monarch.[150] However, a wholesale exclusion of the entirety of the peerage would also appear to be problematic.

Some changes in attendance may doubtless be required for any coronation—and some are desirable, such as to reflect the changed and diminished role of the House of Lords. This could, for instance, be achieved by including the Lord Speaker of the House of Lords, but not necessarily by excluding the peers. Typically, and rather unsatisfactorily, the new post of Lord Speaker, first held by Baroness Hayman from 4th July 2006, was granted rank and precedence after the Speaker of the House of Commons, by royal warrant of 4th July 2006.[151] As the Speaker of the Upper House she should, of course, arguably have had precedence before the Speaker of the House of Commons.[152] Hereditary peers have, since the House of Lords Act 1999, and the House of Lords (Hereditary Peers) Act 2024 been excluded from the House of Lords, but it must be questioned whether their constant attendance at coronations for a thousand years—predating Parliament—can simply end because they are (mostly) not members of the House of Lords. This deprives them at once of their role in the acclamation (election) and the homage.

[149] Hansard, Lords, 27 January 1953, cols 4–13.

[150] In 1953 fealty was rendered first by Geoffrey Fisher, Archbishop of Canterbury (all the bishops present, and Cyril Garbett, the Archbishop of York, repeated the words, substituting their own names), then the royal dukes individually, led by the Duke of Edinburgh, followed by Duke of Gloucester, and lastly the Duke of Kent (the Prince of Wales was a child, and the other royal duke, Windsor, was not present). The temporal peerage was led by the Duke of Norfolk, then the Marquess of Huntly (in place of the elderly Winchester), Earl of Shrewsbury, Viscount of Arbuthnott (in place of Herford), and Baron Stourton, Seagrave and Mowbray (in place of Baroness de Ros). In 2023 only the premier royal duke (Cornwall) rendered homage personally.

[151] College of Arms register I.85/194.

[152] For precedence generally, see Squibb, G. D., *Precedence in England and Wales* (1981).

Peers have attended the coronation of their Sovereign since coronations began. Their legislative role was, then and now, in a sense, immaterial. They represented the continuity of the constitution in a manner that the elected members of the House of Commons, however important they may be on a day-to-day basis, cannot do. They should not be wholly excluded, not least because of their pivotal role in the rendering of homage. In 2023, however, the decision was taken, most likely primarily in light of the twin factors of the limitation in overall attendance to 2200, and the passage of the House of Lords Act 1999, that only peers in Parliament were eligible for participation in the ballot to receive an invitation. The only peers in attendance would be the Earl Marshal and those peers who have a hereditary role (including the Prince of Wales), a group of parliamentary peers which may include hereditary peers from amongst the 90 remaining members of the House of Lords,[153] and those who were to be invited as friends of King Charles III. These represented a small proportion of a total of 806 hereditary peers, including 29 dukes (five royal dukes),[154] 34 marquesses, 189 earls, 111 viscounts, and 443 barons.[155]

Other than the lords temporal or lay peerage, the prelates, the Lords Spiritual, also were for long amongst the primary regular attendees at a coronation. Their presence, like that of the lay peerage, was to enable them to acclaim the new Sovereign, and swear allegiance through individual—and now collectively by degree—homage. Presence at a coronation was not a question of social or economic privilege, but rather their constitutional function. Those who needed to be there, for the acclamation, the oath, the anointing, the investiture with regalia, the crowning,

[153] The House of Lords Act 1999, s 2, provided for 90 elected hereditary peers, and two ex officio members, the Earl Marshal and the Lord Great Chamberlain. Whilst the former is vested in the Dukes of Norfolk since 1672, the latter is also entitled to a seat in the House of Lords, if a peer. Since the current Lord Great Chamberlain, Lord Carrington, was an elected hereditary peer, the accession of King Charles III had the effect of creating a vacancy in the House for another elected hereditary peer. The Earl of Erroll and the Earl of Dundee are also elected members of the House, but Lord Hastings and the Earl of Loudoun are not.

[154] The Dukedom of Edinburgh was conferred, for life, on the Prince Edward, Earl of Wessex, in 2023; House of Lords Act 1999, s 2; *The London Gazette*, no 63995, p. 4994, 14 March 2023.

[155] The College of Arms, "The Roll of the Peerage", <https://www.college-of-arms.gov.uk/resources/roll-of-the-peerage>.

and the homage, would be there for constitutional, political, social and theological reasons.

At the same time the total attendance was severely restricted, and the number of peers cut, care was taken to widen the range of ordinary (non-peer or official) guests. In 2023 attendees included 450 recipients of the British Empire Medal.[156] The acclamation of the Sovereign was also altered for the times. Prior to the private prayer by the Sovereign at the Chair of Estate, the King was greeted by a "Young Person" (a Chapel Royal chorister), who asked: "Your Majesty, as children of the Kingdom of God we welcome you in the name of the King of Kings". To this welcome the King replied, "In his name, and after his example, I come not to be served but to serve".[157] The servant kingship model of kingship is emphasised over the constitutive role of the sovereign, or the homage of the magnates. Likewise, before the Recognition the Archbishop of Canterbury provided a fuller introduction to the service (as is now customary with a Eucharist), with the words:

> The grace of our Lord Jesus Christ, the love of God, and the fellowship of the Holy Spirit be with you. And with thy spirit. Alleluia. Christ is risen. He is risen indeed. Alleluia. Dearly beloved, we are gathered to offer worship and praise to Almighty God; to celebrate the life of our nations; to pray for Charles, our King; to recognise and to give thanks for his life of service to this nation, to the realms, and to the Commonwealth; and to witness with joy his crowning and anointing, as he is set apart and consecrated for the service of his people. Let us dedicate ourselves alike, in body, mind, and spirit, to a renewed faith, a joyful hope, and a commitment to serve one another in love.[158]

[156] These were 450 British Empire Medal recipients in recognition of the contributions made by remarkable volunteers, charity representatives and community champions up and down the country; "Over 850 community and charity representatives invited to enjoy the Coronation service from Westminster Abbey", <https://www.royal.uk/over-850-community-and-charity-representatives-invited-enjoy-coronation-service-westminster-abbey>, 9 April 2023.

[157] *The Authorised Liturgy for the Coronation Rite of His Majesty King Charles III For use on Saturday 6th May 2023, 11:00am at Westminster Abbey* (2023).

[158] Ibid.

The Archbishop's opening words are also an indication that the service of Holy Communion is beginning; in 1953, by contrast, the Recognition lay outside the Holy Communion service, which began only after the oaths and the presentation of the *Bible*. Now the short responsory provided liturgical recognition that the Coronation service is taking place in the season of Easter. Both changes indicated that the peerage, as the survivors of the great men of the realm, were no longer the primary focus of the coronation—its religious nature, as a eucharist (in pre-Reformation terms, a coronation mass), and the almost sacrificial dedication of the king to servant leadership, now predominated.

The Queen Consort

Turning now from the peers, spiritual and temporal, it is perhaps surprising that the Queen consort of a king is not, strictly, legally entitled to be crowned, although since mediæval times it has been customary for them to be crowned in a brief ceremony which echoes, in some respects, that of a king or queen regnant. This reflects the fact that, unlike the spiritual and temporal peers, the consort had no constitutional function as counsellor to the Sovereign—however much they might have actually exercised that function—but were the domestic and intimate partner of the Sovereign. Some consorts have not been crowned. As an example, we have the exclusion of Queen Caroline in 1821 from the coronation of her estranged husband, George IV. Caroline of Brunswick-Wolfenbüttel (1768–1821) and the Prince of Wales, later the Prince Regent, were ill-matched, and within a year of their marriage they lived apart. After an official inquiry into allegations of adultery by the princess, it was said that Caroline's behaviour was open to "very unfavourable interpretations". Later, after the Prince of Wales became King, the government prepared a Bill of Pains and Penalties,[159] to deprive her of the status of Queen, and to divorce her. This was heard in the House of Lords. Although few people thought her to be innocent, many of those at the sitting disliked the whole procedure, and the Bill was withdrawn before it could go to the House of Commons.

Queen Caroline sought to attend the coronation of her husband, although she did not have an invitation; she tried to gain admittance

[159] Parliamentary Archives, HL/PO/JO/10/8/517.

at every door of the Abbey but was turned away because she did not have a ticket. Her fruitless and unbecoming activities provoked hostility from the crowd, undermining any lingering sympathy she may have had (which mainly derived from hostility to the King, rather than any affection towards her personally). She was hooted and hissed until she left.[160] Her exclusion from the coronation did, however, help confirm the principle that no one except the Sovereign had an unfettered and undeniable right to attend.[161]

It is perhaps not surprising that the Queen Consort has no automatic right to be crowned. The status of the wife of a king is somewhat ambiguous. On the one hand she is quite unlike any other person in the realm, on the other, she has no constitutional role. The wife of a king has been styled Queen since late Saxon times, although the first and only Saxon queen so styled was Ælfthryth, wife of Edgar—and she was also the first to be anointed.[162] It is common world-wide practice for the wife of a King to be styled Queen, though there are exceptions. Generally speaking, these are when marriages are or may be plural, or are of the so-called morganatic form. The initially proposed arrangement for the former Duchess of Cornwall, wife of the then Prince of Wales—already treated in some respects almost as if this were a morganatic marriage (she was styled Duchess of Cornwall although she was, by marriage, Princess of Wales)—would have been unique. At the time of their marriage, it was said that she would, in the fulness of time, be known as Princess Consort rather than as Queen.[163]

Three questions arose as a result of this proposed arrangement. Firstly, whether the consort of a King is automatically styled Queen, secondly, what legal mechanisms, if any, were needed to ensure that Camilla Duchess of Cornwall became Camilla Princess Consort and not Queen Camilla, and thirdly (more broadly) what was the status of the spouse of the Sovereign. A Princess Consort would not, presumably, be crowned; a Queen Consort, however, would be crowned. Addressing these questions, or these complications, was neatly avoided with the announcement, on the occasion of her Platinum Jubilee, by Queen Elizabeth II, that

[160] Robins, Jane, *The Trial of Queen Caroline* (2006).

[161] *Queen Caroline's Claim to be Crowned* (1821) 1 State Trials NS 949.

[162] Huneycutt, L. L., *Matilda of Scotland* (2003), p. 35.

[163] "Clarence House press release", Clarence House. 10 February 2005.

it was her wish that Camilla be crowned as queen in due course.[164] This was duly honoured, although Queen Camilla was initially styled Queen Consort, rather than simply Queen, a curious departure from custom perhaps intended to prevent any confusion with the late Queen regnant.[165]

The first and third questions can be briefly answered. The wife of a King regnant is styled the Queen Consort. A Queen Consort remains a private citizen, but enjoys distinct prerogatives and privileges. If crowned, this is done at the coronation of their spouse, subsequently to the king's crowning.

At common law the husband of a Queen regnant is a private citizen, but he is usually granted special honorific privileges either by letters patent or by Act of Parliament. The formal position of the husband of a Queen regnant has varied considerably, according to the personal and constitutional circumstances of each case.[166] They have no automatic role at a coronation, although the Duke of Edinburgh led the homage by members of the Royal Family, as was his privilege according to his place in the order of precedence rather than his status as a royal duke—of which he was the junior.[167] He also had a key role in planning the coronation.

The purpose of crowning and investing a queen consort is to emphasise their status as the closest individual to the Sovereign, the mother of the next king (as is usually the case), and therefore ancestress of the next generations of rulers. Again, this is not for their personal glory, something

164 "The Queen's Accession Day message", 5 February 2022, https://www.royal.uk/queens-accession-day-message.

165 See, for example, the use in the *London Gazette*; "Attendees at the Accession Council", 10th September 2022, "HM The Queen Consort".

166 The husband of Queen Victoria, Prince Albert of Saxe-Coburg and Gotha, had the special title of Prince Consort conferred upon him by letters patent on 25th June 1857 (*London Gazette*, 26th June 1857). The husband of Queen Mary, who succeeded to the throne upon the enforced abdication of her father James II in 1688, was declared William III in his own right by the Bill of Rights (1688 or 1689). The husband of Elizabeth II was His Royal Highness Philip, Duke of Edinburgh, Earl of Merioneth and Baron Greenwich (*London Gazette*, 21st November 1947). He was invested by Elizabeth II, with precedence next to herself, shortly after her accession on 6th February 1952. He was granted the style and title of a Prince of the United Kingdom by letters patent of the Queen on 22nd February 1957.

167 Squibb, G. D., *Precedence in England and Wales* (1981).

some of Henry VIII's wives may have forgotten, to their ultimate personal cost.

The Legal Function of a Coronation

On the question of the legal necessity for a coronation, we have something of a dilemma. An early case (*Calvin's Case*[168]) appears to establish that a coronation is not a legal necessity, because the succession to the Crown is automatic, according to the law of succession—there has been a clearly established doctrine of immediate succession since at least 1399. However, it should more properly be held that *Calvin's Case*[169] only established, as a matter of law, the doctrine of immediate succession; it did not follow that the coronation was not a legal necessity for some other reason than to establish the king in his kingship. It also leaves unsettled the question of whether a coronation was legally necessary prior to 1399. Manifestly, although it may not be easily traced before the eighth century, nonetheless, well before 1399 few, if any, commentators would have argued that a coronation was anything other than a legal and constitutional necessity for any new King (or rarely, Queen). It is here postulated that a coronation is a legal necessity, not because it makes a Sovereign, for even in the earliest times it did not do so, but because it proclaims and affirms the legal reality. As such, it is of critical and central constitutional importance.

Calvin's Case[170] itself concerned a child born in Scotland, after the Union of the Crowns under King James VI and I in 1603. The immediate question considered by the Court of Exchequer Chamber[171] was their status under the common law, as an alien, and whether they could hold land in both kingdoms. The judges noted that.

[168] (1608) 7 Co Rep 1a; 77 ER 377.

[169] Ibid.

[170] Ibid.

[171] This court, existing in various forms from the fourteenth century, was an appellate court, hearing civil appeals from common law courts of King's Bench and the Court of Exchequer. It was abolished as part of the reforms of the 1870s; O'Keefe, David, "Sir George Jessel and the Union of Judicature" (1982) 26 American Journal of Legal History 227–251.

> the title is by descent; by Queen Elizabeth's death the Crown and kingdom of England descended to His Majesty, and he was fully and absolutely King, without any essential ceremony or act to be done ex post facto, and that coronation was but a Royal ornament, and outward solemnisation of the descent.[172]

It was observed that King Henry VI was not crowned until the eighth year of his reign. The logical fallacy of *Calvin's Case*[173] is not hard to identify. The method by which the new Sovereign establishes their title to the Crown may vary, as outlined in a previous section, and includes parliamentary title, common law, custom and election; more usually, a combination of these is present. There was formerly often a brief interregnum, until the heir apparent established a clear title, or (more rarely) until a usurper was able to convert de facto authority into de jure authority. However the title was established—and indeed after 1399 there was deemed to be immediate succession—the necessity for a coronation was not doubted, even if it was not itself the basis for royal authority, if indeed it ever had been. The necessity for a coronation did not lie in it being the basis for a de jure or de facto kingship, but rather for deeper and more nuanced constitutional reasons. The decision with respect to coronations in *Calvin's Case*[174] was in any event *obiter dicta* rather than *ratio decidendi*, and therefore not strictly binding as a precedent.[175]

Likewise, the proclamation of the Sovereign does not make them king or queen, but is an integral part of the accession nonetheless. The accession council, which assembles to proclaim a new Sovereign, does not make the Sovereign or effect the accession, it merely publicises the accession, which took place immediately on the death of the previously reigning monarch, by the operation of common law (or rather constitutional law, as it predates the common law in its origins), and may be regulated by statute law. The proclamation of the new Sovereign is an older tradition (at least from Edward VI in 1547), but the idea that an accession council makes it dates only to the accession of James I in 1603, when the fact that

[172] (1608) 7 Co Rep 1a; 77 ER 377. Due to the importance of the case, there were fifteen judges, led by the Lord Chancellor (Thomas Egerton, Lord Ellesmere, later Viscount Brackley). Two judges dissented.

[173] (1608) 7 Co Rep 1a; 77 ER 377.

[174] Ibid.

[175] Cross, Rupert and J. W. Harris, *Precedent in English Law* (4th ed., 1991).

James VI was in Scotland required immediate action in London—waiting for his arrival could have been politically dangerous. In the event it took two weeks for the new King James VI and I to reach London,[176] the new king's journey from Edinburgh having something of the character of a triumphal procession.

However the title to the Crown is founded, whether it be election, strict hereditary succession, parliamentary title, cession, abdication, conquest, or a combination of some of these, one element remains common—the coronation. This is so even if, as in the past, it was delayed—or in the case of King Edward VIII, omitted altogether because of the brevity of his reign.[177] As a political and constitutional ritual dating back well before the Norman Conquest, it has unrivalled antiquity—not itself perhaps a basis for legal necessity, but then it could be argued that the coronation, as a constitutional device, precedes the common law, and is such an ancient part of the constitution that it is indispensable.

In addition, the provisions of the Coronation Oaths Act 1688[178] may also be interpreted as requiring a coronation, rather than any other form of inauguration. The introductory words of the Act state that:

> Whereas by the Law and Ancient Usage of this Realme the Kings and Queens thereof have taken a Solemne Oath upon the Evangelists at Their respective Coronations to maintaine the Statutes Laws and Customs of the said Realme and all the People and Inhabitants thereof in their Spirituall and Civill Rights and Properties But forasmuch as the Oath itselfe on such Occasion Administred hath heretofore beene framed in doubtfull Words and Expressions with relation to ancient Laws and Constitutions at this time unknowne To the end therefore that One Uniforme Oath may be in all Times to come taken by the Kings and Queens of this Realme and to Them respectively Adminstred at the times of Their and every of Their Coronation.

[176] Croft, Pauline, *King James* (2003), p. 49.

[177] Edward VIII had initially been reluctant to have a coronation at all (asking the Archbishop of Canterbury whether it could be dispensed with), but conceded that a shorter service would be acceptable; his desire for a lower-key event led to the planned abandonment of the royal procession through London the following day, the thanksgiving service at St Paul's Cathedral and the dinner with London dignitaries; Strong, Sir Roy, *Coronation* (2005), pp. 421–422.

[178] Will & Mary c 6.

Similarly Sect. 4.2 of the Act of Settlement 1700[179] requires that every new Sovereign must make, subscribe and repeat, at their coronation, a declaration of their religious orthodoxy.[180] The Act states that.

> ... And that every King and Queen of this Realm who shall come to and succeed in the Imperiall Crown of this Kingdom by vertue of this Act shall have the Coronation Oath administred to him her or them at their respective Coronations according to the Act of Parliament made in the First Year of the Reign of His Majesty and the said late Queen Mary intituled An Act for establishing the Coronation Oath and shall make subscribe and repeat the Declaration in the Act first above recited mentioned or referred to in the Manner and Form thereby prescribed.

The Coronation Oath Act 1688[181] specifies, in s 2,

> May it please Your Majesties That the Oath herein Mentioned and hereafter Expressed shall and may be Adminstred to their most Excellent Majestyes King William and Queene Mary (whome God long preserve) at the time of Their Coronation in the presence of all Persons that shall be then and there present at the Solemnizeing thereof by the Archbishop of Canterbury or the Archbishop of Yorke or either of them or any other Bishop of this Realme whome the King's Majesty shall thereunto appoint and who shall be hereby thereunto respectively Authorized which Oath followeth and shall be Administred in this Manner That is to say,
>
> > (section 3)
> > The Arch-Bishop or Bishop shall say,
> > Will You solemnely Promise and Sweare to Governe the People of this Kingdome of England and the Dominions thereto belonging according to the Statutes in Parlyament Agreed on and the Laws and Customs of the same?
> > The King and Queene shall say,
> > I solemnly Promise soe to doe
> > Arch Bishop or Bishop,
> > Will You to Your power cause Law and Justice in Mercy to be Executed in all Your Judgements.

[179] 12 & 13 Will III. c. 2.

[180] Her Majesty The Queen made the declaration on opening Parliament, in the presence of both Houses of Parliament, on 4th November 1952.

[181] 1 Will. III & Mary c. 6.

King and Queene,
I will
Arch Bishop or Bishop.
Will You to the utmost of Your power Maintaine the Laws of God the true Profession of the Gospell and the Protestant Reformed Religion Established by Law? And will You Preserve unto the Bishops and Clergy of this Realme and to the Churches committed to their Charge all such Rights and Priviledges as by Law doe or shall appertaine unto them or any of them.
King and Queene.
All this I Promise to doe.
After this the King and Queene laying His and Her Hand upon the Holy Gospells, shall say,
King and Queene
The things which I have here before promised I will performe and Keepe Soe help me God.
Then the King and Queene shall kisse the Booke.
(section 4)
And the said Oath shall be in like manner Adminstred to every King or Queene who shall Succeede to the Imperiall Crowne of this Realme at their respective Coronations by one of the Archbishops or Bishops of this Realme of England for the time being to be thereunto appointed by such King or Queene respectively and in the Presence of all Persons that shall be Attending Assisting or otherwise present at such their respective Coronations Any Law Statute or Usage to the contrary notwithstanding.

All are instructive, but s 4 of the Coronation Oaths Act 1688[182] is particularly significant. The clear assumption of the Act as a whole is that a coronation oath is a constitutional requirement, and its sole and proper setting is in the context of a coronation. The precise form and content of the coronation itself is not thereby specified or settled, and is probably not legally significant in respect of the Coronation Oaths Act 1688,[183] provided it qualifies as a coronation as distinct from some other ritual or occasion. This probably entails adhering to the form and structure of the coronation as it has evolved over the past millennia, and specifically the provisions of the *Liber Regalis*.

[182] Ibid.

[183] Ibid.

Additionally, the Court of Claims had long been held to hear petitions relating to attendance and service at coronations.[184] The first recorded such court was held in 1377 before the Lord High Steward, John of Gaunt, Duke of Lancaster. Since the time of Henry VII commissioners have been appointed in lieu of the Lord High Steward (whose office has generally been vacant since 1421, and is now only filled temporarily for the coronation, for an impeachment—the last being in 1806[185]—and formerly for the trial of peers[186]), and the Court of Claims now consisted, in modern times, of a royal commission appointed under the Great Seal.[187] The modern practice had been for the Lord Chancellor to preside, though since 2006 the Lord Chancellor is no longer a senior judge,[188] so this would be inappropriate now. However, this is a moot point since no Court of Claims was constituted ahead of the 2023 coronation of King Charles III[189]; the abolition of the judicial procedure was recommended in a report by the Constitution Unit of University College London in 2018.[190] This was on the basis that its functions could be

[184] See, generally, Wollaston, Sir Gerald, *Coronation Claims* (1903).

[185] Hutchison, Gary D. "'The Manager in Distress': Reaction to the Impeachment of Henry Dundas, 1805–7" (2017) 36(2) Parliamentary History 198–217.

[186] This later was abolished in 1948 by the Criminal Justice Act 1948 (11 & 12 Geo. VI c. 58), the last trial being in 1935, under the Lord Chancellor (Viscount Hailsham), who presided as Lord High Steward *pro tempore*, over the trial of Edward Russell, 26th Baron de Clifford, on a charge of manslaughter in a motor vehicle accident—he was acquitted.

[187] In modern times, this Court sat in the Whitehall Council Chamber used by the Judicial Committee of the Privy Council (until it was co-located with the new Supreme Court in 2009).

[188] The effect of the Constitutional Reform Act 2005, with the Lord Chief Justice becoming the Head of the judiciary in England and Wales. As a consequence, the Lord Chancellor was given a new oath, reflecting their changed role:

> I, (name), do swear that in the office of Lord High Chancellor of Great Britain I will respect the rule of law, defend the independence of the judiciary and discharge my duty to ensure the provision of resources for the efficient and effective support of the courts for which I am responsible. So help me God.

Constitutional Reform Act 2005 s 17.

[189] Torrance, David, "The Coronation: history and ceremonial" (House of Commons Library Research Briefing, number CBP9412, 6 December 2022), p. 20.

[190] Morris, R. M., *Inaugurating a New Reign* (2018), p. vii.

achieved more cost-effectively by administrative means. In any even the court might refer any claim to the Sovereign's pleasure, and the Sovereign might withdraw a claim from the commission and transfer it to another tribunal.

The Sovereign cannot establish, merely by the exercise of the royal prerogative, a court to administer any law but the common law,[191] so the Court of Claims may perhaps best be conceived as a quasi-judicial tribunal, or an irregular court the origins of whose jurisdiction lie in the earliest years of the realm and may be regarded as existing by prescription.[192] The existence of a duly constituted court to determine claims for personal and official attendance at a coronation attests at once to the social and political importance of attendance, and to the seriousness with which the matter was dealt with; no purely optional or symbolic ceremony would have such a provision. Although the Court of Claims is ancient, its formal necessity may be questioned since it exists at the behest of the Sovereign, to whom recourse may be had. The reports of previous Courts of Claims have however proved to be invaluable sources for historical and constitutional research,[193] and helpful in planning coronations. The decision to dispense with the Court of Claims in 2023 was unsurprising, but does little to negate the legal importance of the coronation.

The antiquity and indeed constitutional necessity of the coronation itself is grounded in the earliest years of the state and cannot be ascribed to any single Act of Parliament—for it predates Parliament—or any royal instrument. It, like the royal prerogative,[194] pre-dates both common and statute law. Parliament, as a permanent or semi-permanent legislative body, far post-dates the establishment of the coronation.[195]

The content and structure of the coronation also provides evidence of its irreducible constitutional role and importance. As noted earlier,

[191] *In re the Lord Bishop of Natal* (1864) 3 Moo PCC NS 115; 16 ER 43.

[192] A comparison may be made with the Court of Chivalry; Squibb, G. D., *The High Court of Chivalry* (1959).

[193] Wollaston, Sir Gerald, *Coronation Claims* (1903).

[194] Cox, Noel, *The Royal Prerogative and Constitutional Law* (2021).

[195] Maddicott, J. R., *The Origins of the English Parliament, 924–1327* (2010); Weiler, Björn, "Describing Rituals of Succession and the Legitimation of Kingship in the West, ca. 1000–ca. 1150", in Alexander Beihammer, Stavroula Constantinou, and Maria G. Parani (eds.), *Court Ceremonies and Rituals of Power in Byzantium and the Mediæval Mediterranean* (2013), pp. 113–140.

there may be said to be seven elements to a coronation, the recognition or acclamation, the oath, the anointing, the investiture with regalia, the crowning, the enthroning, and the homage. For a Sovereign basing their title on election, the first is vitally important—and indeed it is when their claim may be disputed, for whatever reason.

The contemporary wording of the recognition or acclamation is instructive. At the north, south, east and west sides of the central theatre within Westminster Abbey, the archbishop calls for the recognition of the Sovereign, with the words,

> I here present unto you King Charles, your undoubted King, Wherefore all you who are come this day to do your homage and service, are you willing to do the same?[196]

This is a clear survival of the time when the kingship was elective within the royal family, with the assembly in the Abbey representing the *witan*. After the people acclaim the Sovereign at each side, the archbishop administers an oath to the Sovereign—the coronation oath now having statutory authority. A form of social compact may be identified in this element of the ceremony, though one must exercise due care in ascribing anachronistic interpretations to older practices. Like the homage and fealty from the Lords temporal and spiritual respectfully, the acclamation may be seen as a survival of the ancient process of election by the magnates; even after the creation of a separate House of Commons for the burghers and knights of the shires, the commons were not called upon to render homage at a coronation as they were not, unlike the peerage, hereditary counsellors to the Sovereign.

In likely recognition of constitutional and societal change, in addition to the Archbishop of Canterbury, in 2023, participating in the act of Recognition of His Majesty, whereby the King was presented to the Congregation, were an eclectic group, comprising Baroness Amos, LG (representing the oldest Order of Chivalry in England), Lady Elish Angiolini, LT (representing the oldest Order of Chivalry in Scotland),

[196] *Authorised Liturgy for the Coronation Rite of His Majesty King Charles III For use on Saturday 6th May 2023, 11:00am at Westminster Abbey* (29 April 2023); The only difference in 1953 was that the question began, "Sirs"; *The Form and Order of Service that is to be performed and the Ceremonies that are to be observed in The Coronation of Her Majesty Queen Elizabeth II in the Abbey Church of St. Peter, Westminster, on Tuesday, the second day of June, 1953* (1953).

and Christopher Finney, GC, Chair of the Victoria Cross and George Cross Association.[197] This was contrary to the earlier modern practice for the presentation of the monarch to the people by the Archbishop of Canterbury accompanied by the Lord High Chancellor, the Lord Great Chamberlain, the Lord High Constable and the Earl Marshal, with Garter Principal King of Arms preceding them, and the recognition of the monarch by the people. The Great Officers of State were present, but their role in this essential first stage of the coronation was relinquished in favour of a more representative group. The role of the Lord High Chancellor, in particular, was diminished, due to the reduction in the latter's functions.[198] The new group individually addressed the assembled congregation: "I here present unto you King Charles, your undoubted King: Wherefore all you who are come this day to do your homage and service: are you willing to do the same?"[199] Rather than the Great Officers of State addressing an audience comprised largely of the peerage and political elite, in the 2023 coronation a more diverse group (still giving due tribute to tradition) addressed a more eclectic congregation.

After the Communion service is interrupted, the anthem "Come, Holy Ghost"[200] is recited, as a prelude to the act of anointing. The translation "Come Holy Ghost, our souls inspire" was by Bishop John Cosin in 1625, and has been used for all subsequent British coronations.[201] After this anthem, the Archbishop of Canterbury (or the archbishop or bishop

[197] Press Release, "Roles to be performed at the Coronation Service at authorised Westminster Abbey". The Royal Family. 27 April 2023.

[198] The effect of the Constitutional Reform Act 2005, with the Lord Chief Justice becoming the Head of the judiciary in England and Wales.

[199] *The Authorised Liturgy for the Coronation Rite of His Majesty King Charles III For use on Saturday 6th May 2023, 11:00am at Westminster Abbey* (29 April 2023).

[200] "*Veni Creator Spiritus*", is a traditional hymn believed to have been written by Rabanus Maurus, a ninth-century German monk, teacher, and archbishop. As an invocation of the Holy Spirit, *Veni Creator Spiritus* is sung during liturgical celebrations on the feast of Pentecost (at both Terce and Vespers). It is also sung at occasions such as the entrance of Cardinals to the Sistine Chapel when they elect a new pope, as well as at the consecration of bishops, the ordination of priests, the sacrament of Confirmation, the dedication of churches, the celebration of synods or councils, the coronation of monarchs, the profession of members of religious institutes, and other similar solemn events.

[201] The translation "Come Holy Ghost, our souls inspire" was by Bishop John Cosin in 1625, and has been used for all subsequent British coronations; Aquilina, Ivan D., *The Eucharistic Understanding of John Cosin and His Contribution to the 1662 Book Of Common Prayer* (2002), p. 6.

acting in his place) recites a prayer in preparation for the anointing, which is based on the ancient prayer "Deus electorum fortitude" also used in the anointing of French kings.[202] After this prayer, the coronation anthem "Zadok the Priest" is sung by the choir. The Sovereign is anointed seated on the coronation chair, under which is the Stone of Scone (nowadays to be borrowed from its permanent home in Scotland[203]). The archbishop then concludes the ceremonies of the anointing by reciting a prayer that is a modified English translation of the ancient Latin prayer "Deus, Dei Filius", recited in the consecration of other Christian sovereigns.[204]

This rite arguably serves the constitutional purpose of establishing the new Sovereign as an anointed king or queen in the tradition of the ancient near eastern kings. Likewise, the investiture with regalia, and the crowning symbolically, and therefore practically, invests the new Sovereign with a sacred and secular authority, in a form of Weberian historical legitimacy.[205] The homage, like the acclamation, represents and in some part creates, acceptance of the new regime.

The coronation assumes greater relevance if the title to the Crown is disputed, however unmeritorious the claim of another might be. For example, in *Britain's Real Monarch*, a historical documentary presented by Sir Tony Robinson and first shown on Channel 4 in the United Kingdom on 3rd January 2004, historian Dr Michael Jones advanced a thesis that King Edward IV was illegitimate, and that, as a consequence, all subsequent Sovereigns were without title to the throne. According to this thesis, the rightful Sovereign was now Michael Abney-Hastings, 14th Earl of Loudoun, who was to die in 2012. This contention was however without basis in law or fact. Whether or not Edward IV was

[202] Zupka, Dušan, "Power of rituals and rituals of power: Religious and secular rituals in the political culture of mediæval Kingdom of Hungary", in *Historiography in Motion* (2010), pp. 29–42.

[203] Breeze, David, and Graeme Munro, *The Stone of Destiny* (1997).

[204] *The Form and Order of Service that is to be performed and the Ceremonies that are to be observed in The Coronation of Her Majesty Queen Elizabeth II in the Abbey Church of St. Peter, Westminster, on Tuesday, the second day of June, 1953.*

[205] Collins, Randall, *Weberian Sociological Theory* (1986); Weiler, Björn, "Describing Rituals of Succession and the Legitimation of Kingship in the West, ca. 1000–ca. 1150", in Alexander Beihammer, Stavroula Constantinou, and Maria G. Parani (eds.), *Court Ceremonies and Rituals of Power in Byzantium and the Mediæval Mediterranean* (2013), pp. 113–140.

illegitimate, the title of subsequent Kings and Queens is undoubted, in part because of their coronation, with the multifaceted recognition and inauguration which they entail. Even a de facto king becomes a de jure one over time.[206] Sir Nicholas Bacon, the Lord Keeper of the Great Seal, advised that "the Crowne once worn quite taketh away all Defects whatsoever".[207]

By the fifteenth century the principle had developed that any aberrant settlement of the succession had to be justified by the consent of the estates of the realm, in addition to the rituals of the coronation—though not in place of them. This was done for the Tudors, who succeeded shortly after Edward IV's death, and has been done on a number of occasions since then—especially by the Act of Settlement 1700.[208]

Equally importantly, the title of the present King derives also from his hereditary right as the heir of generations of Kings and Queens since then. A claim by a distant heir of Edward III against a Sovereign descended from Henry VII would be legally and historically extremely weak. But this is not the only potential challenge to the succession.

Rival Claims

The laws of succession are at the very heart of hereditary monarchy. Yet while (with the exception of the Abdication of King Edward VIII in 1936) there had been no changes in Great Britain since 1701 until 2013, the law of succession was historically often a matter of uncertainty. Not every sovereign who ruled in England was the rightful heir. As a consequence of the statutory exclusion of Roman Catholics from 1689, and due to the irregularity of succession which occurred at the time of the Wars of the Roses, there remain even today a number of potential claimants to the throne, aside from the dubious claim ascribed to the Earl of Loudoun.

There are few surviving representatives of the lineage of the mediæval royal family of England, due to the depredations of wars and later more

[206] Brookfield, F. M., "Some aspects of the Necessity Principle in Constitutional Law" (1972) University of Oxford DPhil thesis.

[207] Duncan, Sarah and Valerie Schutte (eds.), *The Birth of a Queen* (2016), p. 80.

[208] 12 & 13 Will III c 2.

peaceful extinctions. The current, 15th, Earl of Loudoun[209] is the heir of Margaret Countess of Salisbury (sister of Warwick), if the children of King Edward IV and Elizabeth Woodville are regarded as illegitimate. Margaret was the daughter of George Duke of Clarence, descended from Edward III. But this family never obtained the throne, which was seized by Henry Tudor, a man with an even weaker claim. Yet, once established as de facto king, Henry's title was legally good..[210] In addition, Lady Caroline Child Villiers, daughter of the Earl of Jersey, could raise a claim based on descent in accordance with Henry VIII's Third Act of Succession,[211] as could Teresa Freeman-Grenville, 13th Lady Kinloss.

Prince Franz, Duke of Bavaria is now the Senior Representative of the House of Stuart.[212] His ancestress Princess Maria Beatrice of Savoy (1792–1840) married her maternal uncle Duke Francesco IV of Modena (1779–1846) in a marriage which would be invalid in English law for reasons of consanguinity. However, as a marriage which is valid where contracted is recognised by English law, unless contrary to the nature of marriage,[213]

These potential claimants lack the legitimacy of being proclaimed, acclaimed, anointed and crowned—possession of the Crown is not, perhaps, legally equivalent to the maxim that possession is nine-tenths of legal title[214]—but coronation, and the legitimacy which that imparts, bolsters any claim to the throne and, conversely, weakens and ultimately

[209] Born 1974, he succeeded his father 2012. Created 1633, he is 15th in line. He is also co-heir to the English baronies of Botreaux (1368), Stanley (1456), and Hastings (1461).

[210] Brookfield, F. M., "Some aspects of the Necessity Principle in Constitutional Law" (1972) University of Oxford DPhil thesis.

[211] Succession to the Crown Act 1543 (35 Hen. VIII c. 1).

[212] The line of Jacobite succession is James VII and II 1685-1701, James VIII and III 1701-66, Charles III 1766-88, Henry I and IX 1788-1807, Charles IV 1807-19, Victor 1819-24, Mary II 1824-40, Francis 1840-75, Mary III 1875-1919, Robert IV and I 1919-55, Albert 1955-96, Francis II (born 1933) since 1996.

[213] The formal validity of a marriage is governed by the *lex loci celebrationis*. A marriage is formally valid if it complies with the formal requirements of the *lex loci celebrationis*, even though it does not comply with the formal requirements of the law of the parties' domicile; *Berthiauem v Dastous* [1930] AC 79 (PC).

[214] *Parker v British Airways Board* [1982] 1 QB 1004.

destroys and expunges, any lingering claim by a pretender and their heirs.[215]

The importance of a definitive assertion of authority in a coronation cannot be overstated, particularly when the title to the throne is weak, or there are rival claimants—however distant their claims might be. Legitimacy is derived, inter alia, from the coronation, where a de facto king becomes a de jure king, and defects in title are corrected. This is especially important when the kingship exercises significant political power, but is also relevant even in a limited or constitutional monarchy.

European Counterparts to the English/British Coronation

The English and later British position is not markedly dissimilar to that of other European countries, particularly the old kingdom of France and the kingdoms of western and central Europe—Hungary and Poland perhaps excepted. The coronation at once proclaims and dedicates the new king for their rule. The modern situation in Scandinavia presents an interesting contrast, however. The coronations in Denmark, Norway, and Sweden, were abolished for reasons unique to each kingdom—but in none of these states could the coronation be said to have the same multifaceted role as in Britain.

Denmark, nominally an elective monarchy until 1660, held coronations from 1170 to 1840, mostly in Lund Cathedral, St Mary's Cathedral, Copenhagen, and the chapel of Frederiksborg Palace in Hillerød.[216] The constitutional evolution of Denmark was reflected in the nature of the coronation. The elective monarchy used a typical mediæval coronation service, though ironically perhaps the absolute monarchy (from 1660) introduced anointing and dispensed with the crowning—though the crown was worn –and the advent of the constitutional monarchy in 1848 saw the demise of the coronation altogether in favour of a simple proclamation. Frederick VII granted a constitution within a couple of months of succeeding and was therefore the last absolute king and the first constitutional king of Denmark.[217] The coronation was thus linked to the

[215] Brookfield, F. M., "Some aspects of the Necessity Principle in Constitutional Law" (1972) University of Oxford DPhil thesis.

[216] Bak, János M. (ed.), *Coronations* (1990).

[217] Hoffman, Erich, "Coronation and Coronation Ordines in Mediæval Scandinavia", in János M. Bak (ed.), *Coronations* (1990), pp. 125–143.

constitutional evolution of the kingdom, and in its fullness, consecrated and inaugurated a king—effectively fulfilling a constitutive function. The absolute monarchy had less need of this, the royal legitimacy being independent of anything suggesting the approval or approbation of anyone else was required. The demise of absolute monarchy rendered the coronation, thus conceived, unnecessary.

Coronations were held in Norway from 1164 to 1906, mostly in Nidaros Cathedral in Trondheim. In 1905 the union between Norway and Sweden was dissolved, and the last coronation was in 1906 for the first king of an independent Norway since 1387, Haakon VII. His successor, Olav V, was not crowned on his accession in 1957, following the repeal of article 9 of chapter B of the 1814 Constitution—coronations being seen by then as undemocratic—and kings are now (from 1958) inaugurated in a simple ritual of benediction.[218] The coronation was perceived as a mediæval relic, and perhaps, as tainted by association with the joint Swedish-Norwegian kingdom from 1387. Rather than being retained as a uniquely Norwegian institution, it was discarded almost as soon as it was restored as a solely Norwegian coronation, possibly as an assertion of the independence of Norway and in defiance of the old ways. The argument was that a modern monarchy has limited powers and therefore no need of a ritual which savoured of personal authority and status.

Sweden, in turn, abolished the coronation in 1907 because, as in Norway, they were seen as inconsistent with democracy. The last coronation had been in 1873.[219] Sweden, like Denmark, initially had a nominally elective monarchy, and the coronation served the purpose of legitimising their rule.[220] As in Norway, in a modern era, where the king lacked personal authority except as an instrument of his ministers and Parliament, a ceremony which suggested or even hinted at personal legitimacy outside the ambit of the Constitution, was politically too charged to survive.

Unlike the Scandinavian countries, where coronations were associated with autocracy, or at least a kingship which accorded a significant independent political role to the king, in Britain a very different path had

[218] János M. Bak (ed.), *Coronations* (1990).

[219] Woolley, Reginald Maxwell, *Coronation Rites* (1915).

[220] Hunt, Alice, *Drama of Coronation* (2008).

been followed. Effectively side-lined by politicians accountable to Parliament after 1815, British sovereigns relatively early pioneered the concept of the constitutional monarchy. The coronation, always a public spectacle as well as a legal, political, and theological ritual, acquired a greater role in forming the popular monarchy, especially in the course of the twentieth century.[221] The rationale for abolition followed in Norway, Sweden or Denmark therefore did not apply in the United Kingdom.

The rationale for the abolition—or technically merely suspension—of the papal coronation is even less applicable to the United Kingdom. The first recorded papal coronation was of Pope Nicholas I in 858. The Holy See ceased using coronations in 1978, largely because it was felt that the coronation emphasised the temporal power of the papacy rather than the religious role of the Holy See. The reforms of Vatican II had also led to the abolition of most of the ancient papal household, including many posts which were hitherto present at papal coronations. The last papal coronation was therefore that of Pope Paul VI in 1963. The ceremony was not, however, abolished, so it remains possible for a new pope to choose to be crowned, however unlikely that may now be.

The legal role of a coronation in the British tradition depends not simply on the constitutive effect of the coronation, or on its symbolic function. It is deeply embedded in the constitution. It has symbolic functions which are not suggestive of autocratic power or personal superiority, indeed its emphasis has long been on a kingship bound by the recognition and acceptance of the people, the approbation of the church, the fealty and homage of the magnates, secular and ecclesiastical (which establish reciprocal obligations), and a royal oath to reign in accordance with tradition and custom. As such, its legal and constitutional function is quite dissimilar to most other states, and its survival for this reason alone, unsurprising even in a democratic age.

Conclusion

Upon the demise of the Crown there are certain steps which are followed to ensure the smooth commencement of the new reign. This was particularly important when matters of high policy—particularly religious—might render a succession uncertain. Each step, in conjunction with the

[221] Kuhn, William. *Democratic royalism* (1996).

coronation, forms a part of a practical, legal and political assertion of legitimacy.

Only the coronation provides the fullest endorsement of the Sovereign, and the clearest assertion and establishment of their title. This is true of all ancient monarchies, though less true of states whose constitutional constructs are based on modern codified constitutions. The situation in the United Kingdom, with constitutional government having a largely unbroken heritage of 1,500 years[222]—even William I's accession may be explained and justified in terms of then contemporary law and practice—is exceptional in the modern world. In this context the coronation must be seen as a profoundly significant element in the (unwritten) constitution.

The constitutive function of the coronation, like the ancient Egyptian coronation ceremonies, lies in the cumulative effect of its many parts. Sacred and profane, the coronation's discrete elements all contribute towards confirming and proclaiming the title of the sovereign. This title derives from hereditary right, parliamentary grant and acclamation and recognition (as a survival of election by the magnates), with the investiture with regalia, the vesting in imperial (and sacerdotal) robes, and the anointing with holy oil elevating the candidate for kingship to king indeed. As in mediæval times, even today the coronation is vital to the legitimation of the Sovereign.[223]

Since the title to the Crown does not depend upon statutory title alone, or hereditary title alone, but is a mixture of contributing elements, so the coronation sets the seal upon the king, as the chosen of God (or the people). His—or her in the case of a queen regnant—title is only fully established in their coronation. During the period between accession and coronation the king or queen is truly the sovereign, for there is no interregnum, but like the King of the Romans awaiting a papal coronation

[222] The Egyptian monarchy lasted from c.3100 BC to 30 BC, more than twice as long, though there were many changes of dynasty during that time. In contrast, as already mentioned, the Japanese imperial dynasty is ancient, even discounting the legendary period, and is as old as the English; Shillony, Ben-Ami, *The Emperors of Modern Japan* (2008).

[223] Weiler, Björn, "Describing Rituals of Succession and the Legitimation of Kingship in the West, ca. 1000–ca. 1150", in Alexander Beihammer, Stavroula Constantinou, and Maria G. Parani (eds.), *Court Ceremonies and Rituals of Power in Byzantium and the Mediæval Mediterranean* (2013), pp. 113–140.

to become Holy Roman Emperor, a further step is required to achieve the fullness of the title, to turn it from being in pretence to being in reality. But the coronation does not, of itself, suggest an absolute kingship—indeed the coronation oath, in particular, emphasises the limits on the king's powers.

No coronation alone created a sovereign, whether in the British tradition, or that of Egypt or Rome, and even in the Holy Roman Empire the requirement for a papal coronation was arguably a special case (partly grounded on the succession being determined by approval of the senate, people and army—and later of the electoral princes,[224] and partly on the assertion of *imperium*). It would be false logic to suggest that the question of whether or not a coronation is a legal necessity can be answered simply by asking whether a coronation makes a king. The answer, it must be said, almost ubiquitously, is that the coronation does not make the king, but rather that the king makes the coronation. Only the coronation can provide the ultimate endorsement and *imprimatur* for a king; but only a king can be crowned—queens regnant and consort excepted.

The coronation was never of itself intended to "make" a king—many early kings were crowned later in their reigns, and a few were crowned, or at least anointed, more than once. But none, once coronations became established as obligatory (by at least the tenth century, and probably for several centuries before then), doubted the necessity for a coronation, in order to provide the sacred and profane recognition needed for a successful reign.

As a constitutive exercise, the British coronation is quite dissimilar to any of the Scandinavian or papal coronations, for instance, thus rendering any argument for abolition or radical reform based upon those precedents constitutionally dangerous. The argument that other European countries abolished, or never had, coronations, ignores the facts that Britain is the last great European monarchy, and has its own tradition of coronations, and cannot be compared to modern practice in newer states, nor indeed to those of older states—such as Denmark and Sweden—which have quite dissimilar constitutional histories. There is scant rationale for abandoning what has been regarded universally (or almost universally) as a necessary

[224] Vale, M. G. A., *The princely court* (2001).

step in the accession to the throne. There is much sound reason for the preservation of a constitutional step which has the most profound antiquity and which pre-dates every modern organ of government except the kingship itself—and in England, possibly also office of the Archbishop of Canterbury.

CHAPTER 5

The Political Function of a Coronation

Introduction

Each stage of the coronation reflects, to varying degrees, the political role of the Sovereign as monarch—or head of state as we might perhaps today anachronistically, and arguably inappropriately, style the monarch.[1] The political function of the coronation is distinct from the legal or theological functions but is not completely divorced from either of these. Indeed, to some extent at least it links the legal and theological functions of the

[1] Aside from the question of whether there is, in British constitutional law, such a legal entity as the state, "Head of State" is perhaps more properly reserved for the realm of international law; Foakes, Joanne, *The Position of Heads of State and Senior Officials in International Law* (2014). Chapter II, Section 61 of the Commonwealth of Australia Constitution Act 1900, states the position of the Sovereign more accurately, and in a manner more consistent with Westminster constitutional history:

> The executive power of the Commonwealth is vested in the Queen and is exercisable by the Governor-General as the Queen's representative, and extends to the execution and maintenance of this Constitution, and of the laws of the Commonwealth.

N. Cox, *The Political, Legal, and Theological Functions of the Ceremony in the British Tradition*,
https://doi.org/10.1007/978-3-031-88960-8_5

ritual of the coronation and reflects the contemporary as well as the timeless elements of the political role of the monarch in the state or polity. For instance, several of the seven key elements of a coronation can be seen as illustrating this distinction between the political or practical function of a coronation and its theological and legal functions. The recognition or acclamation, the oath, the anointing, the investiture with regalia, the crowning, the enthroning, and the homage are all key aspects of the coronation, but each represents or involves different aspects of the constitutional role of the coronation. For example, whilst the recognition or acclamation may be seen as reflecting, at least in some respects, the elective aspects of the Crown, it also has a more overtly political role than, for example, the anointing. Likewise, the homage, with its notions of fealty and allegiance, reflects the relationship between Sovereign and people, albeit in a very particular and specific—and individualised—formalised manner. It also carries with it imputations of feudalism, though its origins and meaning go much further into the past even than that era.

This chapter considers some aspects of the political function of the coronation, from the conceptual and practical role of the monarch to the nature of the state, or realm. It will cover the development of the role of the Sovereign, and the influence of the office on the evolution of the polity. The coronation reflects not the king's personal magnificence, but their role as sovereign of the kingdom—or kingdoms. As such, the rites of the coronation manifest aspects of that relationship, rather than any solely personal status, just as the Egyptian pharaohs were often invested with the joint crowns of Upper and Lower Egypt, symbolising in their person and in their attire the unity of the (united) kingdom. In any system which exhibits the joint characteristics of continuity, longevity and an unwritten—or uncodified—constitution, the authority of the regime cannot be ascribed purely to majoritarian electoral endorsement. More profound structural factors are present, and these are predominantly based on continuity, acquiescence and conformity with inherited forms, rituals and symbolism.[2]

In the course of this chapter, we will consider how the role and status of the Sovereign has changed, including the functional role of the king as law-maker, their symbolic and practical role in the state, and their contribution to legitimacy. In the latter discussion we will consider the

[2] See Hobsbawn, Eric and Terence Ranger, *The Invention of Tradition* (1983).

symbolic role of the Crown, and the Sovereign's specific contribution there to legitimacy and continuity. Each of these aspects is reflected, directly or indirectly, in the coronation. The relationship of the Sovereign with the realms, and most profoundly, that with the United Kingdom, are manifested in the ritual of the coronation. Elements of the coronation also reflect the public role of the Sovereign, including their legislative, executive, judicial (and ecclesiological) roles, and their central role in establishing and maintaining legitimacy.

The first section considers the role of the king as law-maker. From the sole source of law in Saxon times, through to the King-in-Parliament, the Sovereign has long been the quintessential authority for law-making. This has also long been reflected in the presence of the Lords Temporal and Spiritual at a coronation, the acclamation, homage, and most crucially, the coronation oath. Law-making was an is an exercise in sovereign authority, but also long exhibited, in the British tradition, a collectivist modality and political—if not initially democratic—accountability.

The second section of the chapter expands on the feudal elements of the monarchy, and the echoes of these to be found in the coronation. Although the coronation, in some respects, both predates feudalism and also has post-feudal elements, there is an inevitable overlay of feudal forms and language, even if these are sometimes more apparent than real.

The third section considers imperial kingship, with its links to a Roman past—it was not a coincidence that in 973 Edgar was crowned in Bath, with its significant Roman remains (undoubtedly much more obvious then than they are now, despite nineteenth century and later restoration and reconstruction work on the Roman baths). The pre-feudal and feudal kingship sought to acquire the status and authority which was throughout Europe being asserted by renewed claims to a past golden age of the Roman *imperium*. Imperial is to be understood not in relation to the modern British empire,[3] but rather in respect to the claim to sovereignty and authority equal to the hitherto ubiquitous claims of universal *imperium* of the Holy Roman Empire, as successor to the authority of Rome. The coronation of King Edgar included a procession

[3] In particular the First (seventeenth and eighteenth centuries), Second (eighteenth and nineteenth centuries), and Third British empires (nineteenth and twentieth centuries); See Keith, A. B., *Constitutional History of the First British Empire* (1930); Madden, F. and D. Fieldhouse (eds.), *The Classical Period of the First British Empire, 1689–178* (1985), vol. 2; Halstead, J. P., *The Second British Empire* (1983).

through the streets of Bath, during which the king was carried on a litter by four prominent nobles. The ceremony also included a series of oaths and pledges, in which Edgar promised to rule justly and to protect the rights and liberties of his subjects.

The development of the English state, however, only partly relied upon feudal or imperial authority. It was the result of a long series of wars and alliances between and among the Saxon kingdoms, and the gradual assimilation of the non-Saxon dominated parts of the country, particularly the south west, and later still Wales. This development was both driven by, and in turn influenced, the nature of kingship. The rediscovery of Roman law later aided in the development of the modern state. These developments were reflected in the assumption of Roman elements in the coronation ritual, some via the Carolingian empire, or West Francia, and some directly from Byzantium (or Constantinople).

But the growth of a state presupposes that such a polity has, or will acquire, legitimacy. In the next section we consider the establishment and preservation of legitimacy. We see how legitimacy can be acquired—and challenged—in circumstances where the acquisition of legitimacy might reasonably be questioned. The acquisition of authority by the Saxon kings ultimately depended upon conquest or settlement, or a combination of the two. Yet, after the passage of some 1500 years it would be a brave person to suggest that the kings and queens of the United Kingdom lacked legitimacy, even allowing for irregularities in the succession. No new dynasty has assumed regnal power without a link to the previous dynasty since the Anglo-Saxon settlement of England, and as will be discussed later, the House of Wessex may indeed have originally been of British (Celtic) descent,[4] and therefore even more ancient.

As will be discussed, legitimacy depends upon a number of factors, only one of which is the ballot box. It can be earned over time, particularly when the sovereign follows what we now know as the rule of law. The coronation oath was always central to this process, just as the acclamation and the homage were central to the broader acquisition of legitimacy.

The Commonwealth realms, while independent, share the British monarch, raising questions about their role in the coronation. Historically, separate coronations for Scotland highlighted national distinctiveness, but modern ceremonies rely on symbolic inclusions like national

[4] Parsons, D., "British Caraticos, Old English Cerdic" (1997) 33 Cambrian Mediæval Celtic Studies 1–8.

emblems and realm representatives. The 1953 and 2023 coronations incorporated evolving Commonwealth representation, such as realm flags and Governors-General, while maintaining a primarily British structure. Future ceremonies may further adapt symbolism to reflect constitutional changes without altering the traditional format.

The King as Primary Law-Giver

First and foremost of the various aspects of the political function of the coronation may be said to be its reflection of the function of the king or queen regnant as law-giver, a concept not altogether defunct even in a time of limited constitutional monarchy; laws are made in the Sovereign's name and authority under the royal prerogative, and in the name of the King-in-Parliament for statutory laws and statutory subordinate legislation. Even the common law, or judge-made law, is the product of the King's judges, operating in the King's courts, and in his name.[5]

In much earlier times, the function of kingship was also one of law-making, as one of the pivotal roles of a leader has always been to make laws. This was, in the English tradition, early closely linked to the practice of taking the coronation oath, in which the newly anointed and crowned Sovereign—or one about to be anointed and crowned—promised, on their honour and before God and people, to uphold the laws, and to govern according to the ancient customs of the realm. Such an oath served at once to cement political support, to emphasise the historical continuity of rule—particularly important at a time of civil war, disputed succession, or even usurpation—and to garner the support of the church. The oaths were also, particularly in the mediæval period, closely linked with notions of fealty and allegiance on the part of the magnates. William the Conqueror, following practice from the tenth century (and possibly as far back as the eighth century), bound himself by a threefold promise. This was to preserve peace and protect the church, to maintain good laws and abolish bad, and to dispense justice to all. He also made, as an addition of his own, the solemn promise that he would treat the English

[5] This is true, in England at least, even of ecclesiastical courts, the combined effect of the Statute of Appeals 1532 (24 Hen VIII c 12); Ecclesiastical Licences Act 1533 (24 Hen VIII c 21); Act of Supremacy 1534 (26 Hen VIII c 1) and later legislation; *Bishop of Lincoln v Smith* (1668) 1 Vent 3; 86 ER 3; *ex parte Medwin* (1853) 1 E & B 609; 118 ER 566.

people as well as the best of their kings had done.[6] Whether he lived up to any of these undertakings might legitimately be questioned, but the symbolic and political importance of taking the coronation oath was great. This is true also of its religious significance, in an age when oaths before God carried great weight—it was also an oath by Harold upon which William relied heavily for his claim to the throne.[7]

As already noted, the early coronation oaths were peculiarly English in nature. They stemmed, in part, from the native legal and cultural landscape. This enshrined feudalism (though greatly predating it), but also a relatively strong monarchy, and a comparatively weak nobility. Laws were made more by the central government than by local potentates. The kingdom was not wholly unitary, but it was certainly not federal nor a confederation. The king was the supreme and primary law-maker, whose authority extended across the length and breadth of the country. His reach was also seen in the kingdom-wide royal prerogative.[8]

The Tradition of the Common Law

A second key aspect of the political landscape was the nature of English law itself. The common law, by which we mean that body of laws common to all, and which are to be distinguished from local custom, royal prerogative and all other exceptional or special law,[9] is remarkable historically for its formulary nature, and its longevity. Legal memory dates from the coronation 3rd September 1189 of Richard I.[10] Though this is a technical doctrine concerned merely with prescriptive rights, it does however illustrate the longevity of the common law, whose root indeed go back centuries earlier than that date. In its origins English law drew from two distinct traditions. The Anglo-Saxon law, from the dooms of

[6] Richardson, H., "The English Coronation Oath" (1941) 23 Transactions of the Royal Historical Society 129–158.

[7] Barlow, Frank, *Edward the Confessor* (1970).

[8] Cox, Noel, *The Royal Prerogative and Constitutional Law* (2021).

[9] Including the statute law because that was formerly rare.

[10] Anon, "Note: The nation's memory: 1838–1988, 1189–1989" (1989) 10(1) The Journal of Legal History 110–113.

Æthelberht (c.602),[11] and the laws of Ine (c.694),[12] the ordinances of Ælfred (c.893), to the code of Canute (c.1020), constitute one of these sources. The other is the French or Frankish tradition, the capitularies of the Carlovingian emperors and the Merovingian kings to Childeric, who led the Franks to Gaul. In the case of the Doom Book, *Dōmbōc*, Code of Ælfred or Legal Code of Ælfred the Great, Ælfred codified three prior Saxon codes—those of Æthelberht of Kent, Ine of Wessex, and Offa of Mercia (c.786).[13]

The King of the English was expected to publish laws at a time when hardly anyone else in western Europe was attempting any such feat—the dooms of Canute are probably the most comprehensive of any code in eleventh century Europe.[14] Ælfred promoted education so that his laws could be understood more widely, but also so that religious works reached a wider readership. The function of the king as law-giver and judge was gradually emphasised at the expense of self-regulation by leading figures in the community, as a consequence of the Christianising of kingship, with the *Bible*'s stories about great judges and Christian law. From Ine to Æthelred II the tradition of assembling the pronouncements, administrative regulations and laws of their predecessors led to the development of a recognisable body of Anglo-Saxon law. Saxon times saw many influences which could have either weakened or strengthened the kingship. The balance between the king and the community as the fount of law and the dispenser of justice was perceptibly altered in favour of the king by Ælfred's time. To make and proclaim the law became a mark of kingship. A new king was expected to accept and abide by those laws, though they might be adjusted as required.[15]

The Normans by contrast with the Saxons, had little if any written law to bring with them, and had perforce to rely on the comparatively well-developed Saxon legal and administrative structure (itself partly a product

[11] Stenton, Frank, *Anglo-Saxon England* (1971), pp. 59–60.

[12] Wormald, Patrick, *The Making of English Law*, Vol I, (1999).

[13] Preston, Todd, *King Alfred's Book of Law* (2012).

[14] In western Europe law codes were rare until the twelfth century, when a whole new jurisprudence appeared, as the Roman law of Justinian became better understood and diffused—Attenborough, F. L. (ed. & trans.), *Laws of the earliest English kings* (1922); Robertson, A. J., *Laws of the Kings of England* (1925); Gluckman, M., *Politics law and ritual in tribal society* (1977), pp. 196–202.

[15] Maine, Sir Henry Sumner, *Early Law and Custom* (1890).

of necessity, in particular as a consequence of the *danegeld*, levied from 991 to 1162[16]).

The king's role as law-giver and judge became central to the identity of kingship, with laws becoming a mark of sovereign authority. The common law's development in England reinforced the political authority of kings by centralising legal power and establishing continuity in governance. The coronation and royal continuity symbolised and strengthened the common law's stability and longevity, distinguishing it from local customs and emphasizing the monarchy's role as the source of universal justice. This legacy positioned the king as both protector and enforcer of a unified legal framework, crucial for his political authority and legitimacy.

Kingly Authority

Making the laws placed the king at the apex of the legal framework. They were both the arbiters of legal disputes, and at the same time the one definitive source of legal authority, even as Parliament developed, the whole being under the sovereignty of the Crown (later the Crown-in-Parliament).[17] The law served to develop the powers of kings, but also to direct and limit their action. Kings and their officers became increasingly central as sources of law,[18] particularly after the legal reforms of Henry II.[19] People were increasingly made aware of the kings' religious and moral responsibilities. The coronation was a unique and ideal occasion for this educative function, as well as the occasion for the king to confirm his allegiance to the ancient laws of the realm.

Royal authority was founded on the constitutional history and structure of society, including the role of the king as the official representative

[16] Campbell, James, *Essays in Anglo-Saxon History* (1986), p. 167.

[17] *R. v. Secretary of State for Foreign and Commonwealth Affairs* [1982] Q.B. 892, 911 per Lord Denning M.R. (C.A.).

[18] Robertson, A.J., *Laws of the Kings of England* (1925).

[19] Nicholas, Michael, "King Henry II and his Legal Reforms" (2019) 6(2) The Histories Article 5. Available at: https://digitalcommons.lasalle.edu/the_histories/vol6/iss2/5.

of the community. Yet even the Saxon kings were more than mere officials, as popular reverence for their real or imagined pedigree showed. The king was also not just the chosen of the people, but the chosen of God. He was able to command greater resources than any potential rival, unlike the King of France, who was often dominated by over-powerful vassals[20]; including, at times, the Kings of England (for their French domains).

The Norman conquest brought few changes in the idea or practice of English rulership, indeed these latter insular concepts could strengthen the Conqueror's authority in the face of an alternative Norman tradition of aristocratic freedom.[21] Despite this, the consent of the nascent Parliament was sometimes necessary.[22]

The king's duty to maintain the peace in his kingdom and provide justice for his subjects underwent a major transformation in the twelfth century, which emphasised the king's authority throughout England and made more explicit his obligations and the parameters within which he ruled. His role as judge and law-maker was revolutionised,[23] but not abolished, though both were to later be circumscribed by the development of the courts and of Parliament. From the thirteenth century in England, as in France, the monarch was powerful, but this power was checked, in Bracton's formulation, by the notion that the king "must not be under man but under God and under the law, because law makes the King"[24]; his authority was not absolute in nature.

Because of the uncomfortable paradox of monarchy and the unsuitability of some kings it came to be believed over the course of the thirteenth and fourteenth centuries that one could separate the Crown from the wearer, so that it became possible to correct or even remove the king. Discussion along these lines tended to decline in the fifteenth

[20] Anson, Sir William, *The Law and Custom of the Constitution* (3rd ed., 1907), vol II Part I, pp. 16–17.

[21] Nelson, Janet L., "Kingship and empire", in J. H. Burns (ed.), *Cambridge History of Mediæval Political Thought c.350-c.1450* (1988), pp. 211–251, 241.

[22] Maddicott, J. R., *The Origins of the English Parliament, 924–1327* (2010), pp. 424–425.

[23] Cannon, John and Ralph Griffiths, *The Oxford Illustrated History of the British Monarchy* (1988), p. 110.

[24] I.e. *rex non debet esse sub homine, sed sub Deo et lege, quia lex facit regem*: Bracton, Henry de, lib. 1 C. 8; 12 Co. Rep. 65; Fleta 2 c. 5; Chitty, Joseph, *A Treatise on the Law of the Prerogatives of the Crown; And the Relative Duties and Rights of the Subject* (1978), p. 5.

century because of the relatively weak title of the usurpers in that century. There was no practical alternative to hereditary rule.[25] Establishing title through the coronation—and usually statute law—was vital.

In the time from Henry VIII to the accession of William and Mary, as never before, the court was at the very centre of political power. But the power of the king was limited by a tradition of consultation,[26] though this may not have been much more a feature of the English monarchy than the French, despite the belief to the contrary held by Fortescue and Smith.[27] For a strong king consultation had a very different meaning than it did for a weak one; Henry VIII generally obtained whatever concessions he wished from his Parliament, though even he sometimes had to compromise.[28]

The repudiation of papal authority and the insistence upon the Crown's imperial status under Henry VIII, though of great symbolic and legal importance, did not in themselves materially alter the Crown's position vis-à-vis Parliament and the courts.[29] The king remained the primary law-giver, and, as for some centuries, this was predominantly through Parliament. Although the nature of Parliament was to change over time, first with the withering, during the eighteenth century, of the role of the Sovereign, and the decline of the House of Lords during the nineteenth century, nevertheless it was the King-in-Parliament which comprised the centrepiece of constitutional government.

The central role of the Sovereign, today largely reduced to what Bagehot's terms the dignified part of government,[30] leaves the efficient part of government, such as ministers of the Crown, responsible for the actual conduct of government in the King's name, very largely without his personal involvement, except formally. In the words imputed to King

[25] Cannon, John and Ralph Griffiths, *The Oxford Illustrated History of the British Monarchy* (1988), p. 217.

[26] Fortescue, Sir John, *In Praise of the laws of England (De Laudibus Legum Angliæ)* ed. S. B. Chrimes (1942).

[27] Cannon, John and Ralph Griffiths, *The Oxford Illustrated History of the British Monarchy* (1988), p. 299.

[28] For example, in his (third) Succession to the Crown Act 1543-4 (35 Hen VIII c 1).

[29] Cannon, John and Ralph Griffiths, *The Oxford Illustrated History of the British Monarchy* (1988), p. 322.

[30] Bagehot, Walter, *The English Constitution* (2001).

Charles II: "my words are my own, and my actions are my ministers".[31] This leads to a clear separation between what we today might term the functions of the head of state and the head of government, a division only strengthened after the development during the eighteenth century and into the nineteenth century of the office of Prime Minister. However, whether the king is the effective—or efficient in Bagehot's taxonomy—or the dignified part of government, or both, the solemnity of the coronation proclaims, in an overt and explicit manner, the dominance of their conceptual, practical or legal authority.

The coronation was at once the proclamation of the king's political and legal supremacy (along with Parliament, and personally) and an opportunity to publicly rein in the over-powerful lords (especially in the oath and homage). The king's role as law-maker was both emphasised and proclaimed in the coronation. But, crucially, it was at the same time limited by both coronation oath and sacred obligation. To illustrate the point, the first part of the oath from the eighth century to 1274 was.

> *Haec tria populo Christiano et mihi subdito in Christi Qomine promitto. In primis ut ecclesia Dei et omnis populus Christianus veram pacem nostro arbitrio in omni tempore setvet* ("I promise these three things to the Christian people and to my subjects in the Church of Christ. First of all, that the church of God and all the Christian people may establish true peace at our discretion at all times").[32]

31

We have a pretty witty king,

Whose word no man relies on;

He never said a foolish thing,

Nor ever did a wise one.

– John Wilmot, 2nd Earl of Rochester, about King Charles II of England, as quoted in Blackwood's Edinburgh Magazine Vol. XLIV (January–June 1857) p. 592; It is said to that this was written on the door of Charles II's bedchamber, and that on seeing it, the king replied, "This is very true: for my words are my own, and my actions are my ministers ....".

32 Legg, L. G. W., *English Coronation Records* (1901), p. xxxi.

The unity of the kingdom was reflected in the coinage, in the royal style and titles, and in the coronation. Even at Edgar's coronation, the homage—or submission—of tributary kings (or sub-kings) acknowledged as publicly as was possible the pre-eminence if not hegemony of the king, and the unity (or relative unity) of the kingdom, as well as the King's pre-eminent status even beyond the territory of his realm. Such a unity and status is also seen in, for instance, the decorations on the 1821 sword of offering, in which the stones are arranged to form roses, thistles, shamrocks, oak leaves and acorns, to represent the constituent parts of the United Kingdom.[33]

Even a king owing his title to force of arms could not afford to ignore legal form and continuity, particularly as he invariably based his claim on hereditary right, not mere military success. The coronation at once illustrated this and provided a perfect opportunity to proclaim and declare the new king's status. Aside from the coronation oath, the homage may be seen as another aspect of the reciprocal relationship between king and people; in 2023 the greeting by a Child of the Chapel Royal, the King's response, the King's Prayer, and the Homage of the People, all reflected an enhanced emphasis upon the reciprocal role of servant kingship. The homage was particularly significant in the context of feudalism, to which we shall shortly turn, though homage may be said to have preceded feudalism, as a means for the formalisation of relationships.

The coronation was a key political event that affirmed the king's supreme authority while highlighting the limits of his power. By taking an oath, the king publicly committed to uphold the realm's laws, symbolising a balance between absolute authority and responsibility. The ceremony reinforced the king's duty to justice, unity, and moral governance under divine authority, while also formalising subjects' loyalty through public homage, solidifying both the king's and his subjects roles in the kingdom.

Feudal Kingship

The coronation is neither the product of feudalism, nor strongly influenced or shaped by it, despite the appearance to the contrary. However, the feudal era—broadly the ninth to the fifteenth centuries, or in England, primarily from the Norman Conquest in 1066 to the early fourteenth

[33] Keay, Anna, *The Crown Jewels* (2011).

century—did not leave the coronation untouched, nor did the coronation lack in particular contemporary relevance to kings in the context of a feudal system. The ritual of homage, with its pivotal role in creating and reinforcing reciprocal relationships is a principal example. Although feudalism only prevailed during some of the lifetime to date of the English coronation, nevertheless, as a system with legal, political and theological aspects, we cannot fail to consider the influence of feudalism on the coronation, and in particular, the political function of the coronation through the lens of feudalism in its nascent, full and decayed forms.

Whether we use a wide[34] or a narrow[35] definition of feudalism, the system, with political, economic and social aspects which permeated through society in its heyday, did leave its impact on the coronation, particularly in the creation and retention of certain hereditary offices and roles.

Feudalism added a gloss to the coronation, but did not radically change it (many of the feudal services related to the coronation banquet), and the same can be said of the evolving conception of the kingship under the influence of sub-Roman thought, and later mediæval political theology. The fact remains, however, that although the mediæval English king always had as one of his principal functions the granting of laws to his subjects, he was never in any way above the law. Kings did not have exclusive legislative authority either, but were relatively free from formal and permanent limitations on their powers and freedom of action. When the nobility felt that kings had gone too far, they occasionally sought (and even fought) to restrain them. Earthly pressures, including rebellion, were used against English kings on at least six occasions from 1327 to 1485,[36] at the risk to the perpetrators of grave consequences in heaven and on earth. These feudal ideas of mutual duties provided no substantive sanctions except the renunciation of fealty (*diffidatio*), and, in the last resort, war on the autocratic king.[37] Centuries later the Rump of the House of Commons were to use this reasoning to justify their war

[34] The wide definition may be taken from Bloch, Marc, *Feudal Society* (1965); Maitland, Frederic, *Domesday Book and Beyond—three essays on the early history of England* (1966).

[35] Stenton, Frank, *The First Century of English Feudalism 1066-1166* (2nd ed., 1961); Clanchy, M. T., *England and its Rulers, 1066-1272* (1983), p. 83.

[36] Cannon, John and Ralph Griffiths, *The Oxford Illustrated History of the British Monarchy* (1988), p. 205.

[37] Ibid, p. 113.

against Charles I, however self-serving and cynical their actions were.[38] As St Columba warned Áedán mac Gabráin, the king of Dál Riata, at his coronation in 574, so long as he obeyed God's laws, then none of his enemies would prevail against him, but the moment he broke God's laws, divine protection would end.[39]

The King at the Apex of Society

The feudal era saw the king as the apex of a complex formal arrangement of relationships. The king, hitherto the law maker, and war band leader, now also assumed the role of supreme land owner, responsible for a number of tenants-in-chief, who in turn owed responsibility for a larger number of sub-tenants.[40] The whole edifice, developed during the dying days of the Roman Empire, with its dearth of willing taxpayers and public servants, was based on reciprocal obligations, and was closely aligned to land ownership—or at least possession—as the one asset which could not fall victim to the depredations of civil war, Vikings, Barbarians or brigands.[41] The system, in theory, contributed to social and economic stability, but could also encourage an increasing centralisation of authority,[42] as well as social and political rigidity.

Though the nature of feudalism depended upon land ownership, its defining characteristic was that of obligation. In the early Carolingian empire this protective relationship, which was set up by one free man over another, was called *patrocinium*. An individual—the vassal—placed himself in this position by an act of commendation (*commendatio*). This created the obligation of serving and respecting the vassal's superior (*dominus*), but only so far as compatible with the maintenance of the vassal's status as a free man. In his turn the lord—the superior—was to aid and support his vassal, such as with food, clothing and (military or even legal) protection, as required. Although the various obligations

[38] Russell, Conrad, *The Fall of the British Monarchies 1637–1642* (1991).

[39] Adomnán of Iona, *The life of St Columba* ed. Richard Sharpe (trans.) (1995).

[40] Barlow, Frank, *The Feudal Kingdom of England, 1042-1216* (2nd ed., 1961).

[41] Bloch, Marc, *Feudal Society* (1965).

[42] Moreland, John, "Land and Power from Roman Britain to Anglo-Saxon England?" (2011) 19(1) Historical Materialism 175–193.

became more specialised over time, this was essentially a contractual arrangement,[43] intended principally for mutual benefit.

The parallels between feudal obligations and the ancient Roman social practice of patronage (*clientela*) are obvious, though they may be coincidental. *Clientela* was the distinctive relationship between the *patronus* (the patron) and their *cliens* (client).[44] It was the formalisation of such reciprocal relationships, in a time of military, political, social and economic upheavals, that made the early feudal era distinct.[45]

Feudalism prevented the break-up of the Carolingian state in tenth century France onwards, because, although the supremacy of the king had become purely theoretical, vassalage remained a real legal and practical bond.[46] Until late in the twelfth century the French king could only exercise power outside the royal domain in a feudal capacity, but the reciprocal bonds of feudalism was of lasting value, as even a weak bond was still better than nothing at all. Monarchical sovereignty, per se, was only clearly recognised by a few, and most reliance was placed on the feudal authority of the lord-vassal reciprocity. Even the king might owe feudal loyalty to the pope, as did King John, or to the emperor.

Unlike in France, the basis of royal power in Germany was not vassalage (although this was common), but the surviving organisation of the Carolingian state, and the use of the hierarchy of the Roman Catholic Church until the struggle with the Pope over investiture in the second half of the eleventh century. Frederick Barbarossa tried to reform the state on a feudal basis in the second half of the twelfth century, and from the re-grant of the lands of Henry the Lion all imperial grants were of fiefs directly held of the emperor (the imperial princes or *Reichsfürsten*). But this approach did not give the empire the strength it needed, because fiefs which escheated had to be re-granted, effectively preventing the formation of any considerable royal domain.[47] Just as the late Roman empire sought to stave off collapse by new innovations or the revival or

[43] Ganshof, Francois, *Feudalism* trans. Philip Grierson (1952), pp. 5–8.

[44] Wallace-Hadrill, Andrew (ed.), *Patronage in Ancient Society* (1989).

[45] Lot, Ferdinand, *The End of the Ancient World and the Beginnings of the Middle Ages* (1931).

[46] Hinde, G. W., D. W. McMorland and P. B. A. Sim, *Land Law* (1978), vol 1, pp. 7–8; Cheshire, G. C., *Modern Law of Real Property* ed. J. H. Burn (13th ed., 1982), p. 10.

[47] Ganshof, Francois, *Feudalism* trans. Philip Grierson (1952), pp. 145–149.

strengthening of old concepts,[48] so too, in Germany, such attempts were ultimately only to serve to delay the coming collapse.[49]

Across the English Channel the situation was rather different from that in both France and Germany—and even more so from that in Italy or the territories of the (Eastern) Roman empire. Although there were clear signs that feudalism was gaining a foothold in Britain pre-1066, it was the Norman Conquest which truly established a feudal polity in all its fullness, grafted onto an English state which was already benefitting from a comparatively robust central administration. The Norman kings were thereby potentially far stronger than their Saxon predecessors. This was in part due to their position as conquerors, which left them fully in command of a military, social, and political structure,[50] able, for instance, to undertake wholesale land re-distribution on a scale wholly in excess of that attempted somewhat later in Europe by Emperor Frederick Barbarossa. It was also because, with the advent of the feudal system of land tenure and its associated social and economic structures, the king became far more the apex of society than he had been to the Saxons. The relationship of king and subject extended not just to the great tenants-in-chief but to everyone possessed of an interest in land. The eleventh and twelfth century renaissance across Europe, and the accompanying economic expansion, also benefited the Normans.[51]

Under feudalism, every estate or interest in land was held directly or indirectly of the king, and to avoid sub-vassals from being used by tenants-in-chief against the king, an oath of fealty or allegiance was occasionally demanded, as at Salisbury in 1086. By the Salisbury Oath all freemen were bound to swear allegiance directly to the king instead of to the immediate lord from whom they held their lands.[52] This move,

[48] Lot, Ferdinand, *The End of the Ancient World and the Beginnings of the Middle Ages* (1931).

[49] Wilson, Peter H., "Bolstering the Prestige of the Habsburgs: The End of the Holy Roman Empire in 1806" (2006) 28(4) The International History Review 709–736.

[50] Cheshire, G. C., *Modern Law of Real Property* ed. J. H. Burn (13th ed., 1982), p. 12.

[51] Anson, Sir William, *The Law and Custom of the Constitution* (3rd ed., 1907), vol II Part I, pp. 8–9.

[52] Cheshire, G. C., *Modern Law of Real Property* ed. J. H. Burn (13th ed., 1982), p. 13.

backed no doubt by William's newly victorious army, was to prove a decisive step in establishing a strong central government in England.

There were multiple advantages in imposing an oath of allegiance or fealty on a wide scale. This method was used especially for the purpose of designating the heir and obtaining (theoretically irrevocable) promises of support, as for William Rufus in 1087, and Henry I in 1100. All those swearing allegiance became liegemen of the king. The growth in the use of the tenure of scutage and the replacement of military service by payment made the Crown more independent of the feudal levy.[53]

Feudalism throughout Europe made the king the supreme landowner (particularly in England, due to the radical effect of the Conquest) and invested the relation of king and subject with a contractual character, rights to service and protection. In England the association of land ownership and the rights of the Crown tended also to assimilate the descent of the Crown to the descent of an estate in land, and inevitably increased the emphasis on the hereditary at the expense of the elective character of kingship. The obligation on the king's part however, of providing good government—a particular concern of late Saxon kings—remained. The *Witan* of the Saxon kings gave way to the *Commune Concilium* of the Normans, a body which was much more dominated by the landed interest, because land-ownership was the primary and safest source of wealth and a sign of importance far more to the Norman than perhaps it was to the Saxon.[54]

Feudalism and the Coronation

In such a hierarchical system the role and importance of the coronation—and especially (in its English form) the coronation oath and homage—is clear. But neither element was exclusively derived from feudal ideas. In addition, in typical feudal fashion certain individuals participate or formerly participated on account of various feudal tenures—such as the Lord of the Manor of Worksop, whose duty from 1327 it was to provide white kid gloves and support the king's right arm during the Coronation

[53] Ganshof, Francois, *Feudalism* trans. Philip Grierson (1952), pp. 149–151.

[54] Anson, Sir William, *The Law and Custom of the Constitution* (3rd ed., 1907), vol II Part I, pp. 8– 9.

while the Royal Sceptre was in his hand.[55] The simple device of tenure (in this case grand serjeanty[56]) serves as a reminder of the late Roman practice, perpetuated in the feudal system, of requiring service in return for land tenure.

What began often as comparatively menial tasks became, over time, more distinguished and even sought after, and subject to many disputed claims in the Court of Claims. The claim to be Chief Butler of England, for instance, was taken to the 1902 Court of Claims, but not resolved. The position was held by grand serjeanty, by the Lord of the Manor of Kenningham, Norfolk, which had been granted by Henry I to William d'Aubigny before 1101.[57] It was later inherited by the Dukes of Norfolk, who sold the manor in 1872 to John Oddin Taylor of Norwich. In 1902 the Duke of Norfolk, Mr Taylor of Kenninghall, and a descendant of William de Albini, all claimed the role. As an office by grand serjeanty logically it should have been assigned to Taylor, as the owner of the manor, but no discussion was had and no decision necessary as there was to be no coronation banquet, at which the Chief Butler was to serve.[58] Since then the manor has been sold several times, most recently in 1986 to Ingalill de Joussineau, Countesse de Tourdonnet, of Stockholm.[59]

No aspects of the coronation can be categorised as purely feudal in nature, with the limited exception of those offices (though not necessarily the function they perform or performed) which retain tenure by grand serjeanty.[60] These include the King's Champion, in right of the

[55] In 1953 the manor was under corporate ownership, so the Chancellor of the Duchy of Lancaster (Lord Woolton) presented the Glove; *Coronation of Her Majesty Queen Elizabeth the Second* (1952).

[56] By the Tenures Abolition Act 1660 s 7 (repealed), the majority of honorary services of grand serjeanty were preserved. They were again preserved by the Law of Property Act 1922 s 136 (repealed), although the tenure itself was abolished.

[57] "Aubigny, William d' [William de Albini; known as William d'Aubigny Pincerna](d. 1139)", *Oxford Dictionary of National Biography* (2004).

[58] Wollaston, Sir Gerald, *Coronation Claims* (1903).

[59] Norfolk Record Office Online Catalogue, File NRS 2375, 11D4—Manor of Kenninghall court roll. < https://nrocatalogue.norfolk.gov.uk/index.php/manor-of-kenninghall-court-roll-5 >.

[60] Examples include the Lord of the Manor of Bardolf-in-Addington (or Addington), the site of Addington Palace, the summer residence of the Archbishops of Canterbury 1807–1897, who had the duty of serving a mess—or meal—of Dillegrout, or Malepigernout (a form of spiced chicken porridge, stew, soup or pottage, which likely

office of Lord of the Manor of Scrivelsby since the time of the Anarchy,[61] whose role in a coronation has been limited since the abolition (or at least suspension) of the coronation banquet, but whose proper role was evocative of a grand mediæval feudal rite. In 2023 the then Lord of the Manor, Francis Dymoke, was assigned the role of carrying the Royal Standard.[62] Other tenures, all formerly covered in detail in the proceedings of the past Courts of Claims,[63] were feudal incidences but not necessarily feudal offices per se.

Grand serjeanty is to be distinguished from offices held hereditarily in gross, which were not incidents of lands. The senior and most significant examples of these offices held in gross include the Lord Great Chamberlain.[64] Related specifically to the coronation, the duty to carry the spurs at a coronation (today vested in the 5th Baron Churston, and the co-heirs of the Baron Hastings (in abeyance since 1960),[65] by descent from the Hastings Earls of Pembroke via Baron Grey of Ruthyn), is also an office held in gross.[66] The 22nd Earl of Shrewsbury and Waterford, the premier Earl in England and Ireland, in his hereditary capacity as Lord High Steward

consisted of almond milk, the brawn of capons, sugar and spices, chicken parboiled and chopped) at coronations, from after 1086 until 1821; Round, J. Horace. *The King's Serjeants & Officers of State with their Coronation Services* (1911).

61 The 35th Honourable the King's Champion is the 34th Lord of the manor of Scrivelsby, Thornton and Dalderby, Francis John Fane Marmion Dymoke, DL (born 1955), a landowner and chartered accountant, who carried the Royal Standard. The office of Champion descends through the female line (from 1377) from the original grantee, Robert Marmion, at the time of the Anarchy. The Marmion family claimed descent from the lords of Fontenay, hereditary Champions of the Dukes of Normandy; Lodge, Samuel, *Scrivelsby, The Home of the Champions* (1893). Although the title has passed by hereditary descent since the eleventh century, it is not strictly a hereditary office, since it is not held in gross, but is rather linked to the ownership of the manor of Scrivelsby (initially from the feudal barony of Tamworth); Sanders, Ivor John, *English Baronies* (1960), p. 145, "Tamworth, Nottinghamshire".

62 Press Release, "Roles to be performed at the Coronation Service at Westminster Abbey". The Royal Family, 27 April 2023.

63 Wollaston, Sir Gerald, *Coronation Claims* (1903).

64 Round, J. Horace, "The Lord Great Chamberlain" (June 1902) 7(21) Monthly Review 42–58.

65 The co-heirs are the descendants of the 20th Baroness: Simon Abney-Hastings, 15th Earl of Loudoun (born 1974); Mrs Sheena Williams (born 1941); Mrs Flora Purdie (born 1957); and Norman Angus MacLaren (born 1948).

66 "Lord Grey de Ruthin", *The Times*, 26 October 1963, p. 10.

of Ireland, may carry a white staff.[67] Other offices are either wholly obsolete or disputed; as noted above, many relate to the now abandoned coronation banquet.

Not all coronation offices are hereditary, but some may be attached to an office. In 2023 the Coronation Claims Office accepted the claim of the Dean of Westminster to advise the King on the proper procedure during the ceremony. For nearly a thousand years he and his predecessor deans and abbots have kept an unpublished Red Book of practices. It also accepted the claim of the Bishop of Durham and the Bishop of Bath and Wells to walk beside the King as he entered and exited the Abbey and to stand on either side of him through the entire coronation ritual.[68] Though similar to the role of the King's Champion, in that it was a function assigned to a particular office, it was not strictly hereditary, as the office of bishop itself was not hereditary, but was rather a corporation sole. The hereditary and other functions belonging to certain individuals and offices which were not required—as, for example, because of the abovementioned abandonment of the coronation banquet—were explicitly preserved in 1952 and again in 2023, albeit in a modified form.[69] Others were retained as subordinate to other hereditary offices, such as (in 2023) the Earl of Crawford and Balcarres, who acted as Deputy to the Great Steward of Scotland, the Prince of Wales.[70]

The evolution of coronation ceremonies and associated offices reveals the intricate blending of feudal traditions and broader historical influences, such as Roman administrative practices. While some roles, like those held by grand serjeanty, originate from feudal obligations tied to land tenure, others transcend these origins, reflecting shifts in their symbolic and functional significance over time. The continuation or adaptation of such traditions into modern coronations, even as some practices become obsolete, underscores the enduring importance of historical precedent in the ceremonial representation of authority. This synthesis

[67] *Coronation of Her Majesty Queen Elizabeth the Second* (1952).

[68] Ibid.

[69] See the Coronation Proclamation dated 6 June 1952, where the services usually performed in Westminster Hall or in the procession there were dispensed with, saving the rights and privileges of persons claiming to perform them at any future coronation: see the *London Gazette* Extraordinary, 6 June 1952, p. 3165.

[70] Press Release, "Roles to be performed at the Coronation Service at Westminster Abbey". The Royal Family, 27 April 2023.

of continuity and evolution exemplifies the coronation's role as both a historical and living tradition, accommodating change while preserving its ritualistic essence.

The King and Constitutionalism

The combination of English and Norman kingship paved the way for what could have become an institutional despotism operating through prerogative rights that could only be checked by rebellion and, theoretically, by the application of feudal ideas of mutual duties. The feudal theories which were the basis of the right of counsel found in chapter 14 of magna carta, for instance, were only put forward when feudalism as a method of government was already in decay.[71] These feudal ideas of mutual duties provided no substantive sanctions except the renunciation of fealty (*diffidatio*), and, in the last resort, war on the autocratic king.[72] Centuries later the Rump of the House of Commons were to use this reasoning to justify their war against Charles I, however self-serving and cynical their actions were.[73]

Monarchy was not the only system of government the twelfth and thirteenth century jurists knew, but it was the only one they treated seriously and extensively. Ruler, nobility, clergy, and people were part of a mediæval constitutionalism, a *societas Christiana*, that encompassed all (or almost all) of Christian Europe.[74] The canonists' corporate theory explained the relationship between the head of a *universitas* and its members. In the thirteenth century this led to a new theory of government, based in part on Aristotle's mixed constitution (a mixture of monarchy, aristocracy, and democracy). Aquinas perceived this system in ancient Israel.[75] At the beginning of the fourteenth century John of Paris combined the

[71] Barlow, Frank, *The Feudal Kingdom of England, 1042-1216* (2nd ed., 1961), pp. 112–113.

[72] Ibid, p. 113.

[73] Russell, Conrad, *The Fall of the British Monarchies 1637–1642* (1991).

[74] Pennington, Kenneth, "Law, Legislative authority and theories of government, 1150-1300", in J. H. Burns (ed.), *The Cambridge History of Mediæval Political Thought, c.350-c.1450* (1988), pp. 424–453, 443.

[75] Aquinas, *Summa Theologiae* ed. J. Gilbey (1964-80), 1.2 q 1051.

corporate theory and Aquinas' mixed constitution, and applied it to the government of the Church.[76] It was soon to extend further.

Kingship conferred a coercive jurisdiction, with the king a dispenser of justice, and repressor of evil. But a king could also be a guide to the end for which the state was ordained. In this, the king disposed of moral authority which could command obedience. Belief in this attribute of kingship was revived under the influence of Aristotelian teleology,[77] where there was philosophical support for monarchy.[78]

By 1377 Parliaments were almost annual occurrences, and the monarchy was regularly dependent upon the commons for financial aid, though in theory the king was to continue for a long time to rely primarily upon his own hereditary revenues, perquisites, and large, expensive borrowings. By the time of the so-called "Good Parliament" of 1376 it had become possible for the commons to organise and launch a far-reaching attack on the conduct and policies of the government, and yet still be allowed to remain in session for more than two months.[79] Richard II tried, ultimately unsuccessfully, to revive the personal monarchy which had been on the decline since the last years of his grandfather Edward III.[80]

Fifteenth century England was a limited monarchy, limited by the reliance of the king on laws made by the king in Parliament.[81] The first attempt to wrest actual control of the direction of affairs from the king is found in the Provisions of Oxford (1258), though the council established under it lasted only eighteen months.[82] The king could do no wrong, and his ministers took the blame for decisions even in that century.[83] The

[76] John of Paris, *De potestate regia et papali, Johannes Quidort von Paris Über Königliche under päpstliche Gewalt* ed. F. Bleienstein (1969), ch 19.

[77] Dunbabin, Jean, "Government", in J. H. Burns (ed.), *The Cambridge History of Mediæval Political Thought c.350-c.1450* (1988), pp. 477–519, 482–483.

[78] "Monarchy is the best form of government" —Aristotle, *Ethica Nicomachea* ed. R. A. Gauthier (1972–74), viii 10, 1160b.

[79] Chrimes, S. B., *Lancastrians, Yorkists and Henry VII* (2nd ed., 1966), p. 4.

[80] Ibid, p. 32.

[81] Chrimes, S. B., C. D. Ross, and R. A. Griffiths (eds), *Fifteenth-century England 1399-1509* (1972), p. 30.

[82] Cannon, John and Ralph Griffiths, *The Oxford Illustrated History of the British Monarchy* (1988), p. 208.

[83] Ibid, p. 32.

interdependence of king and nobility, with the church, was to continue to be reflected in their respective attendance and role in the coronation.

The coronation highlighted the king's central role in a complex and evolving political system, balancing personal authority with accountability to other institutions like Parliament and the church. By publicly affirming mutual duties, feudal theories of kingship underscored the coronation as a moment of allegiance and limited authority, checked by duties to counsel and justice, as reflected in Magna Carta. The coronation also symbolised the king's dual role. This helped legitimise the monarchy within a mixed government structure, sustaining monarchic authority while acknowledging its constitutional limits.

The Homage

The homage itself could be thought to be a feudal addition to the coronation, yet it predates feudalism, being found in the coronation of Edgar in 973, if not earlier. It involved the establishment of relationships. These relationships were essential to governance. This was true in pre-feudal, feudal and post-feudal times.

Henry VII took over the Yorkist monarchy, used its methods and institutions, extended and improved them, and made them more efficient.[84] Continual wars had led to the need for working arrangements between king and subjects in Parliament.[85] Kings came to rely more and more on their councillors.[86] These counsellors had to be incorporated into the royal government, and encouraged in their allegiance, through a combination of rewards—such as grants of manors, monopolies, grand serjeanty, and service at coronations—and punishment, in particular, through the treason laws, but also by the removal of inducements, and patronage. Reciprocity was at the heart of the constitution.

The homage, as part of the coronation, is a survival and reminder of this early development of the constitution, yet even today not entirely obsolete, especially in that we are reminded of the ongoing status (at

[84] Ibid, p. 178.

[85] Cannon, John and Ralph Griffiths, *The Oxford Illustrated History of the British Monarchy* (1988), p. 211.

[86] Ibid, p. 213.

least until recently) of the peerage as individual and collective counsellors to the Sovereign, and indeed of the role of the Lords Spiritual in Parliament and the episcopate. It must be recalled that the homage both preceded feudalism and survived it. The reasons are apparent from the (contemporary) wording of the homage:

> I, N., Duke [Marquess, Earl, Viscount, Baron or Lord] of N., do become your liege man of life and limb, and of earthly worship; and faith and truth will I bear unto you, to live and die, against all manner of folks. So help me God.[87]

The same form was used by the (modern) Princes of Wales, for the later King Charles III, at his investiture as Prince of Wales in 1969 (a modern revival of a traditional investiture of a peer, abandoned otherwise in 1621[88]).

> I, Charles, Prince of Wales, do become your liege man of life and limb and of earthly worship, and faith and truth I will bear unto thee, to live and die against all manner of folks.[89]

It is an oath of allegiance, such is still generally used throughout the world, in a variety of forms. In feudal times, a person would also swear allegiance to his feudal superiors, but the Sovereign had no superior save God. The Lords Spiritual take a similar oath upon being called to Parliament, and the Lords Temporal, likewise. The wording used in 2023 was.

> I, Justin, Archbishop of Canterbury, will be faithful and true, and faith and truth *I will* bear unto you our Sovereign Lord, *Defender of the* Faith, and *unto your* heirs *and successors according to law*. So help me God.[90]

[87] *The Form and Order of Service that is to be performed and the Ceremonies that are to be observed in The Coronation of Her Majesty Queen Elizabeth II in the Abbey Church of St. Peter, Westminster, on Tuesday, the second day of June, 1953.*

[88] Wagner, Sir Anthony and J. C. Sainty, *The Origin of the Introduction of Peers in the House of Lords* (1967), pp. 132–134.

[89] Oath of fealty taken by the Prince of Wales at his investiture at Caernarfon Castle, 1st July 1969.

[90] Ibid.

This had been similar in 1953, but earlier use was.

> I, N., Archbishop [or Bishop] of M., will be faithful and true, and faith and truth bear unto you our Sovereign Lord, and your Heirs Kings [and Queens] of England [Great Britain, etc], and I shall do and truly acknowledge the lands which I claim to hold of you, as in right of the Church. So help me God.[91]

This differed from that of 2023 (and in 1953) in several ways. The addition of Defender of the Faith, and removal of "King of the United Kingdom etc." is significant, but most important as is the removal of the reference to lands. The inclusion of "according to law" brings the archbishop's oath into general conformity with oaths of allegiance. The effect is perhaps rather to emphasis the spiritual rather than the temporal role of the bishops. It also reflects the changes in the administration of church lands.

The ceremony of homage in the coronation was, in mediæval times, perceived rather differently, however, to what it was later seen as. Homage (from the mediæval Latin *hominaticum*, literally, "pertaining to a man") in the Middle Ages was the ceremony in which a feudal tenant or vassal pledged reverence and submission to his feudal lord, receiving in exchange the symbolic title to his new position or land (investiture). The oath known as fealty implied lesser obligations than did homage. Further, one could swear fealty to many different overlords with respect to different land holdings, but homage could only be performed to a single liege, as one could not be "his man" (such as committed to military service) to more than one "liege lord".

The most significant material difference between fealty and homage today from what it was in past centuries, is that, whereas all manner of offices and appointments require the oath of allegiance, only the Lords Spiritual and Temporal traditionally rendered fealty and homage at a coronation. An opportunity, perhaps, for a change in a future coronation which would not significantly affect the scheme and purpose of the coronation, would be to include additional individuals and office-holders amongst those giving their homage, in addition to the Lords Spiritual (in 2023 the Archbishop of Canterbury alone) and Temporal (in 2023, likewise only the Prince of Wales).

[91] Legg, L. G. W., *English Coronation Records* (1901), pp. lvi.

In 2023, the Homage of the Royal Blood was confined solely to the Prince of Wales, who used the following words of homage

> I, William, Prince of Wales, pledge my loyalty to you and faith and truth I will bear unto you, as your liege man of life and limb. So help me God.[92]

The King responded, rather prosaically, "thank you, William".[93] There was no homage by the Royal Dukes, or any peers. There was instead the so-called Homage of the People. This took the following form, with the Archbishop saying.

> I now invite those who wish to offer their support to do so, with a moment of private reflection, by joining in saying 'God save King Charles' at the end, or, for those with the words before them, to recite them in full.[94]

The Homage of the People was the source of some controversy. The original wording of the Archbishop's invitation, and the response, was.

> Archbishop of Canterbury: I call upon all persons of goodwill of The United Kingdom of Great Britain and Northern Ireland, and of the other Realms and the Territories to make their homage, in heart and voice, to their undoubted King, defender of all. All who so desire, in the Abbey, and elsewhere, say together:
> All: I swear that I will pay true allegiance to Your Majesty, and to your heirs and successors according to law. So help me God.[95]

This was widely seen as something of an imposition (though constitutionally quite orthodox), and was quietly abandoned almost at the last minute, in favour of a less assertive invitation. In neither wording was

[92] *The Authorised Liturgy for the Coronation Rite of His Majesty King Charles III For use on Saturday 6th May 2023, 11:00am at Westminster Abbey* (29 April 2023).

[93] *The Roll of Claims and Proceedings at the Coronation of His Most Sacred Majesty Charles the Third by the Grace of God of the United Kingdom of Great Britain and Northern Ireland and of His other Realms and Territories, King, Head of the Commonwealth, Defender of the Faith, and of Her Majesty Queen Camilla, His Consort* (2024) (*Coronation Roll*, 2023).

[94] *The Coronation of Their Majesties King Charles III and Queen Camilla Saturday, 6th May, 2023 at 11.00 a.m.* (2023).

[95] *The Authorised Liturgy for the Coronation Rite of His Majesty King Charles III For use on Saturday 6th May 2023, 11:00am at Westminster Abbey* (2023).

the peoples' participation strictly a homage, however, but rather the first was a means of taking of the oath of allegiance, an altogether different thing, and the second form, that actually used, contained a much vaguer declaration of support.[96] Curiously, the style "Defender of the Faith" was replaced in the original approved rite by "defender of all", although the wording of the liturgy did not explicitly suggest an intention to formally replace the former style. However, perhaps wisely this was abandoned.

Fealty was theoretically a lesser obligation than homage, and was required of the lords spiritual because they held their lands on behalf of the church and not for themselves; land being held as an estate subject to the eminent domain, or overlordship of the monarch. Homage was essentially an oath based on tenure. However, if we recall Edgar's coronation, the allegiance sworn by the tributary kings present was perhaps not dissimilar in nature, and may be thought of in terms of submission and allegiance rather than in specifically feudal theory and practice.

The existence of hereditary offices, and the wording of the homage, suggested a feudal origin, but as with all aspects of the coronation, the reality was very different. The coronation, as a pre-feudal rite, reflected much more the wider political complexion of the country, including its relationship with the European continent. This includes its relationship, such as it was, with the former Roman empire, and its successor states. The death of feudalism in the course of the thirteenth and fourteenth centuries, and the abolition of its remaining incidental privileges and obligations (excepting some honorary services) in England and Wales in 1660,[97] and in Scotland in 2000,[98] has not inherently changed the purpose of the homage undertaken as part of the coronation, as it had long been seen to be distinct from any feudal implications. It is a formal declaration of loyalty, personal and collective. The state, or polity, exists independently of feudalism, and the allegiance of its population, however constituted, forms a key element in the unity of the realm.

The king, at the apex of the feudal hierarchy, was scarcely dissimilar to the late Saxon, or early modern king. All three enjoyed their status primarily due to birthright, aided by election and acclamation, and the

[96] Maqbool, Aleem and Andre Rhoden-Paul, "Coronation: No drama over swearing allegiance, says archbishop", BBC News, 3 May 2023, <https://www.bbc.com/news/uk-65458470>.

[97] Tenures Abolition Act 1660 (12 Car 2 c 24).

[98] The Abolition of Feudal Tenure etc. (Scotland) Act 2000.

endorsement of the church. In a feudal world the oath and the homage spoke to different aspects of the reciprocity which formed the basis of societal bonds. But the crowning, investing and especially the anointing also reflected contemporary concerns with the sacred bonds which held society together. Whilst all the elements of the coronation held importance in the mediæval mind, perhaps the mutual obligations of king and subject, and the sacredness of the office to which the king was called, held greatest weight.

Imperial Kingship

England, as a political entity in the British Isles which evolved in the late sub-Roman era, was rarely wholly divorced from a wider European world, with its profound Roman legacy, and its newer Germanic and Frankish influence. From an English perspective, the kings of England were (at least from the tenth century) compared with the authority of the emperor, just as some late Roman, sub-Roman and Saxon rulers had defined their own status in light of the Roman political model, however weak the empire might then have been. Ideas have inherent strength, just as powerful, if not more so, than armies, and the image of imperial Rome, more than most.[99]

The example of Carolingian kingship brought a renewed emphasis on a tradition of royal war-leadership and an idea of empire,[100] neither of which were novel ideas. The king was in the place of a father, as Christ's representative.[101] The old insular ideas of imperial kingship (partly fed by recollections of the *imperium* of Rome) gained new impetus, not only from the extension of the West Saxon power, but also from English acquaintance with Ottonian and Salian courts.[102]

The use of the styles emperor and empire was not simply mediæval, nor influenced solely by the Holy Roman Empire of the early mediæval period. It had earlier antecedents. A sixth century poem from Wales refers

[99] Nicols, John, *Idea of Rome, idea of Europe* (2005).

[100] Nelson, Janet L., "Kingship and empire", in J. H. Burns (ed.), *Cambridge History of Mediæval Political Thought c.350-c.1450* (1988), pp. 211–251, 213–229.

[101] Wulfstan of York, *An Werk Erzbischof Wulfstans von York—Die "Institutes of Polity, Civil and Ecclesiastical"* ed. K. Jost (1959), pp. 40–42.

[102] Nelson, Janet L., "Kingship and empire", in J. H. Burns (ed.), *Cambridge History of Mediæval Political Thought c.350-c.1450* (1988), pp. 211–251, 239–240.

to Arthur as *ameraudur* or "emperor".[103] Earlier still, in 286, the soldier in command of the *Classis Britannica* (Roman fleet around the coast of Britain), Marcus Aurelius Mausaeus Carausius, had declared himself emperor in Britain and northern Gaul (*Imperium Britanniarum*). The Britannic empire was, however, short-lived, the territory being regained by Rome from his successor and assassin Allectus, in 296.[104] Subsequently, following a revolt in Britain in 406, the army backed successively Marcus (406) and Gratian (406–407). Constantine III (407–411, recognised as co-emperor with Honorius and Constans II from 409) also sought the purple, but seems to have only weakened the empire and drained Britain of its garrisons just when they were needed most.[105]

Later on, several Kings of England displayed imperial ambitions, at least in nomenclature, in the period from 930 to 1066, using a variety of what would have been considered by contemporaries to be imperial styles and titles. The most common title was *basileus*, but *imperator*, *princeps*, *augustus*, and *caesar* were all used at times. Each suggested equality or equivalence with the Roman emperor (whether western, eastern, or Holy), in at least a de facto sense. The direct impetus for this was perhaps the resurgence of the imperial title in the west, from Charlemagne (800) onwards, though the empire had only fully passed in the west in the eleventh century (with the loss of the last parts of southern Italy[106]), with eastern emperors previously having periodically and temporarily asserting sovereignty over parts of the west,[107] and western states occasionally mimicking imperial institutions and titles (such as *Imperator totius*

[103] Bollard, J. K., *Arthur in the Early Welsh Tradition* in *The Romance of Arthur* (1994), pp. 11–12.

[104] Casey, P. J., *Carausius and Allectus* (1994).

[105] Higham, Nicholas J., *Rome, Britain and the Anglo-Saxons* (1992); Birley, Anthony R., *The Roman Government of Britain* (2005).

[106] Wickham, Chris, *Early Medieval Italy* (1981).

[107] The western imperial court at Ravenna was closed in 554, but the last possession, Bari, did not fall until 1071.

Hispaniae 866,[108] and the Holy Roman Empire 962[109]), as well as Bulgaria (913),[110] Serbia (1345),[111] and Russia (1547).[112]

The first king of England that we know used such imperial styles since late- or sub-Roman times was Æthelstan or Athelstan, (c. 895–939), a collector of imperial relics, who had himself proclaimed "*imperator*" in 930, six years after the death of the last Carolingian emperor,[113] Berengar of Friuli, who himself was elected to succeed the deposed Charles the Fat. Variants that Æthelstan used throughout his reign included such formulations as "king of the Anglo-Saxons and emperor of the Northumbrians" (*Rex Angulsexna* and *Norþhymbra imperator*).[114] Like the successors of Charlemagne, the emperors in the west, and those claiming imperial styles, bore little resemblance to the ancient western emperors, and scarcely any more to those of the east. But they maintained a status nonetheless overtly and explicitly distinct from mere kingship. They also, occasionally, enjoyed the recognition of Constantinople.

Æthelstan was also one of many rulers in England to use the Anglo-Saxon royal title of *Bretwalda* ("wielder of the strength of Britain", or *Brutenwealde*).[115] Like the Irish title of high king (or High King of Tara),[116] the title of *Bretwalda* may have meant an overlord whose status was rather more *primus inter pares* than *imperium*. As such, it also resembled *Imperator totius Hispaniae*. But equally it suggests an imperial ambition in the sense of not recognising any jurisdictional superior. It may also have been inspired by a dim recollection of the universal authority of

[108] Cullinan, Margaret M., "*Imperator Hispaniae*: The Genesis of 'Spain'" (1975) City University of New York PhD dissertation.

[109] Latowsky, Anne A., *Emperor of the World* (2013).

[110] Mladjov, I. S. R., "The Crown and the Veil: Titles, Spiritual Kinship, and Diplomacy in Tenth-Century Bulgaro-Byzantine Relations" (2015) 13 History Compass 171–183.

[111] Soulis, George Christos, *The Serbs and Byzantium during the reign of Tsar Stephen Dušan (1331–1355) and his successors* (1984).

[112] Kotilaine, Jarmo and Marshall Poe (eds.), *Modernizing Muscovy* (2004).

[113] Le Goff, Jacques, *La civilisation de l'Occident médieval* (1964).

[114] Hare, Kent G., "Athelstan of England: Christian King and Hero" (Spring 2004) 7 The Heroic Age 1–12.

[115] Colebrooke, Thomas Edward, *On Imperial and Other Titles* (1877), pp. 34–36.

[116] From Máel Sechnaill mac Máel Ruanaida (c.852) to Edward Bruce, Earl of Carrick (died 1318); Byrne, Francis John, *Irish Kings and High-Kings* (1973); Duffy, Seán (ed.), *Robert the Bruce's Irish wars* (2002).

the emperor as the ruler of the civilised world; later Russian pretensions to the title definitely were reinforced, if not inspired by the final collapse of the eastern Roman empire in 1453,[117] and Russian perception of itself as the successor to the imperial mantle.[118]

King Edgar the Peaceful (c. 943–975) legendarily took homage from five (or eight) lesser kings during an excursion on the River Dee, after his coronation.[119] During his lifetime, he issued royal charters proclaiming himself as *Anglorum Basileus* and *totius Albionis Basileus*, among other variants.[120] As noted earlier, it was not for nothing that Edgar chose to be crowned in Bath, by Dunstan Archbishop of Canterbury by the ruins of Roman Aquae Sulis, rather than the usual Kingston.[121] The language of a restored *imperium* was too powerful to ignore, and also helped to link his kingship to the pre-Saxon age, unifying Saxon and Briton alike.[122] Æthelred the Unready (c. 966–1016) was also noted for being especially fond of high titles during his reign.[123]

[117] Melville-Jones, John R., *The Siege of Constantinople 1453* (1972).

[118] Bulgaria, 919–1018 and 1185–1396, used the style "Tsar" for its ruler—the revived use 1908–1946. Serbia used the term tsar 1346–1371. Most famously, Russia used Tsar 1547–1721, officially imperator 1721-1917; Margeret, J. *The Russian Empire and Grand Duchy of Muscovy* (1983).

[119] Shortly after the coronation at Bath, other kings of Britain came and gave their allegiance to Edgar at Chester (the former Roman *castrum*, Deva Victrix). Six kings in Britain, including Kenneth II, the King of Scots, Máel Coluim, King of Strathclyde, and four kings from Wales pledged their faith that they would be the king's liege-men on sea and land. Later chroniclers made the kings into eight, all plying the oars of Edgar's state barge on the River Dee. The traditional location of Edgar's royal residence in Chester is known as Edgar's Field, a park in Handbridge, near the old Dee bridge. The barge is thought to have been rowed from Edgar's residence up the Dee to the Minster Church of St John the Baptist on the opposite bank; Huscroft, Richard, *The Norman Conquest* (2013), p. 21.

[120] Colebrooke, Thomas Edward, *On Imperial and Other Titles* (1877), pp. 34–36.

[121] The city became a spa with the Latin name *Aquae Sulis* ("the waters of Sulis") c. 60 AD when the Romans built baths and a temple in the valley of the River Avon. The likely contemporary state of the town is described in the eighth or ninth century Anglo-Saxon poem, "The Ruins", which is probably based on Bath; Leslie, R. F. (ed.), *Three old English elegies* (Rev. ed., 1988).

[122] A monastery was founded at an early date, reputedly by St David although more probably in 675 by Osric, King of the Hwicce; Sims-Williams, Patrick, "The Settlement of England in Bede and the Chronicle" (1983) 12 Anglo-Saxon England 1–41; Falconer, David, *Bath Abbey* (1999).

[123] Richard Green, John, *The Conquest of England* (1884), p. 356.

The choice of Kingston, or Kingston-upon-Thames, was equally significant. The earliest surviving record of Kingston is from 838 as the site of a meeting between King Egbert of Wessex and Ceolnoth, Archbishop of Canterbury. Kingston lay on the boundary between the kingdoms of Wessex and Mercia, until in the early tenth century when King Athelstan united both to create the kingdom of England. According to the *Anglo-Saxon Chronicle*, two tenth century kings were consecrated in Kingston, Æthelstan (925), and Æthelred the Unready (978). There are certain other kings who are also said to have been crowned there, although the records are less certain. These include Edward the Elder (902), Edmund I (939), Eadred (946), Eadwig (956), Edgar the Peaceful (circa 960), and Edward the Martyr (975).[124] Just as did Scone in Scotland, and Tara in Ireland, Kingston held a central, though often contested role, as a king-raising site.

Sweyn Forkbeard (ruled 1013–1014) and his son Canute the Great (1016–1035), and Canute's son Harthacnut (1040–42) ruled England, Norway, and Denmark through personal union and lacked formal imperial title during their lifetime, though they followed Anglo-Saxon tradition in their governance; sub-Roman pretensions seem to have not interested them. The lands which they ruled are commonly referred to as the North Sea Empire (*Norþ Sǣ Rīce*) (1013–42). The ephemeral nature of the transmarine kingdom, however, mitigated against its establishment as a real rival to the Holy Roman Empire, although at its height it was second only to that Empire, at least in extent, if not wealth, population or institutional resilience. Canute himself, in 1027, had attended the coronation in Rome of Conrad II as Holy Roman Emperor.[125]

Edward the Confessor (c. 1003–1066) continued the occasional use of imperial titles after the restoration of the House of Wessex, but the kings of England largely ceased referring to themselves as emperors following the Norman conquest.[126] Subsequently the use of the style and title of emperor and the notion of an empire was less overt—ironically perhaps at

[124] Malden, H. E. (ed.), "Colleges: Collegiate chapel of St Mary Magdalen, Kingston", in *A History of the County of Surrey* (1967), pp. 125–127; Keynes, Simon, "Kingston-upon-Thames", in Michael Lapidge, John Blair, Simon Keynes, and Donald Scragg (eds.), *The Blackwell Encyclopedia of Anglo-Saxon England* (2001), pp. 106–119.

[125] Lawson, M. K., *Cnut* (2nd ed., 2004), p. 49.

[126] Colebrooke, Thomas Edward, *On Imperial and Other Titles* (1877), pp. 34–36.

a time when a (new) transmarine kingdom was in existence. It also coincided with the beginning of the Great Schism (1054),[127] which ultimately led, along with the gradual decline of the power of the eastern empire, to a lessened influence for Constantinople. But it did not, it would seem, lessen the symbolic allure of Roman styles, titles, modes of dress, and imperial ceremonial, especially the coronation (other ceremonies seem to have had little, if any, influence upon practices in the British Isles, or indeed, in western Europe).

The English coronation ceremony historically blended Roman and European influences, emphasising England's connection to broader imperial traditions. From the tenth century, English kings adopted imperial titles, like Æthelstan's use of *imperator*, inspired by Charlemagne's revival of the Western Empire. These titles reinforced the king's authority within England and aligned coronation rites with the legacy of Rome and the Holy Roman Empire, lending it historical weight and legitimacy.

European—and Roman—Influences

Had the Norman dynasty lasted in England, and not expired within two generations, the earliest wave of Franco-Norman settlers might perhaps have been assimilated in time without radically affecting the broad lines of indigenous development of the law, with its Germanic/Saxon origins, and perhaps have weakened the attraction of imperial styles and titles. But with the death in 1120 of William's grandson William the Ætheling[128] in the *White Ship*,[129] the Crown went to a count of Boulogne, a member of the House of Blois, and then a count of Anjou.[130] With the sons and descendants of Henry II the influence of Aquitaine on England was profound.[131] As under Canute, where the Danish influence brought

[127] Nichols, Aidan, *Rome and the Eastern Churches* (2010).

[128] As noted earlier, Ætheling, or aetheling, atheling or etheling, was an Old English word (æþeling) used in Anglo-Saxon England to designate princes of the royal dynasty who were eligible for the kingship; Abels, Richard, "Royal Succession and the Growth of Political Stability in Ninth-Century Wessex" (2002) 12 The Haskins Society Journal: Studies in Mediæval History 83–97.

[129] Spencer, Charles Spencer, Earl, *The White Ship* (2020).

[130] Leyser, Karl, "The Anglo-Saxon Succession 1120-1125" (1990) 13 Proceedings of the Battle Conference on Anglo-Norman Studies 225–241.

[131] Barlow, Frank, *The Feudal Kingdom of England, 1042-1216* (2nd ed., 1961), p. 108.

a broader European influence, so under the Plantagenets, rather more than William I himself, this influence once again became dominant in England,[132] as it had been during the hegemony of Rome. This was to affect the development of the law, of the kingship, the realm or state, and indeed even the coronation, although significant indigenous distinctions were to remain.

Reminders of the Roman past, the pseudo-Roman present (in the Frankish, Carolingian, and later Holy Roman Empires), were to long influence English kingship. The revival if not rediscovery of the imperial legacy of Rome during the twelfth century Renaissance and later was also significant.[133] This conception of kingship was often profoundly legalistic in nature. In the course of the early mediæval period civil law began to exhibit strong signs of the influence of canon law. The juristic theory of territorial sovereignty, with the king being supreme ruler within the confines of his kingdom, was originally two distinct conceptions. The king owned no superior in temporal matters, and within his kingdom the king was emperor.[134] The (Roman) emperor either had legal supremacy, or he did not. If the former, theories of the sovereignty of kings were not needed, as they swayed merely de facto power. Sovereignty remained essentially de jure authority.[135] The legacy of Roman hegemony meant that for long centuries a widespread perception was that the only true source of authority was from an emperor crowned by a pope. It was only in post-mediæval times that a Holy Roman emperor would dare to use the title without a papal coronation.[136]

Bartolus and Baldus led the way towards recognition of a legal sovereignty of kings. The Holy Roman emperor had a genuine de jure sovereignty within the *terrae imperii*. Other powers could obtain true sovereignty on a purely de facto basis. This was not merely power without

[132] Gillingham, John, *The Angevin Empire* (2nd ed., 2001).

[133] Bauer, Susan Wise, *The History of the Renaissance World* (2013).

[134] Ullmann, Walter, "This Realm of England is an Empire" (1979) 30(2) The Journal of Ecclesiastical History 175–203.

[135] Canning, J. P., "Law, sovereignty and corporation theory, 1300-1450", in J. H. Burns (ed.), *The Cambridge History of Mediæval Political Thought c.350-c.1450* (1988), pp. 454–476, 465–467.

[136] Stollberg-Rilinger, Barbara, *The Emperor's Old Clothes* (2020), p. 13.

legitimacy.[137] However, in the later Middle Ages it was widely believed that England was an independent sovereign monarchy answerable only to God—in mediæval parlance an empire, self-contained and sovereign,[138] despite the paucity of imperial language after the Conquest. The focusing of the Crown's activities almost exclusively on the realm of England after 1216 encouraged such thinking, but this may not have been the source of them. Sir John Fortescue remarked that

> From of old English kings have reigned independently, and acknowledged no superior on earth in things temporal.[139]

This was a fundamental feature of English monarchy by the fifteenth century, at least partly based on precepts of Roman law.[140] They rejected a Holy Roman Empire that had been narrowly German for several centuries, and the temporal authority of the Pope. The French had asserted their own empire for very similar reasons by 1200, though it took until Napoleon in 1804 for the actual style to be used,[141] when the self-made ruler of France wore a golden laurel wreath recalling the Roman Empire, as well as a replica of Charlemagne's crown.[142] In such a conceptual environment it would be inconceivable that there would not be some implications for the coronation.

Perhaps under the influence of continental political theory, the imagery and conception of the kingship in England was to gradually change. Henry V especially emphasised his legal status as an emperor in his

[137] Canning, J. P., "Law, sovereignty and corporation theory, 1300-1450", in J. H. Burns (ed.), *The Cambridge History of Mediæval Political Thought c.350-c.1450* (1988), pp. 454–476, 467–471.

[138] In 1485 Chief Justice Huse observed that the king was superior to the pope within his realm, and answerable directly to God—YB Hil 1 Hen VII fo 10 pl 10.

[139] Fortescue, Sir John, *The Governance of England*, notes by Charles Plummer (1979).

[140] Majesty, the sense of awe-inspiring greatness, in particular, the attribute of divine or sovereign power, was part of the legacy of Rome. The *maiestas* of the Republic or the people of Rome had become that of the emperor, the *maiestas augustalis*. Western emperors were frequently called majesty after the letter of Q. Aurelius Symmachus to Theodosius I (c.390). Eastern emperors were styled μεγαλειοτεσ. The Holy Roman emperors were styled majesty from the time of Louis the Pious (813–840).

[141] Dwyer, Philip, "'Citizen Emperor': Political Ritual, Popular Sovereignty and the Coronation of Napoleon I" (2015) 100(339) History 40–57.

[142] Roberts, Andrew, *Napoleon* (2014), p. 355.

kingdom. His son Henry VI was occasionally called "Most Imperial Majesty", and he was the first to wear a new imperial Crown of state—a closed or arched Crown with four curved hoops meeting in the centre above the diadem itself, and surmounted by a cross,[143] although William the Conqueror had adopted a hoop crown in order to not appear inferior to the emperor.

Royal and Imperial Robes

The use of imperial titles and styles was to be reflected not merely in the use of an imperial crown. The regalia of the Sovereign, as well as the ritual of the coronation, as seen in the third recension, borrowed heavily from the coronation ritual of the Holy Roman Emperors, especially the *Pontificale Romano-Germanicum*, a liturgical text compiled in Mainz in 961. Examples of liturgical developments in England derived from imperial practice include the Imperial Robe of purple velvet, and the *supertunica*. The first is the robe worn at the conclusion of the ceremony, on the exit from the abbey. It comprises an embroidered ermine cape with a train of purple silk velvet, trimmed with ermine and fully lined with pure silk satin. The purple recalls the imperial robes of Roman Emperors,[144] purple being reserved for emperors by the fourth century.[145]

The *Supertunica* is the second robe with which the sovereign is invested. It is a long coat of gold silk which reaches to the ankles and has wide-flowing sleeves. It is lined with red or rose-coloured tabby or taffeta silk, trimmed with gold lace, woven with national symbols and fastened by a sword belt. It derives from the formal full dress uniform of a consul of the Eastern Roman Empire,[146] as used by the eastern Roman emperors. Its use has been attested since at least the fifteenth century in

[143] Cannon, John and Ralph Griffiths, *The Oxford Illustrated History of the British Monarchy* (1988), p. 203.

[144] Cox, Noel, "The Coronation Robes of the Sovereign" (1999) 5(1) Arma 271–280.

[145] St Clair, Kassia, *The Secret Lives of Colour* (2016), pp. 162–164. The colour purple was early reserved for the king, although scarlet was more usual; Cox, Noel, "Tudor sumptuary laws and academical dress: An Act against wearing of Costly Apparel 1509 and An Act for Reformation of Excess in Apparel 1533" (2006) 6 Transactions of the Burgon Society 15–43.

[146] Cox, Noel, "The Coronation Robes of the Sovereign" (1999) 5(1) Arma 271–280.

its present form, and is mentioned in the *Liber Regalis* in the fourteenth century.

More examples, both of liturgy and dress, could be given, such as the Imperial State Crown. The style of the Crown does not suggest empire in the sense of the First, Second or Third British empires.[147] Rather, it refers to the imperial ambitions and pretensions of the kings who wore these crowns.[148] The Imperial Crown of India, on the other hand, was made in 1911 expressly for the King's trip to India for his Durbar,[149] and might be considered an imperial crown in a wider sense, as it was made for the Emperor of India.[150] St Edward's crown, conversely, represents a much older tradition, that of using the ancient crown of Edward the Confessor (now a copy of it), as part of an assertion of legal, constitutional, political and theological continuity from late Saxon times.[151] King Edward had left his coronation regalia for use by all subsequent kings, something that was traditionally done from the thirteenth to the seventeenth centuries.[152] The use of the term "imperial" has recently been eschewed in official language, partly because of the likelihood of confusion over its meaning; in the liturgy for the coronation of King Charles III in 2023, the imperial mantle or Robe Royal or Pall of cloth of gold was invariably called

[147] In particular, the First (seventeenth and eighteenth centuries) and Second British empires (nineteenth and twentieth centuries); See Madden, F. and D. Fieldhouse (eds.), *The Classical Period of the First British Empire, 1689-1783* (1985), vol. 2; Halstead, J. P., *The Second British Empire* (1983).

[148] The imperial state crown, with its closed arch, certainly makes its earliest known appearance at the coronation of Henry IV in 1399, but the clear identification of this with imperial claims was only settled in the sixteenth century; Grierson, Philip, "The origins of the English sovereign and the symbolism of the closed crown" (28 January 1964) British Numismatic Society, available at http://www.britnumsoc.org/publications/Digital%20BNJ/pdfs/1963_BNJ_33_19.pdf.

[149] Kaul, Chandrika, "Coronation, Colonialism and Cultures of Control: The Delhi Durbar, 1911", in *Communications, Media and the Imperial Experience* (2014), pp. 19–70.

[150] The Imperial Crown of India is the only crown of a British sovereign to have eight half-arches, in the style of continental European crowns, departing from the tradition of British crowns having two arches or four half-arches; Mears, Kenneth J., Simon Thurley, and Claire Murphy, *The Crown Jewels* (1994).

[151] The coronation crown of England, St Edward's Crown, was made for Charles II's coronation in 1661; Keay, Anna, *The Crown Jewels* (2011); Twining, Edward Lord, *A History of the Crown Jewels of Europe* (1960).

[152] Keay, Anna, *The Crown Jewels* (2011).

the robe royal (which is, however, also correct), and the accompanying prayers shorn of the word "imperial".[153] "Receive this Imperial Robe, and the Lord your God endue you with knowledge and wisdom, with majesty and with power from on high: the Lord clothe you with the robe of righteousness, and with the garments of salvation. Amen",[154] became "Receive this Robe. May the Lord clothe you with the robe of righteousness, and with the garments of salvation".[155] The term imperial mantle was, however, in general use, without explanation offered.

The English kings, both pre- and (later) post-Conquest, often portrayed themselves as equals to the emperors, ancient and mediæval. This was reflected in both title and coronation ritual, including robes. Influences on the coronation which were closer to home included the constitutional legitimacy of the kingdom, to which we will now turn our attention.

The Establishment and Preservation of Legitimacy

Mere assertion of the unity of the kingdom in the Saxon era—by right of conquest, restoration of lost Roman unity, or otherwise—would not, of itself, give rise to a lasting unity of the realm. This required more robust elements. At its heart it necessitated a degree of legitimacy—such as the House of Wessex acquired, at least temporarily, from their pivotal role in the defeat of the Danes. As noted above, the British royal house descends, through the female line, from the House of Wessex in the early sixth century, and thus, broadly speaking, the one family has held the kingship since before the creation of the Kingdom of England.[156] The

[153] *The Authorised Liturgy for the Coronation Rite of His Majesty King Charles III For use on Saturday 6th May 2023, 11:00am at Westminster Abbey* (2023).

[154] *The Form and Order of Service that is to be performed and the Ceremonies that are to be observed in The Coronation of Her Majesty Queen Elizabeth II in the Abbey Church of St. Peter, Westminster, on Tuesday, the second day of June, 1953.*

[155] *The Authorised Liturgy for the Coronation Rite of His Majesty King Charles III For use on Saturday 6th May 2023, 11:00am at Westminster Abbey* (2023).

[156] The Royal House of Japan claims significant antiquity, as does that of the former kingdoms of Georgia, and the empire of Ethiopia. The Imperial House of Japan, otherwise known as the Yamato dynasty, traditionally dates back to 660 BC, and can be historically attested from AD 781. The Bagrationi of Georgia date (as sovereigns) from 813. The Solomonic dynasty of Ethiopia claim descent from Solomon (ruled 970–931BC); Vadala, Alexander Atillio, "Elite Distinction and Regime Change: The Ethiopian Case" (2011)

dynasties which mark the development of the constitution over time are distinguished by the various breaks in regular succession or when there is succession through a female. In more modern times, from the early mediæval period at least, the law and the church aided the kingdom, by offering a form of legitimacy derived from the approbation of the church, and from revived interest in and appreciation of Roman law.

Within the constitutional structure of those countries which have retained the form and theory of British constitutional monarchy the Crown is important legally because it holds the conceptual place held by the State in those legal systems derived from or influenced by the Roman civil law.[157] Not only does the Crown provide a legal basis for governmental action, but it provides much of the legal and political legitimacy for such action. Symbolism can be very important as a source of authority, and is not merely indicative of it.[158]

The Crown remains an important source of traditional legal, though not necessarily political, authority. Thus, in traditional terms, the Crown is the embodiment of governmental authority, and a focus of legal sovereignty. But the Crown, as distinct from the Sovereign or (in the realms) the Governor-General (who is appointed by and represents the Sovereign, and who equates to Head of State in most respects), is also important as a source of constitutional or political legitimacy, which supplements that conferred through more directly democratic processes. This is the legitimacy derived from continuity, and acquiescence. This is partly based on traditional, inherited authority. To many today obedience looks more like a matter of lingering habit, expediency, or necessity, but no longer a matter of reason and principle, and of deepest sentiment and conviction.[159] But a claim that any public institution's authority is in any sense innate will probably fail to convince the majority.

10(4) Comparative Sociology 636–653; Suny, Ronald Grigor, *The Making of the Georgian Nation* (2004); Shillony, Ben-Ami, *The Emperors of Modern Japan* (2008).

[157] Though the term "State" is used in popular (and scholarly) writing, and there are some instances of official use, it has been said to have an uncertain legal meaning in New Zealand except as a synonym for the Crown; Goldfinch, Shaun, "The State", in Raymond Miller (ed.), *New Zealand Government and Politics* (2001), pp. 11–20.

[158] Warhurst, John, "Nationalism and Republicanism in Australia" (1993) 28 Australian Journal of Political Studies 100–120. See also Collins, Randall, *Weberian Sociological Theory* (1986).

[159] Schaar, John H., "Legitimacy in the Modern State", in William Connolly (ed.), *Legitimacy and the State* (1984), pp. 104–133, 104–106.

As Lord Devlin has said:

> The law, both criminal and civil, claims to be able to speak about morality and immorality generally. Where does it get its authority to do this and how does it settle the moral principles which it enforces? Undoubtedly, as a matter of history, it derives both from Christian teaching. But I think that the strict logician is right when he says that the law can no longer rely on doctrine in which citizens are entitled to disbelieve. It is necessary therefore to look for some other source.[160]

Although Devlin's reasoning might, in its turn, be questioned—a sort of constitutional *reductio ad absurdum* would lead us to reject all legitimacy—the legal crisis facing many states today is partly due to the fact that the law of Western civilisation had been in its origins Christian law, but its faith has been increasingly humanist.[161] Traditional legitimacy derived from inherited legal forms is not, in an egalitarian and democratic age, itself sufficient.[162] The Crown, and any other possessor of traditional legitimacy, has to accommodate itself to a society which has largely ceased to respect tradition, much less to regard it as a source of legitimacy.[163]

Even more significant is where the political, social and economic context has become, for whatever reason, fundamentally different to what it had been when what might be termed the original legitimacy is established. In some respects, legitimacy due to continuity and tradition is perpetual, yet there may come a time when, for instance, the form and substance of the constitution bears little relationship to its original design and context—the American constitution being an example.[164]

Legitimacy is a more supple and inclusive idea than sovereignty, or of continuity.[165] Legitimacy offers reasons why a given State deserves the

[160] Devlin, Patrick, *The Enforcement of Morals* (1959), p. 9.

[161] Rushdoony, Rousas John, *The Institutes of Biblical Law* (1973), p. 69.

[162] Barker, Rodney, *Political Legitimacy and the State* (1990); Laski, Harold Joseph, *Authority in the Modern State* (1919). For specific instances, see Tarifa, Fatos, "The quest for legitimacy and the withering away of utopia" (1997) 76(2) Social Forces 437–473; Larmour, Peter, *Legitimacy, Sovereignty and Regime Change in the South Pacific* (1992).

[163] Bogdanor, Sir Vernon, *The Monarchy and the Constitution* (1995), p. 303.

[164] Cox, Noel, *Constitutional paradigms and the stability of states* (2012).

[165] Barker, Rodney, *Political Legitimacy and the State* (1990), p. 4; Brookfield, F. M., "Some aspects of the Necessity Principle in Constitutional Law" (1972) DPhil thesis, University of Oxford; and Brookfield, F. M., *Waitangi and Indigenous Rights* (1999).

allegiance of its members. Weber identifies three bases for this authority—traditions and customs; legal-rational procedures (such as voting); and individual charisma.[166] Some combination of these can be found in most political systems.

With the dominance of democratic concepts of government, it might be thought that if the people believe that an institution is appropriate, then it is legitimate.[167] But this scheme leaves out substantive questions about the justice of the State and the protection it offers the individuals and groups who belong to it.[168] It is generally more usual today to maintain that a State's legitimacy depends upon its upholding certain human rights.[169] Such an approach also omits consideration of the contribution to legitimacy of societal ethos, continuity and history.

Three current alternative definitions of legitimacy are firstly, that it involves the capacity of the system to engender and maintain the belief that the existing political institutions are the most appropriate ones for that society.[170] Second, in the tradition of Weber, legitimacy has been defined as "the degree to which institutions are valued for themselves and considered right and proper".[171] Third, political legitimacy may be defined as the degree of public perception that a regime is morally proper for a given society.[172]

Whichever definition is preferred, all are based on belief or opinion, unlike the older traditional definitions which revolved around the element

[166] Collins, Randall, *Weberian Sociological Theory* (1986).

[167] Brook Cowen, Penelope, "Neo Liberalism" in Raymond Miller (ed.), *New Zealand Politics in Transition* (1997), pp. 341–349, 341.

[168] Which is illustrated by the study of the application of the model to Mummar Qadhafi's Libya; Al Namlah, S., "Political legitimacy in Libya since 1969" (1992) Syracuse University PhD thesis.

[169] Rawls, John, *Political Liberalism* (1993); Honderich, Ted (ed.), *The Oxford Companion to Philosophy* (1995), p. 477; Swanson, M., "The Social extract tradition and the question of political legitimacy" (1995) University of Missouri-Columbia PhD thesis.

[170] Lipset, Seymour Martin, *Political Man* (1960), p. 77.

[171] Bierstedt, Robert, "Legitimacy", in J. Gould and W. Kolb (eds.), *A Dictionary of the Social Sciences* (1964), p. 186.

[172] Merelman, Richard, "Learning and Legitimacy" (1966) 63 American Political Science Review 548–461.

of law or right.[173] These traditional concepts of legitimacy were built upon foundations external to and independent of the mere assertion or opinion of the claimant.[174] These normative or legal definitions included laws of inheritance, and laws of logic. Sources for these included immemorial custom, divine law, the law of nature, or (historically much more rarely) a constitution.[175]

Legitimacy is sought through the advancing and acceptance of a political formula, a metaphysical or ideological method that justifies the existing exercise or proposed possession of power by rulers as the logical and necessary consequence of the beliefs of the people over whom the power is exercised.[176] Just what this formula is depends upon the history and composition of a country. In modern democratic societies, popular elections confer legitimacy upon governments. But legitimacy can also be independent of the mere assertion or opinion of the claimant, or even of voters. This was particularly important in late twentieth century discussion of indigenous rights.[177] Majoritarian authority is not sufficient to establish legitimacy.

The Crown, of which the King is the personification—is more than just the mechanism through which government is administered. It is also itself one of the sources of governmental authority, as a traditional source of legal sovereignty. Sovereignty has assumed different meanings and attributes according to the conditions of time and place, but at a basic level it requires obedience from its subjects and denies a concurrent authority to any other body.[178] In the United Kingdom and in the

[173] In an extreme form, the divine right of kings; Figgis, J. N., *The theory of the Divine Right of Kings* (2nd ed., 1914).

[174] Schaar, John H., "Legitimacy in the Modern State", in William Connolly (ed.), *Legitimacy and the State* (1984), pp. 104–133, 108; Waskan, Jonathan, "De facto legitimacy and popular will" (1998) 24(1) Social Theory and Practice 25–56.

[175] Arendt, Hannah, "What was authority" in Carl Friedrich (ed.), *Authority* (1958), pp. 81–112.

[176] Tarifa, Fatos, "The quest for legitimacy and the withering away of utopia" (1997) 76(2) Social Forces 437–473.

[177] See, for example, Lauterpacht, Sir Eli, "Sovereignty – myth or reality?" (1997) 73(1) International Affairs 137–150.

[178] Philpott, Daniel, "Sovereignty" (1995) 48(2) Journal of International Affairs 353–368.

realms, the Sovereign is formally responsible for the executive government, and indeed is specifically so appointed by the Constitutions of most Commonwealth countries of which His Majesty is head of State.[179]

It will be immediately apparent that there is a divergence between abstract (and even substantive) law and political reality, for substantial political power is vested in politicians rather than the Sovereign. Political orthodoxy also appears to hold that for a constitution to be legitimate it must derive (in some manner) from the people. Yet, our constitution is not apparently based legally on the sovereignty of the people, but rather on that of the King-in-Parliament. The coronation, likewise, can perhaps be taken to suggest a greater authority or status is vested in the Sovereign than the day-to-day political and constitutional reality suggests. It is Parliament, and Ministers responsible to it, in contrast to the Crown, which is widely regarded as being the focus of political power.[180] Joseph assumes therefore that it is the people rather than Parliament who is sovereign.[181] But it would seem to more closely match the legal reality, and constitutional history and evolution, to observe that sovereign authority is legally vested in the Crown-in-Parliament, and politically in the people. The coronation more nearly suggests this, particularly in the acclamation, oath and homage.

The authority of government is based upon several sources. Even were authority legally derived from the people, as it appears to now be in Australia,[182] it is not clear how this is to be understood in the context of

[179] See, for example, the Barbados Independence Order 1966, the Schedule of which is the Constitution of Barbados. Section 63(1): "The executive authority of Barbados is vested in Her Majesty". Barbados became a republic 30 November 2021, so King Charles III never reigned over that particular realm; Constitution (Amendment) (No. 2) Act, 2021.

[180] See Kornberg, Allan and Harold D. Clarke, *Citizens and Community – Political Support in a Representative Democracy* (1992); Harlow, C., "Power from the People?", in Patrick McAuslan, and John F. McEldowney (eds.), *Law, Legitimacy and the Constitution Essays marking the Centenary of Dicey's Law of the Constitution* (1985), pp. 62–74; Mallory, James Russell, "The Appointment of the Governor General" (1960) 26 Canadian Journal of Economics and Political Science 96–107.

[181] Joseph, Philip A., *Constitutional and Administrative Law in New Zealand* (1993), pp. 284–285.

[182] The Australian Constitution has been held to be based on popular sovereignty, as it was adopted by popular vote; *Australian Capital Television Pty Ltd v Commonwealth,* (1992) 177 CLR 106 at 138 per Mason CJ; *Theophanous v Herald & Weekly Times Ltd*

the 1707 Act of Union, let alone the quasi-federal system now operating de facto if not de jure in the United Kingdom.

Executive authority is also formally vested in the Crown.[183] The government does not require parliamentary approval for most administrative actions; nor need it necessarily show popular approval or consent for these actions—though the rule of law and political expediency, and the strictly limited range of powers held by the Crown, prevent authoritarian Crown government.[184]

The authority of a country could be vested in a president, the Governor-General, or the King, irrespective of the basis of sovereignty. But in our constitutional arrangements the sole focus of legal authority is the Crown-in-Parliament, in most (if not all) of the realms. This institution enjoys full legal sovereignty or supremacy, subject, where one exists, to an entrenched written constitution. The Crown itself is allocated executive functions, and, within a limited (and increasingly restricted) field,[185] requires no other legal authority than its own prerogative.[186]

This approach has the advantage of simplicity, leaving broader questions of sovereignty unanswered.[187] As such it owes much to the British tradition of a constitution as something which evolves, and for which theory is sometimes developed subsequent to the evolution of the practice.[188] One aspect of this paucity of theory, if it may be so called, is the weakness—or absence, of a general theory of the State.[189]

(1994) 182 CLR 104 at 171 per Deane J; *McGinty v Western Australia* (1996) 186 CLR 140 at 230, 237 per McHugh, J.

[183] Harris, B. V., "The 'Third Source' of Authority for Government Action" (1992) 109 Law Quarterly Review 626–651.

[184] For an example of the application of such limits on government see *Fitzgerald v Muldoon* [1976] 2 NZLR 615.

[185] Cox, Noel, *The Royal Prerogative and Constitutional Law* (2021).

[186] Harris, B. V., "The 'Third Source' of Authority for Government Action" (1992) 109 Law Quarterly Review 626–651.

[187] Which suits most political leaders and the general public alike; Interview with Sir Douglas Graham, in Auckland, New Zealand (24 November 1999).

[188] By contrast Australia's Constitution may be described as a social covenant drawn up and ratified by the people; La Nauze, John Andrew, *The Making of the Australian Constitution* (1972).

[189] David Bercuson, David and Barry Cooper, "From Constitutional Monarchy to Quasi Republic" in Janet Ajzenstat (ed), *Canadian Constitutionalism, 1791-1991* (1992), pp. 15–36; cf Smith, David, *The Republican Option in Canada, Past and Present* (1999),

There have been no pressing technical or practical reasons for these difficult questions of the sources of governmental authority to be answered in the United Kingdom. To some extent, the asking of such questions was also avoided.[190] Thus, the existence of the Crown, whilst providing a convenient legal source for executive government, has also acted as an inhibitor of abstract constitutional theorising. As a consequence, in Laski's view, the Crown covered a "multitude of sins".[191] Whilst this might not be desirable, it provides a convenient cover behind which the business of government is conducted, unworried by conceptual difficulties which might exercise academics. Bagehot's distinction between the dignified and the efficient elements of government has some validity.[192]

The Crown provides a significant element of legitimacy for government, through legal and historical continuity. This itself influences the form of government, specifically the preservation of the concept of the Crown. The traditional governance of kings, from Saxon times onwards, also provides a legitimacy of continuity to the British polity—a legitimacy which is only partly based on popular will, and which provides a counterweight to popularism or majoritarian dictatorship. It was not for nothing that coronation oaths have long included promises to govern according to the laws and customs of the realm.

This is true whenever there might be a conceptual or practical challenge to the authority of the ruler. King Edgar, in 973, saw the importance of symbolically linking his status to an earlier age—as did William I in 1066, who could have relied solely upon the right of conquest. In both cases broader and more nuanced appeals to legitimacy were made. Likewise, in the coronation not one but multiple assertions to legitimacy are

p. 18; Interview with Sir Douglas Graham, in Auckland, New Zealand (24 November 1999).

[190] Interview with Hon Georgina te Heuheu, in Auckland, New Zealand (7 December 1999).

[191] Laski, Harold, "Responsibility of the State in England" (1919) 32 Harvard Law Journal 447–472.

[192] Bagehot, Walter, *The English Constitution* (2001).

offered, and each is important. However, since only the first—acclamation—has any direct link with modern notions of democratic government, this might suggest a disconnect between constitutional theory underpinning the coronation and contemporary concepts of governance. This raises the possibility of challenges to the inherited traditional legitimacy manifested in the coronation.

Sovereignty

The acquisition of what we today classify as sovereignty over the British Isles can be divided, roughly, into eras. Crudely these include the pre-Roman settlements, the Roman settlement—or occupation—of much, but by no means all, of the British Isles, the Saxon invasions and settlements, the Danish invasions or settlements, and ultimately the Norman Conquest. Each led to the replacement, partially or completely, of previous governance structures. None however completely supplanted the previous population, as has been confirmed by modern DNA studies.[193]

The modern realms, as well as the Republic of Ireland, are the consequence of a series of revolutionary or evolutionary changes, some spanning centuries. Like the pre-1840 Māori people of New Zealand, the various native populations might have wished for a different future; unlike them, however, most if not all of these changes occurred without an overt attempt to ameliorate the consequences for the indigenous populations. The exception, perhaps, was in the post-Conquest settlement after 1066. Although the new ruling class was overwhelmingly Norman and French (if they could be so termed at such an epoch, given that the Norsemen had been in Normandy for scarcely a century[194]), the relative weakness of a Norman governance and legal tradition, coupled with the comparative strength of the Saxon fiscal and legal systems, and William's own claim to rule based on tradition rather than simply conquest, led to a gradual growth of a unified realm.

Legitimacy, even in the most contested circumstances, can develop and gain its own authority. In part, in England unlike in France, this was aided by a relatively early development of indigenous law, and a late reception

[193] Oppenheimer, S., *The Origins of the British* (2006).

[194] Brown, R. Allen, *The Normans* (1994).

of Roman law.[195] In part because of a tradition of royal charters, and the coronation oath, kings generally aspired—or portrayed themselves as ascribing—to rule justly, wisely, and according to law, in a manner which later was categorised as the rule of law. This they promised in the setting of a coronation ritual already centuries old.

Today, in the United Kingdom the primary challenge to legitimacy and the unity of the realm is devolution, and, to a lesser extent, regionalism. Both of these historically have been met with an assertion of royal unity—the Dukes of Normandy and Aquitaine were symbolically represented at coronations until 1820, despite the loss of the duchies in 1259 and 1337 respectively, apart from the Channel Islands.[196] George IV's coronation, the first since the Union of the Parliaments of Great Britain and Ireland, consciously and overtly emphasised the unity of the realm.[197] Perhaps most fundamentally, the coronation oath has, for centuries, been a pivotal assertion of the rule of law, and a crucial statement of the political function of a coronation.

A Commonwealth Perspective on the Coronation

The Commonwealth realms, wholly independent politically, judicially and legally from the United Kingdom, nonetheless possess the same person as their respective Sovereigns. Whilst their status and evolution varies between the realms, for historical constitutional reasons, yet their independence places them in a similar position with respect to the coronation as the Kingdom of Scotland between 1603 and 1707. King James VI of Scotland (later James I of England) was crowned King of Scotland at the Church of the Holy Rude in Stirling, on 29th July 1567, just after his first

[195] Seipp, David J., "The reception of canon law and civil law in the common law courts before 1600" (1993) 13(3) Oxford Journal of Legal Studies 388–420.

[196] Legg, L. G. W., *English Coronation Records* (1901); Powicke, Frederick Maurice, *The Loss of Normandy, 1189-1204* (1999).

[197] Union with Scotland Act 1706 (6 Anne c 11), art II; Union with Ireland Act 1800 (39 & 40 Geo III c 67) art 2; Ireland Act 1949 (12 & 13 Geo VI c 41) s 1 (1).

birthday.[198] His son, Charles I, was crowned at the Palace of Holyroodhouse, in Edinburgh, on 18th June 1633,[199] eight years after his accession and coronation in England.

The son of St Charles, King and Martyr, Charles II, was crowned King of Scotland, 1st January 1651, at Scone, in the last coronation, to date, in Scotland.[200] James II was crowned 23rd April 1685 in London, but was deposed before he could be crowned in Scotland. His successors, William II and Mary II, were crowned in London 11th April 1689, and finally, Queen Anne, on 23rd April 1702; none had a Scottish coronation. Arguably, although the coronation in London remained resolutely Anglican (if it could be so called, given the antiquity of much of the ritual), it was thereafter not thought necessary for there to be a separate coronation in Scotland. Such a rite was probably also thought particularly unnecessary after the unions of the Parliaments in 1707.

In the course of the twentieth century, and into the twenty-first century, constitutional and political changes have rendered the position less clear. Always a distinct legal entity, devolution has returned much of constitutional autonomy to Scotland.[201] At the same time the development of separate crowns in the form of the realms raised the question of the appropriateness of inclusion of Commonwealth, and Scottish elements in the London coronation, if not indeed a separate coronation in Scotland at least.

In 2013 the General Assembly of the Church of Scotland supported a call to crown monarchs separately in a newly independent Scotland.[202] In an ideal world it might be thought that the realms could have their own coronations (or at least inaugurations), but really this is not necessary; Scotland was between 1603 and 1707 and still today is in a distinct

[198] Lyall, Roderick J., "The Medieval Scottish Coronation Service: Some Seventeenth-Century Evidence" (1977) 28(1) Innes Review 3–21.

[199] Shaw, Dougal. "St. Giles' church and Charles I's coronation visit to Scotland" (2004) 77(198) Historical Research 481–502.

[200] Gross, George William Cullen, "1651: The Last Coronation in Scotland — An Anomaly?" (2021) 26(3) The Court Historian 229–245.

[201] Scotland Act 1998.

[202] 23 May 2013. This was based on a Joint Report by the Church and Society Council, the Committee on Ecumenical Relations, and the Legal Questions Committee on the implications for the Church of Scotland of independence for Scotland, 15 May 2013. The Report itself didn't conclude that a coronation was necessary, but the General Assembly endorsed that more specific sentiment.

position from the realms. During that time there was only two coronations in Scotland, in 1633 and 1651, and those for very specific political reasons. In 2023, and in 1953, there were, however, solemn ceremonies at which the Scottish regalia, or Honours of Scotland, were presented to the new Sovereign; a ceremony described erroneously by more than one source in 2023 as a Scottish coronation. Indeed, in 1953, Sir Winston Churchill was said to have advised the Queen to dress relatively informally at the National Service of Thanksgiving in Edinburgh, so as to avoid any impression that it was a Scottish coronation.[203]

Conversely, in 2023 the National Service of Thanksgiving and Dedication had a strong coronation-like character. For instance, the Duke of Hamilton and Brandon (Hereditary Bearer of the Crown of Scotland) presented the Crown, saying: "By the symbol of this Crown, we pledge our loyalty, entrusting you to reign as our King in the service of all your people". The King replied: "In receiving this Crown, I so promise by God's help".[204] The Scottish service of Thanksgiving and Dedication, following the coronation, modelled a very different approach, with representatives of non-Christian faiths, including humanism, being fully integrated into the service and offering prayers directly to the new king. This was quite unlike the Westminster coronation, which included only the combined blessing from Christian leaders, and the inaudible prayers of non-Christian religious leaders, offered as the King's procession was leaving the Abbey. This latter arrangement was to preserve the essentially Christian nature of the service, but was also a concession to the sensitivities of at least one religious representative—the Chief Rabbi of the United Hebrew Congregations of the Commonwealth, Rabbi Sir Ephraim Mirvis, to comply with Jewish Shabbat law for a ceremony held on a Saturday, not only walked to the coronation (having been invited to spend the previous night in St James's Palace), but was unable to use any sound projection equipment.[205]

[203] Mack, Douglas S., "Can the Scottish subaltern speak?", in Caroline McCracken-Flesher (ed.). *Culture, Nation, and the New Scottish Parliament* (2007), pp. 141–157, 146.

[204] "Order of Service released for a National Service of Thanksgiving and Dedication at St Giles' Cathedral, Edinburgh" (PDF). <www.churchofscotland.org.gov.uk>.

[205] Joshi. Jitendra, "King Charles praised for helping chief rabbi observe Shabbat at coronation", *The Times of Israel*, 5 May 2023.

Although the coronation remains structurally derived very much from the English *ordo*, as we have seen these derive from a wider European and near eastern ancestry. Today, elements have been added or changed to ensure the representation of other parts of the United Kingdom—most notably in 2023, in the use of music; These include a *Kyrie eleison* sung before the Recognition (wholly in Welsh, the first time that language had been used in a coronation in England), and a plainsong *Veni Creator Spiritus* (used since the time of Dunstan in 973) before the anointing, in Welsh, Scots Gaelic, Irish Gaelic, and English.[206]

Commonwealth Representations in the Coronation Attire and Insignia

Queen Elizabeth II was crowned for the whole Commonwealth in 1953. This was reflected in the coronation dress worn by the Queen. This replaced the crimson surcoat and purple surcoat that would be worn by a king. Commissioned in October 1952 and designed by the couturier Norman Hartnell, the coronation dress was made by a team of three seamstresses and six embroiderers. It is of white satin silk, encrusted with thousands of tiny seed pearls and crystals, each in a small silver saucer, to create a lattice-work appearance and to catch the effect of movement. The gown is embroidered in pastel-coloured silks, pearls, diamonds, pale amethysts, golden crystals, gold and silver bullion and sequins for the details. The embroidery depicts the emblems of the United Kingdom and the Commonwealth. There are Tudor roses (for England), thistles (Scotland), shamrock (Ireland), leeks (Wales), lotus (two different types, for India and Ceylon), protea (South Africa), wattle flower (Australia), wheat cotton and jute (Pakistan), maple leaf (Canada), and fern (New Zealand) designs embroidered.[207] As Trepanier notes, "the gown was intended to signify that the one physical person wearing it is the embodiment of eleven countries".[208] Such an approach is not new; Queen Alexandra (1902)

[206] *The Authorised Liturgy for the Coronation Rite of His Majesty King Charles III For use on Saturday 6th May 2023, 11:00am at Westminster Abbey* (2023).

[207] Cho, Youn-Yung and Sook-In Yang, "A Study on Queen Elizabeth II's Dress: Focusing on the Dress and Role Enactment" (2010) 13(1) The International Journal of Costume Culture 12–22.

[208] Trepanier, Peter, *Some Visual Aspects of the Monarchial Tradition* (2004).

made her coronation dress designed and woven in India.[209] Royal robes, and especially those used at a coronation, are replete with imagery.[210]

The royal stole also represented the Commonwealth realms symbolically in 1953. This is a richly and heavily embroidered cloth-of-gold scarf, with gold and silver thread and set with jewels. It has a square panel at either end, each with a red St George's Cross on a silver background. On a background of floral emblems of the Commonwealth are the emblems of the four Evangelists. There are also St Edward's Crowns, imperial eagles, and the dove of the Holy Ghost, as well as the flags of St Patrick, St Andrew and St George. The lining is of rose-coloured silk, and there are gold fringes at each end. It is kept in the Tower of London.[211]

In 2023 a new stole was commissioned for the coronation as the traditional gift of the Worshipful Company of Girdlers, also bearing significant Christian iconography, including the gridirons of St Lawrence (the patron saint of the Girdlers Company), and palm branches. Palms are both a symbol of martyrdom but also a reminder of the humble entry of Jesus as a Servant King into Jerusalem.[212] The 2023 stole features a series of roundels, set in a gold chain framework and applied to cloth of gold. Each roundel features an embroidered image, including the four emblems of the United Kingdom; a dove of peace (representing the Holy Spirit); a Tudor Crown; and a pattern inspired by the Cosmati Pavement in Westminster Abbey.[213] The absence of Commonwealth emblems might be ascribed simply to the practical difficulty of including more than a dozen countries on a small item, though it had been just possible in 1953.

The royal stole itself was derived from the λοροσ(loros), a jewelled scarf of the eastern emperors. This originated as the *stola* worn by noble ladies in the early Roman Empire. Senators and consuls were required to wear a coloured pall or scarf over the alb and *paenula* by the sumptuary Codex of Theodosius (382). Shortly afterwards it became a distinctive badge of

209 Strasdin, Kate, "Empire Dressing—The Design and Realization of Queen Alexandra's Coronation Gown" (2012) 25(2) Journal of Design History 155–170.

210 Sutton, Anne, "The coronation robes of Richard III and Anne Neville" (1979) 13(1) Costume 8–16.

211 Keay, Anna, *The Crown Jewels* (2011).

212 *The Authorised Liturgy for the Coronation Rite of His Majesty King Charles III For use on Saturday 6th May 2023, 11:00am at Westminster Abbey* (2023).

213 "Coronation outfits worn by Their Majesties King Charles III and Queen Camilla to go on display at Buckingham Palace", Royal Collection Trust, 19 May 2023.

episcopal status. The stole as a liturgical vestment is today confined to the major orders of the Christian ministry—deacons, priests and bishops. It is worn over the alb or surplice when performing religious functions. Although now widely used in the Anglican Church, it was replaced at the time of the Reformation with the scarf, a broad band of black silk. The *Liber Regalis* requires its use by the Sovereign at their coronation (though the stole predates that document) —an example was found on the body of Edward I (crowned 1274, died 1307) when his coffin was opened in 1774[214]—although it has only been regularly used since James I.[215] While the *colobium sindonis* resembles the surplice, which may now be worn by laymen, and the *supertunica*, the dalmatic of the deacon, the stole as worn over both shoulders is proper only to the major or higher orders of priest and bishop. It is worn by the king uncrossed (like a bishop), but over the dalmatic (*colobium sindon*).

Also a gift from Commonwealth countries in 1953, the presentation of the armillae, or bracelets, was a restoration of a practice which seems to have been last used for the coronation of Edward VI, although "coronation bracelets" are recorded as being in the Tower of London in 1649,[216] and bracelets were made in 1661. The new armillae are single-piece round bracelets made of 22 carat gold lined with crimson velvet, with a concealed hinge and spring catch. Under the velvet lining they are described as being.

> Presented for the Coronation of Her Majesty Queen Elizabeth II by the Governments of the United Kingdom, Canada, Australia, New Zealand, South Africa, Pakistan, Ceylon and Southern Rhodesia.[217]

The respective flags of the realms were also borne at the coronation by the High Commissioners; though by 2023 the position had changed, and the flags of the realms, which preceded the Governors-General and Prime

[214] Davenport, Cyril, *The English Regalia* (1897), p. 14.

[215] Cox, Noel, "The Coronation Robes of the Sovereign" (1999) 5(1) Arma 271–280.

[216] Legg, L. G. W., *English Coronation Records* (1901), pp. xliv.

[217] "Queen Elizabeth II's Armills 1952-53", <https://www.rct.uk/collection/31724/queen-elizabeth-iis-armills>.

Ministers, were borne by a variety of individuals; that of New Zealand was borne by Sergeant Hayden Smith, RNZAF.[218]

While the 2023 royal stole was devoid of explicit Commonwealth iconography, a new item, the anointing screens, more clearly incorporated this—though significantly all member countries were included, and not just the realms.[219]

Vesture aside—and some insignia and minor regalia—the coronation remained at its core the British (if not English) ceremonial. This probably accurately reflected the nature of the constitutional relationship which prevailed between the realms—or dominions—in 1953. However, it does not accurately reflect the constitutional relationship between the realms today. Although it is an exaggeration to say the one person being, for instance, King of the United Kingdom, and King of Australia, is a coincidence, or a mere accident of history, nevertheless, from a political perspective, the appropriateness of the one coronation being held for all realms might be questioned, however convenient it might be.

Likewise, after the abandonment of the coronation of the King of Scotland, was the coronation of the King of Great Britain, and then the United Kingdom, in London, sufficient for the United Kingdom let alone the realms? In 1953 efforts were made—such as the involvement of the Moderator of the General Assembly of the Church of Scotland—to accommodate Scotland,[220] but the coronation remained overwhelmingly English.

This probably suggests the likely line of future development. Greater symbolic representation of realms—and the constituent countries of the United Kingdom—may be included, but the structure of the rite would not necessarily change. This is, perhaps ironically, reminiscent of the coronation of Edgar, and the most appropriate way of retaining faithfulness to the nature of the coronation. Equally important will be acknowledging

[218] Baker Wilson, Kim, "NZ Defence Force contingent heading to London for King's coronation", *1 News*, 23 April 2023.

[219] Press Release, "The Anointing Screen", The Royal Family, 29 April 2023.

[220] The Moderator presented a *Bible*, as had been done since 1689; The Archbishop of Canterbury, "Archbishop of Canterbury receives the Coronation Bible at Lambeth Palace". 20 April 2023. The presentation of the *Bible*—again by the Moderator—was moved from after the administration of the Oath, to before, a more logical place; *The Authorised Liturgy for the Coronation Rite of His Majesty King Charles III For use on Saturday 6th May 2023, 11:00am at Westminster Abbey* (2023).

religious and social changes since 2023, again without disrupting the inherited form of the coronation.

Just as efforts were made after 1707 and 1801 to reflect the changing constitutional reality, so to in 1953 the dominions were acknowledged and symbolically included. It might be expected that greater efforts will be made to involve the realms in the next coronation, but, as previously, limited to symbolism rather than structural changes in the coronation. This would be consistent with the practice surrounding the accession proclamations. |

The political role and function of the coronation, particularly at a time of greater pluralism and diversity, cannot be underestimated. Ironically, it may have increased, just as it has done at any time of social, economic or political turmoil or change. Arguably, the presence of the standards of the various realms, the flora of those countries on royal fabrics, and a new piece of regalia donated by the realms, would not be enough to reflect the constitutional changes which have occurred since 1953. In that year only six years had passed since Indian independence, and the empire was transitioning into the Commonwealth.

Today, the constitutional relationship between the realms and the United Kingdom is quite different to what it was in 1953. It is possible that this should be reflected in either a significantly greater or a significantly lesser presence in the coronation, just as the perception of the Sovereign has been managed in different ways in the major realms.

In 2023 there were some changes from 1953 which reflected the changing status of the realms. In addition to the various realm Prime Ministers, and their respective national flags, Governors-General were now in the procession in the Abbey. At the conclusion of the service, having acknowledged the greeting from faith leaders, the king turned to greet the Governors-General. The King acknowledged their greeting and proceeded to the Gold State Coach.[221] Whether that is constitutionally and symbolically sufficient remains to be seen.

[221] *The Authorised Liturgy for the Coronation Rite of His Majesty King Charles III For use on Saturday 6th May 2023, 11:00am at Westminster Abbey* (2023).

The Political Function of a Coronation

The political function of the coronation is primarily to establish and declare that the king is sovereign of the realm or realms, and both that this is settled and unquestioned and that there is a corresponding unity to the realm.

In the many centuries since Saxon times, and during the centuries since the Tudors, the monarchy in England expanded to include Scotland, Wales and (Northern) Ireland, as well as the overseas territories of the Crown—not to mention the overseas realms. The role of the Crown greatly changed over this time, from actual governance to largely—though not entirely—a ceremonial and symbolic function.

Sometimes, in the quest for legitimacy, kings used the coronation quite explicitly (and even cynically). The oil used at the coronation of Henry IV (ruled 1399–1413) in 1399 was believed to have been miraculously given to the Archbishop of Canterbury Thomas Becket (in office 1162–1170) by the Virgin Mary. This wondrous oil had allegedly only recently been discovered hidden away in one of the darker corners of the Tower of London's cellars.[222] The oil, whatever its real origin, was a useful addition in Henry's search to legitimise his usurpation of the throne from Richard II (ruled 1377–1399). The link with the martyred archbishop and the Blessed Virgin Mary was particularly potent in this era.[223]

Equally, the seizure by Edward I of the Stone of Destiny, or Stone of Scone, in 1296, was subsequently used to bolster English claims to sovereignty over Scotland, the stone having allegedly been the traditional crowning site of the Kings of the Scots.[224] It was, and has been used, at every English coronation since then, although since 1996 it has again been stored in Scotland—though not at Scone. Whether the Stone is truly that used to enthrone Scottish kings since at least 906 (if not the late fifth century), or is the legendary Biblical stone pillow of Jacob, or a fourteenth century substitute by the Scots, or by Edward I himself, we do know that it was upon this stone that every English king and queen regnant has been

[222] Ullmann, Walter, "Thomas Becket's miraculous oil" (1957) 8(1) The Journal of Theological Studies 129–133.

[223] McKenna, John W., "The Coronation Oil of the Yorkist Kings" (1967) English Historical Review 102–104.

[224] Breeze, David, and Graeme Munro, *The Stone of Destiny* (1997).

crowned since 1308.[225] The symbolism of claimed hegemony over the Scots soon gave way to its own autochthonous authority, as a new king-stone. The stone's use in England from 1296 to 2023 (and counting), compared with its use in Scotland 906 to 1296 (assuming it was a genuine article and not a substitute by Edward or the Scots), means that it had spent 727 years in English use, almost twice as long as the 390 years in Scottish use. Since 1603 it might also reasonably be described as having a joint use as the coronation stone for the King of Scotland in England.

The political factors which led to the importance of the coronation as a royal, church and state ritual remained, through varied political fortunes. The idea of the need to gain popular support for a new monarch by making the ceremony a spectacle for ordinary people, started with the coronation in 1377 of Richard II, a 10-year-old boy. Although George IV's 1821 coronation may have over-played the role, in the course of the twentieth century, when the role of the Sovereign was at its nadir, arguably the importance of the coronation grew, as a means of establishing and maintaining governmental legitimacy.

The tone was set during the late nineteenth century. *The Times*, in regretting Queen Victoria's apparent withdrawal from government after the death of her husband, Prince Albert, the Prince Consort, warned that,

> No reigning House can afford to confirm in its views those who suggest that the Throne is only an antiquarian relic and Royalty itself a ceremony.[226]

But by the end of the 1860s it too was acknowledging that the future of the monarchy lay in its ceremonial and not in its political functions.[227] Official efforts were made to capture and enhance this perception, as the

[225] Historically kept in the now-ruined Scone Abbey, near Perth, in 1996 it was moved to Edinburgh Castle and put with the Honours of Scotland (the Scottish regalia) in the Crown Room of the Castle. In 2024 was moved again, this time to the Hall of Destiny in Perth City Hall.

[226] 15th December 1864, p. 8.

[227] 21st October 1869, p. 6. See also Shearman, Deirdre, "Image of Victoria" (1996) Brandeis University PhD thesis. The conscious development of ceremonial from late Victorian times has often been remarked; Kuhn, William, "Ceremony and Politics" (1990) Johns Hopkins University PhD thesis; Hobsbawn, Eric and Terence Ranger, *The Invention of Tradition* (1983).

monarchy was consciously promoted by Disraeli as a symbol of imperial unity (a source of legitimacy). Governments—in Bagehot's terms the efficient part of government[228]—conducted business behind the smokescreen and legitimacy of the dignified part of government—the Crown. This however may overly simplify the situation, drawing an absolute distinction between dignified and efficient. The reality was and remains that there is a much more nuanced relationship between the day-to-day government and the role of the King.

Weber's conception of traditions and customs as a basis for legitimacy provides a useful standpoint.[229] Legitimacy offers reasons why a given state deserves the allegiance of its members, but also why the authority of an institution is respected and enforced. As noted earlier, Max Weber identified three bases for this authority – traditions and customs; legal-rational procedure; and individual charisma.[230] The coronation, as a key ritual of monarchy, ushering in a new reign, is pivotal in establishing legitimacy through traditions and customs.

As was observed by the Constitution Unit, University College London, in two reports in 2018,[231] the population and constitution of the United Kingdom has changed dramatically since 1953, the year of the then most recent coronation. However, the population and constitution of England, Great Britain, and the United Kingdom had also changed dramatically in the almost one thousand years between 973 and 1953. The political role of the coronation remained important, though the details of the coronation may have gradually, and sometimes radically, changed over time. The coronation is, primarily, an assertion of legitimacy and authority.

At the Enthroning, the Archbishop of Canterbury prays the following Exhortation.

> Stand firm, and hold fast from henceforth the seat and state of royal and imperial dignity, which is this day delivered unto you, in the Name and by the Authority of Almighty God, and by the hands of us the Bishops and servants of God, though unworthy. And the Lord God Almighty, whose

[228] Bagehot, Walter, *The English Constitution* (2001).

[229] Collins, Randall, *Weberian Sociological Theory* (1986).

[230] Ibid.

[231] Hazell, Robert and R. M. Morris, *Swearing in the New King* (2018); Morris, R. M., *Inaugurating a New Reign* (2018).

> ministers we are, and the stewards of his mysteries, establish your Throne in righteousness, that it may stand fast for evermore. Amen.[232]

The legitimacy represented by the coronation is not that of a transitory shared values,[233] nor is it pluralist. It is that of a Christian monarchy, rooted, in Weberian terms, traditions and customs, legal-rational procedures (the acclamation, homage, and the coronation as a whole); and individual charisma.[234] But it also allows for the emotional and practical inclusion of the non-religious, as well as Christian and non-Christian, within the framework of an Anglican liturgy, though one which originally predates not just the Reformation, but the Great Schism between the eastern and western churches. As has been observed, the coronation has been viewed as a more or less unproblematic occasion of national unity or even national communion.[235]

As the various contributors to a collection edited by Hazell and Morris argue, the public look to the monarchy in European countries to represent continuity, stability and tradition, but also want it to be modern, to reflect modern values and be a focus for national identity.[236] Such a contradictory attitudes present challenges for monarchs and their advisers, whatever the formal or actual constitutional functions, their day-to-day political functions, or their ceremonial functions might be. The combination, however, a markedly different political environment than, for example, one hundred years ago.

Conclusion

The political, rather than legal, legitimacy of a regime depends on factors which extend well beyond mere adherence to legal norms and rules. The king or queen may no longer be a law-maker, in their own

[232] *Proceedings of the Coronation of Her Majesty The Queen*, 2nd June 1953 (1953).

[233] Cf. Birnbaum, Norman, "Monarchs and Sociologists: A reply to Professor Shils and Mr. Young" (1955) 3(1) Sociological Review 5–13.

[234] Collins, Randall, *Weberian Sociological Theory* (1986).

[235] Örnebring, Henrik, "Revisiting the coronation" (2004) 25(1–2) Nordicom Review 175–195.

[236] Hazell, Robert and R. M. Morris (eds.), *The Role of Monarchy in Modern Democracy* (2022).

right (apart from some limited special exceptions), but the King-in-Parliament remains the ultimate source of authority. In a sophisticated dynamic, authority is traced to institutions which have evolved, formed and reformed over the centuries, with the person of the Sovereign, as a personal and political body, acting as a constitutional linchpin for the whole. Such a corporation sole or corporation aggregate—the personification of the Crown—does not simply assume the throne on the death of their parent or other predecessor. They assume the crown, as part of a process which has continued for over a thousand years, which involves a coronation.

This incorporates political and religious elements. The former includes, in terms which might be recognised by Weber, Hobsbawn, and Ranger,[237] tradition and custom. It is more than merely a veneer to disguise where the real authority in government lies—for that authority is vested in the Sovereign, as part of a sacred trust from God and people, reflected in the words of the coronation oath (and in 2023 in particular, elsewhere in the liturgy). The dependence of the Sovereign on the loyalty of the people is reflected in the acclamation. The coronation is an opportunity for reaffirming the connection between the monarchy, the Church of England, and the state, as the sovereign pledges to uphold the laws and govern in line with the nation's values.

Feudalism may have long ago decayed and passed as a socio-economic and political model of governance, but some of its forms survive—most notably in land tenure, which remains, for the most part, in free and common socage. Homage, a similar concept, though one which is more ancient still, also survives, though in an attenuated form. The homage rendered by prelates, peers and members of the Royal Family, echo the acclamation and the coronation oaths. Sovereignty may be a sacred charge, but even the Divine Right of Kings allowed that the King exercised his authority on trust.

The event often draws international leaders, emphasising the United Kingdom's global cultural influence and fostering diplomatic relations.

The coronation ritual affirms the sovereign's role as head of state and reinforces the monarchy's constitutional legitimacy. It formalises the new monarch's authority, although this authority is symbolic under the parliamentary system. Legitimacy, as a key element of any political institution,

[237] Hobsbawn, Eric and Terence Ranger, *The Invention of Tradition* (1983).

may be acquired by a variety of means. Changing political and social landscapes can bring into question the legitimacy of government, but can also provide new forms of legitimacy. The coronation can, and does, incorporate these. But in order to achieve this the coronation must be true to the traditional form, and not an inauguration in all but name, shorn of much or all the solemnity, and historical meaning of the ritual, for reasons of economy, modernising, inclusivity, or any other non-germane justification. In order to fulfil its political purpose, the coronation must be consistent with the ancient form and content of the ritual, or it risks undermining both its purpose and the legitimacy of the Sovereign, and by extension, the governance of the country.

From a political perspective, perhaps the most important factor today is the role of the Sovereign in relation to national unity. Just as the Saxon kings contributed in large part to the development of a unified English kingdom by the tenth century, and the later Tudor kings and queens provided the basis upon which the modern state arose, so too, in face of devolution, and social and economic change, the monarch today can and does provide a focus for national unity—perhaps, indeed, the most important one. In such a situation, the new king or queen does not simply assume their status upon the death of the previous Sovereign.

The event serves as a unifying symbol for the nation, offering a moment for collective celebration and reflection on shared values and history. The ceremony underscores the continuity of the British constitutional system and the stability of the monarchy amidst changes in government or society.

Through its grandeur and ritual, the coronation weaves the political structure, national identity, and cultural heritage into a single ceremony. The status of the Sovereign also reflects the changing structure of the kingdom—or kingdoms. Just as James I and VI and Charles I and were crowned Kings of Scotland, as well as of England, so too, in a post-imperial era, the new Sovereign may be crowned king or queen of more than one realm. Indeed, in 1953 Queen Elizabeth II was concurrently Sovereign of seven realms—the United Kingdom, Canada, Australia, New Zealand, South Africa, Pakistan, and Ceylon. The extent to which this reality is reflected, or not reflected, in the coronation rituals, is an important question, as is the gradual change in the relationship between the realms. We will now consider this issue.

CHAPTER 6

The Theological Function of a Coronation

Introduction

The notion that the coronation has a theological function in the twenty-first century, when only about half the population of the United Kingdom affirm a Christian identity[1]—however loosely—and the number who attend church regularly is markedly less, may seem quaint. Further, as was observed by the Constitution Unit, University College London, in two reports in 2018,[2] the population of the United Kingdom is today much more diverse than it was in 1953. The population of the Commonwealth realms are even more diverse, ethnically, and religiously, though indeed they were in 1953 also. However, rather than diminishing the importance of the theological function of the coronation, conversely this diversity may serve to increase it. The coronation is an unashamedly Christian ritual, but in a country which is notionally at least, Christian

[1] "Religion, England and Wales: Census 2021", https://www.ons.gov.uk/peoplepopulationandcommunity/culturalidentity/religion/bulletins/religionenglandandwales/census2021.

[2] Hazell, Robert and R. M. Morris, *Swearing in the New King* (2018); Morris, R. M., *Inaugurating a New Reign* (2018).

N. Cox, *The Political, Legal, and Theological Functions of the Ceremony in the British Tradition*,
https://doi.org/10.1007/978-3-031-88960-8_6

(there is an established church in England and Scotland),[3] and representing an institution which has enjoyed Christian approbation for over a thousand years, that is arguably unremarkable. A humanist or multi-faith coronation is not entirely unthinkable, but would be a radical move, and a significant constitutional risk for any new Sovereign. It would also be practically impossible without statutory amendments, such as to the Coronation Oath Act 1688.[4]

As we have noted, in 574, Áedán mac Gabráin, the king of Dál Riata, reputedly came to the monastery at Iona (or possibly the hill of Dunadd) to be crowned by St Columba, in the earliest recorded coronation in Britain and Ireland.[5] Thus, from the beginning the coronation was a religious ritual, not a purely secular ceremonial. Although the pre-Christian rulers of Britain doubtless had their own inauguration traditions, the advent of Christianity brought with it a new tradition of coronation, one drawn into and from the rich heritage outlined in Chapter 2.

For centuries the unbroken tradition continued. No Sovereign—or their advisers—dared depart from time-honoured custom, for fear of the social, political and theological consequences. Even the break with Rome did not alter the coronation markedly. On 20th February 1547 King Edward VI was crowned, in the first post-Reformation rite. Although the ceremony was largely unchanged, there were certain noticeable and significant points of departure. Thomas Cranmer, Archbishop of Canterbury, prior to the anointing of the nine-year old king, gave an address in which he observed, *inter alia*, that "solemn rites of coronation have their ends and add utility, yet neither direct force or necessity", and that "the oil, if added, is but a ceremony". The sacred rite was transformed—in his mind at least—into a type of drama, though a very necessary one.[6]

Yet, nearly five hundred years later the theological function of the coronation remains, and is perhaps better understood today for its

[3] Church of Scotland Act 1921 (11 & 12 Geo. V c. 29); Ecclesiastical Appeals Act 1532 (24 Hen VIII c 12); Submission of the Clergy Act 1533 (25 Hen VIII c 19).

[4] 1 Will. III & Mary c. 6.

[5] Adomnan of Iona, *The life of St Columba* ed. Richard Sharpe (trans.) (1995), vol 3, 5 and translator's note 358; Broun, Dauvit, "Aedán mac Gabráin", in Michael Lynch (ed.), *The Oxford Companion to Scottish History* (2001), p. 5; Byrne, Francis John, *Irish Kings and High-Kings* (1973), p. 159; Yorke, Barbara, *The Conversion of Britain* (2006), p. 241.

[6] Hunt, Alice, *Drama of Coronation* (2008), chapter 3, pp. 77–110.

historical and theological meaning. Through the centuries, pre- and post-Reformation, the theological rationale and effect of the coronation remained central to it. That is not because the Sovereign is Supreme Governor of the Church of England[7]—for before the Reformation they were not; nor is it because they are Defender of the Faith[8] (for it preceded that by a thousand years). It is because the coronation is the setting aside and dedication of the Sovereign by the church universal in the name of God, in the tradition of Zadok the priest and Nathan the prophet for King David, the Patriarchs for the Eastern Roman Emperors, and the Popes for the Holy Roman Emperor. It reflects both the Sovereign's *persona mixta* and the sacred nature of kingship. The nature of the royal person, the monarchy, and the political entity—the polity—can not be divorced from the ancient Christian ethos inherited from the Byzantines, the Franks and the mediæval European states.

This chapter will consider the development of the underlying Christian nature of the polity—still not completely expunged in a largely post-Christian (if not indeed anti-Christian) world. It commences by looking at the foundations of the Christian basis of the state, and the contribution of a religious ethos to the evolution of the early kingdom. It then will consider the role of the Sovereign as a sacred person, as distinct from their political or social role (insofar as the three elements can be distinguished). There will then be a brief discussion of the establishment of the church in England, and the relationship between king and church. The result of all of this is that the coronation remains pre-eminently a Christian ritual and solemnity, a sacred hallowing of kingship in the service of God, kingdom and realms.

The Early Sub-Roman Foundations of the Christian Basis of the State

The pluralist Roman state—despite the imperial *cultus*—was gradually to come under the sway of a new monotheistic religion the fourth century of the present era. This affected the nature of the state throughout the

[7] *Thirty-Nine Articles of Religion*, enacted in 1562, and confirmed in 1571 by the Subscription (Thirty-Nine Articles) Act 1571 (13 Eliz. I c. 12).

[8] The title of Defender of the Faith dates from 1521, when Pope Leo X conferred upon King Henry VIII the title of *Fidei Defensor*. The title was settled on the king and his successors in perpetuity by the King's Style Act 1543 (35 Hen. VIII c. 2).

Roman world, including in the British provinces of the empire. A Christian ethos prevailed across the empire—and well beyond, especially into the lands of those whom the Romans had characterised as Barbarians. Former provinces of the empire, client states, and those tribal states and kingdoms which bordered Rome, could not fail to be affected by both Roman civilisation—including government and law—and from the fourth century the new Roman state religion. The classical world was transforming, not without considerable chaos, into the early mediæval European and Mediterranean world.[9]

This, and a general collapse of the economy, centralised government, and what we might today call law and order, brought new challenges, for which solutions had to be sought. These latter included the utilisation, across the empire, of formerly Barbarian peoples to provide (at least temporarily) much needed manpower to resist the advance of less Romanised—and more hostile and threatening—peoples.[10] Often the response was decentralised. The rescript of Honorius, a response from the western emperor in Ravenna, in 410, to a request for imperial support, was to the effect that the people of Britain were (at least temporarily) on their own in the face of invasion.[11]

In the British Isles the mass movement of people involved the arrival, apparently in a series of waves, of Angles, Saxons and Jutes, from what is now northern Germany and southern Denmark. According to Bede, in his *Historia ecclesiastica gentis Anglorum*, written around 731 but relying on earlier sources such as Gildas (his *De Excidio et Conquestu Britanniae* dates from c.510–530), these first arrived in 449.[12] Although the accuracy of these accounts, and the extent to which the newcomers were subsequently to displace the native population, before long little remained of the Roman era human and even physical infrastructure, thanks to decades of depredations, famine and war. The modern view generally prefers the

[9] Lot, Ferdinand, *The End of the Ancient World and the Beginnings of the Middle Ages* (1931).

[10] Frere, Sheppard Sunderland, *Britannia* (3rd, revised ed., 1987), p. 357.

[11] Salway, Peter, "The end of Roman rule", in *Roman Britain* (2nd edn, 2015), pp, 97–108.

[12] Colgrave, Bertram and R. A. B. Mynors (eds.), *Bede's Ecclesiastical History of the English People* (1969), Book 1, chapter 15.

concept of a Saxon elite ruling a population largely of Britons,[13] much as the Normans were later to prevail over the far more numerous Anglo-Saxons. But despite vigorous efforts at self-defence against the invaders, over time Britain declined in population, economic and social standing.[14]

But not all was lost. We have already remarked on the coronation of Edgar in 973 being amid the ruins of Roman Bath.[15] Ironically, perhaps, those parts of Britain which were most Romanised in 350 were those that by 550 were most securely under Anglo-Saxon control, and the least Romanised areas in 350 (including what we now call Wales) were those that two hundred years later would arguably still retain at least some vague continuity with a Roman, or sub-Roman, past,[16] perhaps as a way of asserting a separate identity from the invaders, but also in an attempt to to identify with the legacy of a golden age, even if it means engaging in mythopoeic reconstruction of imperial lineage.

There are many reasons why this might have been so, but it is worth noting that Christianity appears to have penetrated through even distant rural parts of Britain, and that brought with it elements of a Roman identity.[17] Like the rest of pre-Roman Britain, the departure of the legions in the face of empire-wide crisis, led to political fragmentation, even if possibly based on pre-Roman tribal lines. After c.500 politics were dominated by kings with territorial kingdoms.[18] The legitimacy of the kingship

[13] Higham, Nicholas J., and Martin J. Ryan, *The Anglo-Saxon World* (2013), pp. 104–105.

[14] Woolf, Alex, "The Britons: from Romans to barbarians", in Hans-Werner Goetz, Jörg Janut, and Walter Pohl (eds.), *Regna and Gentes. The relationship between Late Antique and Early Mediæval Peoples and Kingdoms in the Transformation of the Roman World* (2003), pp. 345–380.

[15] See the eighth or ninth century Anglo-Saxon poem, "The Ruins", which is probably based on Bath; Leslie, R. F. (ed.), *Three old English elegies* (rev. ed., 1988).

[16] Charles-Edwards, T. M., *Wales and the Britons, 350-1064* (2012), pp. 31–3; Sargent, A., "The North-South Divide Revisited: Thoughts on the Character of Roman Britain" (2002) 33 Britannia 219–226 (the division was not north-south but rather north and west versus south and east).

[17] Dowding, Janka, "The prevalence of Christianity in Roman Britain to AD 410" (2005) 3 Hirundo: The McGill Journal of Classical Studies 53–63.

[18] Davies, Wendy, *Patterns of Power in Early Wales* (1989), p. 32.

was of paramount importance,[19] the proper attainment of power was by dynastic inheritance or military proficiency.[20]

Even in those parts of the island which were under the sway of the Saxons, such as Wessex, the intermingling of settlers and natives may have been significant, including at an elite level—the Wessex royal line was traditionally founded by a man named Cerdic, a probably Celtic name identical to Ceretic, the name given to two British kings, and ultimately derived from the Brittonic Caraticos.[21] Cerdic, who may have been legendary, was said to have founded the Kingdom of Wessex in 519, and in c.650 his successor, Cenwalh, became a Christian. The royal line may therefore have been Britons, who became Anglicised under the prevailing hegemony of Saxon settlement and expansion. If so, his descendants, of the House of Windsor, are of British (probably Romano-British) rather than Anglo-Saxon (or Norman), origin.

The Welsh of Gwynedd remained conscious of their Romano-British heritage and an affinity with Rome survived long after the empire had retreated from Britain, particularly with the use of Latin in writing and by sustaining the Christian religion.[22] The British ruling classes in what was later to become Wales continued to emphasise Roman ancestors within their pedigrees as a way to link their rule with the old imperial Roman order, suggesting stability and continuity with that old order.[23] Edgar was not the first to attempt to gain prestige and political capital by reference to the ghost of a departed glory.

In the fourth century, the Roman Empire's shift to Christianity reshaped governance, including in Britain. As Roman control waned, local elites adapted Christian symbols and Roman traditions to reinforce their rule amidst political fragmentation. Despite Anglo-Saxon conquests, regions like Wales retained elements of Roman-Christian identity, using Latin and Christian practices to assert continuity with the past. This

[19] Davies, Wendy, *Wales in the Early Middle Ages* (1982), p. 122.

[20] Ibid, pp. 121–5; Davies, Wendy, *Patterns of Power in Early Wales* (1989), p. 38.

[21] Parsons, D., "British Caraticos, Old English Cerdic" (1997) 33 Cambrian Mediæval Celtic Studies 1–8.

[22] Davies, John, *A History of Wales* (1993); Ward-Perkins, Bryan, "Why Did the Anglo-Saxons Not Become More British" (2000) 115 English Historical Review 513–533.

[23] Ibid.

early integration of Christian ideals laid groundwork for the mediæval European state, blending Roman influence with local traditions.

Saxon Expansion

As the post-Roman states in the Anglo-Saxon dominated parts of the island fell under the influence of the church, so the foundations of the Christian basis of the state were formed. Although there was later to be conflict between the late sub-Roman Celtic church and the newer Roman church (re-)established by Gregory the Great's mission from 597, this was largely to be resolved by Oswiu of Northumbria at the synod of Whitby in 664, which adopted Roman practices in preference to Celtic[24]—if we take the traditional view of the council as a watershed moment in church history—thus returning the British church to its "imperial" origins.

With the gradual conversion of the Saxon kingdoms, Britain slowly became markedly Christian, aided by the reforms of St Theodore of Tarsus, Archbishop of Canterbury, who from 673 extended a parish structure across England.[25] The country became wholly, or at least predominantly, Christian. Long before that stage was reached, however, the mutually beneficial alliance between the Kings of Wessex and the Archbishop of Canterbury had established a pattern which was to shape the kingdom for more than a thousand years.[26] The former unifying influence of Roman imperial civil and military infrastructure gave way to a unifying church, now linked, for the most part, in an alliance with the kings. The alliance between king and bishop—especially the Archbishop of Canterbury—helped the kings to establish the sacred nature as Christian kings.[27]

The consequence of this on the kingship was significant. Primitive kingship was the focus of racial emotions far stronger than those that generally subsist today. His potency was representative, and his sacred

[24] Abels, Richard, "The Council of Whitby: A Study in Early Anglo-Saxon Politics" (1984) 23(1) Journal of British Studies 1–25.

[25] Pounds, N. J. G., *A history of the English parish* (2000).

[26] The alliance between the Kings of Wessex and the Archbishops of Canterbury began in the early ninth century; Kelly, Susan, *Charters of Malmesbury Abbey* (Oxford University Press, Oxford, 2005), p. 89; Blair, John P., *The Church in Anglo-Saxon Society* (Oxford University Press, Oxford, 2005).

[27] Higham, Nicholas J., *The convert kings* (1997).

figure was independent of his capacity as a ruler. It is often difficult to distinguish between the acts of the king and those of the *Witan*—it was impossible, and probably considered improper, for the king to rule without the help and advice of his elders.[28] Kingship was moving rapidly to a new level of sanctity and formality, where the king, as well as his subjects, found themselves morally and spiritually bound to discharge duties and obligations to one another.[29] But if a king broke his oath the restraints were moral and religious.[30] The nature of this relationship might not always have been explicit, but it was reflected in the stages of the coronation, each of which represented continuity, legitimacy and dynastic, religious and formalistic and ritualistic links to the past. The oath was and is both a promise and contract, in terms of governance, but it is also a binding (and sacramental) promise before God, integral to the other rites.

This went hand in hand with an ongoing emphasis upon continuity and history, especially the great kings of the past, real or legendary. Just as late post-Roman tribal communities in parts of Britain sought to bolster their continued self-identity and independence by recalling Roman precedent, so later English rulers emphasised their links to a past golden age—real or imagined (it mattered little which). In later centuries the decision of Henry VII to name his eldest son, the Prince of Wales, Arthur (1486–1502), was not accidental.[31]

Following the collapse of Roman rule, Anglo-Saxon Britain gradually adopted a Christian foundation for the state. The church's influence, initially divided between the Celtic and Roman traditions, favouring Roman practices. This shift helped establish a close alliance between kings and the church, especially the Archbishop of Canterbury, shaping governance and reinforcing the sacred nature of kingship. Over time, Christian rites, including coronation oaths, formalised the moral duties between rulers and subjects. Later rulers continued to draw on past Roman and legendary symbols to reinforce continuity.

[28] Barlow, Frank, *The Feudal Kingdom of England, 1042-1216* (2nd ed., 1961), pp. 43–44.

[29] Ganshof, Francois, *Feudalism* trans. Philip Grierson (1952), pp. 5–8.

[30] Cannon, John and Ralph Griffiths, *The Oxford Illustrated History of the British Monarchy* (1988), p. 124.

[31] Gunn, Steven and Linda Monckton, *Arthur Tudor, Prince of Wales* (2009).

The King as the Sacred Head of the State

The implications of the early sub-Roman foundations of the Christian basis of the state are important, and influence still the nature and attributes of the king as the sacred head of the state. The Sovereign is a layman, in the sense that they are not an ordained Christian cleric in the major holy orders of deacon, priest or bishop, or even in the (now obsolete) minor orders of subdeacon, doorkeeper, reader, exorcist and acolyte. Yet, such a distinction is of itself insufficiently nuanced. Within the total body of the *laos*—the people of God—the sharpest distinction has tended to come between the clergy and those called laity (that is, in common parlance, those members of the *laos* who are not clergy). The sharpness of the distinction has varied from time to time and from place to place. The existence of many in minor orders, who might proceed to major orders, or might revert to completely secular status,[32] helped to create confusion over the difference.

Kings were surrounded by clergy. Like the kings of Egypt, those of Israel had a role in ordering the creation. This is set out most clearly in Psalm 72, where his administering divine justice and establishing divine righteousness [divine order] affects both creation and human society.[33] This was understood and mirrored in later Christian kingship. It also reflected a primal sacral kingship, deriving from shamanism,[34] which also influenced the coronation, as, for instance, in the anointing. The kingship and its rituals reflected the relationship between king and polity.

Azfar Moin and Strathern distinguish between immanentist and transcendentalist models of power.[35] In the first, rulers are assigned priestly roles, in a world of spirits, ancestors, and gods[36]; the second, which took shape in certain first millennium BC societies in Greece, Israel, northern India, and China, sacred kingship was reformed and constrained by being

[32] In the western church before 1207 subdeacons might revert to a laicised state, unlike those in major orders, which were—generally at least—of an indelible nature; Collins, John N., "Ordained and Other Ministries: Making a Difference" (2006) 3(1) Ecclesiology 11–32.

[33] Barker, Margaret, *The Hebrew Kings* (2023) unpublished paper.

[34] Hani, Jean, *Sacred Royalty* (2011); Maine, Sir Henry Sumner, Early Law and Custom (1890), pp. 125–144.

[35] Azfar Moin, A., and Alan Strathern, *Sacred Kingship in World History* (2022).

[36] Ibid, p. xii.

ethicised.[37] Israeli kingship has been conceived as a Deuteronomist model at odds with the more ancient, immanentist, Egyptian monarchy.[38] This transcendentalist conception later brought to the English monarchy a servant-king model, but equally importantly, one reflecting the perennial need for the indivisible sovereign power to be represented in one figure; and the aesthetic, and indeed sacral, dimensions of authority that grounded the legitimacy of rulership.[39] That authority, though represented in the one person, is not wholly secular or wholly sacred, but has characteristics of each aspect. The king is but a man, but a man with a special role, for which he is set apart—as, for example, in the anointing, and indeed in the presentation, the receiving of regalia, and the coronation oath.

This theology of servant kingship was first formulated in the early 1100s by the Norman Anonymous (previously known as Anonymous of York),[40] and developed more fully in the fourteenth century by John Wycliffe.[41] In this developed form, the king is the living embodiment of Christ the king (*Rex imago Christi*). As Bond has argued, the ideals of human rights and ruling with justice and mercy slowly grew out of the hope for holiness, the living prayer that the love of God be manifested and generously poured out on crown and kingdom, in an anointed monarch.[42] At their anointing the sovereign assumes spiritual and secular duties, and more importantly, *gemina persona*, that is, a twinned person, human by nature and divine by grace, a reverse image of Christ, who is divine by nature and human by grace.[43] Although understood today in somewhat different ways to the early middle ages, yet the servant king

[37] Ibid, pp. xii–xiii, 9.

[38] Assmann, Jan, "Pharaonic Kingship and Its Biblical Deconstruction", in A. Azfar Moin and Alan Strathern (eds.), *Sacred Kingship in World History* (2022), pp. 94–110.

[39] Yelle, Robert A. "Hobbes the Egyptian: The Return to Pharaoh, or the Ancient Roots of Secular Politics", in A. Azfar Moin and Alan Strathern (eds.), *Sacred Kingship in World History* (2022), pp. 223–248.

[40] Williams, George H., *The Norman Anonymous of 1100 AD* (2009).

[41] Bond, Susan E. "Anointing the King: Hallowing Hope for the World in the English Coronation" (2019) Georgetown University DLS thesis.

[42] Bond, Susan E. "Anointing the King: Hallowing Hope for the World in the English Coronation" (2019) Georgetown University DLS thesis.

[43] Kantorowicz, Ernst, *The King's Two Bodies* (1957).

model or conception still resonates; it was also to be particularly strongly emphasised in the 2023 coronation of Charles III.

Kings, like deacons, priests and bishops, had special responsibility, not because (unlike the major orders) they were *in persona Christi capitis*, but because they were charged with responsibility for the temporal wellbeing, rather than the spiritual welfare, of the people entrusted to their authority. It was a sacred charge, just as it had been perceived in the ancient near eastern kingdoms of Sumeria, Egypt and indeed Israel. This attitude, at times encouraged and at other times restrained by the church, was to prevail through the early centuries of western constitutional development, through the mediæval period, and into modern times. The origins of this are clear. After Joash's election as king, the high priest Jehoiada "made a covenant between the Lord and the king and the people that they should be the Lord's people; and also between the king and his people".[44]

The king himself, in both pre-Christian and Christian times, held a position which rendered his classification as purely secular overly simplistic. The early tribal Angles, Saxons and Jutes ascribed the authority of their chieftains and kings to a mixture of military prowess and descent from a dread ancestor; the royal pedigrees generally trace their descent from Wōden (Odin).[45] Like ancient near eastern rulers, descent from deities gave kings a sacred character, even if they were not themselves divine. Likewise, though by a different route, it was so with the pagan Roman emperors, at least after the development of the imperial *cultus*. The Romans relied on the approbation of senate, army and people to make an emperor. But once an individual had assumed the purple,[46] they were no longer like other men, but possessing divinely sanctioned authority (*auctoritas*) making them worthy of *cultus*; and on their deaths they might assume fully divine status (*divus*), if the Senate accorded recognition to their apotheosis.[47] The latter of course reflected their reputation during their reign and also influenced their subsequent reputation

[44] 2 Kings 11:17.

[45] Sisam, Kenneth, "Anglo-Saxon Royal Genealogies" (1953) 39 Proceedings of the British Academy 287–348.

[46] Avery, William T., "The 'Adoratio Purpurae' and the Importance of the Imperial Purple in the Fourth Century of the Christian Era" (1940) 17 Memoirs of the American Academy in Rome 66–80.

[47] Brent, A., *The imperial cult and the development of church order* (1999).

and legacy, just as a great mediæval or later king might be canonised or the subject of a spontaneous—or politically orchestrated *cultus*.[48]

English kingship, drawing from these and other traditions, from the late Saxon and early Norman period onwards (and perhaps even drawing on the Romano-British and tribal traditions of the sub-Roman states) relied upon popular approval, the approbation of the nobility (particularly through the approval of the *Witan*), and the approval of the church, combined with hereditary title, and very much later, legal title derived from the common law, and later still, from Parliament (the modern descendant of the Saxon *Witan*).[49] However, once chosen, and anointed and crowned, the new king was set apart from the rest of society. He was not simply *primus inter pares*, he was the sacred head of the state—insofar as the concept of the state existed at this time. As Christianity became prevalent, and then dominant, the sacred nature of kingship was couched in Christian rather than pagan language, but the concept remained essentially equivalent. Rather than a descendant of a god, the king was perceived as God's vicar on earth (though not in the same manner as the Bishop of Rome), charged with the welfare of his people. The anointing, in particular, was the means by which grace was bestowed upon the king. As Shakespeare was to later write

> Not all the water in the rough rude sea
>
> Can wash the balm off from an anointed king; The breath of worldly men cannot depose
>
> The deputy elected by the Lord.[50]

Whilst the selection of the king made him thereafter special, in later centuries, and especially after the general reception of Christianity, it was the sacred rite of coronation, and especially the anointing, which truly

[48] Like, for instance, Edward the Martyr (978), and Charles I (1649). Edward the Confessor (1066) was the only English king formally canonised by Rome; Watson, Tom, "The Enduring Cult of Edward the Martyr" (2021) 43 Southern History 1–19; Stewart, Byron, "The Cult of the Royal Martyr" (1969) 38(2) Church History 175–187; Bozoky, Edina, "The Sanctity and Canonisation of Edward the Confessor", in Richard Mortimer (ed.), *Edward the Confessor* (2009).

[49] Maddicott, J. R., *The Origins of the English Parliament, 924–1327* (2010).

[50] *Richard II*, Act III, Scene 3.

set him apart from all others. As was later said (again by Shakespeare), "for who can stretch forth his hand against the Lord's anointed and be guiltless?"[51] David's anger against King Saul's assassin derives from his temerity in killing the Lord's anointed.[52] Indeed, this belief in the sacredness of the anointing grew so strong in France that the most important part of the French ceremony was not the coronation itself, but the *Sacre*—the anointing or unction of the king.[53] As we have seen, anointing, though not as common as crowning across Europe, has arguably even more ancient origins. It also has the distinction of being invariably sacred rather than profane in both origin and nature, unlike the crowning. Secular rule—even when not anointed (Romans 13: 4)—has a divinely instituted character.

The consequences of the king having a sacred character were significant. If the king was a priest, or at least priest-like, he could hardly be deposed by mere men, and as an early example of this, the deposed Æthelred II was still regarded as the rightful king even in exile.[54] Cannon and Griffiths believed that Matilda's cause was immeasurably weakened after Stephen's coronation in 1136, and when he was captured in 1141 her inability to eliminate him was due to her reluctance to wrest the Crown from an anointed king.[55] In the twelfth century John of Salisbury noted that ordinary people still believed that a crowned king had the spiritual authority of a priest.[56] This attitude persisted into the later middle ages, and was reflected in the constitutional crises of the seventeenth century.[57] It was also to linger in such traditions as touching for the King's Evil, to which we will return shortly.

[51] Samuel 26; 9.

[52] 2 Sam 1:14.

[53] Jackson, Richard A., *Ordines Coronationis Franciae* (1995–2000).

[54] Craig thought that no number of years could extinguish a dormant title—*The Right of Succession to the Kingdom of England* (1703, first published 1602), pp. 91, 338. Parsons argued that time does not run against the king; *Conference About the Next Succession* (1594), part 2 pp. 158, 189.

[55] Bradbury, Jim, *Stephen and Matilda* (2009).

[56] John of Salisbury, *Policraticus, sive de nugis curialium et de vestigiis philosophorum*, ed. Cary J. Nederman (1990).

[57] See, for example, Filmer, Robert, *Patriarcha and other writings* Johann P. Sommerville (ed.) (1991).

Bradley has explored the theme of sacred kingship, its origins in primal religion, its central role in both the Old and New Testaments of the *Bible*, and its representation in modern popular culture. In particular, he explains the Christian symbolism of the coronation, and the unique significance of Christian monarchy in the history of the British Isles, believing that the monarchy may be the one institution that still has a chance of uniting the diverse peoples of the United Kingdom.[58] The monarchy symbolises spiritual values, promoting order and stability in the midst of chaos (as did kings in ancient times), "standing for public good against private gain", representing faith against secular materialism, and "acting as a focal point for unity" in a society that is increasingly fragmented.[59]

The conception of the king as a sacred individual was not unique to England, as has been noted, and was particularly strong in the eastern Roman empire, and later, in imperial Russia. In the latter example, in particular, it formed much of the ideological and philosophical basis for governance. For example, Article 1 of the Fundamental Laws of the Russian Empire (1832), stated that

> the Emperor of All Russia is an autocratic and unrestricted monarch. To obey his supreme authority, not only out of fear but out of conscience as well, God himself commands.[60]

The 1906 Constitution, which replaced the 1832 absolutist Fundamental Laws of the Russian Empire, introduced constitutional monarchy, but did not radically alter the emperor's position. Chapter One (Articles 4–24) concerned "the essence of the supreme autocratic power", declaring that the emperor possessed "supreme sovereign power", and that obedience to his commands was mandated by God himself (Article 4). It provided for the ruler's prerogatives, while making him personally inviolable (Article 5).

Church policy held that the Russian monarch must be anointed and crowned according to the Orthodox rite to have a successful reign, and the Russian Orthodox Church considered the Tsar to be wedded to

[58] Bradley, Ian, *God Save the King* (2023).

[59] James, Graham, *God Save the King* by Ian Bradley (28 April 2023) *Church Times*.

[60] "Chapter One On the Essence of Supreme Sovereign Power, Article 7", Russian Imperial House: Official site of the Romanov Dynasty. See Wortman, Richard, "The Russian Coronation: Rite and Representation" (2004) 9(1) The Court Historian 15–31.

his subjects in the Orthodox coronation service.[61] The modern coronation, introducing western European-style elements, replaced an older style crowning ceremony and was first used for Catherine I in 1724.[62] Like the coronation in England, it included the full panoply of elements, including anointing, crowning (the emperor himself placing the crown on his head, following the eastern Roman custom)—and a coronation banquet afterwards. In part this explains how damaging and inauspicious the Khodynka Tragedy which occurred at the post-coronation festivities of Nicholas II in 1896, were to be seen.[63] Much weight was placed on the coronation as a statement of regal authority.

In England, as in Russia, royal propaganda such as ceremonial and an open display of royal munificence, were used to promote stability, and enhance royal status and reputation.[64] In England, additionally, and especially in Anglo-Saxon times, there was also the promotion of the origin-myths of the royal line, something which was gradually abandoned, perhaps as the Saxon blood became thinner, only to be replaced by a renewed emphasis upon Arthur (in the time of Henry VII),[65] and even earlier British antecedents under James I and Charles II, as well as the imagery of Britannia.[66]

Once installed, the persons of monarchs represented a fusion of two fundamental sources of authority, feudal (or earlier, tribal) lordship and sacral kingship. Adomnán of Iona claimed that divine punishment fell on the assassin of Irish King Diarmait mac Cerbaill.[67] The person of the king exhibited an indwelling sacredness. They relied much on homage, and anointing, and even King John was regarded by his enemies as having a sacred character due to his having been anointed. That was not of course

[61] Oldenburg, Sergei S., *Last Tsar* (1975), vol 1, pp. 59–60.

[62] Wortman, Richard S., *Scenarios of Power* (2006).

[63] Baker, Helen, "Monarchy discredited? Reactions to the Khodynka coronation catastrophe of 1896" (2003) 16(1) Revolutionary Russia 1–46.

[64] Cannon, John and Ralph Griffiths, *The Oxford Illustrated History of the British Monarchy* (1988), p. 76.

[65] Gunn, Steven and Linda Monckton, *Arthur Tudor, Prince of Wales* (2009).

[66] Dresser, Madge, "Britannia", in Raphael Samuel (ed.), *Patriotism* (1989), vol. 3, pp. 26–49.

[67] Adomnán of Iona, *The life of St Columba* ed. Richard Sharpe (trans.) (1995).

an infallible safeguard, as Edward II's allegedly grisly, and supposedly apposite demise reminds us.[68]

However, assuming no such misfortune occurred, the inviolancy which unction conferred upon the person of the king was not simply passive and defensive. He emanated a potent *mythos* and aura. This is seen in the widespread belief in the efficacy of touching for the king's evil,[69] and similar thaumaturgical powers. Touching for the King's Evil—Scrofula, a tuberculous condition of the lymphatic glands, and earlier still for other conditions also—was found only in England and France, where it survived only until the reigns of George I (1714) and Charles X (1825) respectively.[70]

In Greek writings the term *thaumaturge*, usually translated into English as "wonderworker," referred to a saint through whom God works miracles, not just occasionally, but as a matter of course. These included such individuals as St Nicholas (270–343) and St Anthony of Padua (1195–1231). Those invested with the gift of miracles possessed a spiritual gift (*charismata*) mentioned by St Paul in his First Epistle to the Corinthians.[71] Such individuals were ministers of God in the sense that the miracles worked were those of God, for the strengthening of the faith, and not for the personal benefit of the wonderworker. Kings ideally fitted the model of the category of individual who might be graced with such a gift, given their great potential for good.

Even in a more prosaic and less theological sense the sacredness of the king's person had its effect, such as in the value of a king's hand-given peace.[72] Violation of the peace given by the king's own hand was a crime unatoneable by money,[73] and might be punished by loss of limb.[74]

[68] Phillips, Seymour, *Edward II* (2011).

[69] Sturdy, David J., "The Royal Touch in England", in Heinz Duchhardt, and Richard A. Jackson (eds.), *European Monarchy* (1992), pp. 171–184.

[70] Sturdy, David J., "The Royal Touch in England", in Heinz Duchhardt, and Richard A. Jackson (eds.), *European Monarchy* (1992), pp. 171–184; Brogan, Stephen, *The Royal Touch in Early Modern England* (2015).

[71] Grudem, Wayne A. (ed.), *Are Miraculous Gifts for Today?* (1996).

[72] Harding, Alan, *Mediæval Law and the Foundations of the State* (2002).

[73] Downer, L. J. (ed & tr), *Leges Henrici Primi* (1972).

[74] From Strickland, Matthew, "Against the Lord's anointed: aspects of warfare and baronial rebellion in England and Normandy 1075-1265", in George Garnett, and John

Eventually the king's peace became country-wide, and its origins lost in the mists of time.[75]

The religious role of the king aside, strong links developed between the kings and the Church, and both were to benefit from this, as when Oswiu of Northumbria at the synod of Whitby in 664 adopted Roman practices in preference to Celtic, because to do so would strengthen his political control.[76] Offa of Mercia, anxious that his only son Ecgfrith should succeed him, persuaded papal legates visiting England to anoint Ecgfrith as a king in 787, in what may be the first anointing in Anglo-Saxon England, certainly the first in the lifetime of a king,[77] as far as we know. A similar procedure had been adopted by Charlemagne in 781,[78] and doubtless inspired the Mercian move. Offa himself was styled King of Mercia "by the divine controlling grace", and Ecgfrith and Cenwulf were both "the Lord's anointed". This was during the heyday of the Mercia kingdom, the so-called Mercian Supremacy between c.716 and c.825.[79] The spiritual nature of the kingship itself was reinforced by coronation, the ritual for which was formalised in Wessex by the end of the ninth century.[80]

The Norman Conquest nearly undermined this alliance, however. William I was far less indulgent towards the native ecclesiastical establishment than had been Canute. This was perhaps hardly surprising since one of the publicised aims of William's invasion (or crusade as he called it) was the removal of the schismatic Archbishop Stigand of Canterbury

Hudson, *Law and Government in Mediæval England and Normandy* (1994), pp. 56–79, 57–60.

[75] Allen, Sir Carleton, *The Queen's Peace* (1953).

[76] Abels, Richard, "The Council of Whitby: A Study in Early Anglo-Saxon Politics" (1984) 23(1) Journal of British Studies 1–25; Cannon, John and Ralph Griffiths, *The Oxford Illustrated History of the British Monarchy* (1988), p. 23.

[77] Williams, Ann, "Ecgfrith king of Mercia", in Ann Williams, Alfred P. Smyth and D. P. Kirby (eds.), *A Biographical Dictionary of Dark Age Britain* (1991).

[78] Cannon, John and Ralph Griffiths, *The Oxford Illustrated History of the British Monarchy* (1988), p. 26.

[79] Webster, Leslie and Backhouse, Janet, "The Mercian Supremacy", in L. Webster, and J. Backhouse, (eds.), *The Making of England, Anglo-Saxon Art and Culture, AD 600–900* (1991), pp. 193–253.

[80] The *ordo* of Wessex; Cannon, John and Ralph Griffiths, *The Oxford Illustrated History of the British Monarchy* (1988), p. 27.

and the encouragement of Church reform.[81] However, as subsequent developments showed, the alliance between king and church was later strengthened, to the mutual advantage of both. The king's duties were made clear to him and by him in his coronation oath, formalised in the tenth century. He was to defend and preserve the Church and Christian people, to ensure peace and order in the kingdom, and to ensure justice and mercy in their judgments.[82] This was a sacred charge.

The convention of hereditary succession ordinarily dictated the descent but it was not deep-rooted enough to resist every political and personal pressure, as during the so-called Wars of the Roses. Perhaps it never could do so long as kings had considerable powers that could be abused, and so long as ambitious and ruthless men felt that they could get away with challenging even an anointed king.[83] But only in 1215–1216 did subjects come close to undermining the foundation of Christian kingship itself. Magna Carta was mainly an attempt to define anew the king's power and his duties towards his subjects. It was inspired by Henry I's coronation charter of 1100,[84] and by evolving principles of canon law.[85]

The Christian quality of the kingship had rather less practical importance in the later Middle Ages, as perhaps also did the alliance of Church and Crown.[86] Appropriately, anointing kings had essentially a religious significance, though with an increased emphasis on their legal status.[87] But by the sixteenth century, if not earlier, there was increasing questioning of what had hitherto been accepted positions. During the Reformation this came to a head. In England the Church reformers sought to lessen the religious significance of anointing, as in Archbishop Cranmer's comments at the coronation of Edward VI referred to above.[88]

[81] Cannon, John and Ralph Griffiths, *The Oxford Illustrated History of the British Monarchy* (1988), p. 164.

[82] Ibid, p. 30.

[83] Ibid, p. 215.

[84] Ibid, p. 125.

[85] Helmholz, Richard, "Magna Carta and the *ius commune*" (1999) 66 University of Chicago Law Review 297–371.

[86] Ibid, p. 199.

[87] Dale, Johanna, "Christus Regnat: Inauguration and images of kingship in England, France and the Empire c.1050-c.1250" (2013) University of East Anglia PhD thesis.

[88] Hunt, Alice, *Drama of Coronation* (2008), chapter 3, pp. 77–110.

A coronation might not exclusively rely upon the sacredness of the royal office, but nor could it ignore it altogether.

The anointing, and the role of the Sovereign within the liturgy (which is set within the context of a eucharist or mass), is fundamental to understanding the sacred nature of kingship. Just as Zadok the priest anointed Solomon,[89] thereby setting him aside for the sacred duties of kingship—one of the most important being in his responsibility as mediator between God and the kingdom—so too the "Lord's anointed" held, and continues to hold, a special place in human society. As always, this is not primarily for their own glory—indeed many kings since Solomon's time and before have sought, sometimes vainly and sometimes with temporary or long-lasting success, to cast off the burden of responsibility. Not for nothing did Shakespeare write, "uneasy lies the head that wears a crown".[90] Yet the transformation of the faithful, in Christ, through baptism, moves them from one degree of glory to another.[91] By the tenth century, like their Israelite predecessors, the king became the embodiment of the people, through their anointing.

As with the Russian emperors, the eastern Roman emperors, and the kings of France, and others in a long tradition, the kings of England were entrusted by God with sacred responsibility, echoed and reinforced in the coronation rite, as God's vicegerent in matters temporal, and (insofar as a layman might, and subject to the church hierarchy) in matters spiritual too.

The situation was quite different after the Reformation, though no easier for the king. Henry VIII himself did not trust the orthodoxy of the bishops of his day, and for this reason himself intervened in theological arguments – the *King's Book* (1543) was more catholic than the *Bishop's Book* (1539),[92] and his retention of the title Defender of the Faith was perhaps not wholly unjustified even after the break with Rome. The title of Defender of the Faith (*Fidei Defensor*), which dates from 1521, had been conferred by Pope Leo X (pope 1513–21) upon King Henry

[89] 2 Samuel 8:16-19.

[90] In Act III, Scene I, of the William Shakespeare play, "King Henry IV".

[91] 2 Corinthians 3:18.

[92] Haugaard, William, *Elizabeth and the English reformation* (1968), p. 5.

VIII. In spite of its papal origin, the title was settled on the king and his successors in perpetuity by Act of Parliament in 1543.[93]

McCoy argues that older notions of sacred kingship expanded during the political and religious crises from the Reformation to the Civil War.[94] Contemporary commentators grappled with the symbolic and substantive power of kingship. But the suppression of the sacrifice of the mass, and the Real Presence of Christ in the Eucharist, was met with a corresponding renewed emphasised upon the sacred kingship. A new conception of the state under Henry VII, the supremacy of the king over church and state under Henry VIII, and a more ambiguous religious settlement under Elizabeth I, were reflected in a gradually changing emphasis in the coronation, reaching its pinnacle under the later Georgians, as primarily a political spectacle.

The Sovereign retains, even today, a sacred status. As noted earlier. the Archbishop of Canterbury, Justin Welby, speaking on the Platinum Jubilee of Queen Elizabeth II, argued that her role as monarch could be said to be like "a lifelong religious vocation", and the coronation like "the vows for religious ministry".[95] In this the modern Sovereign of the United Kingdom retains a status not dissimilar to that of ancient Israel.

This kingship is very much a servant kingship, understood in explicitly Christian terms. This was always present in kingship, and reflected in the coronation, In 2023 this was seen, not just in the King's Prayer, discussed above,[96] but also in the greeting of the King by a Child of the Chapel Royal, and his reply, "In his name, and after his example, I come not to be served but to serve".[97] Both of these innovations, and the iconography of the anointing screen,[98] strongly emphasising not merely the Christian nature of the coronation service, but also of the monarchy, and explicitly a servant-kingship model. It is entirely consistent with the tradition of royal

[93] King's Style Act 1543 (35 Hen. VIII c. 2), repealed by the See of Rome Act 1554 (1 & 2 Philip & Mary c. 8), s. 4, repeal confirmed by the Act of Supremacy 1558 (1 Eliz. I c. 1), s. 4.

[94] McCoy, Richard C., *Alterations of State* (2002).

[95] Sean Coughlan and Nicholas Witchell, "Justin Welby: Queen set example at Philip's funeral", BBC News, 5 February 2022, https://www.bbc.com/news/uk-60231239.

[96] *The Authorised Liturgy for the Coronation Rite of His Majesty King Charles III For use on Saturday 6th May 2023, 11:00am at Westminster Abbey* (2023).

[97] Ibid.

[98] Press Release, "The Anointing Screen", The Royal Family, 29 April 2023.

service, reflected, for example, in the coronation oaths but renewed. This is quite possibly an entirely personal decision by the king himself, whose political and religious beliefs were strongly influenced by his mother. Her own spiritual conception of monarchy has been well attested to.[99]

Part of the complex equation which constituted the working constitution was the relationship between the church and the Crown. From the beginnings of Christianity in England—or at least its re-founding by St Augustine in 597—kings sought the approbation of bishops, and prelates and secular rulers alike enjoyed (or occasionally suffered from) this symbiotic relationship.[100] The church both upheld the king and checked him, and the central role of the Archbishop of Canterbury in coronations since at least as early as the tenth century is no coincidence. The role of the church today remains important in other respects, as in England at least, the Church of England remains the established church, and the Church of Scotland has an equivalent status in Scotland.[101]

This relationship between king and church was represented, vividly, in the presence at the coronation of King Charles III in 2023, of the St Augustine Gospels, for the first time. This illuminated manuscript book is believed to date from the Gregorian Mission of 597 and is the oldest surviving illustrated Latin Gospel book,[102] and oldest non-archaeological artefact of any kind to have survived in England, continuously owned and in use for 1,400 years.[103] It was carried in procession by the Master of Corpus Christi College Cambridge, Professor Christopher Kelly, from St Edward's Shrine, and used as the Gospel by the Gospeller, the Dean of the Chapel Royal (and Bishop of London), at the King's request.[104]

[99] Butcher, Catherine and Mark Greene, *The Servant Queen and the King she serves* (2016).

[100] The complex relationship between Henry II and Thomas Beckett, is well known; Barlow, Frank, *Thomas Becket* (1986).

[101] See the Papal Jurisdiction Act 1560 c. 2.

[102] Also known, to the Church of England, as the Canterbury Gospels.

[103] Corpus Christi College, Lib. MS. 286; De Hamel, Christopher, *Meetings with Remarkable Manuscripts* (2016). It was in St Augustine's Abbey, Canterbury (598-1538), by the tenth century, and was given to Parker Library, Corpus Christi College, Cambridge, in 1575, by Matthew Parker, Archbishop of Canterbury.

[104] "Fit for a King: Sixth-century Augustine Gospels to be used in the Coronation of King Charles III", Corpus Christi College, Cambridge, https://corpus-christi-college.shorthandstories.com/a2f9d2ef-d0e0-43f8-850b-0bd1807f2650/.

Like the Pharaohs of Egypt, a series of rituals both emphasise, and in a manner achieve, a change in status. This is reflected in the words of the Archbishop of Canterbury, at the anointing, as used for Queen Elizabeth II in 1953:

> Let us pray
>
> O Lord and heavenly Father, the exalter of the humble and the strength of thy chosen, who by anointing with Oil didst of old make and consecrate kings, priests, and prophets, to teach and govern thy people Israel:
>
> Bless and sanctify thy chosen servant ELIZABETH, who by our office and ministry is now to be anointed with this Oil, and consecrated Queen: Strengthen her, O Lord, with the Holy Ghost the Comforter; Confirm and stablish her with thy free and princely Spirit, the Spirit of wisdom and government, the Spirit of counsel and ghostly strength, the Spirit of knowledge and true godliness, and fill her, O Lord, with the Spirit of thy holy fear, now and for ever; through Jesus Christ our Lord. Amen.[105]

In 2023, this prayer, which may be said to be more of a blessing of the Sovereign, was replaced with a prayer of thanksgiving for the holy oil.[106]

The change in status which the Sovereign underwent, can be characterised as legal, or political, but equally theological. One might be King because the law says so, and sovereign because the political reality is constitutional monarchy, but the change in theological status also reflects the theory and reality that a crowned, anointed and sworn Sovereign holds a sacred trust, from God and people, and is not simply the holder of an office.

The Legal Status of the Church

The respective role of church and State in modern society is markedly different to what has often been the historic role. Today, rulers (at least in liberal democracies) protect individual freedom of choice. The ruler is not the arbiter and defender of his or her people's particular faith,

[105] *Proceedings of the Coronation of Her Majesty The Queen*, 2nd June 1953 (1953).

[106] *The Authorised Liturgy for the Coronation Rite of His Majesty King Charles III For use on Saturday 6th May 2023, 11:00am at Westminster Abbey* (2023).

though he or she may be a defender of faith in the abstract.[107] Secular State laws usually assert ecclesiastical autonomy, and generally are based on the premise of the freedom and equality of religions.[108] This leaves the relationship between church and State at times difficult.

The King or Queen of the United Kingdom enjoys a special relationship with the churches. In each country comprising the United Kingdom this relationship differs. In England and Scotland, the church is established (though in markedly different ways); in Northern Ireland and Wales it is dis-established.[109] In principle, churches, in their relationship with the State, may be classified as established, quasi-established,[110] dis-established, or non-established. All but the first are normally based on the principle of consensual compact, in which it is the voluntary membership of the church which alone imposes binding or mandatory obligations upon members.[111] They are, in secular terms, voluntary associations in which all obligations are internally mandated, and which have no implications outside the church.

[107] As suggested by the then Prince of Wales (now King Charles III), in a remark which may appear surprising to a common law audience as it may appear a constitutional commonplace to the citizens of most continental countries; Watkin, Thomas Glyn, "Church and State in a changing world", in Norman Doe, Mark Hill and Robert Ombres (eds.), *English Canon Law* (1998), pp. 82–92, 88.

[108] See Art. 18 of the International Covenant on Civil and Political Rights, Adopted and opened for signature, ratification and accession by General Assembly resolution 2200A (XXI) of 16th December 1966, protecting freedom of religion.

[109] Donaldson, Gordon, *The Scottish Reformation* (1960). In its purest form establishment meant mutual recognition of Church law and secular law, and equal validity within their respective spheres; Coriden, James, *An Introduction to Canon Law* (1991), p. 18.

[110] Under secular legislation the Church of England in Nova Scotia [Mutiny Act 1758 (32 Geo. II c. 5) (G.B.)], New Brunswick [Trade with America Act 1786 (26 Geo. III c. 4) (G.B.)], and Prince Edward Island [Indemnity Act 1802 (43 Geo. III c. 6) (U.K.)] enjoyed certain statutory privileges over other Churches.

[111] Though *Scandrett v. Dowling* [1992] 27 N.S.W.L.R. 483 (N.S.W.) would appear to support the proposition that church members are associated only on the basis of a shared faith without legal sanction for its enforcement; McPherson, Mr. Justice Bruce, "The Church as consensual compact, trust and corporation" (2000) 74 Australian Law Journal 159–174, 171.

The Royal Supremacy

The Church of England remains formally established by law in England.[112] Some of the other Churches of the British Isles,[113] have been dis-established. The ecclesiastical law is a part of the laws of England, but not part of the common law.[114] It was enacted in 1553 by Parliament that England was "an Empire governed by one supreme head and king".[115]

The Sovereign's office of Supreme Governor of the Church of England is to be distinguished from the mere title of Defender of the Faith, which dates from 1521. In that year Pope Leo X conferred upon King Henry VIII the title of *Fidei Defensor*.[116] In spite of its papal origin, the title was settled on the king and his successors in perpetuity by Act of Parliament in 1543.[117] At the time of the 2023 coronation the non-sectarian (though originally, and historically, Roman Catholic) style "Defender of the Faith" was used in New Zealand, and Canada, though that of Supreme Governor of the Church of England was not, since the Church of England was not established in either country. Canada abandoned the usage the following year.[118] Despite the establishment of the church in England—and an equivalent status in Scotland—the title Defender of the Faith should not

[112] See, for instance, the *Thirty-Nine Articles of Religion*, enacted in 1562, and confirmed in 1571 by the Subscription (Thirty-Nine Articles) Act 1571 (13 Eliz. I c. 12).

[113] By the Irish Church Act 1869 (32 & 33 Vict. c. 42) (U.K.), the Church of Ireland is now a voluntary association; *State (Colquhoun) v. D'Arcy* [1936] IR 641. The independent Church in Wales was created by the Welsh Church Act 1914 (4 & 5 Geo. V c. 91) (U.K.), though dis-establishment was delayed until after the end of the First World War; Suspensory Act 1914 (4 & 5 Geo. V c. 88) (U.K.); Welsh Church (Temporalities) Act 1919 (9 & 10 Geo. V c. 65) (U.K.). The Scottish Episcopal Church was dis-established in 1689 ((Claim of Right Act 1689 c. 28) (Scot.)).

[114] *Evers v. Owen* (1627) Godbolt's Report 432; New canon law could only be created by Act of Parliament, and now by Measure, under the Church of England Assembly (Powers) Act 1919 (9 & 10 Geo. V c. 76) (U.K.). Any canon is binding on clergy in ecclesiastical matters; *Matthew v. Burdett* (1703) 2 Salk. 412.

[115] Appointment of Bishops Act 1533 (25 Hen. VIII c. 20).

[116] Pope Julius II had earlier made King James IV of Scotland, "Protector and Defender of the Christian Faith" (1507); Macdougall, Norman, *James IV* (1997), p. 22.

[117] King's Style Act 1543 (35 Hen. VIII c. 2), repealed by the See of Rome Act 1554 (1 & 2 Philip & Mary c. 8), s. 4, repeal confirmed by the Act of Supremacy 1558 (1 Eliz. I c. 1), s. 4.

[118] Royal Style and Titles Act, 2023 (Canada), The new style became "Charles the Third, by the Grace of God King of Canada and His other Realms and Territories,

be understood as referring to the established churches, but rather to the Christian faith.

It is important to emphasise that the pre-Reformation history of the Anglican Church was that of the Roman Catholic Church—at least after the early adoption of the Latin hierarchy[119]—and that the legacy of the Church of England was principally that of the Rome-centred western patriarchate.[120] The universal church as represented—if not embodied—by those national and particular Churches in communion with the See of Rome, was strongly juridical. This was so especially after the era of the great lawyer-popes,[121] and this tradition survived the break with Rome.

Because the Church was constituted by jurisdictional break, rather than being an artificial creation, or the result of theological dispute, the degree of continuity which existed—and which largely survives—was very considerable. This is today reflected in the survival of significant elements of the pre-Reformation legal infrastructure. The Church remained the One Holy Catholic and Apostolic Church.[122]

The Church of England has a role in the coronation service not because of the establishment of the church, for it predates the modern concept of establishment, but because from the earliest coronations Christian prelates, whatever the relationship between king and church, represented the spiritual realm. The approbation of the church was essential to the successful reign of any king. Sometimes the Archbishop of Canterbury and the king enjoyed good relations, and sometimes not. Occasionally the church was a direct target of kings in search of more funds, but—even during the reign of Henry VIII—this was restricted in scope. For instance, during the reign of King Henry III (1216–1272),

Head of the Commonwealth"; Proclamation Establishing for Canada the Royal Style and Titles: SI/2024-4 (8th January 2024).

[119] After the Synod of Whitby (664). Full unification, and integration with the Church of Rome and the authority of the Pope was finally achieved at the councils of Hertford in 673 and Hatfield 680, under the diplomatic guidance of St Theodore of Tarsus, Archbishop of Canterbury; Lapidge, Michael (ed.), *Archbishop Theodore* (1995); Cubitt, Catherine, *Anglo-Saxon church councils c.650-c.850* (1995).

[120] French historian Bruno Neveu, Directeur de la Maison Française d'Oxford, regarded the outward heritage of the Church of England as a revelation, a survival of a lost world; Rogister, John, "Bruno Neveu", *The Independent*, 14th April 2004.

[121] Tierney, Brian, *Church law and constitutional thought in the Middle Ages* (1979).

[122] See Doe, Norman, *Canon Law in the Anglican Communion* (1998).

many alien priories were suppressed by Simon de Montfort's Parliament (the Parliament of Leicester, 1265), and their revenues were taken into the king's hands. This practice repeated, with intervals in which the priories were returned to their mother houses. Most alien priories finally came to an end under Henry V in 1414, with a few exceptions surviving.[123] In contrast, native houses, except in occasional reforms, were rarely touched by kings, until the Reformation.

The relationship between the church and the kings evolved over the centuries. It was ultimately caught up in Europe-wide developments in the papacy and its interaction with secular power, including the Holy Roman Empire. As churchmen were prime, though not sole, contributors to the coronation ritual—for centuries the Earl Marshal has held secular responsibility, and both Archbishop and Earl Marshal were subject to the king's wishes—their influence on its form was profound. Framed within the context of a mass (later called holy communion or eucharist), the church contribution to the coronation was to emphasise the king's reliance upon, and responsibility to, God. This meant priority was given to the anointing, but even the oath and homage have theological aspects. Were there no formal relationship between church and state (to use the modern expression), it is possible that the coronation would have a weaker theological aspect, but would not necessarily be markedly different.

In pre-Reformation times the church and the state were intertwined in a manner which can be traced to the earlier times; bishops and other senior clerics served in Parliament, the courts (at least as early as the thirteenth century), and bureaucracy. The relationship did not radically alter in 1533; the removal of the jurisdiction of the pope and its replacement with that of the king was not, at least initially, as profound as the misleading notion that Henry VIII created the Church of England. It remained incumbent upon the church to sanctify the new king, just as St Columba anointed Áedán mac Gabráin king of Dál Riata at Iona in 574.

In a Christian state, or one in which the majority, or a significant minority of the population are nominally Christian, it was appropriate for the coronation to be a religious ritual. Even where only a minority of the population to be Christian, and even if the Church of England were not established in its present sense, it would still be right and proper for

[123] McHardy, Alison and Nicholas Orme, "The Defence of an Alien Priory: Modbury (Devon) in the 1450s" (1999) The Journal of Ecclesiastical History 303–312.

the Church of England to have a leading role in the coronation. This is because the ritual was formed and composed in a time when state and church rituals were a seamless whole, reflecting the sacred nature of kingship and God's approval of the new king. Although the sacred nature of kingship might be questioned—or at least open to being questioned—today, the ritual of crowning and anointing has such a strong religious element that it would not be a coronation without these elements. An inauguration, at which the crown might make a cursory appearance, and in which no anointing occurred, would be such a radical departure from more than a thousand years of practice that it would raise serious questions about the nature of the new king's reign, if not its legitimacy. No coronation made a king, but no king felt secure unless crowned and anointed by the duly appointed prelates of the Church.

The Theological Function of a Coronation

A state has some elements of an ethos, or an underlying philosophical or moral identity.[124] One of the aspects of twenty-first century Western culture which is most remarkable is the widespread intellectual dominance of secularism. This has not been without its effects on the constitution of states—despite the oft-quoted principle of the separation of Church and State. It has left the State, in many societies, unable to provide the degree of conceptual unity of focus which it might be expected to do. While secularism seeks to remove religious influence from public life, the State itself cannot exist as a morally neutral entity; it inherently carries elements of an ethos, or an underlying philosophical or moral identity. The absence of a shared moral framework leads to fragmentation and polarisation, leaving the State struggling to fulfil its role as a unifying force. The theological function of coronation goes beyond ceremony, reinforcing the monarch's role as a leader with both political and divine authority. This tradition, rooted in Christian heritage, has historically unified kingdoms under a shared moral order, as seen in the coronation of early English kings like Edgar.

Even in a secular age, these rites offer a reminder of values beyond temporal power, suggesting that governance is a duty to both the state

[124] Cox, Noel, *Constitutional paradigms and the stability of states* (2012).

and a higher moral ideal. Thus, coronations continue to provide continuity and purpose, linking historical tradition to modern governance. This intersection highlights the unique ability of coronations to serve as both a unifying symbol and a moral compass. In embodying the integration of the sacred and the secular, the ritual gestures towards a vision of leadership that transcends the merely administrative. It roots the exercise of power in service, accountability, and a commitment to the common good—a stark contrast to the fragmented ethos often seen in contemporary political discourse. As such, coronations act not only as relics of the past but as enduring reminders of a state's capacity to inspire a shared identity through a moral and spiritual framework. This can be seen most starkly in the anointing.

Anointing

The Christian nature of the monarchy was reflected in the coronation service, and the strong ongoing relationship between what we would now call Church and State. St Dunstan, archbishop of Canterbury 961–988, who anointed and crowned three kings (Edgar 973, Edward the Martyr 975, and Æthelred the Unready 978), saw anointing as being on the same level as baptism and confirmation, and thus the prostration of the king at the beginning of the liturgy emphasised their rebirth as an anointed king. Just as the early Church used oil in baptism and confirmation, so the Church also used oil for anointing Christian kings—and kings, like priests and bishops, used chrism, although church practice with respect to baptismal anointing in general varied.[125] For this reason, it was confirmation, as distinct from baptism, that provided one of the key liturgical foundations for royal anointing.[126] The practice of anointing kings owed much to the Old Testament of the *Bible*.[127] The similarity of the rite

[125] Spinks, Bryan, *Early and Medieval Rituals and Theologies of Baptism—From the New Testament to the Council of Trent* (2006). From the origin, the Fourth Recension's rubrics allow for the use of two oils, Catechumens on the body and Chrism on the crown of the head, until later three anointings with Chrism only, becomes the norm.

[126] Austin, Gerard, *Anointing with the Spirit: the rite of confirmation: the use of oil and chrism*. Vol. 2. (1985).

[127] Generally, see O'Brien, Conor, "The Origins of Royal Anointing" (2023) 59 Studies in Church History 27–47.

of the coronation, in the Second Recension, with the consecration of a bishop, Is, also, too great to be a mere coincidence.[128]

St Dunstan brought order to the coronation rites, fostered the importance of the role of the clergy in the investing of the king with regalia, the centrality of the involvement of the Archbishop of Canterbury, and the reciprocity implicit and explicit in much of the rite.

In the early use of the Fourth Recension of the coronation rite the king is anointed with two oils. The oil of Catechumens (known at the time as Unction) is used to anoint the king on his hands, breast, between the shoulders, on the shoulders, on both elbows and on the head in the form of a cross, from a silver phial. Then the king's head is anointed a second time with Oil of Chrism, from a gilt vial.[129]

The importance of the chrismation of the king remained great, even as the wider society became more secular. The holy oil used for the 2023 coronation of King Charles III was consecrated in Jerusalem on 3rd March 2023, at the Church of the Holy Sepulchre, built on the site where it is believed Jesus died and was buried. The oil was consecrated by Theophilos III, Patriarch of Jerusalem, and Hosam Naoum, the Anglican Archbishop in Jerusalem. It has been the custom at most coronations in modern times to consecrate the holy oil on the day of the coronation either on the High Altar of Westminster Abbey or at St Edward's Shrine, so this was an innovation. In 2023 ingredients included oil from olives grown in two groves on the Mount of Olives, one of which was at the Monastery of Mary Magdalene, which is where the King's grandmother, Princess Alice of Greece (Prince Philip, Duke of Edinburgh's mother), is buried. The second was at the Monastery of the Ascension, on the traditional site of the Ascension of Jesus. The olives were pressed just outside

[128] Woolley, Reginald Maxwell, *Coronation Rites* (1915), pp. 193–196.

[129] Ibid.

Bethlehem.[130] The new oil included olive oil scented with a mix of essential oils, sesame, rose, jasmine, cinnamon, neroli, benzoin and amber, with orange blossom also added.

The old notion of the anointing conferring grace was, consistent with post-Reformation theology, more fluid. The Archbishop of Canterbury was quoted as saying

> Since beginning the planning for the Coronation, my desire has been for a new Coronation Oil to be produced using olive oil from the Mount of Olives. This demonstrates the deep historic link between the Coronation, the Bible and the Holy Land. From ancient kings through to the present day, monarchs have been anointed with oil from this sacred place. As we prepare to anoint The King and The Queen Consort, I pray that they would be guided and strengthened by the Holy Spirit.[131]

The anointing invoked the descent of the Holy Spirit on the candidate for kingship, making him a new man, transmitting through the anointing the divine grace by which alone he would be able to fulfil his royal *ministerium* as defender of the Church. Kingship became an office within the Church without bestowing on it any priestly status. This did not change markedly over time—even the Reformation arguably did not entirely alter the position. From the earliest times anointing was held to confer grace upon the king, although at the coronation of James I in 1603,[132] and in the context of a catholic and reformed liturgy, it was argued that the king received anointing so that he may receive grace, rather than receiving grace as a result of being anointed.[133] Though a small distinction, perhaps, it reflected a changed perception of the sacred role and

[130] The new holy oil did not include any ingredients derived from animals, omitting the usual civet oil (from the glands of small cat-like animals), and ambergris (from the digestive system of sperm whales). Musk—a glandular secretion from a musk deer—was also omitted. "The consecration of the Coronation Oil", Buckingham Palace, 3 March 2023, https://www.royal.uk/consecration-coronation-oil; Coughlan, Sean, "Sacred coronation oil will be animal-cruelty free", BBC 4 March 2023, https://www.bbc.com/news/uk-64836101.

[131] "The consecration of the Coronation Oil", Buckingham Palace, 3 March 2023, https://www.royal.uk/consecration-coronation-oil.

[132] Jack, Sybil M., "'A Pattern for a King's Inauguration': The Coronation of James I in England" (2004) 21(2) Parergon 67–91.

[133] Hunt, Alice, "British Coronation: A History", Gresham College, 2 May 2023.

status of the king. In 2023 this ritual underscored the monarch's role in service to the people under divine authority, with the anointing seen as a dedication rather than a sacramental grace that transforms the monarch. The Archbishop of Canterbury emphasised that Charles III was to be anointed as one who is called to serve under God's will.

The coronation services remained replete with pre-Reformation ritual, though conducted in the vernacular, with the blessing (restored under James II, though in a form acceptable to the established church),[134] censing and prayers to the saints alone deleted. A second crowning was possible, but not a second anointing; though King Henry III obtained a papal dispensation for this latter in 1220.[135]

The coronation ceremony has long symbolised the monarch's dedication to serve under divine authority, blending secular leadership with spiritual commitment. The 2023 coronation of King Charles III upheld this tradition, with anointing oils from the Holy Land and a focus on service rather than sacramental transformation. Despite evolving interpretations, the ceremony preserves an ancient connection between monarchy and faith, uniting tradition with modern purpose.[136]

The coronation liturgy's theological underpinnings, rooted in both Old Testament precedent and Christian sacramental practice, highlight the enduring sacredness of anointing as a divine commissioning rather than mere ritual formality. This sacred act, whether understood as conferring grace or as dedicating the monarch to divine service, remains central to the coronation's symbolism, bridging pre-Reformation traditions with contemporary interpretations of kingship as service under God's will.

Priestly Kingship

Pope Gelasius I, in a letter to the Eastern Roman Emperor Anastasius I in 494, wrote that "two there are, august emperor, by which this world is chiefly ruled, the sacred authority of the priesthood and the royal power".[137] Today the former may be weaker, at least in the West, and the

[134] Hunt, Alice, Drama of *the Coronation* (2008).

[135] Carpenter, David A., *The Minority of Henry III* (1990), pp. 137–137.

[136] Garnett, George, "Long Live the Ancien Régime! The coronation of Charles III was dense with meaning. It's complicated; and easy to misunderstand" (2023) 73(8) History Today 106–109.

[137] Tierney, Brian, *The Crisis of Church and State, 1050–1300* (1964).

latter is now pre-eminent (though now the "royal power" is more likely than not to be wielded by a politician accountable to the electorate). As we are told, we should "Render therefore unto Caesar the things which be Caesar's, and unto God the things which be God's" (Luke 20:25, and Matthew 22:21). But in early mediæval times rulers were often cast as *Christus Domini* (literally as though they were in the place of Christ on earth). The notion of priestly kingship in mediæval and early modern Europe fused sacred and secular roles, portraying the monarch as both a political leader and a spiritual guardian. "Let every soul be subject unto the higher powers. For there is no power but of God: the powers that be are ordained of God" (Romans 13:1). The king had a sacred role, not as mediator, or part of the cosmic order, as the Pharoahs of Egypt, but as someone entrusted with the care of God's people. This was in the context of a society in which church and state were but two sides of the one community.

While mediæval rulers drew on religious language to legitimise authority, conflicts like the Investiture Controversy revealed underlying tensions between ecclesiastical and royal power. The papacy was concerned with the idea of sacral kingship, which it saw as a potential threat to its authority, as they implied that monarchs could possess an almost priestly status that might challenge the pope's spiritual leadership.[138]

In response, the Church sometimes attempted to limit the sanctity of royal authority, including by questioning or controlling the practice of royal anointing. By declaring that royal anointing was not a sacrament, the Church aimed to reassert its own unique claim to sacramental authority, although such a stance varied across regions and periods.[139]

Today the anointing survives in Europe only in the United Kingdom, the surviving continental European monarchies having either never been granted the privilege of using holy oil, or having abandoned the rite, usually due to revolution (as in Spain) or a desire to modernise (in Scandinavia). However, modernising is dangerous if it means abandoning an element which was once seen as an integral part of establishing a royal title. Conversely, the desire to deny the Sovereign any religious or even

[138] Tierney, Brian, *Church law and constitutional thought in the Middle Ages* (1979).

[139] Blumenthal, Uta-Renate. *The investiture controversy* (1988).

historical mandate was behind most moves to modernise. This inherently weakens the legitimacy of the Sovereign, threatening to render them wholly dependent upon the mandate of Parliament, by ignoring the much older and more sophisticated nature of the legitimacy of the Crown. Most critically, any abandonment of the key ritual of king-making threatens to undermine the legitimacy of the monarch by departing from the conceptual basis of monarchy.

The hallowing of the Sovereign remains vital, if less a part of the church-regulated sacramental authority, and more of their setting aside and dedication for service. St Augustine of Hippo wrote at the beginning of the fifth century during the first great wave of barbarian incursions into the western empire. He described (in *The City of God*) two societies, of the spirit and of the world. Despite Christianity's designation as the official religion of the empire, Augustine declared its message to be spiritual rather than political. Christianity, he argued, should be concerned with the mystical, heavenly City of Jerusalem rather than with Earthly politics. The book presents human history as being a conflict between what Augustine calls the City of God and the City of Man (a conflict that is destined to end in victory for the former). The City of God is marked by people who forego earthly pleasure and dedicate their lives to the promotion of Christian values. The City of Man, on the other hand, consists of people who have strayed from the City of God.[140] The coronation symbolises the sovereign's role as a bridge between Augustine's City of God and City of Man, embodying a spiritual mission within the temporal realm.

As a physical manifestation of such ideas, King Henry III rebuilt Westminster Abbey 1245–72 to create a suitable place for royal burials and a grand setting for coronations.[141] This work included the Cosmati Pavement of 1268 and the Quire, forming a Coronation Theatre placed before the Shrine of St Edward the Confessor and the High Altar.[142] The cosmological significance of the pavement was not accidental, and like Egyptian

[140] Augustine of Hippo, St, *The City of God*. Translation by William Babcock, notes by Boniface Ramsey (2012).

[141] Wilkinson, James and Charles S. Knighton, *Crown and Cloister* (2010).

[142] Grant, Linda and Richard Mortimer, *Westminster Abbey*, Courtauld Institute Research Papers, 3 (2002); Coldstream, Nicola, "The Abbey and Palace as Theatres for Coronation", in Warwick Rodwell, and Tim Tatton-Brown (eds.), *Westminster Part I* (2015).

conceptions of monarchy, the preservation of the balance of nature was an important message.

In 1937 Archbishop Lang emphasised the sacred role of the coronation in the Official Souvenir Programme for the Coronation of George VI

> But the significance of the ceremony is that the King does not crown himself. His Crown is brought from God's Altar and put upon his head by the Archbishop, in token that his kingship is a solemn trust committed to him by Almighty God .... the ultimate source and sanction of all true civil rule and obedience is the Will and Purpose of God, that behind the things that are seen and temporal are the things that are unseen and eternal.[143]

As a more recent Dean of Westminster put it.

> At its heart, the anointing of the Sovereign, and clothing with priestly garments that precede the coronation itself, resemble the ordination of a priest or the consecration of a bishop. The coronation is a setting apart for service after the pattern of Jesus Christ.[144]

It may be said that the coronation no longer determines a sovereign's image,[145] and especially in a religious context. However, in a 2012 revised edition of a book originally published in 2002, Bradley puts forward the counter-cultural proposition that the monarchy still has a vital role, and crucially, that this role is primarily spiritual:

> It involves symbolizing spiritual values, embodying the sacred, representing and defending religious faith against unbelief and secular materialism, promoting order in the midst of chaos standing for the public good against private gain, and acting as a focal point for unity in a society which is increasingly fragmented and fissiparous.[146]

The idea that the Sovereign is above politics—which can be traced to *The Patriot King*, a 1714 essay by the statesman and philosopher Henry St John Viscount Bolingbroke—does not render the coronation oath any

[143] *Official Souvenir Programme for the Coronation of George VI.*

[144] Hall, John, *Queen Elizabeth and Her Church* (2012), p. 2.

[145] Monod, Paul, "Coronations", in *Early Modern Court Culture* (2021), pp. 215–230.

[146] Bradley, Ian, *God Save the Queen* (2012), p. 250.

less important, or necessarily diminishes the spiritual or political role of the Sovereign. It becomes, like the anointing, part of the hallowing and dedication of the Sovereign as a national figure.

While the Christian beliefs of Queen Elizabeth II were well known, those of King Charles III were perhaps less well understood. Yet he is remarkable as a philosopher-King, who genuinely strives to bring some sense to the place of religion in society. This role is as relevant to the atheist and agnostic as it is to the believer.

There is no inconsistency with Christianity remaining at the heart of the political system, despite the long-established principle of freedom of religion. Freedom for individuals to choose does not mean that the state must be atheist or agnostic—for that is adopting a stance on—or rather against—religion. If a Sovereign reflects and adheres to a religious belief system it gives them a sense of moral purpose which is often lacking in political figures.

The coronation reinforces the monarchy's sacred role, symbolising the sovereign's dedication to serve both God and nation. Rooted in priestly tradition, it affirms the monarch as a bridge between spiritual and secular realms. Despite a secular age, the ceremony preserves values of service, unity, and faith, underscoring the monarchy's enduring significance in modern society.

The priestly dimension of kingship reflects a deeply theological view of leadership, where the sovereign is not merely a ruler but also a custodian of moral and spiritual order. This aspect connects to the biblical tradition of anointing kings like David, who were consecrated as both leaders and servants under God. This duality of roles—sacred and secular—requires a delicate balance. While the monarch symbolises divine sanction, their authority is exercised within a political framework that demands accountability, illustrating the enduring tension between religious heritage and modern governance. Though the overt spiritual authority of the monarch has waned, the coronation ceremony remains a powerful symbol of moral responsibility, uniting faith and nation even in secular times.

The Coronation as a Christian Rite

The coronation remains an unashamedly Christian ritual. As arrangements were made for the first coronation in 70 years, Pepinster asked whether 2022 was the time to jettison an ancient rite and, as she put it, reinvent the coronation to appeal to multicultural Britain. Conversely, she asked whether the nation ought to embrace tradition and reassert its Christian heritage in the new Carolean age.[147] Such a stark choice, perhaps unsurprisingly, would be both difficult and controversial. In 2015 the religious think tank Theos had published a report, *Who wants a Christian Coronation?*[148] Relying on a telephone survey,[149] the report concluded that there were no majorities for a secular coronation or for the view that a Christian coronation would alienate those of other faiths or none. A majority (57 per cent) thought the ceremony should be Christian compared with 19 per cent who thought it should be multi-faith and 23 per cent who thought it should be secular. The authors also noted that there were majorities saying they would not feel alienated by a Christian ceremony, even among religious minorities and those of no religious faith.

However, conversely, Morris argued that

> the size and composition of the Abbey congregation, the length of the service and its feudal and eucharistic elements all require radical review. This is not simply on grounds of cost, but more on how a modern, forward looking and confident state should choose to present itself to itself and for view from outside.[150]

The reasoning behind these latter conclusions appears to be insufficiently developed—the feudal elements of the coronation, for instance, being more apparent than real, given that the basic form of the coronation predated feudalism. The eucharistic elements are there for the simple reason that the coronation ritual is a church service, conducted in Westminster Abbey since 6 January 1066,[151] and involves the sacrising and anointing of a Sovereign by the church. To omit this aspect would bring into question the whole nature of the coronation, and thereby raise difficult and nuanced issues of legitimacy and authority. A modern, forward looking

[147] Pepinster, Catherine, *Defenders of the Faith* (2023).

[148] Theos, 1 September 2015 at http://www.theosthinktank.co.uk/publications/2015/09/01/who-wants-a-christiancoronation.

[149] Theos—Coronation Polling, ComRes, Theos—Coronation Polling, ComRes at http://www.theosthinktank.co.uk/publications/2015/09/01/who-wants-a-christian-coronation.

[150] Morris, R. M., *Inaugurating a new reign* (2018), p. 34.

[151] Page, William, "Benedictine monks: St Peter's abbey, Westminster", in *A History of the County of London* (1909), vol. 1, "London Within the Bars, Westminster and Southwark", pp. 433–457; Cannadine, Sir David (ed.), *Westminster Abbey* (2019).

and confident state should have the confidence to retain its core values, customs and rituals, rather than assume that they should be abandoned in favour of some uncertain alternative.

That is not to say that changes cannot or should not happen. Advances in œcumenism, for instance, ensured that a number of denominations were represented at the coronation of King Charles III in 2023, as well as non-Christian religious figures. Christian leaders joined in the Blessing.[152]

In addition, during the exchange of Swords, Psalm 71 was sung (in Greek) by a Greek Orthodox Choir.[153] The idea of singing a Psalm during the exchange of Swords was a new one; the use of Greek presumably refers to the King's Greek and Orthodox heritage, through his father, born Prince Philippos of Greece and Denmark.

Other innovations in 2023 reflected both a desire to simplify and shorten the liturgy—whilst remaining faithful to its meaning—and show a more open and inclusive spirit. For example, the words "for the terror and punishment of evildoers, and for the protection and encouragement of those that do well" were amended in the 2023 prayer over the Sword of Offering to "to resist evil and defend the good". The Archbishop's words of presentation, beyond "Receive this kingly Sword", were new for 2023. However, the prayer following the King's girding with the Sword was unaltered, with the exception of the addition of the words "and all people of goodwill".[154] The words used by the Archbishop when presenting the Spurs was also new, reflecting a modernised conception of their role: "Receive these spurs, symbols of honour and courage. May you be a brave advocate for those in need".[155]

The formula for the presentation of the Armills was significantly truncated, omitting the words "and also for symbols and pledges of that bond which unites you with your Peoples: to the end that you may be strengthened in all your works and defended against your enemies both bodily and

[152] *The Authorised Liturgy for the Coronation Rite of His Majesty King Charles III For use on Saturday 6th May 2023, 11:00am at Westminster Abbey* (2023).

[153] Ibid.

[154] Ibid.

[155] *The Authorised Liturgy for the Coronation Rite of His Majesty King Charles III For use on Saturday 6th May 2023, 11:00am at Westminster Abbey* (2023). The Spurs are traditionally presented without a form of words, but one has been invented for the 2023 service; this is entirely an innovation.

ghostly, through Jesus Christ our Lord".[156] Ensuring the involvement of Anglican churches outside the Church of England, the Archbishop of Armagh brought the Sovereign's Orb to the Archbishop of Canterbury, and the Sceptre with the Cross and St Edward's Rod were presented to the Archbishop of Canterbury by The Archbishop of Wales and The Primus of Scotland respectively.[157]

Aside from the innovative involvement of the Anglican Archbishop of Armagh in presenting the Orb, the words "remember the whole world is subject to the Power and Empire of Christ our Redeemer" were amended to "remember always the kingdoms of this world are become the kingdoms of our Lord, and of his Christ". In 2023, the Sceptre with Cross and Sceptre with Dove were presented simultaneously, without separate prayers; there was, rather, a single new prayer, entirely new:

> May the Spirit of the Lord which anointed Jesus at his baptism, so anoint you this day, that you might exercise authority with wisdom, and direct your counsels with grace; that by your service and ministry to all your people, justice and mercy may be seen in all the earth.

The prayer of blessing of the Crown remained largely unchanged, apart from the addition of the words "that he may be crowned with thy gracious favour". While the Archbishop presumably joined in acclaiming the Sovereign in previous Coronations, it was not previously a rubric that the Archbishop says "God save the King!" as (or immediately after) he brings the Crown down onto the King's head. In all likelihood, this provision was intended to replace the tradition of peers putting on their coronets at this point in the service. The prayer of blessing beginning 'God crown you with a crown of glory and righteousness …' was entirely omitted in 2023.

The blessing that latter year involved leaders of all the major Christian denominations, and retained some of the wording of the 1953 blessing; but there was no mention of

[156] *Proceedings of the Coronation of Her Majesty The Queen*, 2nd June 1953 (1953).

[157] *The Authorised Liturgy for the Coronation Rite of His Majesty King Charles III For use on Saturday 6th May 2023, 11:00am at Westminster Abbey* (2023).

> faithful Parliaments and quiet Realms; sure defence against all enemies; fruitful lands and a prosperous industry; wise counsellors and upright magistrates; leaders of integrity in learning and labour; a devout, learned and useful clergy; honest peaceable and dutiful citizens.[158]

Doubtless this was thought to be too archaic in its tone. Likewise, the prayer of enthroning was simplified; the word "imperial" was once again removed, as well as the words "and by the hands of us the Bishops and servants of God, though unworthy. And the Lord God Almighty, whose ministers we are, and the stewards of his mysteries".[159]

The Order of Service for the 2023 coronation of King Charles III also included an explicitly Christian explanation of the nature and significance of the items of royal dress, the *colobium sindonis*, and the *supertunica*, the stole and the imperial mantle

> Once anointed, The King is vested in priestly garments that symbolise both humility (the Colobium Sindonis) and splendour (the Supertunica, Stole, and Robe); reflecting the two natures of Christ who 'though he was in the form of God ... emptied himself ... being born in human likeness' (from Philippians 2: 6–8). The King represents humanity restored to its full dignity and glory in Christ, as 'a chosen race, a royal priesthood, a holy nation' (1 Peter 2: 9).[160]

The coronation as a Christian rite balances tradition with modern inclusivity. The 2023 coronation upheld its religious heritage—if not indeed enhancing that—while incorporating interfaith elements and simplified language, reflecting the monarchy's sacred role and its commitment to a diverse society.

[158] *Proceedings of the Coronation of Her Majesty The Queen*, 2nd June 1953 (1953).

[159] *The Authorised Liturgy for the Coronation Rite of His Majesty King Charles III For use on Saturday 6th May 2023, 11:00am at Westminster Abbey* (2023) cf *Supplement to the London Gazette*, 17th November 1953 (HMSO, London, 1953), pp. 6223–6270 "Ceremonial of the Coronation of Her Majesty Queen Elizabeth II".

[160] *The Authorised Liturgy for the Coronation Rite of His Majesty King Charles III For use on Saturday 6th May 2023, 11:00am at Westminster Abbey* (2023).

Conclusion

The theological functions of the coronation can be traced back to the origins of the state. Christianity reached the British Isles in the early years of the Christian era, when much of the island of Britain was part of the Roman empire. Once raised to the status of the official religion of the empire, under Constantine the Great, Christianity was encouraged, at least at official levels, throughout the empire, including in Britain.

The fall of imperial authority, the withdrawal of the last legions, and increased Barbarian depredations, threw the indigenous population, Roman, Romanised, and non-Romanised alike, on their own devices. The native Christian authorities sought allies amongst the Anglo-Saxon arrivals, and also fought them, in a series of confused and confusing conflicts, the true picture of which is likely to always remain inaccessible.

However, the legacy of imperial Rome had a long reach, and as in what later became the German heartland of the Holy Roman Empire, the recollection of imperial authority remained strong. A ruler might augment their status by mimicking the style and titles of the empire. By the more settled times of Edgar, the new Saxon kingdoms sought to associate themselves with the past but not forgotten glories of imperial Rome. Thus his coronation was in the once splendid—and in the tenth century doubtless still evocative—Roman town of Bath (*Aquae Sulis*). The pre-Roman tribal kingdoms, and the post-Roman kingdoms—British and Saxon alike—all saw the past as something to recover. This was perhaps influenced, after the regained dominance of Christianity, by the analogy of the fall of humanity, at least in those kingdoms which remained, or became, Christian.[161]

Slowly the tribal kings of both British and Saxon principalities and kingdoms assumed to themselves a sacred character, made more overtly Christian as time went on, but nonetheless of a more ancient lineage. In Christian theological terms, the king was a *persona mixta*, neither a layman nor a priest, but having some aspects of the character of both. Even a deposed king held a special status, as, like a priest, this character

[161] Audronis, Domantas, "Un-Roman Empires, post-Roman worlds: Rome and imperial ideology in a comparative European context, 800-1000" (2021) The University of Manchester PhD thesis,

was indelible. Gradually, over time, the status of king grew, so that kingship was seen as the centre of all governance, and the divine right of the king, all but unchallengeable.

This status was not generally questioned by the church, indeed from the mission of St Augustine in 597, onwards, the church and king were largely in alliance. This was reflected in the structure of the coronation, and in particular the anointing and the coronation oath.

The church and the kingdom worked hand-in-hand in a symbiotic relationship. The church offered support to the legitimacy of the king, and the king supported and protected the church. It is no wonder that the rights and privileges of the church loomed large in both magna carta and the coronation oaths. But the relationship was not merely cynical. Kings were, with some notable exceptions, genuine in their religious persuasions, and the church was likewise generally seeking the welfare of the realm and its people. It is worth noting that one of the earliest sources, Gildas, was himself Old Testament prophet-like in his condemnation of the morals of the kings and clergy of sub-Roman Britain.[162] Church and king alike were wedded—or should have been—to the welfare of the people. The coronation upheld, and continues to uphold, that concept, with the Archbishop of Canterbury's sermon (abandoned in 1902, and revived in a shorter form in 1911,[163] abandoned in 1937 and 1953, and restored in 2023[164]) being a particularly significant opportunity to extort the king, and through him the kingdom, to Christian virtue and behaviour.

The British coronation embodies a profound theological tapestry that integrates sacred tradition, Christian doctrine, and the constitutional realities of modern governance. At its core lies the sacred nature of kingship, which is not merely an inherited office but a divinely sanctioned vocation.

[162] See "De Excidio et Conquestu Britanniae" in John Allen Giles (ed.), *The Works of Gildas and Nennius* (1841).

[163] Strong, Sir Roy, *Coronation* (2005), p. 477. Other changes in 1902 included omitting the litany, and the first oblation of the pall or altar cloth and wedge of gold, and curtailing the ceremony of homage. At the coronation of George V, the litany, sermon and first oblation were restored; *Form and Order of the Coronation of George V and Queen Mary*; and *Supplement to the London Gazette*, 27 September 1911. At the coronation of Elizabeth II, the sermon was omitted, and the litany was sung before the service began: see *Supplement to the London Gazette*, 20 November 1953, p. 236.

[164] *The Authorised Liturgy for the Coronation Rite of His Majesty King Charles III For use on Saturday 6th May 2023, 11:00am at Westminster Abbey* (2023).

The anointing of the monarch, echoing Old Testament practices, marks the pivotal moment in the coronation rite, signifying the investiture of divine grace upon the sovereign.

Integral to this theological framework is the concept of servant kingship. The coronation liturgy, shaped by centuries of Christian tradition, underscores the monarch's duty to serve rather than to dominate, reflecting Christ's example of humility and stewardship. The presentation of regalia, such as the orb and sceptre, reinforces this duality, symbolising both the king's divine appointment and his accountability to God and his people.

The intertwining of Church and State finds its origins in the Christianisation of the British Isles and the enduring legacy of Constantine's vision of a Christian state. This unity, however, is not without its complexities. The Church legitimises the monarch's authority through its liturgical and sacramental acts, while the State provides a framework within which the Church itself operates. The coronation thus serves as a reminder of this delicate symbiosis, where ecclesiastical blessing affirms royal authority, yet the sovereign pledges to uphold the faith and protect its institutions.

This sacred covenant between monarch, Church, and nation finds expression in the enduring symbolism of the coronation. Through the invocation of divine favour, the anointing, and the charge to serve, the ceremony transcends a mere constitutional formality to affirm the theological underpinnings of British kingship. It stands as a testament to the enduring relevance of sacred kingship in a modern constitutional monarchy, bridging ancient traditions and contemporary governance. As such, the coronation continues to be a profound ritual that unites history, faith, and national identity in the figure of the anointed sovereign.

Conclusion

The coronation serves a deep constitutional function in the British legal, political and theological context. It is a manifestation of the legitimation of authority, based on an element of constitutional continuity—not, perhaps, entirely unbroken, but nonetheless almost unrivalled in its antiquity.

The Westminster Abbey website, in 2023, said of the coronation that

> In strictly constitutional terms, coronations do not have to take place. In fact, two monarchs, King Edward V and King Edward VIII, did not have a coronation but were still kings. However, a coronation does have three key purposes. First and foremost, it has a religious significance, with the monarch making promises to God as part of a Christian ceremony. Secondly, while the monarch has acquired the status and authority at their accession, it is at the coronation that the monarch makes promises to the people that they serve. Finally, it is a moment for public celebration and affirmation in a way that would be inappropriate in the days and weeks following the accession.[1]

Thus the theological, legal and political functions of the coronation were expressly identified, although the legal was couched particularly

[1] https://www.westminster-abbey.org/about-the-abbey/history/coronations-at-the-abbey/a-guide-to-coronations.

N. Cox, *The Political, Legal, and Theological Functions of the Ceremony in the British Tradition*,
https://doi.org/10.1007/978-3-031-88960-8

(though not expressly) in terms of the social contract of the coronation oath, the political in terms of celebration and affirmation, and the theological in terms similarly of promises. Whether these particular views of the coronation reflected the views of Westminster Abbey, the coronation committee, or even of King Charles III personally, they nevertheless reflect some aspects of the function of the coronation as a constitutional solemnity of great significance. The personal involvement of the Sovereign in planning a coronation may be expected. A significant innovation in 2023 was that vesting the King in the Robe Royal was entrusted to Baroness Merron,[2] and the Prince of Wales, rather than the Groom of the Robes,[3] Lord Great Chamberlain and Dean of Westminster, as hitherto.[4] This was one example of the inclusion of non-Christian participants, as well as the opportunity for the King's heir to perform a personal service for his father, echoing the robing of the then Charles, Prince of Wales, by his mother, Queen Elizabeth II, in 1969.[5]

The coronation forms a pivotal part of the largely unwritten—or at least uncodified—British constitution. The nature of the British constitution is fluid and organic. The constitution, as the result of a thousand years of evolution, is eminently pragmatic rather than based on a formal conceptual model—even the notions of the rule of law,[6] or the separation of powers,[7] have evolved as a means of making theoretical sense of what happens in practice. The coronation itself serves as an occasional reinforcement of the legitimacy of government, through the secular and religious aspects of recognition or acclamation, coronation oath, anointing, investiture with regalia, crowning, enthroning, and homage.

A coronation is the formal hallowing of a new king or queen. Parsons believed that it was the "coronation and admission that maketh a perfect

[2] Chief Executive of the Board of Deputies of British Jews.

[3] Lieutenant-Colonel Jonathan Thompson, Royal Regiment of Scotland, Equerry to the King.

[4] *The Authorised Liturgy for the Coronation Rite of His Majesty King Charles III For use on Saturday 6th May 2023, 11:00am at Westminster Abbey* (2023).

[5] Ellis, John Stephen, *Investiture* (2008).

[6] Bingham, Tom, *The Rule of Law* (2011).

[7] Montesquieu, Charles Louis de Secondat Baron de, "The Spirit of the Laws", in Arend Lijphart (ed.), *Parliamentary versus Presidential Government* (1992), pp. 48–51.

and true king".[8] The succession was based on consent and acceptance, rather than being strictly hereditary. It is commonly said that the title to the Crown was governed at common law,[9] by the feudal rules of hereditary descent formerly applicable to land.[10] It followed that, to complete the title, some formal act, such as a coronation, was needed. In the latter days of Queen Elizabeth I's reign, Peter Wentworth maintained that a coronation was a declaration rather than a creation of right. But no king—or queen—would have felt secure without one.[11] Both Parsons and Wentworth maintained that, as the right to the Crown was not entirely a matter of the automatic operation of the law, a formal coronation was needed. It is submitted that, in part, this was due to the fact that the legal title to the Crown was insufficient, of itself, to establish possession, and that the roots of this lie deep in the law of succession.

In *Calvin's Case* (1608),[12] the Court of Exchequer Chamber decided that a coronation, as a consequence of hereditary succession, was not a legal necessity, though as late as 1483 there was a belief that a coronation enabled a minor king to exercise independent authority without a formal regency or protectorate being necessary.[13] It is to be doubted whether a Sovereign would be fully accepted without a coronation, as may be seen with the still-current attitude towards the uncrowned King Edward VIII[14]; the succession remained a combination of hereditary title, parliamentary grant, and consent—as we were reminded in 1688–89, and

[8] Doleman, R. (pseudonym for Fr. Robert Parsons), *Conference About the Next Succession* (1594), p. 136; Axton, Marie, *The Queen's Two Bodies; Drama and the Elizabethan Succession* (1977), p. 94.

[9] *Halsbury's Laws of England* (4th ed., 1974), vol. 8 para., 845.

[10] This is the substance of the rule as deduced by Sir William Blackstone (see Blackstone, Sir William, *Commentaries on the Laws of England* ed. E. Christian (1978), pp. 192, 193); See 7 Hen IV c 2 (Succession to the Crown) (1405–6); 1 Mar sess 2 c 1 (Legitimacy of the Queen) (1553); 1 Eliz I c 3 (Recognition of the Queen's Title to the Crown) (1558–9); 1 Jac I c 1 (Recognition of the King's Title to the Crown) (1603–4) (all repealed); and the Succession to the Crown Act 1707 (6 Ann c 41).

[11] Wentworth, Peter, *A Pithie Exhortation to Her Majestie for Establishing Her Successor to the Crowne* (1598), p. 54; Craig, Sir Thomas, *The Right of Succession to the Kingdom of England* (1703), p. 21.

[12] (1608) 7 Co Rep 1a; 77 ER 377.

[13] McKisack, May, The *Fourteenth Century* (1959), pp. 399–400; Tuck, Anthony, "Richard II (1367–1400)", *Oxford Dictionary of National Biography* (2004).

[14] See, for example, Brendon, Piers, *Edward VIII* (2016).

indeed in 1936. It is rarely a wise move to make radical changes at the beginning of a reign.

Almost all English kings (as well as their Scottish and Irish counterparts) since time immemorial had been crowned, and since Saxon times English, and later Scottish kings had also been anointed with holy oil—a privilege not accorded by the Church to every ruler in Christendom. The coronation served to publicly declare the king to have come into his own, and allowed the people to welcome him. In this regard the coronation parades were important elements.

The swearing of the coronation oath was important from Anglo-Saxon times, and never lost its constitutional and political significance. Indeed, since 1689 they have enjoyed increased importance, with the coronation now an indispensable rite of passage for a kingship recast since the late eighteenth century as a bulwark of the democratic system which it fostered. Since the claim to the Crown by divine right was weaker, popular support, based on adherence to the ancient constitution, grew in importance, as did the need to affirm the accession symbolically. As the liturgist E. C. Ratcliff puts it, "In a word, the English Coronation Service symbolises national continuity considered *sub specie Christianitatis*".[15]

The king's coronation oath becomes, like the anointing, part of the hallowing and dedication of the Sovereign as a national figure. It strengthens, in Bagehot's taxonomy, the dignified part of the constitution,[16] but not at any cost to the efficient. Indeed, it arguably strengthens the latter also, as it reiterates that government ought to be conducted in a moral and upright manner, consistent with the rule of law.

The oath-taking was not all one way. For a king or queen to have any chance of keeping their oath they had to have the support of their people, hence the importance of the recognition or acclamation and the homage. Not only was the king expected to take the oath, but the king expected the magnates and prelates to reciprocate. This was not primarily a feudal relationship—though it resembles it—but rather a collegial approach to governance. The king was superior, but did not rule alone. The ancient institutions of the *Witan* (*Witenagemot*), the *Magnum Concilium*, the *Curia Regis* and later Parliament, aided and advised the kings, and later

[15] Ratcliff, E. C., *The Coronation Service of Her Majesty Queen Elizabeth II* (1953), p. 23.

[16] Bagehot, Walter, *The English Constitution* (2001).

had a tax raising and legislative function. Even the most absolutist kings could not rule without the support of the leading men—and a few women—of the realm. The homage itself, as a coronation rite, precedes the advent of Parliament (arguably 1215 for the Lords and 1265 for the Commons),[17] as the greater land-owners pledged their loyalty to a new king at their coronation—or occasionally beforehand.

The coronation was expected of a new king—and even as recently as William IV, the economy measures which were followed led to him being lampooned in the less sympathetic press, as having had a "half-crownation" or "penny coronation". Although in strict legal terms the Sovereign accedes the throne immediately on the death of their predecessor, the popular idea that the king hasn't really become king until they are crowned remains fairly common—and who is to say that the title is not made secure only by a coronation, *Calvin's Case*[18] notwithstanding.

Even if poorly understood by the population, or even the political elite, the coronation reaches to a deeper level in the public psyche, and therefore of the constitution. As Shils and Young observed, at the time of the coronation of Queen Elizabeth II in 1953

> To sum up: A society is held together by its internal agreement about the sacredness of certain fundamental moral standards. In an inchoate, dimly perceived, and seldom explicit manner, the central authority of an orderly society, whether it be secular or ecclesiastical, is acknowledged to be the avenue of communication with the realm of the sacred values. Within its society, popular constitutional monarchy enjoys almost universal recognition in this capacity, and it is therefore enabled to heighten the moral and civic sensibility of the society and to permeate it with symbols of those values to which the sensitivity responds. Intermittent rituals bring the society or varying sectors of it repeatedly into contact with this vessel of the sacred values. The Coronation provided at one time and for practically the entire society such an intensive contact with the sacred that we believe we are justified in interpreting it as we have done in this essay, is a great act of national communion.[19]

[17] Maddicott, J. R., *The Origins of the English Parliament, 924–1327* (2010).

[18] (1608) 7 Co Rep 1a; 77 ER 377.

[19] Shils, Edward and Michael Young, "The Meaning of the Coronation" (1953) 1(2) The Sociological Review 63–81, 80.

A "great act of national communion" is neither a legal, nor a political, nor a theological—or ecclesiological—action, but rather sociological. It is constitutional in the sense that it acts to form a bridge between Sovereign and subject, king (or queen) and people. The social, political and economic changes since 1953 may be significant, but the constitutional function of the Sovereign, and therefore of the coronation, remains broadly unchanged.

This Durkheimian functionalism which Shils and Young expounded was rejected by the American sociologist Norman Birnbaum, who argued against any shared values or nationally integrative function for the coronation.[20] In some respects Birnbaum may be correct, but to analyse the coronation primarily in terms of values is to underestimate its constitutional function—it is unlikely that any Saxon or mediæval king would understand his coronation in such modern democratic or sociological terms, or as an expression of shared values or even as a national integrative function.

However, a sociological analysis of the coronation is still useful. Shils and Young argued that

> ... the Coronation was the ceremonial occasion for the affirmation of the moral values by which the society lives. It was an act of national communion ... The Coronation Service itself is a series of ritual affirmations of the moral values necessary to a well-governed and good society. The key to the Coronation Service is the Queen's promise to abide by the moral standards of society ... Over the past century, British society, despite distinctions of nationality and social status has achieved a degree of moral unity equalled by no other large national state.[21]

Here, despite the references to moral standards of society, the emphasis is perhaps more on the personal albeit representational role of the Sovereign. Queen Elizabeth II, in taking her coronation oath, asserted her acceptance, not of any commonly held moral standards of society, but specific promises expected of a good ruler, promising to abide by the customs and laws of the kingdom. Whether this approach is adequate

[20] Birnbaum, Norman, "Monarchs and Sociologists: A reply to Professor Shils and Mr. Young" (1955) 3(1) Sociological Review 5–13.

[21] Shils, Edward and Michael Young, "The Meaning of the Coronation" (1953) 1(2) The Sociological Review 63–81, 67.

in the markedly changed world of 2023 remains unanswered, but the popular appeal of monarchical ceremonies in general, and the relationship of these rituals to both primal and contemporary ritual and belief remain complex and multifaceted questions.

The appeal of the ritual may be described as both deeply personal—for King and observer alike—and drawing on aspects of modern culture and sociological/psychological factors. The contemporary context may be different in 2023 to what it was in 1953, but arguably this has been true for each generation. Coronations have always reflected change and continuity, and the anticipation and management of perceptions.[22] Contemporary culture still has a place for history and tradition—indeed perhaps more today than is usually the case.

Queen Elizabeth II's coronation in 1953 was in the latter days of empire. Theoretically future coronations could follow the 1953 model closely—so far as the service itself is concerned at least—and in principle there is no reason why they should not do so, and good reason why it should. But care would have to be taken to ensure clarity of understanding of its exact role.

In 1953 elements were changed to incorporate Scotland—where the last coronation was in 1651 (Scottish peers and officers of state had been involved in the London ceremony from 1714, as is right and proper)—and the realms, then called dominions.

The changing nature of the United Kingdom was reflected in the course of the twentieth century—for example, in the involvement of the Moderator of the General Assembly of the Church of Scotland in 1953, and it was only to be expected that Welsh-language elements would be introduced in 2023.

In 2023, in a sign that the liturgy of the coronation was more strongly influenced by the clerical participants, and less prescribed by tradition, the Gospel, which had invariably been Matthew 22:15–22, was changed to Luke 4:16–21.[23] From the time of the *Liber Regalis*, and the coronation of Edward III (1327), the first reading has been 1 Peter 2: 13–19 or sometimes finishing at verse 17 "Honour the king;" in 2023 the Epistle was Colossians 1:9–17. Whereas in 1953 the Epistle was read by a bishop,

[22] Lloyd, Daniel, "The Coronation of Charles III from the Perspective of Liturgical Studies" (2023) 2 Ex Fonte–Journal of Ecumenical Studies in Liturgy 363–445.

[23] Shils, Edward and Michael Young, "The Meaning of the Coronation" (1953) 1(2) The Sociological Review 63–81, 67.

in 2023 it was read by the Prime Minister—in the event, a Hindu, Rishi Sunak. The newly selected readings offered a less authoritarian view of kingship, a view made clear in the opening moments of the coronation, in the welcome by a child, and the King's Prayer. It was now more overtly a servant kingship.

The Thanksgiving for the Holy Oil was significantly different from the prayer said before the anointing in 1953, which was a blessing of the Queen rather than a blessing of the oil itself (which might have been more controversial in the Church of England at that time than it is today). The 2023 prayer also drew attention to the priestly and royal anointing of all Christians in baptism. The presentation of the holy oil to the Archbishop by the Anglican Archbishop in Jerusalem was a new development, both œcumenical and inclusive, and emphasising the worldwide nature of the Anglican Communion.

Several changes increased the emphasis upon the coronation as being framed within the setting of a eucharist, including the addition of a Greeting and Introduction by the Archbishop of Canterbury, the expansion of the *Kyrie eleison* into a multilingual sung rendering, and a Gloria in place of an Introit, although a sung Gradual, and a sung Creed, were abandoned in favour of a sung Alleluia (Psalm 47:1–2, 6–7). While the Gloria featured in the 1953 Coronation, it appeared much later owing to the structure of the Holy Communion service in *The Book of Common Prayer*; here it came in the position that would be expected in a service of Holy Communion according to *Common Worship*. However, the Gloria was sung in Latin to a setting by William Byrd—perhaps the first time sung Latin had featured in a Coronation service since the coronation of Queen Elizabeth I in 1559. The coronation collect for 2023 differed quite considerably from that prayed for Elizabeth II in 1953. While the 1953 collect asked for "the Spirit of wisdom and government", the 2023 collect asked for vaguer "gifts of wisdom and love". The mention of the safety of the Church and the monarch's eternal destiny contained in the 1953 collect are omitted; both changes consistent with the image of a servant kingship being fostered.

The Prayer over the gifts was as before—itself derived from the *Liber Regalis*. The Eucharistic prayers however largely followed the modern liturgical practice of the Church of England, including an Offertory

Hymn ("Christ is made the sure foundation"),[24] as in 1953. The Eucharistic prayers all replaced the Roman Canon in the *Liber Regalis*, though the offertory prayers were added in 1953 to echo those of the *Liber Regalis* and represented a renewed interest in returning to ancient sources.

In 2023, as in 1953, the anointing of the Sovereign was veiled from public sight by a screen (replacing the former canopy). As the liturgy noted, "Canopies such as these can be traced back to the Old Testament. In the Middle Ages it was custom for Sovereigns to travel beneath such a canopy. In this context, it is to signify the presence of God over this covenant of anointing".[25] The Queen Consort's anointing was not so hidden, reflecting the distinct, and derivative, nature of their anointing.[26] The moment was not, however, televised directly, the cameras instead focussing on the musicians. This was consistent with long practice, though in 1399 Henry VI chose to be anointed in the view of all attendees.[27]

There were significant contemporary debates about the nature of a future coronation, specifically in the areas of the coronation oaths, both within and outside the churches, about the extent to which the next coronation should include rewritten coronation oaths to take the focus away from maintaining the Protestant religious settlement, and active participation of representatives of non-Christian faiths, and overall tone and ethos. Although there has been considerable discussion about the rewriting of the coronation oath, in particular,[28] apart from an introductory narrative, no revision was made. Although there was a markedly more diverse involvement in the ceremony—racially and with respect to gender and denomination—and non-Christian religious leaders were involved—the ceremony itself remained essentially unchanged.

A radical slash and burn approach to anything thought archaic or feudal would be a serious mistake for a number of reasons, as given above. Some changes may doubtless always be required—and some are desirable

[24] Ibid.

[25] *The Authorised Liturgy for the Coronation Rite of His Majesty King Charles III For use on Saturday 6th May 2023, 11:00am at Westminster Abbey* (2023).

[26] Ibid.

[27] Hunt, Alice, "British Coronation: A History", Gresham College, 2 May 2023.

[28] Hazell, Robert and R. M. Morris, *Swearing in the New King* (2022); see especially Chapter 4 in Morris, R. M., *The coronation of Charles III* (2022), pp. 30–36.

for liturgical or historical reasons (such as the restoration of the sermon, abandoned in 1902, and restored in 2023[29])—and others to reflect the diminished role of the House of Lords. Even this latter step might not be necessary or desirable, as the coronation already included the Speaker of the House of Commons.

The coronation is lengthy because it includes diverse elements, each contributing something to the whole. Some shortening was achieved, for example, by removing the giving of individual fealty and homage by the Lords spiritual and temporal in 1902, in favour of the premier peer of each degree, and the Archbishop on behalf of his spiritual peers. But it should never be subject to a deliberate attempt to reduce its length for brevities sake alone, given its constitutional significance. Nor should economies be taken (either for the coronation service itself, or the parades) on the false argument that the United Kingdom is not, in the twenty-first century, an imperial power, for neither was England, Britain or even the United Kingdom an "imperial power" (as that term might be generally understood today) throughout most of its history. As the international attention paid to the death, lying in state, funeral and interment of Queen Elizabeth II in 2022 clearly showed, the British monarchy had enormous and unequalled international cachet,[30] and a coronation is therefore an investment worth making, from a purely economic perspective, and as an exercise in soft power. No Sovereign can risk their title being questioned. The greatest challenge today is apathy and ignorance, or arguments that society has changed greatly since 1953.

By 1838 the coronation had become a popular spectacle—rather than a state religious rite, or a mere court entertainment—but some were suspecting it as a gigantic extravagance, without any more purpose than to amuse the masses (though that role was important enough—probably far more than contemporary commentators realised). Earl Fitzwilliam argued that the coronation, when the Crown was not in doubt, was not necessary.[31] Even in 1953 there was widespread ignorance of the nature and elements of a coronation, only partly helped by the avalanche of books

[29] Shils, Edward and Michael Young, "The Meaning of the Coronation" (1953) 1(2) The Sociological Review 63–81, 67.

[30] Lloyd, Daniel, "A tradition of invention: Rites and rituals surrounding the death and funeral of Queen Elizabeth II" (2022) 1 Ex Fonte–Journal of Ecumenical Studies in Liturgy 191–237.

[31] Hunt, Alice, *Drama of Coronation* (2008), Chap. 1, pp. 12–38.

on the coronation published at the time. Apathy or downright hostility, fuelled by a desire to save money, could result in the idea that a coronation is an optional extra, or that it can be trimmed and pared back to a mere shadow of the ancient ritual. Nothing could be further from the truth; perhaps both William IV and Edward VIII would have dispensed with the coronation altogether, given the choice. While the ceremony in Westminster Abbey is the last true coronation in western Christendom—there are equivalents in other civilisations—this is because the United Kingdom is the last survivor of the ancient major kingdoms of the west.

The inauguration of lesser European royalty in no way compares with the historic importance of a British coronation. The major cost of a coronation (other than the construction of the theatre in Westminster Abbey), and security (the later costing the Home Office £22m from a total cost in 2023 of £72m[32]), would be the procession, which would doubtless include far fewer military personnel than before—simply because the armed forces of the Crown are now everywhere smaller than in 1953.[33] At that time (1953) there were 868,000 regular military, air and naval personnel. In 2022, by contrast, the British Armed Forces numbered just 148,000 regular personnel. On this basis, even allowing for an increase of some 200,000 due to the Korean War, it was unlikely that more than 7000 troops could be mustered for both parade and street lining purposes, and probably considerably fewer. The actual number was

[32] Howard, Jacqueline, "King Charles's Coronation cost taxpayers £72m", BBC, 22 November 2024, https://www.bbc.com/news/articles/c04lyddv2p5o.

[33] There were 29,000 service personnel in the procession, and another 15,800 lined the route, all under the command of the Field Marshal Commanding Coronation Troops, Field Marshal Viscount Alanbrooke (also Lord High Constable); *Supplement to the London Gazette*, 17 November 1953 (HMSO, London, 1953), pp. 6223–6270 "Ceremonial of the Coronation of Her Majesty Queen Elizabeth II".

In 2023 there were 4000 personnel in the Coronation procession, including 400 personnel from 45 Commonwealth countries; Press Release, "Armed Forces personnel to feature in Coronation", Ministry of Defence, 16 April 2023.

The Coronation Flypast in 1953 was by 168 aircraft, and that of 2023 was planned to number 68 aircraft and helicopters; Press Release, "Armed Forces personnel to feature in Coronation", Ministry of Defence, 16 April 2023; "168 Jets Roared Over The Palace Balcony". Belfast Telegraph. 3 June 1953. See Sawer, Patrick, "King Charles' Coronation military procession to be seven times smaller than late Queen's", *The Telegraph*, 18 April 2023. In the event, in 2023 bad weather meant that only helicopters and the nine jets of the Red Arrows; Sawer, Patrick, "King's Coronation flypast scaled back: Full details of line-up and flight route", *The Telegraph*, 6 May 2023.

confirmed as approximately 6000.[34] But to abolish or severely curtail the parades would be as wrong in the twenty-first century as it would have been in the seventeenth. It would be even more unwise, for the parades are the primary public aspect of the coronation—while it is true that we can all watch a coronation at home on television (or other electronic device), taking part in an event of this nature far transcends merely viewing it from afar.

The trend from the seventeenth century (if not before) has been towards perceiving the coronation as a public spectacle, an occasion for national and later international rejoicing. From 1838—when Buckingham Palace was first used as the point of departure for the coronation—the parade has been longer than it was in ancient times, reflecting the increased (though far from unprecedented) emphasis upon public participation in the spectacle.

Rather than scaling back the parade—because of the unavailability of sufficient troops—it would be desirable to return to the ancient practice of allowing City livery companies, foreign merchants guilds, and their modern equivalents to contribute in their own way. Such pageants as the Queen Mother's 100th birthday parade, in which Her Majesty's charities paraded floats, and the more recent Platinum Jubilee parade in 2022, would be examples of admirable modern interpretations of the ancient coronation procession. In 2023 the King's Procession from Buckingham Palace to Westminster Abbey, and the Coronation Procession, on the return, were traditional aspects surrounding the solemnity of the coronation.[35]

With respect to the service itself the overall structure can scarcely be changed, such is its antiquity and importance. Careful liturgical revisions have already corrected most if not all the errors which had crept in over

[34] In 2022, by contrast to the 1953 figures, the British Armed Forces numbered just 148,000 regular personnel; https://www.statista.com/statistics/579773/number-of-personnel-in-uk-armed-forces/. Press Release, "Armed Forces personnel to feature in Coronation", Ministry of Defence, 16 April 2023.

[35] The King's Procession, accompanied by The Sovereign's Escort of the Household Cavalry. Included the 2012 Diamond Jubilee State Coach. On the return to the Palace, in the Coronation Procession, the 1769 Gold State Coach was used, and the procession included Armed Forces from across the Commonwealth and the British Overseas Territories, and all Services of the Armed Forces, alongside The Sovereign's Bodyguard and Royal Watermen; "The Coronation Procession", https://www.royal.uk/coronation-procession, 9 April 2023.

time, and the only desirable changes would be to make small alterations to further improve it—not wholesale vandalism aimed at "modernising" it, or removing anything seen as feudal, archaic or unnecessary. For instance, the innovation in 1953 of adding a hymn to be sung by the congregation can be built upon—indeed, that it took until the mid-twentieth century for congregational singing to be incorporated, despite the Reformation introducing this as standard in eucharistic liturgies,[36] shows the antiquity and resilience of the ancient rite. Attempting to ensure that the solemnity of the coronation becomes a glorified inauguration, would be both constitutionally risky and historically, aesthetically and liturgically vandalism of the highest order. Changes in 2023 were modest—arguably apart from the exclusion of the peerage from the rite of homage, and its replacement with the homage of the people—but did include a slightly reduced use for the regalia, with the Armills (the use of which was only revived in 1953, having previously fallen out of use), and the Sovereign's Ring being returned to the altar rather than worn. Some prayers were shortened—such as that for the Armills, the Sovereign's Ring, and the Robe Royal.[37] The words of presentation of the Ring were significantly amended, and indeed the Ring's meaning re-imagined. It was no longer "the seal of Catholic Faith' but rather 'a sign of the covenant sworn this day between God and King, King and people", and references in the words of presentation to the King's role as Defender of the Faith were removed. Both changes were doubtless to avoid offence to Roman Catholic and non-Anglicans alike.

On the delicate question of whether to involve representatives of other religions, they could have been included in the parade, or (less desirably perhaps) at a separate service, possibly drawing inspiration from the now-defunct coronation banquet, and held in Westminster Hall; in the event in 2023 they were included at the end, as the King was about to leave the Abbey. The coronation service itself is a Christian church service, of great antiquity, and on that basis alone unsuited to the admixture of non-Christian elements, although it did prove possible to expand the role of other Christian denominations, particularly the Roman Catholic Church and the Orthodox churches. Although these later innovations

[36] Luther regarded music as the greatest gift of God after religion itself; Buszin, Walter E., "Luther on Music" (1946) xxxii Musical Quarterly 80–97.

[37] *The Authorised Liturgy for the Coronation Rite of His Majesty King Charles III For use on Saturday 6th May 2023, 11:00am at Westminster Abbey* (2023).

are, perhaps, unnecessary as the service itself, in its essence, predates both the Reformation and the break with Rome in 1533 and even the Great Schism of 1054, they were sound from an œcumenical perspective.

Equally importantly, the coronation remains an important religious service, the hallowing of the Sovereign. Doubtless the arguments of twenty-first century atheists, and advocates of the separation of Church and State might contradict this. But it is axiomatic nonetheless. The monarchy, like the legal system and the principal institutions of government, is underpinned by Christian concepts[38]; but it has rarely been exclusively Christian. The King is Sovereign alike of Christian and non-Christian subjects, but the mantle of kingship has been hallowed by the Church since the Christianisation of Britain. Evidence suggests that the preservation of the Christian nature of the coronation has broad approval from Christian and non-Christian alike.[39] That is not to say that other faiths are excluded; in 2023, as noted above, at the end of the procession through the Abbey after the coronation, the King received a greeting by Leaders and Representatives from Faith Communities (Jewish, Hindu, Sikh, Muslim, and Buddhist), speaking in unison

> Your Majesty, as neighbours in faith, we acknowledge the value of public service. We unite with people of all faiths and beliefs in thanksgiving, and in service with you for the common good.[40]

Although the United Kingdom and the realms are racially and culturally far more diverse than they were in 1953, it can equally be said that it is a truism that the Sovereign is king or queen of all. The coronation service predates modern society—the social order of Edgar's day was very different to that of Richard II or Edward VI, or that of Elizabeth II, but that is largely immaterial. The coronation speaks to and from the innermost recesses of the constitutional order, of church sanctioned if not divinely approved kingship, of popular acclamation and recognition, and of the allegiance of the great and the good. It confers legitimacy as

[38] Cox, Noel, "Legal aspects of Church-State relations in New Zealand" (2010) 8(1) Journal of Anglican Studies 9–33.

[39] Theos, "Who wants a Christian Coronation?", 1 September 2015 at http://www.theosthinktank.co.uk/publications/2015/09/01/who-wants-a-christiancoronation.

[40] *The Authorised Liturgy for the Coronation Rite of His Majesty King Charles III For use on Saturday 6th May 2023, 11:00am at Westminster Abbey* (2023).

much as any popular election, if not more so. It draws on a deep taproot of constitutionality which characterises the British constitution, of adaptability yet of conformity to the law, of deference but not enslavement to precedent, and of respect for the tradition upon which our ancient system of law and government is built.

Much of twenty-first century thought is critical of ceremonial, opposed to religious symbolism or beliefs, and hostile to tradition. What then is the future of a service which calls down God's blessing on a king, and which involves ancient rites and ceremonies? The danger is that the Government of the day (or even a new, reform minded King) would simply decide that such a supposed extravagance was unnecessary. The cost of a coronation is significant; that of King Charles III in 2023 costing some £72m.[41] But the inauguration of an American president is considerably more expensive,[42] and occurs every four years, whereas a coronation is, by definition, once a generation—and in some cases even less frequent. The return on the investment, whether by tourism or the souvenir trade, or in more intangible terms, are immense.

The coronation also serves, perhaps more today than ever before, as an opportunity to communicate to the masses. The themes and emphases of the reign can be conveyed in the symbolism of the service. In 2023, for instance, sustainability, prudent economy, and respect for tradition, were conveyed by the choices of vestments, chairs, robes and the anointing canopy. The robes of state and estate worn by the King were conserved

[41] Howard, Jacqueline, "King Charles's Coronation cost taxpayers £72m", BBC, 22 November 2024, https://www.bbc.com/news/articles/c04lyddv2p5o.

[42] Dwight D. Eisenhower's 1953 parade included about 22,000 service men and women and 5000 civilians, which included 50 state and organization floats costing $100,000, "1953 Presidential Inauguration", Eisenhower Presidential Library, Museum & Boyhood Home. https://www.eisenhower.archives.gov/all_about_ike/presidential/1953_inauguration.html.

In contrast, the coronation of HM The Queen in 1953 cost £1.57m (the UK:US exchange rate in 1953 was 2.8, hence some US$4.4m). This equates to approximately £36m in 2023 terms; Bank of England Inflation Calculator, https://www.bankofengland.co.uk/monetary-policy/inflation/inflation-calculator?number.Sections%5B0%5D.Fields%5B0%5D.Value=1570&current_year=5.694865713522l8&comparison_year=132.2. However, President Donald Trump's Inauguration cost about $200m in 2017; "How much does an inauguration cost? And who pays for what?", *Washington Post*, 13 December 2016.

and reused from 1937 (when they were worn by King George VI),[43] while the robe of state for Queen Camilla was made in 1953 for Queen Elizabeth II. Only the Queen's purple robe of estate was new, commissioned from Ede and Ravenscroft and embroidered by the Royal School of Needlework.[44]

Likewise, the chairs of estate were made in 1953 for Queen Elizabeth II and the Duke of Edinburgh, and used by the former at her coronation—no chair of estate was actually used by the Duke. The throne chairs, for the enthroning and homage, dated from 1937; the coronation chair, of course, was the ultimate example of economy and sustainability, having been made in 1296 and in use since 1308. In addition, 100 congregation chairs were made, to be sold for charity after the service.[45] Lastly, the *colobium sindonis* dated from the coronation of King Charles III's grandfather, George VI, in 1937, as did the belt or girdle, and coronation gauntlet or glove. The latter still bore the coat of arms of the Dukes of Newcastle, who, as Lords of the Manor of Worksop, once enjoyed the privilege and duty of presenting the glove.[46]

The more valuable, and sacred pieces, the imperial mantle or robe royal dated from the coronation of George IV in 1821, and the *supertunica* from the coronation of George V in 1911.[47] The scarlet surcoat worn before the service, with the scarlet robe of state, and the purple surcoat worn with the purple robe of estate, were new, but were inspired by those worn by George VI in 1937.[48] The King did not wear his Cap

[43] The velvet was conserved by the Royal School of Needlework, and the lining and gold lace were conserved by Savile Row tailors, Ede and Ravenscroft; Magsino, Isiah, "King Charles's Coronation Attire, Explained", Town & Country, 6 May 2023.

[44] Press Release, "A first glimpse at Their Majesties' Coronation robes", The Royal Family, 29 April 2023.

[45] Press Release, "Historic chairs to be reused for the Coronation", The Royal Family, 1 May 2023.

[46] The words accompanying the presentation of the Glove were entirely new in 2023, since there have not previously been any words to accompany the presentation of the Coronation Glove.

[47] Press Release, "Historic Coronation Vestments from the Royal Collection will be reused by His Majesty The King for the Coronation Service at Westminster Abbey", The Royal Family, 1 May 2023.

[48] They were created especially for the occasion by Ede and Ravenscroft, and the purple tunic is made of satin and trimmed with gold artillery lace. These were worn with the King's Royal Naval Trousers, which are regularly worn by His Majesty as part of his Royal

of Maintenance prior to the crowning, though it was present during the coronation.[49]

For the other pieces, only the stole was new,[50] as was the Sovereign's anointing screen. The latter also conveyed a new message; unlike at the coronation of Elizabeth II, when the canopy was borne by four knights of the Order of the Garter, in 2023 the new screen, which was a gift from the City of London Corporation and City Livery Companies, was borne by soldiers of the Household Division (which had Freedom of the City of London).[51] The screen's imagery was of the King as servant of the 56 Commonwealth countries.

The message conveyed by the replacement of the homage of the peers with the homage of the people, the introduction of a new King's Prayer, the welcome to the Abbey by a young person[52]—and the king's response, and the message from the non-Christian faith leaders, all contributed to a clear theme of reciprocity, inclusivity, and proximity, whilst being fully faithful to tradition, and especially a Christian conception of servant-kingship.

The best surety that the coronation will survive in a suitable traditional form is to emphasise that, despite strict legal principle, a coronation—and one with some splendour—is constitutionally, politically and socially necessary, as it is necessary to ensure that the ceremony accords with tradition yet speaks to the age. Every king and queen regnant has been crowned for over a thousand years (except the handful who died, were

Navy full ceremonial uniform. A cream silk overshirt, worn throughout the service, was created especially for the occasion by Turnbull & Asser, the design being inspired by similar items worn by King George V and King George VI at their Coronations. The overshirt's collar and cuffs feature embroidered oak leaves and acorns; "Coronation outfits worn by Their Majesties King Charles III and Queen Camilla to go on display at Buckingham Palace", Royal Collection Trust, 19 May 2023.

[49] It was made especially by Philip Treacy, milliner of London; "King Charles coronation: Irish hat designer Philip Treacy says role in ceremony was 'greatest honour' of his career", www.independent.ie, 8 May 2023.

[50] *The Authorised Liturgy for the Coronation Rite of His Majesty King Charles III For use on Saturday 6th May 2023, 11:00am at Westminster Abbey* (2023).

[51] Press Release, "The Anointing Screen", The Royal Family, 29 April 2023.

[52] After the entry into the Abbey to Parry's "I was Glad", a paraphrase setting of Psalm 122, the use of which is of very ancient precedent; *The Authorised Liturgy for the Coronation Rite of His Majesty King Charles III For use on Saturday 6th May 2023, 11:00am at Westminster Abbey* (2023).

deposed, or abdicated too soon to be crowned[53]). The precedent of a thousand years of history does not necessarily mean that coronations should continue in their traditional form. They have been discontinued in some European countries, but none of these had the same long tradition of coronations, nor the same constitutional arrangements as the United Kingdom. To abandon, or radically change (perhaps in the interests of "slimming it down", "modernising", or removing "archaic and feudal elements") a constitutional ritual and solemnity of such significance would be constitutionally and politically unwise.

The coronation publicly declares, as no other ceremony could, the essential nature of monarchy—the lifelong dedication of an individual to the service of the nation, in the sight of God and people, and the offering of fealty and loyalty in return for the royal undertaking to serve the kingdom in accordance with ancient tradition. This is (in the form used in 1953) to

> solemnly promise and swear to govern the people of this United Kingdom of Great Britain and Northern Ireland and the other realms and territories, according to the statutes in Parliament agreed on, and the respective laws and customs of the same.

Many elements in the coronation help us understand what it means to be the Sovereign, and make it abundantly clear that any authority the King has is derived from God, and that in all things he is His servant. That is not to diminish the role of the people, for though the Sovereign is the elect of God, he is approved by the people. There is also no doubt that Queen Elizabeth II, for example, took her coronation oath seriously.

Doubtless there will be changes in the next coronation, as there always have been. The constitutional position of the realms of the King mean that separate coronations could (or perhaps should) be held in each realm. But this is probably unrealistic—and Scottish coronations ended in 1651 for similar practical reasons. What is more likely is an increase in the involvement of Commonwealth representatives, and probably multi-faith representatives.

It would be more than a pity if any future king were saddled with a "half-crownation", as William IV was, or the "Penny Crowning" of

[53] Edward V (1483) and Edward VIII (1936)—we may perhaps disregard Lady Jane Grey (1553) as she was queen for so brief a period.

Queen Victoria.[54] It would be a national tragedy and shame if it were abolished altogether. A coronation is something which ought to be done well. Over one thousand years of experience of coronations at Westminster Abbey must count for something, even if for ministers and bureaucrats only as a tourist attraction. An appreciation of history, and a deeper understanding of the monarchy and of the kingdoms, suggests that a coronation is a crucial time of re-dedication, and a cathartic exercise in national celebration. The coronation has the function of confirming, affirming and setting aside the Sovereign for the high task they are assigned.

While some may question the necessity of a coronation for a new monarch, it is suggested that it is indeed necessary, as well as beneficial. The coronation is not just legally required or politically expedient, but rather it is a combination of all three aspects woven into the evolution of the kingship and the kingdom over more than a thousand years. Thus, the coronation must adhere to a specific form and structure that has evolved over time. To significantly alter this would risk unforeseeable and potentially significant consequences for the country's fabric and unity. This is why the coronation, as opposed to a mere inauguration, is an integral part of the constitution and has endured for so long.

The many layers of the coronation may be shown in the tribute paid to Queen Elizabeth II by Lord Williams of Oystermouth, former Archbishop of Canterbury

> The coronation service has this much in common with ordination: It singles out someone to occupy a position whose point is to manifest something about the whole community's life—and to do so first by just being there, holding the ideals and aspirations of the community (and also carrying its projections). It is the rationale of the theological tradition that tells us that priesthood is not about an individual's successful or meritorious performance but about fidelity to a position, for the sake of the community's peace and well being. It does not exempt priests from censure and judgement where needed, nor does it confer on them an unchallengeable right to win every argument. That is not the point. They are there so that we can gather around something other than our preferences and

[54] "The coronation and the commonwealth" (1951) 42 The Round Table 165–168, 297–304.

anxieties and prejudices; around a gift of "kinship" in which we can stand together before God.[55]

[55] Williams of Oystermouth, Lord, "Queen Elizabeth, Servant of God", *First Things*, 9 December 2022.

Bibliography

Abels, Richard, "The Council of Whitby: A Study in Early Anglo-Saxon Politics" (1984) 23(1) Journal of British Studies 1–25

Abels, Richard, "Royal Succession and the Growth of Political Stability in Ninth-Century Wessex" (2002) 12 The Haskins Society Journal: Studies in Mediæval History 83–97

Adams, G. B., *The Constitutional History of England* (H. Holt, New York, 1922)

Adomnán of Iona, *The life of St Columba* ed. Richard Sharpe (trans.) (Penguin Classics, London, 1995)

Al Namlah, S., "Political legitimacy in Libya since 1969" (1992) unpublished PhD thesis Syracuse University

Alaichamy, Martin, "An Incarnational Christology of Kingship: The Theological Meaning of Carolingian Royal Unction (751–877)" (2022) Trinity International University PhD dissertation

Alkire, Ti and Rosen, Carol, *Romance Languages: A Historical Introduction* (Cambridge University Press, Cambridge, 2010)

Allen, Sir Carleton, *The Queen's Peace* (Stevens & Sons Ltd, London, 1953)

Allen, James P. *Genesis in Egypt: The Philosophy of Ancient Egyptian Creation Accounts* (Yale Egyptological Study, New Haven, 1988)

Allmand, Christopher T., "The Coronations of Henry VI" (30 April 1982) 32(5) History Today 28–33

Almgren, Bertil, "Helmets, crowns and warriors' dress – from the Roman emperors to the chieftains of Uppland", in Jan Peder Lamm, and Hans-Åke Nordstrom (eds.), *Vendel Period Studies: transactions of the Boat-Grave Symposium in Stockholm, February 2–3, 1981.* Studies – The Museum of

N. Cox, *The Political, Legal, and Theological Functions of the Ceremony in the British Tradition*,
https://doi.org/10.1007/978-3-031-88960-8

National Antiquities, Stockholm. Vol. 2 (Statens Historiska Museum, Stockholm, 1983), pp. 11–16

Alsop, J. D., *The Tudor Coronation Service: A Reformed Liturgy* (Cambridge University Press, Cambridge, 1981)

Anderson, Graham, *King Arthur in Antiquity* (Routledge, London, 2004)

Anon, "Note: The nation's memory: 1838–1988, 1189–1989" (1989) 10(1) The Journal of Legal History 110–113

Anon, *Some Considerations Touching Succession And Allegiance* (Richard Chiswell, London, 1689)

Anson, Sir William, *The Law and Custom of the Constitution* ed. A. B. Keith (5th edn. 1922, Clarendon Press, Oxford, 3rd edn., 1907)

Appendix, Accession Proclamation 1952 (HMSO, London, 1952)

Aquilina, Ivan D., *The Eucharistic Understanding of John Cosin and His Contribution to the 1662 Book Of Common Prayer* (University of Leeds, Leeds, 2002)

Aquinas, St Thomas, *On Kingship*, transl. G. B. Phelan and I. T. Eschmann (Pontifical Institute of Mediæval Studies, Toronto, 1949)

Aquinas, St Thomas, *Summa Theologiae* ed. J. Gilbey et al (Blackfriars, McGaw-Hill, Eyre & Spottiswoode, London, 1964–80), 61 vols

Aquinas, St Thomas, *Summa Theologica* ed. By Fathers of the English Dominican Province (Burns, Oates & Washbourne, London, 1913–42)

Arblaster, Paul, *A History of the Low Countries* (Palgrave Essential Histories, London, 2005)

Arendt, Hannah, "What was authority" in Carl Friedrich (ed.), *Authority* (Harvard University Press, Cambridge, Massachusetts, 1958), pp. 81–112

Aristotle, *Ethica Nicomachea* ed. Gauthier, R. A. (E. J. Brill de Brouwer, Leiden, 1972–74)

Ashcraft, Richard, "The Two Treatises and the Exclusion Crisis", in J. G. A. Pocock, and Ashcraft, Richard (eds.), *John Locke* (William Andrews Clark Memorial Library, University of California, Los Angeles, 1980), pp. 25–114

Assmann, Jan, "Pharaonic Kingship and Its Biblical Deconstruction", in A. Azfar Moin and Alan Strathern (eds.), *Sacred Kingship in World History: Between Immanence and Transcendence* (Columbia University Press, New York, 2022), pp. 94–110

Attenborough, F. L. (ed. & trans.), *Laws of the earliest English kings* (Cambridge University Press, Cambridge, 1922)

Audronis, Domantas, "Un-Roman Empires, post-Roman worlds: Rome and imperial ideology in a comparative European context, 800–1000" (2021) The University of Manchester PhD thesis

Augustine of Hippo, St, *The City of God*. Translation by William Babcock, notes by Boniface Ramsey (New City Press, Hyde Park, NY, 2012)

Austin, Gerard, *Anointing with the Spirit: the rite of confirmation: the use of oil and chrism*. Vol. 2. (Liturgical Press, Collegeville, 1985)

The Authorised Liturgy for the Coronation Rite of His Majesty King Charles III For use on Saturday 6th May 2023, 11:00am at Westminster Abbey (The Archbishop of Canterbury, London, 29 April 2023)

Avery, William T., "The 'Adoratio Purpurae' and the Importance of the Imperial Purple in the Fourth Century of the Christian Era" (1940) 17 Memoirs of the American Academy in Rome 66–80

Axton, Marie, *The Queen's Two Bodies; Drama and the Elizabethan Succession* (Royal Historical Society, London, 1977)

Azfar Moin, A., and Alan Strathern, *Sacred Kingship in World History: Between Immanence and Transcendence* (Columbia University Press, New York, 2022)

Bagehot, Walter, *The English Constitution* (Cambridge University Press, Cambridge, 2001)

Bagehot, Walter, "The English Constitution", in Norman St John-Stevas (ed.), *The Collected Works of Walter Bagehot* (The Economist, London, 1974), vol. 5

Baker, Helen, "Monarchy discredited? Reactions to the Khodynka coronation catastrophe of 1896" (2003) 16(1) Revolutionary Russia 1–46

Baker, Sir John, "English Law and the Renaissance" (1985) Cambridge Law Journal 46–61

Barbero, A., Loring, M. I., "The Catholic Visigothic Kingdom", in Paul Fouracre (ed.), *The New Cambridge Mediæval History I: c.500–c.700* (Cambridge University Press, Cambridge, 2005), pp. 346–370

Bardill, Jonathan, *Constantine, Divine Emperor of the Christian Golden Age* (Cambridge University Press, Cambridge, 2012)

Barker, Brian, *When the Queen was crowned* (Routledge and Kegan Paul, London, 1976)

Barker, Rodney, *Political Legitimacy and the State* (Clarendon Press, Oxford, 1990)

Barlow, Frank, *Edward the Confessor* (University of California Press, California, 1970)

Barlow, Frank, *The Feudal Kingdom of England, 1042–1216* (2nd edn., Longmans, London, 1961, first published 1955)

Barlow, Frank, *The Godwins: The Rise and Fall of a Noble Dynasty* (Routledge, Abingdon, 2013)

Barlow, Frank, *Thomas Becket* (University of California Press, Berkeley, 1986)

Barnard, T. C., *The English Republic 1649–1660* (Routledge, London, 2014)

Barrow, G. W. S., *Feudal Britain: The Completion of the Mediæval Kingdoms, 1066–1314* (Edward Arnold, London, 1956)

Bauer, Susan Wise, *The History of the Renaissance World: From the Rediscovery of Aristotle to the Conquest of Constantinople* (W. W. Norton & Company, New York, 2013)

Beard, Mary, *The Roman Triumph* (The Belknap Press of Harvard University Press, Cambridge, Mass., and London, 2007)

Beard, Mary, J. A., North, and S. R. F. Price, *Religions of Rome: A History* (Cambridge University Press, Cambridge, 1998)

Beck, Hans, Antonio Duplá, Martin Jehne et al. (eds.), *Consuls and Res Publica: Holding High Office in the Roman Republic* (Cambridge University Press, Cambridge, 2011)

Beck, William, *The Draper's Dictionary* (The Warehousemen and Drapers Journal, London, 1886)

Bercuson, David and Cooper, Barry, "From Constitutional Monarchy to Quasi Republic" in Janet Ajzenstat (ed), *Canadian Constitutionalism, 1791–1991* (Canadian Study of Parliament Group, Ottawa, 1992), pp. 15–36

Berger, Carl (ed.), *Imperialism and Nationalism, 1884–1914: A Conflict in Canadian Thought* (Copp Clark, Toronto, 1969)

Bierstedt, Robert, "Legitimacy", in J. Gould, and W. Kolb (eds.), *A Dictionary of the Social Sciences* (The Free Press of Glencoe, New York, 1964), p. 186

Bingham, Tom, *The Rule of Law* (Penguin Books, London, 2011)

Birch, A., *The British System of Government* (9th ed, Routledge, London, 1993)

Birley, Anthony R., *The Roman Government of Britain* (Oxford University Press, London, 2005)

Birnbaum, Norman, "Monarchs and Sociologists: A reply to Professor Shils and Mr. Young" (1955) 3(1) Sociological Review 5–13

Bishop, Olga B., *Canadian Official Publications: Guides to Official Publications* (Elsevier, New York, 2016)

Blackstone, Sir William, *Commentaries on the Laws of England* ed. E. Christian (reprint by Garland Publishing, New York, 1978, 4th edn., Clarendon Press, Oxford, 1770, 1st published 1765)

Blackstone, Sir William, *Commentaries on the Laws of England* (1st ed., 1765–1769; facsimile edition, University of Chicago Press, Chicago, 1979)

Blair, Claude (ed.), *The Crown Jewels: The History of the Coronation Regalia in the Jewel House of the Tower of London* (The Stationery Office, London, 1998), vol 1

Blair, John P., *The Church in Anglo-Saxon Society* (Oxford University Press, Oxford, 2005)

Bloch, Marc, *Feudal Society* (Routledge & Kegan Paul, London, 1965)

Blumenthal, Uta-Renate, *The Investiture Controversy: Church and Monarchy from the Ninth to the Twelfth Century* (University of Pennsylvania Press, Philadelphia, 1988)

Bodley, J. E. C., The *Coronation of Edward the Seventh: a chapter of European and Imperial History* (Methuen & Co, London, 1903)

Bogdanor, Sir Vernon, *The Monarchy and the Constitution* (The Clarendon Press, Oxford, 1995)

Bollard, J. K., *Arthur in the Early Welsh Tradition* in *The Romance of Arthur: An Anthology of Mediæval Texts in Translation* (Routledge, London, 1994)

Bond, Susan E. "Anointing the King: Hallowing Hope for the World in the English Coronation" (2019) Georgetown University DLS thesis

Bonney, N., "The Evolution and Contemporary Relevance of the Accession and Coronation Oaths of the United Kingdom" (2011) 13 The British Journal of Politics & International Relations 603–618

The Book of Common Prayer ... The Book of 1662 with additions and deviations approved in 1927 (Oxford University Press, London, 1928)

Bozoky, Edina, "The Sanctity and Canonisation of Edward the Confessor", in Richard Mortimer (ed.), *Edward the Confessor: the man and the legend* (Boydell Press, Woodbridge, 2009)

Bracton, Henry de, *De legibus et consuetudinibus Angliæ* (4 vols., ed. G. E. Woodbine, transl. S. E. Thorne (Publications of the Selden Society, London, 1968–77)

Bradbury, Jim, *Stephen and Matilda: the Civil War of 1139–53* (The History Press, Stroud, 2009)

Bradley, Ian, *God Save the King: The Sacred Nature of the Monarchy* (Darton, Longman & Todd, London, 2023)

Bradley, Ian, *God Save the Queen: The Spiritual Heart of the Monarchy* (Continuum, London, 2012)

Bradshaw, Paul, "On Revising the Coronation Service" (1993) 96(770) Theology 130–137

Bradshaw, Paul, *The Search for the Origins of Christian Worship* (2nd ed., SPCK, London, 2002)

Breeze, David, and Graeme Munro, *The Stone of Destiny: Symbol of Nationhood* (Historic Scotland, Edinburgh, 1997)

Brendon, Piers, *Edward VIII: The Uncrowned King* (Allen Lane, London, 2016)

Brent, A., *The imperial cult and the development of church order: concepts and images of authority in paganism and early Christianity before the Age of Cyprian* (Brill Publishers, Leiden, 1999)

Brightman, F. E., "Byzantine Imperial Coronations" (1901) II(7)(Old Series) Journal of Theological Studies 359–392

Broadberry, Stephen et al., "English mediæval population: Reconciling time series and sectional evidence" (2010)

Brogan, Stephen, *The Royal Touch in Early Modern England* (Boydell & Brewer, Martlesham, 2015)

Brook Cowen, Penelope, "Neo Liberalism" in Raymond Miller (ed.), *New Zealand Politics in Transition* (Oxford University Press, Auckland, 1997), p. 341–349

Brooke-Little, John, *Royal Ceremonies of State* (Littlehampton Book Services Ltd, London, 1980)

Brookfield, F. M., "Some aspects of the Necessity Principle in Constitutional Law" (1972) University of Oxford DPhil thesis

Brookfield, F. M., *Waitangi and Indigenous Rights: Revolution, Law and Legitimation* (University of Auckland Press, Auckland, 1999)

Broun, Dauvit, "Aedán mac Gabráin", in Michael Lynch (ed.), *The Oxford Companion to Scottish History* (Oxford University Press, Oxford, 2001), p. 5

Brown, R. Allen, *The Normans* (Boydell & Brewer, Woodbridge, 1994)

Bruce, F. F., "Herod Antipas, Tetrarch of Galilee and Peraea" (1963–65) 5 Annual of Leeds University Oriental Society 6–23

Bruce-Mitford, Rupert, *The Sutton Hoo Ship-Burial, Volume 2: Arms, Armour and Regalia* (British Museum Publications, London, 1978)

Brydon, George, *Religious Life of Virginia in the Seventeenth Century* (Virginia 350th Anniversary Celebration Corporation, Williamsburg, 1957)

Buccellatin, Graziella and Holly Snapp (eds.), *The Iron Crown and Imperial Europe* (Mondadori, Milan, 1995)

Butcher, Catherine and Mark Greene, *The Servant Queen and the King she serves* (The Bible Society, London, 2016)

Byrne, Francis John, *Irish Kings and High-Kings* (Batsford, London, 1973)

Campbell, Alistair; Keynes, Simon, *Encomium Emmae Reginae* (Cambridge University Press, Cambridge, 1998)

Campbell, I. C., *Classical Tongan kingship* (Atenisi University, Nuku'alofa, 1989)

Campbell, James, *Essays in Anglo-Saxon History* (Hambledon Press, London, 1986)

Cannadine, Sir David (ed.), *Westminster Abbey: A Church in History* (The Paul Mellon Centre for Studies in British Art, in association with the Dean and Chapter of the Collegiate Church of St. Peter Westminster, New Haven, 2019)

Canning, J. P., "Law, sovereignty and corporation theory, 1300–1450", in J. H. Burns (ed.), *The Cambridge History of Mediæval Political Thought c.350-c.1450* (Cambridge University Press, Cambridge, 1988), pp. 454–476

Cannon, John and Ralph Griffiths, *The Oxford Illustrated History of the British Monarchy* (Oxford University Press, Oxford, 1988)

Cantor, Norman F., *The Civilization of the Middle Ages: A Completely Revised and Expanded Edition of Mediæval History, the Life and Death of a Civilization* (HarperCollins, New York, 1993)

Carile, Maria Cristina, "Globus cruciger", in Dale C. Allison, Jr, Christine Helmer, Volker Leppin, Choon-Leong Seow, Hermann Spieckermann, Barry

Dov Walfish, and Eric J. Ziolkowski (eds.), *Encyclopedia of the Bible and Its Reception*, Vol. 10, Genocide – Hakkoz (De Gruyter, Berlin, 2015)

Carpenter, David A., *The Minority of Henry III* (University of California Press, Berkeley and Los Angeles, 1990)

Carr, Wesley, "This Intimate Ritual: The Coronation Service" (2002) 4(1) Political Theology 11–24

Carr, Wesley, *Westminster Abbey* (Jarrold, Norwich, 1999)

Cartwright, Mark, "The Coronation Ceremony of the British Monarchy", *World History Encyclopedia*. Last modified March 30, 2020. https://www.worldhistory.org/article/1533/the-coronation-ceremony-of-the-british-monarchy/

Casey, P. J., *Carausius and Allectus: The British Usurpers* (Repr. ed., Taylor & Francis, London, 1994)

Catto, Bonnie A., "Venus and Natura in Lucretius: "De Rerum Natura" 1.1-23 and 2.167-74" (1988) 84(2) The Classical Journal 97–104

Chadwick, Owen, *The Reformation* (Harmondsworth: Penguin, 1968)

Charanis, Peter, "Coronation and its constitutional significance in the later Roman empire" (1940) 15 Byzantion 49–66

Charles I, *Eikon Basilike (The Portraiture of His Sacred Majesty in His Solitudes and Sufferings)* ed. Phillip Knachel (Cornell University Press, Ithaca, New York, 1966)

Charles-Edwards, T. M., *Wales and the Britons, 350–1064* (Oxford University Press, Oxford, 2012)

Cheshire, G. C., *Modern Law of Real Property* ed. E. H. Burn (13th edn., Butterworths, London, 1982)

Chibnall, Marjorie, *Anglo-Norman England 1066–1166* (Basil Blackwell, Oxford, 1986)

Chitty, Joseph, *Treatise on the law of the prerogatives of the Crown and the relative duties and rights of the Subject* (Gregg, London, 1969)

Cho, Youn-Yung and Sook-In Yang, "A Study on Queen Elizabeth II's Dress: Focusing on the Dress and Role Enactment" (2010) 13(1) The International Journal of Costume Culture 12–22

Chrimes, S. B., *Lancastrians, Yorkists and Henry VII* (2nd edn., Macmillan & Co. Ltd, London, 1966, first published 1964)

Chrimes, S. B., C. D. Ross, and R. A. Griffiths (eds.), *Fifteenth-century England 1399–1509* (Manchester University Press, Manchester, 1972)

Churchill, Randolph, *The Story of the Coronation* (Derek Verschoyle, London, 1953)

Clanchy, M. T., *England and its Rulers, 1066–1272: Foreign Lordship and National Identity* (Fontana, London, 1983)

Claudius Ptolemaeus, *The Geography of Claudius Ptolemaeus*, trans. by E.L. Stevenson (Dover, New York, 1991)

Cobbett, William (ed.), *The parliamentary History of England* (Bagshaw, London, 1806–20)

Coke, Sir Edward, *Coke upon Littleton* ("First Institutes") (reprint by Garland Publishing, New York, 1979 of 19th edn., 1832)

Coke, Sir Edward, *The First Part of the Institutes of the Laws of England, or, A Commentary on Littleton* ed. F. Hargrave and C. Butler (19th ed., J. & W.T. Clarke, London, 1832, first published 1628)

Coldstream, Nicola, "The Abbey and Palace as Theatres for Coronation", in Warwick Rodwell, and Tim Tatton-Brown (eds.), *Westminster Part I: The Art, Architecture and Archaeology of the Royal Abbey* (Routledge, London, 2015)

Colebrooke, Thomas Edward, *On Imperial and Other Titles* (Trübner & Co., London, 1877)

Colgrave, Bertram and Mynors, R. A. B. (eds.), *Bede's Ecclesiastical History of the English People* (Clarendon Press, Oxford, 1969)

Collins, John N., "Ordained and Other Ministries: Making a Difference" (2006) 3(1) Ecclesiology 11–32

Collins, Randall, *Weberian Sociological Theory* (Cambridge University Press, Cambridge, 1986)

Collins, Roger, *Charlemagne* (University of Toronto Press, Toronto, 1998)

Collins, Roger, *Early Mediæval Spain; Unity in Diversity, 400–1000* (2nd edn., St Martin's Press, New York, 1995)

Comber, Thomas, *Religion and Loyalty Supporting each other* (Robert Clavel, London, 1681)

Conley, Thomas, "The Speech of Ibrahim at the Coronation of Maximilian II" (2002) 20(3) Rhetorica 263–273

Cooney, Kara, *When Women Ruled the World: Six Queens of Egypt* (National Geographic, Washington, DC, 2018)

Corcoran, Simon, "Before Constantine", in Noel Lenski (ed.), *The Cambridge Companion to the Age of Constantine* (Cambridge University Press, Cambridge, 2006), pp. 35–58

Coriden, James, *An Introduction to Canon Law* (Paulist Press, New York, 1991)

Cornwall, Mark, *Last Years of Austria-Hungary: A Multi-National Experiment in Early Twentieth-Century Europe* (2nd ed., University of Exeter Press, Exeter, 2002)

"The coronation and the commonwealth" (1951) 42 The Round Table 165–168, 297–304

Coronation of Her Majesty Queen Elizabeth the Second: minutes of the proceedings of the Court of claims 1952 (Crown Office, London, 1952)

The Coronation of Their Majesties King Charles III and Queen Camilla Saturday, 6th May, 2023 at 11.00 a.m. (Dean and Chapter of Westminster, London, 2023)

Courtney, Alexander, *James VI, Britannic Prince: King of Scots and Elizabeth's Heir, 1566–1603* (Routledge, London, 2024)

Cox, Noel, "The British Peerage: The Legal Standing of the Peerage and Baronetage in the Overseas Realms of the Crown with Particular Reference to New Zealand" (1997) 17(4) New Zealand Universities Law Review 379–401

Cox, Noel, *Church and State in the Post-Colonial Era: The Anglican Church and the Constitution in New Zealand* (Polygraphia, Auckland, 2008)

Cox, Noel, *Constitutional paradigms and the stability of states* (Ashgate, Aldershot, 2012)

Cox, Noel, "The Coronation Robes of the Sovereign" (1999) 5(1) Arma 271–280

Cox, Noel, "The Coronets of Members of the Royal Family and of the Peerage" (2000) 22 The Double Tressure, the Journal of The Heraldry Society of Scotland 8–13

Cox, Noel, "The Law of Succession to the Crown in New Zealand" (1999) 7 Waikato Law Review 49–72

Cox, Noel, *Priest of the Church or priest of a church: the ecclesiology of ordained local ministry* (Rowman & Littlefield, London, 2021)

Cox, Noel, "The rights of peerage" (2007) 5 HPA Newsletter: Journal of the Hereditary Peerage Association 1–3

Cox, Noel, *The Royal Prerogative and Constitutional Law: A search for the quintessence of executive power* (Routledge, London, 2021)

Cox, Noel, "Tudor sumptuary laws and academical dress: An Act against wearing of Costly Apparel 1509 and An Act for Reformation of Excess in Apparel 1533" (2006) 6 Transactions of the Burgon Society 15–43

Craig, Sir Thomas, *The Right of Succession to the Kingdom of England* (M. Bennet, London, 1703, first published 1602)

Crawford, Hariet, *The Sumerian World* (Routledge, London, 2013)

Croft, Pauline, *King James* (Palgrave Macmillan, Basingstoke and New York, 2003)

Croke, Brian, *Roman Emperors in Context: Theodosius to Justinian* (Routledge, London, 2021)

Cross, Rupert and J. W. Harris, *Precedent in English Law* (4th ed., Oxford University Press, Oxford, 1991)

Crouch, Jace T., "Isidore of Seville and the Evolution of Kingship in Visigothic Spain" (1994) 4 Mediterranean Studies 9–26

Cubitt, Catherine, *Anglo-Saxon church councils c.650-c.850* (Leicester University Press, London, 1995)

Cullinan, Margaret M., "*Imperator Hispaniae*: The Genesis of 'Spain'" (1975) City University of New York PhD dissertation

Daalder, Hans, "The monarchy in a parliamentary system" (1991) 1 Res Publica, Tijdschrift voor Politologie, Revue de Science Politique, Belgian Journal of Political Science 70–81

Dagron, Gilbert, *Emperor and Priest: the Imperial Office in Byzantium* (Cambridge University Press, Cambridge, 2003)

Dale, Johanna, "Christus Regnat: Inauguration and images of kingship in England, France and the Empire c.1050-c.1250" (2013) University of East Anglia PhD thesis

Darwish, Ibrahim M., Abdulaziz A. Alzoubi, and Noora Q. Abu Ain, "The Death of Monarchs: Front-Page Reporting of Queen Elizabeth II's Death" (2024) 14(7) Theory and Practice in Language Studies 2046–2052

D'Auria, Sue, *Offerings to the Discerning Eye: An Egyptological Medley in Honor of Jack A. Josephson* (Brill, Leiden, 2010)

Davenport, Cyril, *The English Regalia* (T. & C. Constable, Edinburgh, 1897)

Davies, J. L. and Driver, T. G., "Abermagwr (SN 6688 7416)" (2011) 42 Britannia 320–321

Davies, J. L. and Driver, T. G., "Abermagwr Romano-British villa, Ceredigion, mid Wales: Interim report on its discovery and excavation" (2012) 160 Archaeologia Cambrensis (2011) 39–49

Davies, J. L. and Driver, T. G., "The First Roman Villa in Ceredigion: A summary report on the discovery and excavation of a late Romano-British villa at Abermagwr, near Aberystwyth, 2010–11" (2012) XVI(3) Ceredigion (2011) 1–15

Davies, John, *A History of Wales* (Penguin Group, London, 1993)

Davies, Wendy, *Patterns of Power in Early Wales* (Oxford University Press, Oxford, 1989)

Davies, Wendy, *Wales in the Early Middle Ages* (Leicester University Press, Leicester, 1982)

Day, John (ed.), *King and Messiah in Israel and the Ancient Near East* (Sheffield Academic Press, Sheffield, 2013)

Day, John (ed.), "The Canaanite inheritance of the Israeli monarchy", in John Day (ed.), *King and Messiah in Israel and the Ancient Near East* (Sheffield Academic Press, Sheffield, 2013), pp. 72–90

De Hamel, Christopher, *Meetings with Remarkable Manuscripts* (Allen Lane, London, 2016)

de la Bédoyère, Guy, *Praetorian: The Rise and Fall of Rome's Imperial Bodyguard* (Yale University Press, Yale, 2017)

Deshman, R. E., "The Leofric Missal and Tenth-Century English Art" (1977) 6 Anglo-Saxon England 145–173

Devlin, Patrick, *The Enforcement of Morals* (Oxford University Press, London, 1959)

Dicey, Albert V., *Introduction to the Study of the Law of the Constitution, with introduction & appendix by E. C. S. Wade* (10th ed., Macmillan, London, 1959)

Dillon, Janette, "The Monarch as Represented in the Ceremony of Coronation", in *Representations of Elizabeth I in Early Modern Culture* (Palgrave Macmillan UK, London, 2011), pp. 125–139

Ditmas, E. M. R., "The Curtana or Sword of Mercy" (1966) 29(1) Journal of the British Archaeological Association 122–133

Dodson, Aidan, *Amarna Sunrise: Egypt from the Golden Age to Age of Heresy* (1st ed., The American University in Cairo Press, Cairo, New York, 2014)

Doe, Norman, *Canon Law in the Anglican Communion* (Clarendon Press, Oxford, 1998)

Doleman, R. (pseudonym for Fr. Robert Parsons), *Conference About the Next Succession* (Antwerp, 1594)

Donaldson, Gordon, *The Scottish Reformation* (Cambridge University Press, Cambridge, 1960)

Dowding, Janka, "The prevalence of Christianity in Roman Britain to AD 410" (2005) 3 Hirundo: The McGill Journal of Classical Studies 53–63

Dower, John, *Embracing Defeat* (W. W. Norton & Co., New York, 1999)

Downer, L. J. (ed. & trans.), *Leges Henrici Primi* (Oxford University Press, London, 1972)

Dresser, Madge, "Britannia", in Raphael Samuel (ed.), *Patriotism: the making and unmaking of British national identity* (Routledge, London, 1989), vol. 3, pp. 26–49

Duffy, Seán (ed.), *Robert the Bruce's Irish wars: the invasions of Ireland 1306–1329* (Tempus, Stroud, 2002)

Dufraigne, P., *Aurelius Victor: Livre de Cesars* (Les Belles Lettres, Paris, 1975)

Dumville, D. N., "Sub-Roman Britain: History and Legend" (1977) 62(205) History 173–192

Dunand, Françoise, and Christiane Zivie-Coche, *Cosmonogies, Creation, and Time: Order and Disorder in Creation: Gods and Men in Egypt: 3000 BCE to 395 CE* (Cornell University Press, Ithaca, 2004)

Dunbabin, Jean, "Government", in J. H. Burns (ed.), *The Cambridge History of Mediæval Political Thought c.350-c.1450* (Cambridge University Press, Cambridge, 1988), pp. 477–519

Duncan, Sarah and Valerie Schutte (eds.), *The Birth of a Queen: Essays on the Quincentenary of Mary I* (Palgrave Macmillan, London, 2016)

Dunham, W. H. and C. T. Wood, "Right to Rule in England: Deposition and the Kingdom's Authority, 1327–1485" (1976) 81 American Historical Review 738–761

Dwyer, Philip, "'Citizen Emperor': Political Ritual, Popular Sovereignty and the Coronation of Napoleon I" (2015) 100(339) History 4057

Edie, Carolyn A., "The Public Face of Royal Ritual: Sermons, Medals, and Civic Ceremony in Later Stuart Coronations" (1990) The Huntington Library Quarterly 311–336

Elliot–t, Thomas, *The Christianity of Constantine the Great* (University of Scranton Press, Bronx, 1996)

Ellis, John Stephen, *Investiture: Royal Ceremony and National Identity in Wales, 1911–1969* (University of Wales Press, Cardiff, 2008)

English Historical Documents 1327–1485 ed. A. R. Myers (Eyre and Spottiswoode, London, 1969), pp. 416–417

Enright, M.J., *Iona, Tara, and Soissons: The Origin of the Royal Anointing Ritual* (Arbeiten zur Fruhmittelalterforschung, 17) (Walter de Gruyter, Berlin and New York, 1985)

Erickson, Kyle, "The early Seleucids, their gods and their coins" (2010) University of Exeter PhD thesis.

Erskine May, Sir Thomas, *Parliamentary Practice* ed. C.J. Boulton (21st ed., LexisNexis, London, 1989)

Falconer, David, *Bath Abbey* (Sutton Publishing, Stroud, 1999)

Fallow, Thomas Macall, "Coronation", in Hugh Chisholm (ed.) *Encyclopædia Britannica* (11th ed., Cambridge University Press, London, 1911), pp. 185–187

Farran, C. d'Olivier, "The Law of the Accession" (1953) 16 Modern Law Review 140–147

Favorito, Rebecca, "Constructing Legitimacy: Patrimony, Patronage, and Political Communication in the Coronation of Henry IV" (2016) The Ohio State University PhD thesis

Figgis, J. N., *The theory of the Divine Right of Kings* (2nd edn., Cambridge University Press, Cambridge, 1914)

Filmer, Robert, *Patriarcha and other writings*, Johann P. Sommerville (ed.) (Cambridge University Press, London, 1991)

Flechner, Roy, *The Hibernensis: Volume 2. Translation, Commentary, and Indexes* (The Catholic University of America Press, Washington, DC, 2019)

Fleming, Robin, *Britain after Rome: The Fall and Rise 400 to 1070* (Penguin Books, London, 2010)

Fleming, Robin, *Kings and Lords in Conquered England* (Cambridge University Press, Cambridge, 1991)

Foakes, Joanne, *The Position of Heads of State and Senior Officials in International Law* (Oxford University Press, Oxford, 2014)

Foot, Sarah, *Æthelstan: The First King of England* (Yale University Press, New Haven, 2011)

Fortescue, Sir John, *The Governance of England*, notes by Charles Plummer (reprint Hyperion Press, Westport, Connecticut, 1979, reprint of 1926 edn.)

Fortescue, Sir John, *In Praise of the laws of England (De Laudibus Legum Angliæ)* ed. S. B. Chrimes (Cambridge University Press, Cambridge, 1942)

Frere, Sheppard Sunderland, *Britannia: A History of Roman Britain* (3rd, revised ed., Routledge, London, 1987)

Ganshof, Francois, *Feudalism* trans. Philip Grierson (Longman, London, 1952, first published 1944)

Gardiner, Sir Alan, "The Coronation of King Ḥaremḥab" (1953) 39(1) The Journal of Egyptian Archaeology 13–31

Garipzanov, Ildar H., *The Symbolic Language of Authority in the Carolingian World (c.751–877)* (Brill, Leiden, 2008)

Garnett, George, "Coronation and propaganda: some implications of the Norman claim to the throne of England in 1066" (1986) 36 Transactions of the Royal Historical Society 91–116

Garnett, George, "William's coronation", in *The Norman Conquest: A Very Short Introduction* (Oxford University Press, Oxford, 2009), pp. 19–39

Garland, Lynda, *Byzantine Empresses: Women and Power in Byzantium, AD 527–1204* (Routledge, New York and London, 1999)

Garnett, George, "Long Live the Ancien Régime! The coronation of Charles III was dense with meaning. It's complicated; and easy to misunderstand" (2023) 73(8) History Today 106–109

Gasquet, Francis Aidan, *Edward VI and the Book of common prayer* (2nd ed., John Hodges, London, 1891)

Gauthier, Albert, *Roman Law and its Contribution to the Development of Canon Law* (2nd edn., Faculty of Canon Law, St Paul University, Ottawa, 1996)

Gerstenberger, Erhard S., *Psalms* (Wm. B. Eerdmans Publishing, Grand Rapids, 2001)

Ghazali, Ghazālī, *Book of Counsel for Kings* ("Nas'īat al-mulūk") transl. by F. R. C. Bagley (Oxford University Press, London and New York, 1964)

Gibbons, John R., *Splendour of the Coronation: A History of the Coronation of the British Monarch* (St Martin's Press, New York, 1996)

Giesey, Ralph E., "Inaugural Aspects of French Royal Ceremonials", in János M. Bak (ed.), *Coronations: Mediæval and Early Modern Monarchic Ritual* (University of California Press, Berkeley, 1990)

Gildas, "De Excidio et Conquestu Britanniae" in John Allen Giles (ed.), *The Works of Gildas and Nennius* (James Bohn, London, 1841)

Gillingham, John, *The Angevin Empire* (2nd ed., Hodder Arnold, London, 2001)

Glenn, H. Patrick, *Legal Traditions of the World* (5th edn., Oxford University Press, Oxford, 2014)

Gluckman, M., *Politics law and ritual in tribal society* (Oxford University Press, Oxford, 1977)

Goldfinch, Shaun, "The State", in Raymond Miller (ed.), *New Zealand Government and Politics* (Oxford University Press, Melbourne, 2001), pp. 511–520

Gomaà, Farouk, "Busiris (Abu Sir Bana)," in *Encyclopedia of the Archaeology of Ancient Egypt* (Routledge, London 1999), p. 207

Gosling, Lucinda, *Royal Coronations* (Shire, Oxford, 2013)

Grant, Linda and Richard Mortimer, *Westminster Abbey: The Cosmati Pavements* Courtauld Institute Research Papers, 3 (2002)

Greenhalgh, P. A. L., *The Year of the Four Emperors* (Weidenfeld and Nicolson, London, 1975)

Grierson, Philip, "The origins of the English sovereign and the symbolism of the closed crown" (28 January 1964) British Numismatic Society, available at http://www.britnumsoc.org/publications/Digital%20BNJ/pdfs/1963_BNJ_33_19.pdf

Gross, George William Cullen, "From London to Moscow coronations: perceptions of monarchy" trans. Ju. S. Frolova (2018) 2(26) Systems psychology and sociology 97–110

Gross, George William Cullen, "1651: The Last Coronation in Scotland — An Anomaly?" (2021) 26(3) The Court Historian 229–245

Grudem, Wayne A. (ed.), *Are Miraculous Gifts for Today?* (Zondervan, Grand Rapids, 1996)

Gunn, Steven and Linda Monckton, *Arthur Tudor, Prince of Wales: Life, Death and Commemoration* (Boydell Press, Woodbridge, 2009)

Hall, John, *The Grounds and Reasons of Monarchy*, prefixed to *The Political Works of James Harrington*, ed. J. G. A. Pocock (Cambridge University Press, New York, 1977)

Hall, John, *Queen Elizabeth and Her Church: Royal Service at Westminster Abbey* (Continuum, London, 2012)

Halsbury's Laws of England eds. F. H. Lawson and H. J. Davies (4th ed., Butterworths, London, 1974), vols 1, 8

Halstead, J. P., *The Second British Empire: Trade, Philanthropy, and Good Government, 1820–1890* (Greenwood Press, Westport, 1983)

Hani, Jean, *Sacred Royalty: From the Pharaoh to the Most Christian King* trans Gustavo Polit (Matheson Trust, London, 2011)

Harbin, George, *Hereditary Right to the Crown of England Asserted* (Richard Smith, London, 1713)

Harding, Alan, *Mediæval Law and the Foundations of the State* (Oxford University Press, Oxford, 2002)

Hare, Kent G., "Athelstan of England: Christian King and Hero" (Spring 2004) 7 The Heroic Age 1–12

Harlow, C., "Power from the People?", in Patrick McAuslan, and John F. McEldowney (eds.), *Law, Legitimacy and the Constitution Essays marking the Centenary of Dicey 's Law of the Constitution* (Clarendon Press, Oxford, 1985), pp. 62–74

Harris, B. V., "The 'Third Source' of Authority for Government Action" (1992) 109 Law Quarterly Review 626–651

Harris, Tim, *Revolution: The Great Crisis of the British Monarchy, 1685–1720* (Penguin, London, 2006)

Hassan, H., *In the House of Muhammad Ali: A Family Album, 1805–1952* (American University in Cairo Press, Cairo, 2000)

Haugaard, William P., "The Coronation of Elizabeth I" (1968) 19(2) The Journal of Ecclesiastical History 161–170

Haugaard, William P., *Elizabeth and the English reformation* (Cambridge University Press, London, 1968)

Hayward, Janine, "In search of a treaty partner" (1995) Victoria University of Wellington PhD thesis

Hazell, Robert, "A Constitutional Monarchy: Succession, Accession, and the Coronation" in Anand Menon and Robert Hazell (eds.), *The British Monarchy* (The Constitution Unit, University College London, London, 2023), pp. 9–13

Hazell, Robert, *Future Challenges for the monarchy* (Institute for Government, London, 2022)

Hazell, Robert and R. M. Morris, *Swearing in the New King: The Accession Declarations and Coronation Oaths* (The Constitution Unit, UCL, London, 2018)

Hazell, Robert and R. M. Morris, *Swearing in the New King: The Accession and Coronation swea*

Hazell, Robert and R. M. Morris (eds.), *The Role of Monarchy in Modern Democracy* (Hart Publishing, Oxford, 2022)

Heather, Peter, *The Fall of the Roman Empire: A New History of Rome and the Barbarians* (Oxford University Press, Oxford, 2005)

Helmholz, Richard, "Magna Carta and the *ius commune*" (1999) 66 University of Chicago Law Review 297–371

Herodotus, *The Histories*. translated by Pamela Mensch, with notes by James Romm (Hackett Publishing Co, Indianapolis, 2014)

Heslin, Anne, "The coronation of the Young King in 1170" (1965) 2 Studies in Church History 165–178

Hicks, Carola, *The Bayeux Tapestry: The Life Story of a Masterpiece* (Chatto & Windus, London, 2006)

Higham, Nicholas J., and Martin J. Ryan, *The Anglo-Saxon World* (Yale University Press, New Haven, 2013)

Higham, Nicholas J., *The convert kings: Power and religious affiliation in early Anglo-Saxon England* (Manchester University Press, Manchester, 1997)

Higham, Nicholas J., *King Arthur, Myth-Making and History* (Routledge, London, 2002)

Higham, Nicholas J., *Rome, Britain and the Anglo-Saxons* (B. A. Seaby, London, 1992)

Higley, John and Rhonda Case, "Australia: The Politics of Becoming a Republic" (July 2000) 11(3) Journal of Democracy 136–150

Hilliam, David, *Crown, Orb & Sceptre: The true stories of English Coronations* (Sutton, Stroud, 2001)

Hinchliff, Peter, "Frederick Temple, Randall Davidson and the Coronation of Edward VII" (1997) 48(1) Journal of Ecclesiastical History 71–99

Hoak, Dale, "The Coronations of Edward VI, Mary I, and Elizabeth I, and the Transformation of the Tudor Monarchy", in C. S. Knighton and Richard Mortimer (eds.), *Westminster Abbey Reformed 1540–1640* (Ashgate, Aldershot, 2003), pp. 115–151

Hobsbawn, Eric and Ranger, Terence, *The Invention of Tradition* (Cambridge University Press, Cambridge, 1983)

Hoffman, Erich, "Coronation and Coronation Ordines in Mediæval Scandinavia", in János M. Bak (ed.), *Coronations: Mediæval and Early Modern Monarchic Ritual* (University of California Press, Berkeley, 1990), pp. 125–143

Hohler, C., "Some Service Books of the Later Saxon Church", in D. Parsons (ed.), *Tenth-Century Studies* (Phillimore & Co, Chichester, 1975), pp. 60–83, 217–227

Holbrooke-Jones, Stanley, "The Triumph of Anglo-Catholicism Challenged" (2005) 119(2) Churchman 159–178

Holdsworth, Sir William S., *A History of English Law* (3rd ed., Methuen & Co, London, 1923)

Holt, Edgar, *The Carlist Wars in Spain* (Putnam, London, 1967)

Holtom, D. C., *Japanese Enthronement Ceremonies: With an Account of the Imperial Regalia* (Sophia University, Tokyo, 1972)

Honderich, Ted (ed.), *The Oxford Companion to Philosophy* (Oxford University Press, Oxford, 1995)

Hope, W. H. St John, "The King's Coronation Ornaments" (April 1901) 1 Ancestor 127–159

Hope, W. H. St John, "The King's Coronation Ornaments" (Jul 1902) 2 Ancestor 63–81

Hughes, Andrew, "Antiphons and Acclamations: The Politics of Music in the Coronation Service of Edward II, 1308" (Spring 1988) 6(2) The Journal of Musicology 150–168

Hughes, Andrew, "The Origins and Descent of the Fourth Recension of the English Coronation" (1990) Coronations: Medieval and early modern monarchic ritual 197–216

Huish, Robert, *7An Authentic History of the Coronation of George IV* (T. Kelly, London, 1821)

Huizinga, Johan, *Autumntide of the Middle Ages* (Leiden University Press, Leiden, 2020)

Huneycutt, L. L., *Matilda of Scotland: A Study in Mediæval Queenship* (Anglo-Norman studies. Boydell Press, Woodbridge, 2003)

Hunt, Alice, "All Forms Accustomed': Ritual, precedent and the past at the coronation of Charles II", in *Remembering the English Civil Wars* (Routledge, Abingdon, 2021), pp. 101–121

Hunt, Alice, "The Bright Star of the North: James I and his English Coronation", in M. Twycross, P. King, S. Carpenter, and G. Walker (eds.), *Mediæval English Theatre: 38 The Best Pairt of our Play. Essays presented to John J. McGavin* (Boydell & Brewer, Woodbridge, 2017), Part II, pp. 22–37

Hunt, Alice, "British Coronation: A History", Gresham College, 2 May 2023

Hunt, Alice, *The Drama of Coronation: Mediæval Ceremony in Early Modern England* (Cambridge University Press, Cambridge, 2008)

Hunt, Alice, "The monarchical republic of Mary I" (2009) 52(3) The Historical Journal 557–572

Huscroft, Richard, *The Norman Conquest: A New Introduction* (Longman, London, 2009)

Huscroft, Richard, *The Norman Conquest: A New Introduction* (Taylor & Francis, London, 2013)

Huscroft, Richard, *Ruling England 1042–1217* (Pearson/Longman, London, 2005)

Hutchison, Gary D. "'The Manager in Distress': Reaction to the Impeachment of Henry Dundas, 1805–7" (2017) 36(2) Parliamentary History 198–217

Ishide, Tomoo, *The Royal Dynasties of Ancient Israel: A Study on the Formation and Development of Royal-Dynastic Ideology* (Walter de Gruyter, Berlin, 1977)

Jack, Sybil M., "'A Pattern for a King's Inauguration': The Coronation of James I in England" (2004) 21(2) Parergon 67–91

Jackson, Richard A., *Ordines Coronationis Franciae: Texts and Ordines for the Coronation of Frankish and French Kings and Queens in the Middle Ages* (University of Pennsylvania Press, Philadelphia, 1995–2000)

Jacobson, Paul A., "Sicut Samuhel unxit David: Early Carolingian Royal Anointings Reconsidered", in Larson-Miller, Lizette (ed.), *Medieval Liturgy* (Routledge, Abingdon, 2019), pp. 267–303

Jeep, John M., (ed.), *Mediæval Germany: An Encyclopædia* (Garland Pub., New York, NY:, 2001)

Jiang, Yonglin, *The Mandate of Heaven and The Great Ming Code* (Asian Law Series. Vol. No. 21, University of Washington Press, Seattle, 2011)

John of Paris, *De potestate regia et papali, Johannes Quidort von Paris Über Königliche under päpstliche Gewalt* ed. F. Bleienstein (Ernst Klett Verlag, Stuttgart, 1969)

John of Salisbury, *Policraticus, sive de nugis curialium et de vestigiis philosophorum* [*Policraticus: Of the frivolities of courtiers and the footprints of philosophers*] ed. Cary J. Nederman (Cambridge University Press, Cambridge, 1990)

Joint Report by the Church and Society Council, the Committee on Ecumenical Relations, and the Legal Questions Committee on the implications for the Church of Scotland of independence for Scotland, 15 May 2013

Jones, Adrienne, "The Significance of the Regal Consecration of Edgar in 973" (1982) 33(3) The journal of ecclesiastical history 375–390

Joseph, Philip A., *Constitutional and Administrative Law in New Zealand* (The Law Book Company, Auckland, 1993)

Kaldellis, Anthony, "From 'Empire of the Greeks' to 'Byzantium'", in Jake Ransohoff, and Nathanael Aschenbrenner (eds.), *The Invention of Byzantium in Early Modern Europe* (Harvard University Press, Cambridge, Mass., 2022), pp. 349–367

Kantorowicz, Ernst, *The King's Two Bodies: A Study in Mediæval Political Theology* (Princeton University Press, Princeton, 1957)

Kaplan, Stephen, "Solomonic dynasty", in Bausi, Alessandro, Appleyard, David L., Uhlig, Siegbert, Kaplan, Steven, & Hahn, Wolfgang (eds.), *Ethiopia: History, Culture and Challenges* (LIT Verlag, Münster, 2017), pp. 111–112

Kaul, Chandrika, and Chandrika Kaul, "Coronation, Colonialism and Cultures of Control: The Delhi Durbar, 1911", in Chandrika Kaul (ed.), *Communications, Media and the Imperial Experience: Britain and India in the Twentieth Century* (Palgrave Macmillan, London, 2014), pp. 19–70

Keay, Anna, *The Crown Jewels* (Thames & Hudson, London, 2011)

Keay, Anna, *The Magnificent Monarch: Charles II and the Ceremonies of Power* (Bloomsbury Academic, London, 2008)

Keir, Sir David Lindsay, *The Constitutional History of Modern Britain since 1485* (8th edn., van Nostrand, Princeton, 1966)

Keith, A. B., *Constitutional History of the First British Empire* (Clarendon Press, Oxford, 1930)

Kelly, Susan, *Charters of Malmesbury Abbey* (Oxford University Press, Oxford, 2005)

Kennedy, W. P. M., "Royal Style and Titles" (1953–54) 10 University of Toronto Law Journal 83–87

Keynes, Simon, "Kingston-upon-Thames", in Michael Lapidge, John Blair, Simon Keynes, and Donald Scragg (eds.), *The Blackwell Encyclopedia of Anglo-Saxon England* (Blackwell Publishing, London, 2001), pp. 106–119

Knox, John, "First Blast of the Trumpet", in David Laing (ed), *The Works of John Knox* (Bannatyne Club, Edinburgh, 1846–64), vol IV, pp. 377–378

Kornberg, Allan, and Harold D. Clarke, *Citizens and Community – Political Support in a Representative Democracy* (Cambridge University Press, London, 1992)

Kossmann, E. H., *The Low Countries, 1780–1940* (Clarendon, Oxford, 1988)

Kotilaine, Jarmo and Marshall Poe (eds.), *Modernizing Muscovy: Reform and Social Change in Seventeenth Century Russia* (Routledge, Abingdon, 2004)

Kuhn, William, "Ceremony and Politics" (1990) Johns Hopkins University PhD thesis

Kuhn, William, *Democratic royalism: The transformation of the British monarchy, 1861–1914* (Springer, London, 1996)

La Nauze, John Andrew, *The Making of the Australian Constitution* (Melbourne University Press, Melbourne, 1972)

Lapidge, Michael (ed.), *Archbishop Theodore* (Cambridge University Press, Cambridge, 1995)

Lapsley, G. T., "The Parliamentary Title of Henry IV", in Geoffrey Barraclough, and Helen Cam (eds.) *Crown Community and Parliament in the Later Middle Ages* (Blackwell, Oxford, 1951), pp. 273–336 reprinted from (1934) 94 English Historical Review 423–449

Larkin, James, and Paul Hughes (eds.), *Stuart Royal Proclamations* (Clarendon Press, Oxford, 1973)

Larmour, Peter, *Legitimacy, Sovereignty and Regime Change in the South Pacific: Comparisons Between the Fiji Coups and the Bougainville Rebellion* (Research School of Pacific Studies, Australian National University, Canberra, 1992)

Laski, Harold, *Authority in the Modern State* (Yale University Press, New Haven, 1919)

Laski, Harold, "Responsibility of the State in England" (1919) 32 Harvard Law Journal 447–472

Latowsky, Anne A., *Emperor of the World: Charlemagne and the Construction of Imperial Authority, 800–1229* (Cornell University Press, Ithaca, 2013)

Lauterpacht, Sir Eli, "Sovereignty – myth or reality?" (1997) 73(1) International Affairs 137–150

Lawson, M. K., *Cnut: England's Viking King* (2nd ed., Tempus, Stroud, 2004)

Le Hardy, William, *The Coronation Book: the History and the Meaning of the Ceremonies at the Crowning of the King and Queen* (Hardy & Reckitt, London, 1937)

Leahy, W. J., "'You cannot show me': Two Tudor Coronation Processions, Shakespeare's King Henry VIII and the Staging of Anne Boleyn", in *Shakespearean Criticism* (Vol. 112) (Gale Research Inc., Farmington Hills, 2008)

Lee, Sir Sidney, *King Edward VII* (Macmillan, New York, 1925–27)

Legg, J. Wickham, *The Coronation of the Queen* (Church Historical Society xlii, SPCK, London, 1898)

Legg, Leopold G. Wickham, *English Coronation Records* (A. Constable & Co, Westminster, 1901)

Le Goff, Jacques, *La civilisation de l'Occident médieval* (Arthaud, Paris, 1964)

Leslie, R. F. (ed.), *Three old English elegies* (Rev. ed., University of Exeter, Manchester, 1988)

Leyser, Karl, "The Anglo-Saxon Succession 1120–1125" (1990) 13 Proceedings of the Battle Conference on Anglo-Norman Studies 225–241

Lipset, Seymour Martin, *Political Man: The Social Bases of Politics* (Doubleday, Garden City, New York, 1960)

Lloyd, Daniel, "The Coronation of Charles III from the Perspective of Liturgical Studies" (2023) 2 Ex Fonte–Journal of Ecumenical Studies in Liturgy 363–445

Lloyd, Daniel, "A tradition of invention: Rites and rituals surrounding the death and funeral of Queen Elizabeth II" (2022) 1 Ex Fonte–Journal of Ecumenical Studies in Liturgy 191–237

Loach, Jennifer, "The Function of Ceremonial in the Reign of Henry VIII" (1994) 142 Past & Present 43–68

Locke, John, *Two Treatises of Government* ed. Peter Laslett (Cambridge University Press, Cambridge, 1988)

Lodge, Samuel, *Scrivelsby, The Home of the Champions* (W. K. Morton, Horncastle, 1893)

London Gazette Extraordinary, 8th February 1952 (HMSO, London, 1952), p. 861

Lot, Ferdinand, *The End of the Ancient World and the Beginnings of the Middle Ages* (K. Paul, Trench, Trubner & Company, Limited, Paris, 1931)

Lower, A. R. M., "Origins of Democracy in Canada", in Welf Heick (ed), *History and Myth: Arthur Lower and the Making of Canadian Nationalism* (University of British Columbia, Vancouver, 1975), pp. 26–33

Loyn, H. R., *Anglo-Saxon England and the Norman Conquest* (2nd ed., Longmans, Harlow, 1991)

Lyall, Roderick J., "The Medieval Scottish Coronation Service: Some Seventeenth-Century Evidence" (1977) 28(1) Innes Review 3–21

Macdougall, Norman, *James IV: The Stewart Dynasty in Scotland* (Tuckwell Press, East Lothian, 1997)

Mack, Douglas S., "Can the Scottish subaltern speak?", in Caroline McCracken-Flesher (ed.). *Culture, Nation, and the New Scottish Parliament* (Bucknell University Press, Lewisburg, 2007), pp. 141–157

Macrides, Ruth, Munitiz, J. A. and Dimiter Angelov, *Pseudo-Kodi\nos and the Constantinopolitan Court: Offices and Ceremonies* (Ashgate, Farnham, Surrey, 2013)

Madden, F., and D. Fieldhouse (eds.), *The Classical Period of the First British Empire, 1689–1783: The Foundations of a Colonial System of Government: Select Documents on the Constitutional History of the British Empire and Commonwealth* (Greenwood Publishing Group Westport, 1985), vol. 2

Maddicott, J. R., *The Origins of the English Parliament, 924–1327* (Oxford University Press, London, 2010)

Maine, Sir Henry Sumner, *Early Law and Custom* (John Murray, London, 1890)

Mainstone, Rowland J., *Hagia Sophia: Architecture, Structure, and Liturgy of Justinian's Great Church* (reprint ed., W. W. Norton & Co., London, 1997)

Maitland, Frederic W., *The Constitutional History of England – a course of lectures* ed. H. A. L. Fisher (Cambridge University Press, London, 1980, first published 1908)

Maitland, Frederic W., *Domesday Book and Beyond – three essays on the early history of England* (Norton, New York, 1966, first published 1897)

Maitland, Frederic W., *Equity: A Course of Lectures.* ed. A. H. Chaytor and W. J. Whittaker, revd. J. Brunyate (Cambridge University Press, Cambridge, 2011)

Maitland, Frederic and Sir Frederick Pollock, *History of English Law before the Times of Edward I* (2nd edn., Cambridge University Press, Cambridge, 1895)

Malden, H. E. (ed.), "Colleges: Collegiate chapel of St Mary Magdalen, Kingston", in *A History of the County of Surrey.* Victoria County History. Vol. II (Institute of Historical Research, London, 1905, reissued 1967), pp. 125–127

Mallory, James Russell, "The Appointment of the Governor General" (1960) 26 Canadian Journal of Economics and Political Science 96–107

Margeret, J. *The Russian Empire and Grand Duchy of Muscovy* (University of Pittsburgh Press, Pittsburgh, 1983)

Matyszak, Philip, *The Sons of Caesar: Imperial Rome's First Dynasty* (Thames & Hudson, London, 2006)

May, Henry, *The South African Constitution* (3rd ed., Juta & Co, Cape Town, 1955)

Mayr-Harting, Henry, "Charlemagne, the Saxons, and the Imperial Coronation of 800" (1996) 111 (444) The English Historical Review 1113–1133

Mayr-Harting, Henry, *The Coming of Christianity to Anglo-Saxon England* (University Press Pennsylvania, Pennsylvania, 1992)

McClendon, Charles B., *The Origins of Medieval Architecture: Building in Europe: A.D 600–900* (Yale University Press, New Haven, CT, 2005)

McCoy, Richard C., *Alterations of State: Sacred Kingship in the English Reformation* (Columbia University Press, New York, 2002)

McDougall, Sara, "Illegitimacy and the Making of Mediæval Dynasties *c.*900–*c.*1050", in *Royal Bastards: The Birth of Illegitimacy, 800–1230* (Oxford Studies in Mediæval European History, Oxford, 2016), pp. 94–115

McHardy, Alison and Orme, Nicholas, "The Defence of an Alien Priory: Modbury (Devon) in the 1450s" (1999) The Journal of Ecclesiastical History 303–312

McKenna, John W., "The Coronation Oil of the Yorkist Kings" (1967) English Historical Review 102–104

McKisack, May, *The Fourteenth Century: 1307–1399* (Oxford University Press, Oxford, 1959)

McPherson, Mr. Justice Bruce, "The Church as consensual compact, trust and corporation" (2000) 74 Australian Law Journal 159–174

Mears, Kenneth J., Simon Thurley, and Claire Murphy, *The Crown Jewels* (Historic Royal Palaces Agency, London, 1994)

Mechie, Stewart, *The Office of the Lord High Commissioner* (St Andrew Press, Edinburgh, 1957)

Melville-Jones, John R., *The Siege of Constantinople 1453: Seven Contemporary Accounts* (Adolf M. Hakkert, Amsterdam, 1972)

Menon, Anand and Robert Hazell (eds.), *The British Monarchy* (The Constitution Unit, University College London, London, 2023)

Merelman, Richard, "Learning and Legitimacy" (1966) 60(3) American Political Science Review 548–561

Mladjov, I. S. R., "The Crown and the Veil: Titles, Spiritual Kinship, and Diplomacy in Tenth-Century Bulgaro-Byzantine Relations" (2015) 13 History Compass 171–183

Monod, Paul, "Coronations", in *Early Modern Court Culture* (Routledge, Abingdon, 2021), pp. 215–230

Montesquieu, Charles Louis de Secondat Baron de, "The Spirit of the Laws", in Arend Lijphart (ed.), *Parliamentary versus Presidential Government* (Oxford University Press, London, 1992), pp. 48–51

Moreland, John, "Land and Power from Roman Britain to Anglo-Saxon England?" (2011) 19(1) Historical Materialism 175–193

Morris, Colin, *The papal monarchy: the western church from 1050 to 1250* (Clarendon, Oxford, 1989)

Morris, R. M., *Inaugurating a new reign: Planning for Accession and Coronation* (The Constitution Unit, UCL, London, 2018)

Morris, R. M., *The coronation of Charles III* (The Constitution Unit, University College London, London, 2022)

Murray, K. M. Elisabeth, *The Constitutional History of the Cinque Ports* (Manchester University Press, Manchester, 1935)

Nash, Michael L., "The Jewels of the Kingdom", in *Royal Wills in Britain from 1509 to 2008* (Palgrave Macmillan, London, 2017), pp. 61–86

Nelson, Janet L., *The Annals of St-Bertin* (Manchester University Press, Manchester, 1991)

Nelson, Janet L., "Carolingian Coronation Rituals: A Model for Europe?" (2004) 9(1) The Court Historian 1–13

Nelson, Janet L., "The Earliest Surviving Royal Ordo: Some Liturgical and Historical Aspects", in B. Tierney and P. Linehan (eds.), *Authority and Power: Studies in Mediæval Law and Government presented to Walter Ullmann* (Cambridge University Press, Cambridge, 1980), pp. 29–48; reprinted in Janet L. Nelson, *Politics and Ritual in Early Mediæval Europe* (Hambledon Press, London, 1986), pp. 341–360

Nelson, Janet L., "The First Use of the Second Anglo-Saxon *Ordo*", in Julia Barrow, and Andrew Wareham (eds.), *Myth, Rulership, Church and Charters* (Ashgate, Farnham, 2008), pp. 117–126

Nelson, Janet L., "Kingship and empire", in J. H. Burns (ed.), *The Cambridge History of Mediæval Political Thought c.350-c.1450* (Cambridge University Press, Cambridge, 1988), pp. 211–251

Nelson, Janet L., "Kingship, Law and Liturgy in the Political Thought of Hincmar of Rheims" (1977) 92 English Historical Review 241–279, reprinted in *Politics and Ritual in Early Mediæval Europe* (Hambledon, London, 1986), pp. 133–272

Nenner, Howard, *The Right to be King – The Succession to the Crown of England, 1603–1714* (Macmillan, London, 1995)

Newman, John Henry, *Essays and Sketches* ed. Charles Frederick Harrold (Longans, Green & Co, New York, 1948)

Nicholas, Michael, "King Henry II and his Legal Reforms" (2019) 6(2) The Histories Article 5. Available at: https://digitalcommons.lasalle.edu/the_histories/vol6/iss2/5

Nichols, Aidan, *Rome and the Eastern Churches: a study in schism* (Ignatius Press, San Francisco, 2010)

Nicholson, Oliver and Gwynn, David, "Pontifex Maximus", in Oliver Nicholson (ed.), *The Oxford Dictionary of Late Antiquity* (Oxford University Press, Oxford, 2018)

Nicol, Donald M., "Kaisersalbung. The unction of emperors in late Byzantine coronation ritual" (1976) 2 Byzantine and Modern Greek Studies 37–52

Nicol, Donald M., *The Last Centuries of Byzantium, 1261–1453* (2nd ed., Rupert Hart-Davis Ltd, London, 1993)

Nicolle, David, *The Janissaries* (Osprey Publishing, London, 1995)

Nicols, John, *Idea of Rome, idea of Europe* (Rowman & Littlefield, Lanham, 2005)

Nicolson, Sir Harold, *King George the Fifth His Life and Reign* (Constable & Co, London, 1952)

Nockles, Peter, *The Oxford Movement in Context: High Anglican Churchmanship, 1760–1857* (Cambridge University Press, Cambridge, 1997)

Norrie, Aidan, "The Bishop and the Queen; Or, Why Did the Bishop of Carlisle Crown Elizabeth I?" (2019) 56(1–2) Northern History 25–45

O'Brien, Conor, "The Origins of Royal Anointing" (2023) 59 Studies in Church History 27–47

O'Brien, Harriet, *Queen Emma and the Vikings: The Woman who Shaped the Events of 1066* (Bloomsbury, London, 2006)

O'Connor, David B., Eric H. Cline (eds.), *Amenhotep III: Perspectives on His Reign* (The University of Michigan Press, Ann Arbor, 1998)

O'Donovan, Oliver, *The Desire of the Nations: Rediscovering the Roots of Political Theology* (Cambridge University Press, Cambridge, 1996)

Ogden, Daniel, *The Legend of Seleucus: Kingship, Narrative and Mythmaking in the Ancient World* (Cambridge University Press, Cambridge, 2017)

O'Keefe, David, "Sir George Jessel and the Union of Judicature" (1982) 26 American Journal of Legal History 227–251

Oldenburg, Sergei S., *Last Tsar: Nicholas II, His Reign and His Russia* (Academic International Press, Gulf Breeze, Florida, 1975)

Oppenheimer, Sir Francis, *The Legend of the Ste. Ampoule* (Faber & Faber, London, 1953)

Oppenheimer, S., *The Origins of the British: a Genetic Detective Story* (Constable and Robinson, London, 2006)

Örnebring, Henrik, "Revisiting the coronation" (2004) 25(1–2) Nordicom Review 175–195

Ortenberg, Veronica, "The King from Overseas: Why did Æthelstan Matter in Tenth-Century Continental Affairs?", in David Rollason, Conrad Leyser and Hannah Williams (eds.), *England and the Continent in the Tenth Century: Studies in Honour of Wilhelm Levison (1876–1947)* (Brepols, Turnhout, 2010), pp. 211–236

Osiander, Andreas, "Sovereignty, International Relations, and the Westphalian Myth" (2011) 55(2) International Organization 251–287

Ovid, *Metamorphoses*. translated by A. D. Melville, Introduction and notes by Edward John Kenney (Oxford University Press, Oxford, 2008)

Owen, Matthew and Ingo Gildenhard, *Tacitus, Annals, 15.20–23, 33–45. Latin Text, Study Aids with Vocabulary, and Commentary* (Open Book Publishers, Cambridge, 2013)

Page, Daniel Bennett, "Anointing Judith: Liturgy, Music, and the Coronation of Mary I", in Valerie Schutte and Jessica S. Hower (eds.), *Mid-Tudor Queenship and Memory: The Making and Re-making of Lady Jane Grey and Mary I* (Springer International Publishing, London, 2023), pp. 69–96

Page, William, "Benedictine monks: St Peter's abbey, Westminster", in *A History of the County of London* (Victoria County History, London, 1909), vol 1, "London Within the Bars, Westminster and Southwark", pp. 433–457

Parnell, Geoffrey, *The Tower of London* (Batsford, London, 1993)

Parsons, D., "British Caraticos, Old English Cerdic" (1997) 33 Cambrian Mediæval Celtic Studies 1–8

Penn, Thomas, *Winter King: Henry VII and the Dawn of Tudor England* (Simon & Schuster, New York, 2012)

Pennington, Kenneth, "Law, Legislative authority and theories of government, 1150–1300", in J. H. Burns (ed.), *The Cambridge History of Mediæval Political Thought c.350-c.1450* (Cambridge University Press, Cambridge, 1988), pp. 424–453

Pennington, Kenneth, *Pope and Bishops: The Papal Monarchy in the Twelfth and Thirteenth Centuries* (University of Pennsylvania Press, Philadelphia, 1984)

Pepinster, Catherine, *Defenders of the Faith: The British Monarchy, Religion and the Next Coronation* (Hodder & Stoughton, London, 2023)

Petit-Dutaillis, Charles, *The Feudal Monarchy in France and England: From the Tenth to the Thirteenth Century*. Translated by E. D. Hunt (Harper Torchbooks, New York, 1964)

Pfaff, R., et al., *The Liturgical Books of Anglo-Saxon England*, Old English Newsletter Subsidia 23 (Kalamazoo, MI, 1995), pp. 11–14, 89, 93–94, 100–109

Phillips, Seymour, *Edward II* (Yale University Press, New Haven, 2011)

Philpott, Daniel, "Sovereignty" (1995) 48(2) Journal of International Affairs 353–368

Pocock, J. G. A. and Ashcraft, Richard (eds.), *John Locke* (William Andrews Clark Memorial Library, University of California, Los Angeles, 1980)

Polish, David, "Rabbinic views on kingship – a study in Jewish sovereignty" (Spring 1991) 3(1/2) Jewish Political Studies Review 67–90

Pollard, A. J., *Richard III and the Princes in the Tower* (Alan Sutton Publishing, London, 1991)

Potter, David S., *The Roman Empire at Bay, AD 180–395* (Routledge, London, 2004)

Pounds, N. J. G., *A history of the English parish: the culture of religion from Augustine to Victoria* (Cambridge University Press, Cambridge, 2000)

Powell, J. Enoch, and Keith Wallis, *The House of Lords in the Middle Ages: A History of the English House of Lords to 1540* (Weidenfeld & Nicolson, London, 1968)

Powell, Roger and Peter Beauclerk, *Royal Bastards: Illegitimate Children of the British Royal Family* (History Press, Cheltenham, 2008)

Powicke, Frederick Maurice, *The Loss of Normandy, 1189–1204: Studies in the History of the Angevin Empire* (Manchester University Press, Manchester, 1999)

Pratt, David, *English Coronation Ordines in the Ninth and Early Tenth Centuries*, Henry Bradshaw Society 125 (Boydell Press, London, 2023)

Pratt, David, "The making of the Second English Coronation Ordo" (2017) 46 Anglo-Saxon England 147–258

Preston, Todd, *King Alfred's Book of Laws: A Study of the Domboc and Its Influence on English Identity, With a Complete translation* (McFarland, Jefferson, 2012)

Proceedings of the Coronation of Her Majesty The Queen, 2nd June 1953 (HMSO, London, 1953)

Provinciale (1433) lib. iii. Ut clericalis, etc (Wolfgang Hopyl for William Bretton, London, 1505)

Range, Matthew, *Music and Ceremonial at British Coronation: From James I to Elizabeth II* (Cambridge University Press, London, 2012)

Ratcliff, E. C., *The Coronation Service of Her Majesty Queen Elizabeth II* (SPCK, London, 1953)

Raton, Pierre, *Liechtenstein: History and Institutions of the Principality* (Liechtenstein Verlag, Vaduz, 1970)

Rawls, John, *Political Liberalism* (Columbia University Press, New York, 1993)

Reitan, E. A., "The Civil List in Eighteenth-Century British Politics: Parliamentary Supremacy versus the Independence of the Crown" (1966) 9(3) The Historical Journal 318–337

Report of the Justice and Law Reform Committee on the Imperial Laws Application Bill (House of Representatives, Wellington, 1988) Explanatory Material pp. 57–60

Rex, Peter, *1066: A New History of the Norman Conquest* (Amberley Publishing, Stroud, 2011)

Richard Green, John, *The Conquest of England* (Harper & Brothers, New York, 1884)

Richards, Tessa, *The Coronation Ceremony of the Kings and Queens of England and the Crown Jewels* (HMSO, London, 1992)

Richardson, H. G., "The Coronation in Mediæval England: The Evolution of the Office and the Oath" (1960) 16 Traditio 111–202

Richardson, H. G., "The English Coronation Oath" (1941) 23 Transactions of the Royal Historical Society 129–158

Richardson, John, "The Meaning of *imperium* in the Last Century BC and the First AD", in Benedict Kingsbury, and Benjamin Straumann (eds.), *The Roman Foundations of the Law of Nations: Alberico Gentili and the Justice of Empire* (Oxford University Press, Oxford, 2010)

Richardson, John, "No king but Caesar? The Headship of the Church in Anglican Theology" (2002) 116(4) Churchman 305–325

Ridgeway, H. W., "Henry III (1207–1272)" *Oxford Dictionary of National Biography* (Oxford University Press, online, 2004)

Roberts, Andrew, *Napoleon: A Life* (Penguin Group, London, 2014)

Robertson, A. J., *Laws of the Kings of England* (Cambridge University Press, London, 1925)
Robins, Jane, *The Trial of Queen Caroline: The Scandalous Affair that Nearly Ended a Monarchy* (Free Press, New York, 2006)
The Roll of Claims and Proceedings at the Coronation of His Most Sacred Majesty Charles the Third by the Grace of God of the United Kingdom of Great Britain and Northern Ireland and of His other Realms and Territories, King, Head of the Commonwealth, Defender of the Faith, and of Her Majesty Queen Camilla, His Consort (Clerk of the Crown in Chancery, London, 2024)
Rollason, David W., *Northumbria, 500–1100: Creation and Destruction of a Kingdom* (Cambridge University Press, Cambridge, 2003)
Romano, John F., "The Coronation of Charlemagne as a Liturgical Event" (2020) 82 Mediaeval Studies 149–181
Rose, Tessa, *The Coronation Ceremony and the Crown Jewels* (HMSO, London, 1992)
Rosser, John H., "Introduction", *Historical Dictionary of Byzantium* (Scarecrow, Roth Lanham, MA, 2011)
Round, J. Horace, *The King's Serjeants & Officers of State with their Coronation Services* (Nisbet and Company Ltd, London, 1911)
Round, J. Horace, "The Lord Great Chamberlain" (June 1902) 7(21) Monthly Review 42–58
Rowbottom, Sheila (1994) University of Manchester PhD thesis
Rushdoony, Rousas John, *The Institutes of Biblical Law* (The Craig Press, Craig, 1973)
Russell, Conrad, *The Fall of the British Monarchies 1637–1642* (Clarendon Press, Oxford, 1991)
Russell, Peter H., *Constitutional Odyssey: Can Canadians become a Sovereign People?* (University of Toronto Press, Toronto, 1992)
The Rutland Papers (Camden Society, London, 1842), vol 21 (Henry VII)
St Clair, Kassia, *The Secret Lives of Colour* (John Murray, London, 2016)
Salway, Peter, "The end of Roman rule", in *Roman Britain: A Very Short Introduction* (2nd edn, Oxford University Press, Oxford, 2015), pp, 97–108
Sanders, Ivor John, *English Baronies: A Study of their Origin and Descent 1086–1327* (Clarendon Press, Oxford, 1960), p. 145, "Tamworth, Nottinghamshire"
Sargent, A., "The North-South Divide Revisited: Thoughts on the Character of Roman Britain" (2002) 33 Britannia 219–226
Sawyer, Peter Hayes, *From Roman Britain to Norman England* (Routledge, London, 2002)
Schaar, John H., "Legitimacy in the Modern State", in William Connolly (ed.), *Legitimacy and the State* (Basil Blackwell, Oxford, 1984), pp. 104–133

Schramm, Percy, *A History of the English Coronation*, trans. Leopold G. Wickham Legg (Clarendon Press, Oxford, 1937)

Scott, Jonathon, *Algernon Sidney and the Restoration Crisis, 1677–1683* (Cambridge University Press, Cambridge, 1991)

Scragg, D. G., *Edgar, King of the English, 959–975: New Interpretations* (Boydell & Brewer Ltd, Woodridge, 2008)

Sear, David, *Greek Imperial Coins and Their Values* (Spink Books, London, 1982)

Sebesta, Judith Lynn and Larissa Bonfante (eds), *The World of Roman Costume* (University of Wisconsin Press, Madison, 2001)

Sedlar, Jean W., *East Central Europe in the Middle Ages, 1000–1500* (University of Washington Press, Seattle, 1994)

Seele, Keith C., *The Coregency of Ramses II with Seti I and the date of the great hypostyle hall at Karnack* (Oriental Institute of the University of Chicago, Studies in Ancient Oriental Civilization, no 19, University of Chicago Press, Chicago, 1940)

Sèguin, Rhèal (7 June 2013), "Changes to royal succession face legal fight in Quebec", *The Globe and Mail*

Seipp, David J., "The reception of canon law and civil law in the common law courts before 1600" (1993) 13(3) Oxford Journal of Legal Studies 388–420

Sharman, Campbell, "Australia as a Compound Republic" (1990) 25 Politics 1–5

Sharpe, Kevin, "Archbishop Laud" (August 1983) History Today 26–30

Shaw, Dougal, "Scotland's Place in Britain's Coronation Tradition" (2004) 9(1) The Court Historian 41–60

Shaw, Dougal, "St. Giles' church and Charles I's coronation visit to Scotland" (2004) 77(198) Historical Research 481–502

Shillony, Ben-Ami, *The Emperors of Modern Japan* (Brill, Leiden, 2008)

Shils, Edward and Young, Michael, "The Meaning of the Coronation" (1953) 1(2) The Sociological Review 63–81

Sidney, Algernon, *Discourses concerning Government* ed. Thomas West (Liberty Classics, Indianapolis, 1990)

Sims-Williams, Patrick, "The Settlement of England in Bede and the Chronicle" (1983) 12 Anglo-Saxon England 1–41

Sisam, Kenneth, "Anglo-Saxon Royal Genealogies" (1953) 39 Proceedings of the British Academy 287–348

Smith, David E., "Bagehot, the Crown, and the Canadian Constitution" (1995) 28 Canadian Journal of Political Science 623–624

Smith, David E., *The Invisible Crown: The First Principle of Canadian Government* (University of Toronto Press, Toronto, 1995)

Smith, David E., *The Republican Option in Canada, Past and Present* (University of Toronto Press, Toronto, 1999)

Smith, Julie Ann, "The Earliest Queen-Making Rites" (1997) 66(1) Church history 18–35

Sulovsky, Vedran., "The concept of sacrum imperium in historical scholarship" (2019) 17(8) History Compass e12586

Soulis, George Christos, *The Serbs and Byzantium during the reign of Tsar Stephen Dušan (1331–1355) and his successors* (Dumbarton Oaks Library and Collection, Washington, 1984)

Spelman, Sir John, *The Reports of Sir John Spelman* ed. Sir John Baker (The Seldon Society, London, 1978), vol. 2 Seldon Society 94

Spencer, Charles Spencer, Earl, *The White Ship: conquest, anarchy and the wrecking of Henry I's dream* (William Collins, London, 2020)

Spinks, Bryan, *Early and Medieval Rituals and Theologies of Baptism – From the New Testament to the Council of Trent* (Ashgate, Aldershot, 2006)

Squibb, George D., *The High Court of Chivalry: A Study of the Civil Law in England* (Oxford University Press, Oxford, 1959)

Squibb, George D., *Precedence in England and Wales* (Oxford University Press, Oxford, 1981)

Stadiem, William, *Too Rich: The High Life and Tragic Death of King Farouk* (Carroll & Graf Pub., New York, 1991)

Steele, R., "Crowning the 'Sun of the Aryans': Mohammad Reza Shah's Coronation and Monarchical Spectacle in Pahlavi Iran" (2021) 53(2) International Journal of Middle East Studies 175–193

Stenton, Frank, *Anglo-Saxon England* (Clarendon Press, Oxford, 1971)

Stenton, Frank, *The First Century of English Feudalism 1066–1166* (2nd ed., Oxford University Press, London, 1961)

Stewart, Andrew, *Faces of Power: Alexander's Image and Hellenistic Politics* (University of California Press, Berkeley, 1993)

Stewart, Byron, "The Cult of the Royal Martyr" (1969) 38(2) Church History 175–187

Stewart, Cecil, *Byzantine legacy* (Allen & Unwin, London, 1947)

Stollberg-Rilinger, Barbara, *The Emperor's Old Clothes: Constitutional History and the Symbolic Language of the Holy Roman Empire* (Berghahn Books, New York, 2020)

Strasdin, Kate, "Empire Dressing – The Design and Realization of Queen Alexandra's Coronation Gown" (2012) 25(2) Journal of Design History 155–170

Strickland, Matthew, "Against the Lord's anointed: aspects of warfare and baronial rebellion in England and Normandy 1075–1265", in George Garnett, and John Hudson (eds.), *Law and Government in Mediæval England and Normandy* (Cambridge University Press, Cambridge, 1994), pp. 56–79

Strickland, Matthew, *Henry the Young King: 1155–1183* (Yale University Press, New Haven and London, 2016)

Stróbl, Erzsébet, "The City as Stage: The Coronation Entry of Elizabeth I in 1559" (2021) Art in Urban Space 191

Strong, Sir Roy, *Coronation: A History of Kingship and the British Monarchy* (HarperCollins, London, 2005)

Stubbs, William, *The Constitutional History of England* (4th ed., Clarendon Press, Oxford, 1906)

Sturdy, David J., "The Royal Touch in England", in Heinz Duchhardt, and Richard A. Jackson (eds.), *European Monarchy: Its Evolution and Practice from Roman Antiquity to Modern Times* (Franz Steiner Verlag, Stuttgart, 1992), pp. 171–184

Suny, Ronald Grigor, *The Making of the Georgian Nation* (Indiana University Press, Bloomington, 2004)

Supplement to the London Gazette, 17th November 1953 (HMSO, London, 1953), p. 6223–6270 "Ceremonial of the Coronation of Her Majesty Queen Elizabeth II"

Supplement to the London Gazette, 10th November 1937 (HMSO, London, 1937), p. 7054

Sutton, Anne, "The coronation robes of Richard III and Anne Neville" (1979) 13(1) Costume 8–16

Swanson, M., "The Social extract tradition and the question of political legitimacy" (1995) University of Missouri-Columbia PhD thesis

Swanton, Michael, *The Anglo-Saxon Chronicle* (Routledge, New York, 1996)

Tanner, Lawrence E., "Westminster Abbey and the Coronation Service" (1937) 21(84) History 289–301

Tarifa, Fatos, "The quest for legitimacy and the withering away of utopia" (1997) 76(2) Social Forces 437–473

Taswell-Langmead, Thomas, *English Constitutional History, from the Teutonic Conquest to the Present Time* ed. A. L. Poole (9th edn., Sweet & Maxwell, London, 1929)

Teitler, Hans, "Raising on a shield: Origin and afterlife of a coronation ceremony" (2002) 8 International Journal of the Classical Tradition 501–521

Thirty-Nine Articles of Religion, enacted in 1562, and confirmed in 1571 by the Subscription (Thirty-Nine Articles) Act 1571 (13 Eliz. I c. 12) (Eng.)

Thomas, Andrea, "Coronation Ritual and Regalia", in Julian Goodare, and Alasdair A. MacDonald (eds.), *Sixteenth Century Scotland: Essays in Honour of Michael Lynch* (Brill, Leiden, 2008), pp. 43–68

Thurston, Herbert, "Coronation", in Charles Herbermann (ed.), *Catholic Encyclopedia* (Robert Appleton, New York, 1913)

Thurston, Herbert, *The Coronation Ceremonial* (2nd ed., Catholic Truth Society, London, 1911)

Tierney, Brian, *Church law and constitutional thought in the Middle Ages* (Variorum Reprints, London, 1979)

Tierney, Brian, *The Crisis of Church and State, 1050–1300* (University of Toronto Press, New York, 1964)
Timothy, I., *The Coronation of H.I.M. Emperor Haile Selassie I* (Children of Judah Pub. Co., 1983)
Titley, Brian, *Dark Age: The Political Odyssey of Emperor Bokassa* (McGill-Queen's Press, Quebec, 2002)
Torrance, David, "The Accession of King Charles III" (House of Commons Library Research Briefing, number CBP9621, 29 September 2022)
Torrance, David, "The Coronation: history and ceremonial" (House of Commons Library Research Briefing, number CBP9412, 6 December 2022)
Trepanier, Peter, *Some Visual Aspects of the Monarchial Tradition* (Parliament of Canada, Ottawa, 2004)
Tuck, Anthony, "Richard II (1367–1400)", *Oxford Dictionary of National Biography* (Oxford University Press, Oxford, 2004)
Twining, Edward Lord, *A History of the Crown Jewels of Europe* (B. T. Batsford Ltd, London, 1960)
Ullmann, Walter, "This Realm of England is an Empire" (1979) 30 (2) The Journal of Ecclesiastical History 175–203
Ullmann, Walter, "Thomas Becket's miraculous oil" (1957) 8(1) The Journal of Theological Studies 129–133
Vadala, Alexander Atillio, "Elite Distinction and Regime Change: The Ethiopian Case" (2011) 10(4) Comparative Sociology 636–653
Vale, M. G. A., *The princely court: Mediæval courts and culture in North-West Europe, 1270–1380* (Oxford University Press, Oxford, 2001)
Van der Burg, M., "Transforming the Dutch Republic into the Kingdom of Holland" (2010) 17(2) European Review of History 151–170
Vila, Linda Armengol, *Approach to the History of Andorra* (Institut d'Estudis Andorrans, Perpignan, 1989)
W.G., *Case of Succession to the Crown of England Stated* (a Letter to a Member of the Commons, London, 1679)
Wagner, Sir Anthony and J. C. Sainty, *The Origin of the Introduction of Peers in the House of Lords* (Society of Antiquaries, Oxford, 1967)
Waitz, Georg (ed.) "De unctione Pippini regis nota monachi sancti Dionysii" (1887) 15(1) Monumenta Germaniae Historica, Scriptores 1
Walker, Ian, *Harold the Last Anglo-Saxon King* (Wrens Park Publishing, Stroud, 2000)
Wallace-Hadrill, Andrew (ed.), *Patronage in Ancient Society* (Routledge, London, 1989)
Wandruszka, Adam, *The House of Habsburg: Six Hundred Years of a European Dynasty* (Doubleday, London, 1964)
Ward-Perkins, Bryan, "Why Did the Anglo-Saxons Not Become More British" (2000) 115 English Historical Review 513–533

Warhurst, John, "Nationalism and Republicanism in Australia" (1993) 28 Australian Journal of Political Studies 100–120

Warren, W. L., *Henry II* (Univ. of California Press, Los Angeles, 1973)

Waskan, Jonathan, "*De facto* legitimacy and popular will" (1998) 24(1) Social Theory and Practice 25–56

Watanabe-O'Kelly, Helen, "The Last Habsburg Coronation and What it Means to be Anointed", in Klaas Van Gelder (ed.), *More than Mere Spectacle. Coronations and Inaugurations in the Habsburg Monarchy during the Eighteenth and Nineteenth Centuries* (Berghahn, New Yotk, 2021), pp. 303–312

Watkin, Thomas Glyn, "Church and State in a changing world", in Norman Doe, Mark Hill and Robert Ombres (eds.), *English Canon Law* (University of Wales Press, Cardiff, 1998), pp. 82–92

Watson, Tom, "The Enduring Cult of Edward the Martyr" (2021) 43 Southern History 1–19

Watt, G., "The Coronation Oath" (2017) 19(3) Ecclesiastical Law Journal 325–341

Weber, Max, *Weber: Political Writings* trans. P. Lassman, and R. Speirs (Cambridge University Press, Cambridge, 1994)

Webster, Leslie and Janet Backhouse, "The Mercian Supremacy", in L. Webster, and J. Backhouse (eds.), *The Making of England, Anglo-Saxon Art and Culture, AD 600–900* (British Library, London, 1991), pp. 193–253

Weiler, Björn, "Describing Rituals of Succession and the Legitimation of Kingship in the West, ca. 1000–ca. 1150", in Alexander Beihammer, Stavroula Constantinou, and Maria G. Parani (eds.), *Court Ceremonies and Rituals of Power in Byzantium and the Mediæval Mediterranean* (Brill, Leiden, 2013), pp. 113–140

Weir, Alison, *Britain's royal families: The complete genealogy* (Random House, New York, 2008)

Wentworth, Peter, *A Pithie Exhortation to Her Majestie for Establishing Her Successor to the Crowne. Whereunto is Added a Discourse Containing the Authors Opinion of the True and Lawfull Successor to her Majestie* (Robert Waldegrave, Edinburgh, 1598)

Whaley, Joachim, *Germany and the Holy Roman Empire, Volume I: Maximilian I to the Peace of Westphalia, 1493–1648* (Oxford University Press, Oxford, 2012)

Wheare, K. C., *The Constitutional Structure of the Commonwealth* (Clarendon Press, Oxford, 1960)

Wickham, Chris, *Early Medieval Italy: Central Power and Local Society 400–1000* (Barnes and Noble, Totowa, 1981)

Wilkinson, James and Charles S. Knighton, *Crown and Cloister: The Royal Story of Westminster Abbey* (Scala Publishers, London, 2010)

Wilkinson, Toby A. H., *Royal Annals of Ancient Egypt* (Columbia University Press, New York, 2000)

Williams, Ann, "Ecgfrith king of Mercia", in Ann Williams, Alfred P. Smyth and D. P. Kirby (eds.), *A Biographical Dictionary of Dark Age Britain: England, Scotland, and Wales, c.500-c.1050* (Seaby, London, 1991)

Williams, Ann, "Edgar (called Edgar Pacificus) (943/4–975)", in *Oxford Dictionary of National Biography* (Oxford University Press, Oxford, 2004)

Williams, George H., *The Norman Anonymous of 1100 AD: Toward the identification and evaluation of the so-called Anonymous of York* (Wipf and Stock Publishers, Eugene, 2009)

Willson, David Harris, *King James VI & I* (Jonathan Cape, London, 1963)

Wilson, H. A., "The English Coronation Orders" (July 1901) The Journal of Theological Studies 481–504

Wilson, Peter H., "Bolstering the Prestige of the Habsburgs: The End of the Holy Roman Empire in 1806" (2006) 28(4) The International History Review 709–736

Winterton, George, "Is the House of Lords Immortal?" (1979) 95 Law Quarterly Review 386–392

Woolf, Alex, "The Britons: from Romans to barbarians", in Hans-Werner Goetz, Jörg Janut, and Walter Pohl (eds.), *Regna and Gentes. The relationship between Late Antique and Early Mediæval Peoples and Kingdoms in the Transformation of the Roman World* (Brill, Leiden, 2003), pp. 345–380

Wollaston, Sir Gerald, *Coronation Claims* (Harrison, London, 1903, 1910)

Woolley, Reginald Maxwell, *Coronation Rites* (Cambridge University Press, London, 1915)

Wormald, Patrick, *The Making of English Law: King Alfred to the Twelfth Century*, Vol I, (Blackwell, London, 1999)

Womersley, David. *Divinity and State* (Oxford University Press, Oxford, 2010)

Wortman, Richard, "The Russian Coronation: Rite and Representation" (2004) 9(1) The Court Historian 15–31

Wortman, Richard, *Scenarios of Power: Myth and Ceremony in Russian Monarchy from Peter the Great to the Abdication of Nicholas II* (Princeton University Press, Princeton, 2006)

Wulfstan of York, *An Werk Erzbischof Wulfstans von York – Die "Institutes of Polity, Civil and Ecclesiastical"* ed. K. Jost (A. Francke, München, 1959)

Wyatt, David K., "The Bangkok monarchy and Thai history" (9185) 2(2) Crossroads: An Interdisciplinary Journal of Southeast Asian Studies 131–139

Yelle, Robert A. "Hobbes the Egyptian: The Return to Pharaoh, or the Ancient Roots of Secular Politics", in A. Azfar Moin and Alan Strathern (eds.), *Sacred Kingship in World History: Between Immanence and Transcendence* (Columbia University Press, New York, 2022), pp. 223–248

Yonge, Charlotte, "The Crown of St. Stephen", in *A Book of Golden Deeds Of all Times and all Lands* (Blackie and Son, London, Glasgow and Bombay, 1867), pp. 290–304

Yorke, Barbara, *The Conversion of Britain: Religion, Politics and Society in Britain, c.600–800* (Longman, London, 2006)

Yorke, Barbara, *Wessex in the Early Middle Ages* (A. & C. Black, London, 1995)

Zaller, Robert, "Breaking the Vessels: The Desacralization of Monarchy in Early Modern England" (1998) 29(3) The Sixteenth Century Journal 757–778

Zupka, Dušan, "Power of rituals and rituals of power: Religious and secular rituals in the political culture of mediæval Kingdom of Hungary", in *Historiography in Motion* (Banská Bystrica, Bratislava, 2010), pp. 29–42

Index

N. Cox, *The Political, Legal, and Theological Functions of the Ceremony in the British Tradition*,
https://doi.org/10.1007/978-3-031-88960-8

D

E

I

S

Y

Z

The manufacturer's authorised representative in the EU is Springer Nature Customer Service Centre GmbH, Europaplatz 3, 69115 Heidelberg, Germany. If you have any concerns regarding our products, please contact ProductSafety@springernature.com

Printed and bound by CPI Group (UK) Ltd, Croydon, CR0 4YY
01/10/2026
02225967-0015